Betty Crocker

ANNUAL RECIPES

2·0·0·9

Betty Crocker
ANNUAL RECIPES
2·0·09

RODALE

General Mills

Editorial Director, Jeff Nowak

Manager, Cookbooks, Lois Tlusty

Recipe Development and Testing: Betty Crocker Kitchens

Photography and Food Styling: General Mills Photo Studios

Editor: Anne Egan

Book Designer: Tracey J. Hambleton

Printed in the United States of America
Rodale Inc. makes every effort to use acid-free ∞, recycled paper ♻.

ISBN 10: 1–59486–998–7

ISBN 13: 978–1–59486–998–3

2 4 6 8 10 9 7 5 3 1 hardcover

Cover image: Turtle Tart (page 333)

For more great ideas, visit www.bettycrocker.com

C O N T E N T S

Chicken with Oregano-Peach Sauce

Introduction

Welcome to the expanded 2009 edition of *Betty Crocker Annual Recipes*, where you'll find more than 300 recipes. Each delicious one is sure to please. We've gathered the best recipes from the year's **Betty Crocker** magazines to create this beautiful hardcover volume. Each recipe is accompanied by a spectacular photograph and many offer kitchen tips to help the meals come together with minimal effort. As always, the recipes are thoroughly tested for ultimate ease of preparation, outstanding taste and reliability.

From morning to night, no matter what the occasion, you'll be sure to find the perfect recipe. You can start your day with Tiramisu Waffles, bite into Caesar Chicken Subs for lunch, have tea with a slice of Chai-Spiced Bread and sup on Grilled Italian Steak and Vegetables. Even when time is of the essence, we offer recipes that will allow you to serve a home-cooked meal in a flash. Look for the "Quick" label to find recipes that can be prepared in 30 minutes or less or are ready to cook or bake in 20 minutes or less. With the help of a slow cooker, you can come home to dinner—hearty meals like Chicken Cacciatore, Southwestern Pork Burritos or Sweet and Tangy Short Ribs. Or, gather the family around the table for scrumptious dishes like Barbecue Pizza Wedges, Fire Roasted Tomato-Shrimp Veracruz with Couscous or Dijon Chicken Smothered in Mushrooms, each ready in just 20 minutes.

Knowing that most of us want to keep our fat intake in check (at least some of the time!), you'll find recipes with the "Low Fat" label highlighting dishes that have 10 grams of fat or less per serving (3 grams or less in the sides and desserts) allowing you to enjoy delectable dishes while staying on track. Complete nutritional analyses, including diabetic exchanges on each recipe, makes preparing meals a breeze for those watching their carbohydrates.

Scattered throughout the chapters are sidebars to boost your confidence in the kitchen, including Baking with Confidence and Hosting with Confidence as well as cake baking basics, packing advice for shipping baked goods and easy entertaining tips and tricks.

How sweet it is! Almost one-third of the book is designated to desserts. These luscious treats include cookies, brownies, bars, cupcakes, sweet breads, cakes, pies and more. You'll have fun just reading the recipes besides preparing them for your loved ones. Appealing favorites like Peach Crumble Pie, Black Forest Cake and German Chocolate Picnic Cake as well as some new classics like Chai Latte Cupcakes, Baklava Bars, Cranberry Mousse Torte and Orange Marmalade Crème Brûlée are sure to have your family begging for more.

We hope we've whetted your appetite to dive right into this stunning cookbook and explore all the scrumptious recipes this volume has to offer. Thank you for welcoming us back into your kitchen this year!

Betty Crocker

Easy Entertaining

Menus for Special Times

Whether you're serving cocktails for twenty or pizza for four, entertaining offers the perfect opportunity to welcome friends and family to your home. These twelve stress-free menus will delight your guests while allowing you to enjoy the gathering with minimal work or fuss.

Super Bowl Supper

Creamy Salsa Dip (page 47)
Spicy Chicken Nachos (page 60)
Old-Fashioned Potato Salad (page 75)
Sweet and Tangy Short Ribs (page 201)
Sports Party Cake (page 273)
Chilled Beer and Soft Drinks

Wintry Weekend Gathering

Apple-Gorgonzola Salad with Red Wine Vinaigrette (page 66)
French Peasant Chicken Stew (page 180)
Crusty Rolls
Caramel Latte Cake (page 290)
Crisp White Wine

South of the Border

Fire-Roasted Tomato Gazpacho (page 83)
Latin-Style Flank Steak with Spicy Parsley Pesto (page 204)
Black Beans and Greens (page 124)
Mojito Cake (page 291)
Sangria

Ladies' Lunch

Crab Gazpacho Cocktails (page 143)
Hummus and Cucumber Bites (page 105)
Pimiento-Cheese Spread Appetizers (page 47)
Curried Chicken Salad Cups (page 42)
Ginger-Almond Pears (page 340)
Sparkling Water

Cocktails on the Patio

Ham and Asparagus Rolls (page 39)
Grilled Veggie Platter with Ginger-Mustard Dip
  (page 40)
Grilled Brie with Mango and Raspberries (page 58)
Feta Cheese, Lemon and Chive Turnovers (page 50)
Mojito Melon Kabobs (page 45)
Assorted Wines and Beers

Pool Party

Meatball Mini Burgers (page 120)
Chicken-Gorgonzola Pasta Salad (page 82)
Chili-Cheese Twists (page 56)
Teddy-at-the-Beach Cupcakes (page 243)
Assorted Soft Drinks

Fire Up the Grill

Grilled Blue Cheese Burgers (page 117)
Grilled Corn on the Cob with Herb Butter (page 225)
Primavera Pasta Salad (page 77)
Brownie Ice Cream Cake (page 304)
Frozen Strawberry Margaritas (page 32)
Chilled Beverages

Chili Cook-off

Three-Bean Chili (page 134)
White Bean-Chicken Chili (page 183)
Chili Mole (page 210)
Pecan-Topped Corn Bread with Honey Butter (page 237)
Cool and Creamy Lime Dessert (page 334)
Variety of Soft Drinks

Fall Picnic

Happy Halloween!

Casual Dinner with Friends

Lazy Christmas Morning

Seasonal Selections

COOKING WITH THE SEASONS

Create the perfect meal for every season with the help of this handy guide. Whether you're looking to warm your bones with a hearty bowl of soup in the winter, cool down with a crisp summer salad or find new ways to use the first local spring strawberries, this guide will lead you to the perfect recipe every time.

Spring

Summer

Winter

Anytime

Breads and Breakfasts

Morning Meals and Baked Goods

Canadian Bacon Brunch Pizza with Cheddar-Dijon Sauce
(page 27)

Cinnamon-Crusted Brunch Cake (page 15)

Double-Banana Bread

Prep Time: 15 min   Start to Finish: 3 hr 45 min

Bread

- ³⁄₄ cup sugar
- ¹⁄₄ cup canola oil
- ³⁄₄ cup buttermilk
- 2 teaspoons vanilla
- 1 egg
- 1 cup mashed very ripe bananas (2 medium)
- 2 cups Gold Medal® all-purpose flour
- 1 teaspoon baking soda
- ¹⁄₄ teaspoon salt
- ³⁄₄ cup dried banana chips, chopped
- 2 cups Curves® Honey Crunch cereal, slightly crushed

Topping

- ¹⁄₂ cup Curves Honey Crunch cereal, crushed
- 2 teaspoons sugar
- 2 teaspoons canola oil
- Reserved 2 tablespoons banana chips

1. Heat oven to 350°F. Spray bottom only of 9 × 5-inch loaf pan with cooking spray. In large bowl, beat ³⁄₄ cup sugar and ¹⁄₄ cup oil with electric mixer on low speed until well mixed. Beat in buttermilk, vanilla and egg until blended. Beat in bananas.

2. With spoon, stir in flour, baking soda and salt just until blended. Set aside 2 tablespoons chopped banana chips for topping. Stir remaining banana chips and 2 cups cereal into batter. Spoon into pan; spread evenly. In small bowl, mix topping ingredients until crumbly. Sprinkle over batter in pan.

3. Bake 1 hour 10 minutes to 1 hour 20 minutes or until toothpick inserted in center comes out clean. Cool 10 minutes. Remove from pan to cooling rack. Cool completely, about 2 hours, before slicing.

1 loaf (16 slices)
1 Slice: Calories 210 (Calories from Fat 50); Total Fat 6g (Saturated Fat 1.5g; Trans Fat 0g); Cholesterol 15mg; Sodium 180mg; Total Carbohydrate 35g (Dietary Fiber 2g; Sugars 14g); Protein 3g
% Daily Value: Vitamin A 2%; Vitamin C 4%; Calcium 4%; Iron 10%
Exchanges: 1 Starch, 1¹⁄₂ Other Carbohydrate, 1 Fat
Carbohydrate Choices: 2

Low Fat

Ginger-Topped Pumpkin Bread

Prep Time: 15 min   Start to Finish: 2 hr 35 min

Bread

1	can (15 ounces) pumpkin (not pumpkin pie mix)
1²⁄₃	cups granulated sugar
²⁄₃	cup unsweetened applesauce
¹⁄₂	cup milk
2	teaspoons vanilla
1	cup fat-free egg product for 2 eggs plus 4 egg whites
3	cups Gold Medal all-purpose flour
2	teaspoons baking soda
1	teaspoon salt
1	teaspoon ground cinnamon
¹⁄₂	teaspoon baking powder
¹⁄₂	teaspoon ground cloves

Glaze and Topping

²⁄₃	cup powdered sugar
2 to 3	teaspoons warm water
¹⁄₄	teaspoon vanilla
3	tablespoons finely chopped crystallized ginger

2 loaves (12 slices each)
1 Serving: Calories 70 (Calories from Fat 0); Total Fat 0g (Saturated Fat 0g; Trans Fat 0g); Cholesterol 0mg; Sodium 120mg; Total Carbohydrate 16g (Dietary Fiber 0g; Sugars 9g); Protein 2g
% Daily Value: Vitamin A 30%; Vitamin C 0%; Calcium 0%; Iron 4%
Exchanges: ¹⁄₂ Starch, ¹⁄₂ Other Carbohydrate
Carbohydrate Choices: 1

1. Move oven rack to low position so that tops of pans will be in center of oven. Heat oven to 350°F. Grease bottoms only of 2 (8 × 4- or 9 × 5-inch) loaf pans with shortening or cooking spray.

2. In large bowl, mix pumpkin, granulated sugar, applesauce, milk, vanilla and egg product. Stir in remaining bread ingredients. Pour into pans.

3. Bake 1 hour to 1 hour 10 minutes or until toothpick inserted in center comes out clean. Cool 10 minutes. Loosen sides of loaves from pans; remove from pans to cooling rack. Cool completely, about 1 hour.

4. In small bowl, mix powdered sugar, warm water and ¹⁄₄ teaspoon vanilla until smooth and thin enough to drizzle. Drizzle glaze over loaves. Sprinkle with ginger.

KITCHEN TIPS

✿ You will find crystallized ginger in plastic containers with the other baking ingredients at the grocery store.
✿ Applesauce is the ingredient that adds moistness and depth to this updated favorite; ginger adds a new look and taste.

Quick

Zucchini Bread

Prep Time: 15 min Start to Finish: 3 hr 25 min

3 cups shredded zucchini (2 to 3 medium)

1²⁄₃ cups sugar

²⁄₃ cup vegetable oil

2 tablespoons vanilla

4 eggs

3 cups Gold Medal all-purpose or whole wheat flour

2 teaspoons baking soda

1 teaspoon salt

1 teaspoon ground cinnamon

½ teaspoon ground cloves

½ teaspoon baking powder

½ cup coarsely chopped nuts

½ cup raisins, if desired

1. Move oven rack to low position so that tops of pans will be in center of oven. Heat oven to 350°F. Grease bottoms only of 2 (8 × 4-inch) loaf pans or 1 (9 × 5-inch) loaf pan with shortening or cooking spray.

2. In large bowl, stir zucchini, sugar, oil, vanilla and eggs until well mixed. Stir in remaining ingredients except nuts and raisins. Stir in nuts and raisins. Divide batter evenly between 8-inch pans or pour into 9-inch pan.

3. Bake 8-inch loaves 50 to 60 minutes, 9-inch loaf 1 hour 10 minutes to 1 hour 20 minutes, or until toothpick inserted in center comes out clean. Cool in pans on cooling rack 10 minutes.

4. Loosen sides of loaves from pans; remove from pans and place top side up on cooling rack. Cool completely, about 2 hours, before slicing. Wrap tightly and store at room temperature up to 4 days, or refrigerate up to 10 days.

Cranberry Bread: Omit zucchini, cinnamon, cloves and raisins. Stir in ½ cup milk and 2 teaspoons grated orange peel with the oil. Stir 3 cups fresh or frozen (thawed and drained) cranberries into batter. Bake 1 hour to 1 hour 10 minutes.

Pumpkin Bread: Substitute 1 can (15 ounces) pumpkin (not pumpkin pie mix) for the zucchini.

2 loaves (12 slices each)
1 Slice: Calories 100 (Calories from Fat 40); Total Fat 4.5g (Saturated Fat 0.5g; Trans Fat 0g); Cholesterol 20mg; Sodium 115mg; Total Carbohydrate 13g (Dietary Fiber 0g; Sugars 7g); Protein 2g
% Daily Value: Vitamin A 0%; Vitamin C 0%; Calcium 0%; Iron 2%
Exchanges: ½ Starch, ½ Other Carbohydrate, 1 Fat
Carbohydrate Choices: 1

KITCHEN TIPS

✿ To make muffins: Grease bottoms only of 24 regular-size muffin cups. Fill cups about ¾ full. Bake 20 to 25 minutes or until tops spring back when touched lightly.

✿ Make this recipe a family affair. You can shred the zucchini while one of the kids measures sugar, oil and vanilla. In a separate bowl, have another child or your spouse measure the dry ingredients.

✿ Bake the batter in disposable paper or foil pans. Wrap and decorate for bake sales or gifts.

Zucchini Bread

Quick
Chai-Spiced Bread

Prep Time: 15 min Start to Finish: 3 hr 55 min

Bread

- ³⁄₄ cup granulated sugar
- ¹⁄₂ cup butter or margarine, softened
- ¹⁄₂ cup prepared tea or water
- ¹⁄₃ cup milk
- 2 teaspoons vanilla
- 2 eggs
- 2 cups Gold Medal all-purpose flour
- 2 teaspoons baking powder
- ³⁄₄ teaspoon ground cardamom
- ¹⁄₂ teaspoon salt
- ¹⁄₄ teaspoon ground cinnamon
- ¹⁄₈ teaspoon ground cloves

Glaze

- 1 cup powdered sugar
- ¹⁄₄ teaspoon vanilla
- 3 to 5 teaspoons milk
- Additional ground cinnamon

1. Heat oven to 400°F. Grease bottom only of 8 × 4- or 9 × 5-inch loaf pan with shortening or cooking spray.

2. In large bowl, beat granulated sugar and butter with electric mixer on medium speed until fluffy. On low speed, beat in tea, ¹⁄₃ cup milk, 2 teaspoons vanilla and the eggs until ingredients are well combined (will appear curdled). Stir in remaining bread ingredients just until moistened. Spread in pan.

3. Bake 50 to 60 minutes or until toothpick inserted in center comes out clean (do not underbake). Cool in pan on cooling rack 10 minutes. Loosen sides of loaf from pan; remove from pan to cooling rack. Cool 30 minutes.

4. In small bowl, stir powdered sugar, ¹⁄₄ teaspoon vanilla and 3 teaspoons of the milk, adding more milk by teaspoonfuls, until spreadable. Spread glaze over bread. Sprinkle with additional cinnamon. Cool completely, about 2 hours, before slicing. Wrap tightly and store at room temperature up to 4 days, or refrigerate up to 10 days.

1 loaf (16 slices)
1 Slice: Calories 190 (Calories from Fat 60); Total Fat 7g (Saturated Fat 4g; Trans Fat 0g); Cholesterol 40mg; Sodium 190mg; Total Carbohydrate 30g (Dietary Fiber 0g; Sugars 17g); Protein 3g
% Daily Value: Vitamin A 4%; Vitamin C 0%; Calcium 4%; Iron 6%
Exchanges: 1 Starch, 1 Other Carbohydrate, 1 Fat
Carbohydrate Choices: 2

KITCHEN TIPS

✿ Chai is the Hindi word for tea made with milk and spices such as cardamom, cinnamon, cloves, ginger, nutmeg and pepper.
✿ Serve as a snack or dessert with fresh fruit and tea.

Buttermilk-Lime Tea Bread

Prep Time: 15 min Start to Finish: 1 hr 15 min

1¾ cups Gold Medal all-purpose flour
 ¾ cup sugar
  2 teaspoons baking powder
 ¼ teaspoon salt
  1 egg
  1 cup buttermilk
 ¼ cup vegetable oil
  2 teaspoons grated lime peel
  3 tablespoons lime juice
  1 tablespoon sugar

1. Heat oven to 350°F (325°F for dark or nonstick pan). Grease bottom and sides of 8 × 4- or 9 × 5-inch loaf pan with shortening or spray with cooking spray; lightly flour.

2. In medium bowl, mix flour, ¾ cup sugar, the baking powder and salt; set aside.

3. In another medium bowl, stir egg, buttermilk, oil, lime peel and 1 tablespoon of the lime juice with spoon until well blended. Add buttermilk mixture to flour mixture and stir just until moistened (some lumps will remain). Spread in pan.

4. Bake 50 to 60 minutes or until golden brown and toothpick inserted in center comes out clean. Meanwhile, in small bowl, mix remaining 2 tablespoons lime juice and 1 tablespoon sugar.

5. Brush lime juice mixture over top of warm bread. Cool in pan on cooling rack 10 minutes; remove bread from pan to cooling rack. Cool completely, about 1 hour. When completely cool, wrap in plastic wrap. Bread is best served the next day.

1 loaf (16 slices)
1 Slice: Calories 130 (Calories from Fat 35); Total Fat 4g (Saturated Fat 0.5g; Trans Fat 0g); Cholesterol 15mg; Sodium 120mg; Total Carbohydrate 22g (Dietary Fiber 0g; Sugars 11g); Protein 2g
% Daily Value: Cholesterol 5%; Vitamin A 0%; Vitamin C 2%; Calcium 6%; Iron 4%
Exchanges: 1 Fat, 1 Starch
Carbohydrate Choices: 1½

KITCHEN TIPS

✿ For a tasty spread, stir a tablespoon of sugar and a teaspoon of grated lime peel into a tub of spreadable cream cheese.

Apricot-Oatmeal Muffins

Prep Time: 15 min   Start to Finish: 40 min

¾ cup Gold Medal all-purpose flour
½ cup quick-cooking or old-fashioned oats
1 teaspoon baking powder
¼ teaspoon salt
½ cup packed brown sugar
⅓ cup milk
3 tablespoons vegetable oil
½ teaspoon vanilla
1 egg
⅓ cup finely chopped dried apricots
1 tablespoon quick-cooking or old-fashioned oats, if desired

1. Heat oven to 400°F. Grease bottoms only of 6 regular-size muffin cups with shortening or cooking spray, or line with paper baking cups.

2. In medium bowl, mix flour, ½ cup oats, the baking powder and salt. In small bowl, mix brown sugar, milk, oil, vanilla and egg with fork or wire whisk until blended. Stir milk mixture into flour mixture just until flour is moistened. Fold in apricots. Divide evenly among muffin cups. Sprinkle each with about ½ teaspoon oats.

3. Bake 23 to 25 minutes or until toothpick inserted in center comes out clean. Remove from pan to cooling rack. Serve warm or cool.

6 muffins
1 Muffin: Calories 250 (Calories from Fat 80); Total Fat 9g (Saturated Fat 1.5g; Trans Fat 0g); Cholesterol 35mg; Sodium 200mg; Total Carbohydrate 40g (Dietary Fiber 1g; Sugars 22g); Protein 4g %
Daily Value: Vitamin A 6%; Vitamin C 0%; Calcium 10%; Iron 10%
Exchanges: 1½ Starch, 1 Other Carbohydrate, 1½ Fat
Carbohydrate Choices: 2½

KITCHEN TIPS

❊ To avoid soggy muffins, take them out of the pan immediately after removing them from the oven.
❊ Use an ice cream scoop, if you have one, to add batter to the muffin cups.

Pineapple and Carrot Surprise Muffins

Prep Time: 25 min Start to Finish: 1 hr

2 cups Gold Medal all-purpose flour
¾ cup packed brown sugar
1 teaspoon pumpkin pie spice
½ cup butter or margarine, melted
1 teaspoon baking powder
1 teaspoon baking soda
½ teaspoon salt
2 eggs, beaten
1 cup shredded carrots (about 1½ medium)
1 can (8 ounces) crushed pineapple in juice, undrained
1 package (3 ounces) cream cheese, softened
¼ cup granulated sugar
½ teaspoon vanilla

1. Heat oven to 400°F. Line 12 regular-size muffin cups with paper baking cups (or spray cups with cooking spray or grease with shortening). In large bowl, stir flour, brown sugar, pumpkin pie spice and melted butter with spoon until mixture looks like coarse crumbs. Reserve ½ cup mixture for topping.

2. Stir baking powder, baking soda, salt, eggs, carrots and pineapple into remaining crumb mixture just until moistened; set aside.

3. In small bowl, beat cream cheese, granulated sugar and vanilla with electric mixer on medium speed until well blended.

4. Fill muffin cups two-thirds full with batter. Make indentation in top of each muffin, using back of spoon. Drop about 1 teaspoon cream cheese mixture into each indentation. Sprinkle reserved crumb mixture over batter and filling.

5. Bake 20 to 30 minutes or until golden brown and edges spring back when touched lightly. Cool muffins in pan 5 minutes; remove from pan to cooling rack. Serve warm or cooled. Store covered in refrigerator.

12 muffins
1 Muffin: Calories 265 (Calories from Fat 100); Total Fat 11g (Saturated Fat 7g; Trans Fat 0g); Cholesterol 65mg; Sodium 340mg; Total Carbohydrate 38g (Dietary Fiber 1g; Sugars 21g); Protein 4g
Daily Value: Cholesterol 0%; Vitamin A 35%; Vitamin C 4%; Calcium 6%; Iron 8%
Exchanges: 2 Fat, 2 Starch
Carbohydrate Choices: 2½

Betty Crocker
MAKES IT EASY

Hosting with Confidence

Whether you have overnight guests during the holiday season, or you're looking for an easy way to bring people together early in the day, choose a menu that offers delicious, make-ahead choices such as Overnight French Toast Bake with Berry Topping, page 22.

Making the Table Special

Love the look of mini vases? You don't have to look any farther than your own kitchen to find them. Save empty condiment jars (i.e., mustard, olives, jam), remove the labels and decorate with seasonal charms (found at craft or scrapbook stores) or colorful ribbon. Fill the individual-size jars with bouquets of fresh herbs.

▶ Set the dining table and/or buffet table the day before, if you can.

▶ Set out serving dishes and utensils the day before.

▶ Make two shopping trips: the first one for all the ingredients that will not perish (can be done weeks ahead), the second one for perishables purchased a day or two before the brunch.

▶ Most baked goods can be made ahead and frozen for up to 2 months.

▶ Serve main dishes that can be prepared the day before.

Quick
Fresh Orange Scones

Prep Time: 15 min Start to Finish: 35 min

2½ cups Gold Medal all-purpose flour
1 cup quick-cooking oats
⅓ cup sugar
3 teaspoons baking powder
1 tablespoon grated orange peel
½ teaspoon salt
⅔ cup firm butter or margarine
2 eggs, beaten
½ to ¾ cup half-and-half
2 tablespoons orange juice
2 tablespoons sugar

1. Heat oven to 400°F. Grease cookie sheet with shortening or cooking spray.

2. In large bowl, mix flour, oats, ⅓ cup sugar, the baking powder, orange peel and salt. Cut in butter, using pastry blender (or pulling 2 table knives through ingredients in opposite directions), until mixture looks like fine crumbs. Stir in eggs and just enough half-and-half so dough leaves side of bowl.

3. On lightly floured surface, knead dough lightly 10 times, using floured hands if necessary. Divide dough in half. On cookie sheet, pat or roll each half of dough into 7-inch round, ½ inch thick. Cut each round into 6 wedges with sharp knife that has been dipped in flour, but do not separate wedges. Brush with orange juice; sprinkle each half with 1 tablespoon sugar.

4. Bake 12 to 16 minutes or until golden brown. Immediately remove from cookie sheet; carefully separate wedges. Serve warm.

12 scones
1 Scone: Calories 270 (Calories from Fat 120); Total Fat 13g (Saturated Fat 8g; Trans Fat 0g); Cholesterol 65mg; Sodium 310mg; Total Carbohydrate 33g (Dietary Fiber 1g; Sugars 9g); Protein 5g
% Daily Value: Vitamin A 8%; Vitamin C 0%; Calcium 10%; Iron 10%
Exchanges: 1½ Starch, ½ Other Carbohydrate, 2½ Fat
Carbohydrate Choices: 2

KITCHEN TIPS

❀ Mix together 2 cups powdered sugar and 2 tablespoons fresh orange juice until thin enough to spread. Frost scones, then sprinkle with coarsely chopped pecans.

❀ Try adding 1 cup of raisins or currants to your scones for extra taste and texture.

❀ Place a couple of cooled scones in a cellophane bag, add a tea bag and tie with a pretty ribbon for a tasty gift.

Coconut, Pineapple and Macadamia Scones

Prep Time: 10 min Start to Finish: 25 min

2½ cups Original Bisquick® mix
¼ cup sugar
¼ cup firm butter or margarine
½ cup flaked coconut
½ cup chopped macadamia nuts
¼ cup whipping cream
1 egg
1 can (8 ounces) pineapple tidbits, well drained

1. Heat oven to 425°F. Spray cookie sheet with cooking spray. In large bowl, mix Bisquick mix and sugar. Cut in butter, using pastry blender (or pulling 2 table knives through ingredients in opposite directions), until crumbly. Stir in remaining ingredients.

2. Pat dough into 10 × 7-inch rectangle on cookie sheet (if dough is sticky, dip fingers in Bisquick mix). Cut into 12 rectangles, but do not separate. If desired, sprinkle with additional sugar and coconut.

3. Bake 12 to 14 minutes or until golden brown. Carefully separate scones; serve warm.

12 scones
1 Scone: Calories 250 (Calories from Fat 120); Total Fat 14g (Saturated Fat 6g; Trans Fat 1g); Cholesterol 35mg; Sodium 350mg; Total Carbohydrate 28g (Dietary Fiber 1g; Sugars 12g); Protein 3g
% Daily Value: Vitamin A 4%; Vitamin C 0%; Calcium 4%; Iron 6%
Exchanges: 1 Starch, 1 Other Carbohydrate, 2½ Fat
Carbohydrate Choices: 2

KITCHEN TIPS

✿ Toss together a bowl of assorted fresh fruit pieces or pour glasses of your favorite juice blend to serve with these tropical scones. Don't forget the butter and honey or jam!

✿ Crazy for nuts? Try substituting pecans or almonds for the macadamia nuts, or use a combination of nuts in this sweet scone.

Pull-Apart Caramel Loaf

Prep Time: 10 min Start to Finish: 2 hr 50 min

6 frozen cinnamon rolls (from 36.5-ounce bag)
½ cup packed brown sugar
¼ cup butter or margarine
2 tablespoons light corn syrup
2 tablespoons whipping cream

1. Heat oven to 175°F. Place rolls on cutting board. Let stand 10 minutes or until partially thawed.

2. Meanwhile, in 1-quart saucepan, heat brown sugar and butter over medium heat, stirring constantly, until butter is melted. Stir in corn syrup and whipping cream. Pour brown sugar mixture into 9 × 5-inch loaf pan, covering bottom completely.

3. Cut each cinnamon roll in half crosswise. Arrange roll halves randomly over brown sugar mixture in pan. Cover loosely with plastic wrap sprayed with cooking spray. Place pan in oven and turn off heat. Let rise 1 hour 10 minutes to 1 hour 30 minutes or until loaf has at least doubled in size and top of loaf is 1 inch from top of pan. Remove from oven.

4. Heat oven to 350°F. Remove plastic wrap. Bake loaf 25 to 30 minutes or until golden brown. Place heatproof tray or serving plate upside down over pan; immediately turn tray and pan over. Let pan remain 1 minute to allow caramel to drizzle over loaf; remove pan. Serve warm.

6 servings
1 Serving: Calories 380 (Calories from Fat 150); Total Fat 17g (Saturated Fat 8g; Trans Fat 2g); Cholesterol 40mg; Sodium 210mg; Total Carbohydrate 53g (Dietary Fiber 1g; Sugars 30g); Protein 4g
% Daily Value: Vitamin A 6%; Vitamin C 0%; Calcium 4%; Iron 10%
Exchanges: 1 Starch, 2½ Other Carbohydrate, 3 Fat
Carbohydrate Choices: 3½

KITCHEN TIPS

✿ Corn syrup is available in both a light and dark variety. Light corn syrup, which has a milder, sweet flavor, has been clarified to remove color and cloudiness.

✿ If you like pecans, add chopped pecans to the caramel mixture in the pan.

Pull-Apart Cararmel Loaf

Coconut, Pineapple and Macadamia Scones

Fresh Raspberry Coffee Cake

Prep Time: 20 min Start to Finish: 1 hr 10 min

Coffee Cake

- $1/2$ cup butter or margarine, melted
- $3/4$ cup milk
- 1 teaspoon vanilla
- 1 egg
- 2 cups Gold Medal all-purpose flour
- $1/2$ cup granulated sugar
- 2 teaspoons baking powder
- $1/2$ teaspoon salt
- 1 cup fresh raspberries

Glaze

- $1/2$ cup powdered sugar
- 1 tablespoon butter or margarine, softened
- 2 to 3 teaspoons water
- $1/4$ teaspoon almond extract

1. Heat oven to 400°F. Spray 8- or 9-inch square pan with baking spray with flour.

2. In medium bowl, beat $1/2$ cup butter, the milk, vanilla and egg with spoon. Stir in flour, granulated sugar, baking powder and salt just until flour is moistened. Fold in raspberries. Spread in pan.

3. Bake 25 to 30 minutes or until top is golden brown and toothpick inserted in center comes out clean. Cool 20 minutes.

4. In small bowl, mix glaze ingredients until smooth and thin enough to drizzle. Drizzle glaze over warm coffee cake.

9 servings
1 Serving: Calories 300 (Calories from Fat 120); Total Fat 13g (Saturated Fat 8g; Trans Fat 0g); Cholesterol 55mg; Sodium 340mg; Total Carbohydrate 42g (Dietary Fiber 1g; Sugars 19g); Protein 5g
% Daily Value: Vitamin A 8%; Vitamin C 4%; Calcium 10%; Iron 8%
Exchanges: $1^1/2$ Starch, 1 Other Carbohydrate, $2^1/2$ Fat
Carbohydrate Choices: 3

KITCHEN TIPS

- ❀ This coffee cake is best served warm, but you can microwave a piece for 10 to 15 seconds on High to bring back that fresh-from-the-oven taste.
- ❀ Next time, try making this coffee cake with fresh blackberries instead of raspberries.

Quick

Cinnamon-Crusted Brunch Cake

Prep Time: 15 min Start to Finish: 45 min

¾ cup packed brown sugar
2 tablespoons ground cinnamon
3¾ cups Original Bisquick mix
½ cup packed brown sugar
¼ cup butter or margarine, melted
1⅓ cups milk
1 teaspoon ground ginger
2 eggs
½ cup finely chopped pecans

1. Heat oven to 350°F. Generously grease 12-cup fluted tube cake pan with shortening. In small bowl, mix ¾ cup brown sugar and the cinnamon. Coat pan with cinnamon-sugar mixture; shake out and reserve excess.

2. In medium bowl, stir remaining ingredients except pecans until blended; beat vigorously with spoon 30 seconds. Spoon half of batter into pan.

3. Stir pecans into reserved cinnamon-sugar mixture; sprinkle half of pecan mixture over batter in pan.

Spread remaining batter over pecan mixture. Sprinkle with remaining pecan mixture.

4. Bake 25 to 30 minutes or until toothpick inserted in center comes out clean. Remove from pan to serving plate. Serve warm.

12 servings
1 Serving: Calories 340 (Calories from Fat 120); Total Fat 13g (Saturated Fat 4.5g; Trans Fat 1.5g); Cholesterol 50mg; Sodium 520mg; Total Carbohydrate 50g (Dietary Fiber 2g; Sugars 25g); Protein 5g
% Daily Value: Vitamin A 4%; Vitamin C 0%; Calcium 10%; Iron 10%
Exchanges: 1 Starch, 2½ Other Carbohydrate, 2½ Fat
Carbohydrate Choices: 3

KITCHEN TIPS

✿ Try adding ½ cup of chopped peeled apple to the pecan filling mixture.
✿ Nutmeg can be substituted for the ground ginger.

Peach Melba Pancakes

Coffee Swirl Cake

Quick

Coffee Swirl Cake

Prep Time: 20 min Start to Finish: 3 hr

1/4	cup instant coffee granules or crystals
1	tablespoon hot water
3	cups Gold Medal all-purpose flour
1	teaspoon baking powder
1/4	teaspoon salt
1 1/4	cups butter or margarine, softened
2 3/4	cups sugar
6	eggs
1	cup milk
1/2	cup sour cream

1. Heat oven to 350°F. Grease 12-cup fluted tube cake pan or 10-inch angel food (tube) cake pan with shortening; lightly flour. In small bowl, mix coffee and hot water; cool 10 minutes.

2. In medium bowl, mix flour, baking powder and salt; set aside. In large bowl, beat butter, sugar and eggs with electric mixer on low speed 30 seconds, scraping bowl constantly. Beat on high speed 3 minutes, scraping bowl occasionally. On low speed, beat in flour mixture, milk and sour cream until blended.

3. Remove 1 cup of the batter; stir into cooled coffee. Pour remaining batter into pan. Drop coffee batter by about 12 tablespoonfuls onto batter in pan. Cut through batters with knife for marbled design.

4. Bake 50 to 55 minutes or until toothpick inserted in center comes out clean. Cool 15 minutes in pan on cooling rack; remove from pan to cooling rack. Cool at least 1 hour 30 minutes. Serve warm or cooled.

24 servings
1 Serving: Calories 270 (Calories from Fat 110); Total Fat 12g (Saturated Fat 6g; Trans Fat 0g); Cholesterol 80mg; Sodium 130mg; Total Carbohydrate 36g (Dietary Fiber 0g; Sugars 24 g); Protein 4g
% Daily Value: Vitamin A 10%; Vitamin C 0%; Calcium 4%; Iron 6%
Exchanges: 1 Starch, 1 1/2 Other Carbohydrate; 0 Vegetableetable; 2 Fat
Carbohydrate Choices: 2 1/2

Peach Melba Pancakes

Prep Time: 25 min Start to Finish: 25 min

2	eggs
2	cups Gold Medal all-purpose flour
1 1/2	cups milk
1/4	cup vegetable oil
2	tablespoons sugar
3	teaspoons baking powder
1/2	teaspoon salt
1/2	cup chopped canned (drained) or frozen (thawed and drained) sliced peaches
1/2	cup fresh or frozen (thawed and well drained) raspberries
	Additional peaches and raspberries, if desired
	Raspberry syrup, if desired

1. Heat griddle or skillet over medium-high heat or to 375°F. If necessary, brush griddle with vegetable oil before batter for pancakes is added (or spray with cooking spray before heating).

2. In medium bowl, beat eggs with wire whisk until well beaten. Beat in remaining ingredients except fruit and syrup just until smooth. Stir in 1/2 cup each peaches and raspberries.

3. For each pancake, pour slightly less than 1/4 cup batter onto hot griddle. Cook until bubbly on top, puffed and dry around edges. Turn; cook other sides until golden brown. Serve with additional peaches and raspberries and syrup.

9 servings
1 Serving: Calories 110 (Calories from Fat 40); Total Fat 4g (Saturated Fat 1g; Trans Fat 0g); Cholesterol 25mg; Sodium 160mg; Total Carbohydrate 14g (Dietary Fiber 0g; Sugars 3g); Protein 3g
% Daily Value: Vitamin A 2%; Vitamin C 6%; Calcium 8%; Iron 4%
Exchanges: 1 Starch; 0 Other Carbohydrate; 0 Vegetableeetable; 1/2 Fat
Carbohydrate Choices: 1

KITCHEN TIPS

✿ Adding fruit to your pancakes adds flavor, color, variety and, most of all, extra nutrition. Experts now recommend at least 5 servings of fruits and vegetables per day, and scientists are still uncovering important benefits of those nutrient powerhouses.

Corn Bread Pancakes with Butter-Pecan Syrup

Prep Time: 30 min Start to Finish: 30 min

Butter-Pecan Syrup

2	tablespoons butter or margarine
1/3	cup chopped pecans
3/4	cup maple-flavored syrup

Pancakes

1 1/4	cups Gold Medal all-purpose flour
3/4	cup cornmeal
1/4	cup sugar
2	teaspoons baking powder
1/2	teaspoon salt
1 1/3	cups milk
1/4	cup vegetable oil
1	egg, beaten

1. In 1-quart saucepan, melt butter over medium heat. Add pecans; cook, stirring frequently, until browned. Stir in syrup; heat until hot. Remove from heat.

2. Heat griddle or skillet over medium-high heat or to 375°F. If necessary, brush griddle with vegetable oil before batter for pancakes is added (or spray with cooking spray before heating).

3. In large bowl, mix flour, cornmeal, sugar, baking powder and salt. Stir in milk, oil and egg just until blended.

4. For each pancake, pour about 1/4 cup batter from cup or pitcher onto hot griddle. Cook 2 to 3 minutes or until bubbly on top and dry around edges. Turn; cook other sides 2 to 3 minutes longer or until golden brown. Serve with syrup.

8 servings
1 Serving: Calories 350 (Calories from Fat 140); Total Fat 16g (Saturated Fat 4g; Trans Fat 0g); Cholesterol 35mg; Sodium 350mg; Total Carbohydrate 47g (Dietary Fiber 2g; Sugars 0g); Protein 6g
% Daily Value: Cholesterol 0%; Vitamin A 0%; Vitamin C 0%; Calcium 0%; Iron 0%
Exchanges: 2 1/2 Fat , 2 1/2 Starch
Carbohydrate Choices: 3

Quick

Tiramisu Waffles

Prep Time: 30 min Start to Finish: 30 min

Topping
- 1 teaspoon instant coffee granules
- $\frac{1}{4}$ cup milk
- 1 package (8 ounces) cream cheese, softened
- $\frac{1}{3}$ cup powdered sugar
- $\frac{1}{2}$ teaspoon vanilla

Waffles
- 3 eggs
- $\frac{1}{2}$ cup granulated sugar
- $\frac{1}{4}$ cup vegetable oil
- 2 ounces unsweetened baking chocolate, melted
- $1\frac{1}{4}$ cups milk
- 2 cups Gold Medal all-purpose flour
- 2 tablespoons baking cocoa
- 1 tablespoon baking powder
- $\frac{1}{4}$ teaspoon salt
- 1 ounce semisweet baking chocolate, grated

6 servings
1 Serving: Calories 610 (Calories from Fat 300); Total Fat 33g (Saturated Fat 15g; Trans Fat 0g); Cholesterol 150mg; Sodium 520mg; Total Carbohydrate 67g (Dietary Fiber 4g); Protein 14g
% Daily Value: Vitamin A 12%; Vitamin C 0%; Calcium 12%; Iron 16%
Exchanges: $5\frac{1}{2}$ Fat; $3\frac{1}{2}$ Starch; $\frac{1}{2}$ Meat
Carbohydrate Choices: 2

KITCHEN TIPS

✿ Waffle makers come in different shapes and sizes. The number of waffles you get from the recipe may vary slightly depending on your waffle maker.

1. In small bowl, dissolve coffee granules in $\frac{1}{4}$ cup milk. In medium bowl, beat cream cheese, powdered sugar and vanilla with electric mixer on medium speed until blended. Beat in milk mixture until well blended.

2. Heat waffle maker. If necessary, brush with vegetable oil before batter for each waffle is added (or spray with cooking spray before heating). In large bowl, beat eggs, granulated sugar, oil and melted unsweetened chocolate with wire whisk until smooth. Beat in $1\frac{1}{4}$ cups milk, the flour, cocoa, baking powder and salt just until smooth.

3. Pour about $\frac{1}{2}$ cup batter onto center of hot waffle maker. (Check manufacturer's directions for recommended amount of batter.) Close lid of waffle maker.

4. Bake about 4 minutes or until steaming stops. Carefully remove waffle. Repeat with remaining batter. Serve waffle topped with 1 heaping tablespoon topping and 1 teaspoon grated chocolate.

Whole Wheat Waffles with Honey-Peanut Butter Syrup

Prep Time: 35 min Start to Finish: 35 min

Waffles

3	egg whites
1	cup Gold Medal whole wheat flour
1	cup Gold Medal all-purpose flour
2	cups buttermilk
1	tablespoon sugar
3	tablespoons vegetable oil
2	teaspoons baking powder
1/4	teaspoon salt

Honey-Peanut Butter Syrup

1	cup honey
1/2	cup creamy peanut butter

1. Heat waffle maker. If necessary, brush with vegetable oil before batter for each waffle is added (or spray with cooking spray before heating). In medium bowl, beat egg whites with egg beater until foamy. Beat in remaining waffle ingredients just until smooth.

2. Pour about 3/4 cup batter from cup or pitcher onto center of hot waffle maker. (Check manufacturer's directions for recommended amount of batter.) Close lid of waffle maker.

3. Bake about 5 minutes or until steaming stops. Carefully remove waffle. Repeat with remaining batter.

4. Meanwhile, in small microwavable bowl, mix honey and peanut butter. Microwave uncovered on High 40 to 60 seconds or until warm; stir until smooth. Serve with waffles.

6 servings
1 Serving: Calories 580 (Calories from Fat 170); Total Fat 19g (Saturated Fat 3.5g; Trans Fat 0g); Cholesterol 0mg; Sodium 480mg; Total Carbohydrate 88g (Dietary Fiber 4g; Sugars 0g); Protein 15g
% Daily Value: Cholesterol 2%; Vitamin A 0%; Vitamin C 2%; Calcium 20%; Iron 15%
Exchanges: 3 1/2 Fat, 4 1/2 Starch, 1/2 Milk, 1 Meat
Carbohydrate Choices: 7

KITCHEN TIPS

✿ Top off these hearty, sweet waffles with a sprinkling of crunchy granola.

Quick

Upside-Down Banana-Walnut French Toast

Prep Time: 15 min Start to Finish: 2 hr

1½ cups packed brown sugar

½ cup butter or margarine, melted

¼ cup corn syrup

½ cup chopped walnuts

3 medium bananas, sliced

1 loaf (about 1 pound) sliced unfrosted firm cinnamon bread

6 eggs

1½ cups milk

1 teaspoon vanilla

1. Spray bottom and sides of 13 × 9-inch (3-quart) glass baking dish with cooking spray or grease with shortening. In large bowl, stir together brown sugar, butter, corn syrup and walnuts until smooth. Gently stir in bananas. Spoon banana mixture into baking dish.

2. Reserve heels of bread for another use. Arrange 2 layers of bread on banana mixture, tearing bread to fit if needed.

3. In medium bowl, beat eggs, milk and vanilla with wire whisk until well mixed. Pour over bread. Cover tightly; refrigerate at least 1 hour but no longer than 24 hours.

4. Heat oven to 325°F. Uncover bread mixture; bake 45 to 55 minutes or until knife inserted in center comes out clean. Serve portions upside down, spooning sauce from bottom of dish over each serving.

10 servings
1 Serving: Calories 490 (Calories from Fat 170); Total Fat 19g (Saturated Fat 7g; Trans Fat 0g); Cholesterol 155mg; Sodium 309mg; Total Carbohydrate 72g (Dietary Fiber 3g; Sugars 0g); Protein 11g
% Daily Value: Cholesterol 52%; Vitamin A 10%; Vitamin C 6%; Calcium 10%; Iron 20%
Exchanges: 2½ Fat, ½ Fruit, ½ Meat, 3 Starch,
Carbohydrate Choices: 6

KITCHEN TIPS

✿ This is a perfect dish for company brunch. Do the work the night before, and bake the French toast while you set the table and prepare the rest of the meal in the morning.

✿ Sprinkle powdered sugar over the French toast before serving.

Overnight French Toast Bake with Berry Topping

Prep Time: 20 min Start to Finish: 4 hr 50 min

French Toast Bake

- 12 cups cubed (1 inch) soft French bread (about 13 ounces)
- 8 eggs
- 3 cups half-and-half
- ¼ cup sugar
- 1 teaspoon ground cinnamon
- ½ teaspoon salt
- 2 teaspoons vanilla

Berry Topping

- 1 cup sugar
- 1 tablespoon cornstarch
- ¼ cup orange juice
- 1 bag (12 ounces) frozen unsweetened mixed berries
- 3 cups fresh strawberries, cut into quarters

1. Spray bottom and sides of 13 × 9-inch (3-quart) glass baking dish with cooking spray. Place bread cubes in baking dish. In large bowl, beat eggs, half-and-half, ¼ cup sugar, the cinnamon, salt and vanilla with wire whisk until smooth; pour over bread cubes. Cover tightly; refrigerate at least 4 hours but no longer than 24 hours.

2. Heat oven to 400°F. Uncover dish; bake 25 to 35 minutes or until golden brown and knife inserted in center comes out clean.

3. Meanwhile, in 2-quart saucepan, stir together 1 cup sugar and the cornstarch. Stir in orange juice until smooth. Stir in mixed berries. Heat to boiling over medium heat, stirring constantly. Cook about 6 minutes, stirring constantly, until topping is slightly thickened. Remove from heat.

4. Just before serving, stir strawberries into topping. Serve warm over French toast bake.

8 servings
1 Serving: Calories 496 (Calories from Fat 147); Total Fat 16g (Saturated Fat 8g; Trans Fat 0g); Cholesterol 245mg; Sodium 550mg; Total Carbohydrate 74g (Dietary Fiber 4g; Sugars 40g); Protein 15g
% Daily Value: Cholesterol 82%; Vitamin A 0%; Vitamin C 80%; Calcium 15%; Iron 20%
Exchanges: 2 Fat, 1 Fruit, 3½ Starch
Carbohydrate Choices: 5

KITCHEN TIPS

❈ Use a serrated bread knife to easily cut through the bread slices. Slice off and discard the loaf ends so each slice will readily soak up the egg mixture.

❈ Enjoy this recipe with crisp bacon strips and freshly squeezed orange juice.

Smoked Salmon and Cream Cheese Quiche

Prep Time: 15 min Start to Finish: 2 hr 10 min

1	cup Gold Medal all-purpose flour
$\frac{1}{2}$	teaspoon salt
$\frac{1}{3}$	cup plus 1 teaspoon shortening
2 to 3	tablespoons cold water
$\frac{1}{2}$	pound smoked salmon, skin and bones removed, flaked or chopped
1	package (3 ounces) cream cheese, cut into $\frac{1}{2}$-inch cubes
4	medium green onions, sliced ($\frac{1}{4}$ cup)
6	eggs, beaten
$1\frac{1}{2}$	cups half-and-half
$\frac{1}{2}$	teaspoon salt
$\frac{1}{8}$	teaspoon pepper

1. Heat oven to 425°F. In medium bowl, mix flour and $\frac{1}{2}$ teaspoon salt. Cut in shortening, using pastry blender (or pulling 2 table knives through ingredients in opposite directions), until particles are size of small peas. Sprinkle with cold water, 1 tablespoon at a time, tossing with fork until all flour is moistened and pastry almost leaves side of bowl (1 to 2 teaspoons more water can be added if necessary).

2. Gather pastry into a ball. On lightly floured surface, shape pastry into flattened round. Wrap flattened round of pastry in plastic wrap; refrigerate about 45 minutes or until dough is firm and cold, yet pliable.

3. With floured rolling pin, roll pastry into circle 2 inches larger than upside-down 9-inch glass pie plate. Fold pastry into fourths; place in pie plate. Unfold and ease into plate, pressing firmly against bottom and side. Trim overhanging edge of pastry 1 inch from rim of plate. Fold and roll pastry under, even with plate; flute. Prick bottom and side of pastry thoroughly with fork. Bake 15 to 20 minutes or until light brown. Pat down center if necessary.

4. Reduce oven temperature to 325°F. Spread salmon in bottom of pastry. Top with cream cheese and green onions. In large bowl, beat eggs, half-and-half, $\frac{1}{2}$ teaspoon salt and the pepper with wire whisk until smooth. Pour over salmon mixture.

5. Bake uncovered 35 to 40 minutes or until knife inserted in center comes out clean. Let stand 10 minutes before cutting.

6 servings
1 Serving: Calories 435 (Calories from Fat 274); Total Fat 31g (Saturated Fat 12g; Trans Fat 0g); Cholesterol 250mg; Sodium 526mg; Total Carbohydrate 20g (Dietary Fiber 1g; Sugars 1g); Protein 20g
% Daily Value: Cholesterol 83%; Vitamin A 15%; Vitamin C 4%; Calcium 15%; Iron 15%
Exchanges: $4\frac{1}{2}$ Fat, 2 Meat, 1 Starch
Carbohydrate Choices: 1

Brunch Eggs on English Muffins

Prep Time: 25 min Start to Finish: 25 min

1 teaspoon butter or margarine

2 teaspoons Gold Medal all-purpose flour

1/2 cup milk

1/4 cup shredded Cheddar cheese (1 ounce)

2 teaspoons grated Parmesan cheese

1 teaspoon chopped fresh or 1/4 teaspoon dried basil leaves

Dash of ground red pepper (cayenne)

2 English muffins, split

4 thin slices fully cooked Canadian-style bacon (2 ounces)

8 eggs, beaten

Freshly ground pepper

1. In 1-quart nonstick saucepan, melt butter over low heat. Stir in flour; remove from heat. Gradually stir in milk. Heat to boiling, stirring constantly. Boil and stir 1 minute; remove from heat. Stir in cheeses, basil and red pepper; keep warm.

2. Toast English muffins. In 10-inch nonstick skillet, cook bacon over medium heat until brown on both sides. Remove from skillet; keep warm.

3. Heat same skillet over medium heat. Pour eggs into skillet. As mixture begins to set at bottom and side, gently lift cooked portions with spatula so that thin, uncooked portion can flow to bottom. Avoid constant stirring. Cook 3 to 4 minutes or until eggs are thickened throughout but still moist.

4. Place 1 slice bacon on each muffin half. Top with eggs. Spoon about 2 tablespoons sauce over eggs. Sprinkle with pepper.

4 servings
1 Serving: Calories 300 (Calories from Fat 150); Total Fat 16g (Saturated Fat 6g; Trans Fat 0g); Cholesterol 445mg; Sodium 514 mg; Total Carbohydrate 17g (Dietary Fiber 0g; Sugars 2g); Protein 21g
% Daily Value: Cholesterol 0%; Vitamin A 15%; Vitamin C 0%; Calcium 20%; Iron 15%
Exchanges: 1/2 Fat, 2 1/2 Meat, 1 Starch
Carbohydrate Choices: 1

KITCHEN TIPS

❂ Try reduced-fat cheese for a lower-fat sauce.
❂ Round out this hearty dish with fresh fruit, coffee and freshly squeezed orange juice.

Brunch Eggs on English Muffins

Sausage Oven Pancake Square

Prep Time: 20 min Start to Finish: 50 min

1 package (12 ounces) bulk pork sausage

1 cup shredded American-Cheddar cheese blend (4 ounces)

1 egg

¼ cup milk

2 tablespoons maple-flavored syrup

1 tablespoon vegetable oil

½ cup Gold Medal all-purpose flour

1 teaspoon baking powder

⅛ teaspoon salt

¾ cup maple-flavored syrup

1. Heat oven to 350°F. In 10-inch skillet, cook sausage over medium-high heat 5 to 7 minutes, stirring frequently, until no longer pink. Drain sausage on paper towels. In ungreased 8- or 9-inch square pan, spread cooked sausage. Sprinkle cheese over sausage.

2. In large bowl, beat egg, milk, 2 tablespoons maple syrup and the oil with wire whisk until well blended. Beat in flour, baking powder and salt. Pour batter evenly over sausage and cheese.

3. Bake uncovered 25 to 30 minutes or until golden brown. Serve topped with ¾ cup maple syrup.

6 servings
1 Serving: Calories 405 (Calories from Fat 183); Total Fat 20g (Saturated Fat 8g; Trans Fat 0g); Cholesterol 97mg; Sodium 546mg; Total Carbohydrate 44g (Dietary Fiber 0g; Sugars 0g); Protein 16g
% Daily Value: Cholesterol 32%; Vitamin A 6%; Vitamin C 0%; Calcium 25%; Iron 10%
Exchanges: 1 Fat, 2 Starch, 2 Meat
Carbohydrate Choices: 3

Canadian Bacon Brunch Pizza with Cheddar-Dijon Sauce

Prep Time: 25 min Start to Finish: 45 min
(Photo on page 1)

Crust

   8 cups frozen country-style shredded hash brown potatoes (from 30-ounce bag), thawed, drained
 ¼ cup butter or margarine, melted
   2 eggs, beaten
 ½ cup Gold Medal all-purpose flour
   1 teaspoon salt

Cheddar-Dijon Sauce

   4 ounces prepared cheese product (from loaf), cut into 1-inch cubes (about 1 cup)
   2 tablespoons milk
   1 teaspoon grated Parmesan cheese
 ½ teaspoon Dijon mustard

Topping

   1 package (3.5 ounces) pizza-style sliced Canadian-style bacon
   6 eggs
 ¼ cup milk
 ¼ teaspoon salt
 ⅛ teaspoon pepper
   1 tablespoon butter or margarine
   1 tablespoon chopped fresh chives

1. Heat oven to 425°F. Spray 12-inch pizza pan with cooking spray or grease with shortening. In large bowl, toss potatoes, ¼ cup melted butter, 2 eggs, the flour and 1 teaspoon salt. Press potato mixture in pan. Bake uncovered 20 to 25 minutes or until edges are golden brown.

2. Meanwhile, in small microwavable bowl, cover and microwave cheese product cubes and 2 tablespoons milk on High 1 minute. Stir until smooth. Stir in Parmesan cheese and mustard until well blended. Spread ½ cup of the cheese sauce over potato crust; top with Canadian bacon. Cover remaining sauce to keep warm.

3. Bake 5 to 7 minutes longer or until Canadian bacon is thoroughly heated.

4. Meanwhile, in medium bowl, beat 6 eggs, ¼ cup milk, ¼ teaspoon salt and the pepper with fork or wire whisk until well mixed.

5. In 10-inch skillet, heat 1 tablespoon butter over medium heat just until butter begins to sizzle. Pour egg mixture into skillet. As mixture begins to set at bottom and side, gently lift cooked portions with spatula so that thin, uncooked portion can flow to bottom. Avoid constant stirring. Cook 3 to 4 minutes or until eggs are thickened throughout but still moist.

6. Spoon scrambled eggs over hot crust. Drizzle with remaining ½ cup cheese sauce. Sprinkle with chives. Use spatula to lift servings from pan.

8 servings
1 Serving: Calories 358 (Calories from Fat 234); Total Fat 26g (Saturated Fat 12g; Trans Fat 0g); Cholesterol 250mg; Sodium 910mg; Total Carbohydrate 48g (Dietary Fiber 3g; Sugars 2g); Protein 15g
% Daily Value: Cholesterol 83%; Vitamin A 10%; Vitamin C 25%; Calcium 10%; Iron 15%
Exchanges: 2 Fat, 1½ Meat, 2 Starch
Carbohydrate Choices: 2½

KITCHEN TIPS

✿ Ask your kids to lend a hand with this recipe. Research shows that kids are more likely to eat a good meal after they've helped prepare it.

✿ Use a kitchen scissors to make quick work of chopping the chives.

Make-Ahead Sausage and Mushroom Scrambled Eggs

Prep Time: 30 min Start to Finish: 1 hr

8 ounces bulk pork sausage

1 package (8 ounces) sliced fresh mushrooms (3 cups)

¼ cup finely chopped red bell pepper

¼ cup finely chopped green bell pepper

3 tablespoons butter or margarine

16 eggs

1 cup half-and-half or milk

½ teaspoon dried thyme leaves

½ teaspoon salt

¼ teaspoon pepper

1 can (10¾ ounces) condensed reduced-sodium cream of mushroom soup

2 cups shredded Cheddar cheese (8 ounces)

1. In 12-inch nonstick skillet, cook sausage over medium-high heat 5 to 7 minutes, stirring occasionally, until no longer pink. Add mushrooms and bell peppers; cook 4 to 5 minutes, stirring frequently, until vegetables are tender. Remove mixture from skillet; drain. Wipe skillet clean with paper towel.

2. In same skillet, melt butter over medium heat. Meanwhile, in large bowl, beat eggs. Stir half-and-half, thyme, salt and pepper into eggs. Add egg mixture to butter in skillet. Cook over medium heat about 7 minutes, stirring constantly, until mixture is firm but not moist. Stir in soup.

3. Spray 3- to 4-quart slow cooker with cooking spray. In cooker, place half of egg mixture. Top with half each of the sausage mixture and cheese. Repeat layers.

4. Cover; cook on Low heat setting 30 minutes or until cheese is melted. Mixture can be kept warm on Low heat setting up to 2 hours.

12 servings (¾ cup each)
1 Serving: Calories 280 (Calories from Fat 200); Total Fat 22g (Saturated Fat 10g; Trans Fat 0g); Cholesterol 325mg; Sodium 490mg; Total Carbohydrate 5g (Dietary Fiber 0g; Sugars 3g); Protein 16g
% Daily Value: Vitamin A 15%; Vitamin C 8%; Calcium 15%; Iron 8%
Exchanges: ½ Other Carbohydrate, 2½ High-Fat Meat
Carbohydrate Choices: ½

KITCHEN TIPS

❁ Try using Italian-style soy-protein crumbles in place of the sausage for a vegetarian variation. In nonstick skillet, cook mushrooms and bell peppers in 1 teaspoon oil until tender. Stir in crumbles; cook until warm. Remove mixture from skillet; continue with step 2.

❁ In place of the Cheddar cheese, use an Italian cheese blend.

Make-Ahead Sausage-Potato Egg Bake

Prep Time: 30 min Start to Finish: 10 hr 15 min

1 pound smoked spicy sausage (andouille, chorizo or kielbasa), cut into ³/₈-inch slices

1 large onion, chopped (³/₄ cup)

1 medium red bell pepper, chopped (1 cup)

1 medium green bell pepper, chopped (1 cup)

3 cloves garlic, finely chopped

1 bag (20 ounces) refrigerated home-style potato slices

¹/₂ teaspoon salt

¹/₂ teaspoon pepper

3 cups shredded sharp Cheddar cheese (12 ounces)

12 eggs

³/₄ cup milk

1. Spray 13 × 9-inch (3-quart) glass baking dish with cooking spray. In 12-inch skillet, cook sausage over medium heat 5 to 7 minutes, stirring occasionally, until sausage begins to brown; drain if necessary. Add onion; cook 2 to 3 minutes or until slightly softened. Add both bell peppers; cook and stir 1 minute. Add garlic; cook and stir 30 seconds or until softened.

2. Spread half of potatoes in bottom of baking dish. Sprinkle with ¹/₄ teaspoon each of the salt and pepper. Layer with half of sausage mixture and half of cheese. Repeat layers.

3. In large bowl, beat eggs and milk with wire whisk. Pour over layers in baking dish. Cover; refrigerate 8 hours or overnight but no longer than 24 hours.

4. Heat oven to 350°F. Loosely cover baking dish with sheet of nonstick aluminum foil or regular foil sprayed with cooking spray (nonstick or sprayed side down). Bake 1 hour 30 minutes to 1 hour 40 minutes or until set and potatoes are tender when pierced with a fork. Remove from oven; let stand 5 minutes before cutting.

12 servings
1 Serving: Calories 420 (Calories from Fat 270); Total Fat 30g (Saturated Fat 13g; Trans Fat 0g); Cholesterol 275mg; Sodium 870mg; Total Carbohydrate 14g (Dietary Fiber 1g; Sugars 3g); Protein 24g
% Daily Value: Vitamin A 20%; Vitamin C 30%; Calcium 20%; Iron 10%
Exchanges: 1 Starch, 3 High-Fat Meat, 1 Fat
Carbohydrate Choices: 1

KITCHEN TIPS

❂ This dish needs to be refrigerated at least 8 hours before baking, so it's a great do-ahead recipe.
❂ If you prefer less spicy sausage, use Italian sausage.

Quick

Mixed-Berry Butter Crunch Parfaits

Prep Time: 20 min Start to Finish: 50 min

1	cup Gold Medal all-purpose flour
$\frac{1}{2}$	cup packed brown sugar
$\frac{1}{3}$	cup coarsely chopped pecans or walnuts
$\frac{1}{2}$	cup cold butter or margarine
$1\frac{1}{2}$	cups Fiber One® cereal
$\frac{1}{3}$	cup flaked coconut
6	containers (6 ounces each) Yoplait® Original 99% Fat Free red raspberry yogurt
$1\frac{1}{2}$	cups blackberries, blueberries and raspberries

1. Heat oven to 400°F. In large bowl, mix flour, brown sugar and pecans. Cut in butter, using pastry blender (or pulling 2 table knives through ingredients in opposite directions), until mixture is crumbly. Stir in cereal and coconut. Spread in ungreased 13 × 9-inch pan.

2. Bake 15 minutes, stirring once. Remove from oven; stir and cool 10 to 15 minutes.

3. In each of 6 parfait glasses, layer 1 to 2 tablespoons cereal mixture, $\frac{1}{2}$ container of yogurt and 2 tablespoons berries; repeat layers. Top each with 1 tablespoon cereal mixture. If desired, garnish with additional berries. Store any remaining cereal mixture in refrigerator.

6 parfaits
1 Parfait: Calories 483 (Calories from Fat 197); Total Fat 22g (Saturated Fat 11g; Trans Fat 0g); Cholesterol 44mg; Sodium 260mg; Total Carbohydrate 69g (Dietary Fiber 10g; Sugars 33g); Protein 9g
% Daily Value: Cholesterol 15%; Vitamin A 10%; Vitamin C 15%; Calcium 35%; Iron 20%
Exchanges: 4 Fat, $3\frac{1}{2}$ Starch
Carbohydrate Choices: $4\frac{1}{2}$

KITCHEN TIPS

✿ Feel free to use whatever berries are your favorite. Choose a combo or stick with one kind.

✿ Make the cereal mixture ahead, but wait until serving time to assemble the parfaits to keep the cereal mixture crunchy.

Beverages and Appetizers

Spectacular Starters

Apricot-Chipotle-Cream Cheese Star (page 59)

Frozen Strawberry Margaritas (page 32)

Frozen Strawberry Margaritas

Prep Time: 10 min Start to Finish: 24 hr 10 min

½ can (12 ounces) frozen limeade concentrate, thawed

1 box (10 ounces) frozen strawberries in syrup, thawed, undrained

3 cups water

¾ cup tequila or orange juice

1 bottle (1 liter) lemon-lime carbonated beverage, chilled

10 servings
1 Serving: Calories 145 (Calories from Fat 0); Total Fat 0g (Saturated Fat 0g; Trans Fat 0g); Cholesterol 0mg; Sodium 15mg; Total Carbohydrate 28g (Dietary Fiber 1g; Sugars 26g); Protein 0g
% Daily Value: Cholesterol 0%; Vitamin A 0%; Vitamin C 25%; Calcium 0%; Iron 0%
Exchanges: 1½ Starch
Carbohydrate Choices: 2

1. Place limeade concentrate and strawberries in blender. Cover; blend until smooth. Pour into 2-quart plastic container. Stir in water and tequila. Cover; freeze 24 hours or until slushy.

2. If orange juice was used, let stand at room temperature 2 hours before serving. To serve, place ⅔ cup slush in each glass and fill with ⅓ cup carbonated beverage; stir.

KITCHEN TIPS

✺ Dip rims of margarita glasses in water and then in coarse sugar to add a festive touch.

✺ If you use orange juice instead of the tequila, the mixture will become slushy in about 12 hours. If the mixture freezes solid, allow it to thaw at room temperature for an hour or two before serving.

Quick & Low-Fat

Cranberry-Apple Spritzer

Prep Time: 10 min Start to Finish: 10 min

4 cups chilled dry white wine, nonalcoholic wine or apple juice

2 cups chilled cranberry-apple juice drink

2 cups chilled sparkling water

    Apple slices, if desired

    Fresh mint, if desired

1. In large pitcher, mix wine, juice drink and sparkling water.

2. Serve over ice. Garnish with apple slices and mint.

12 servings
1 Serving: Calories 90 (Calories from Fat 0); Total Fat 0g (Saturated Fat 0g; Trans Fat 0g); Cholesterol 0mg; Sodium 0mg; Total Carbohydrate 9g (Dietary Fiber 0g; Sugars 5g); Protein 0g
% Daily Value: Vitamin A 0%; Vitamin C 25%; Calcium 0%; Iron 0%
Exchanges: 1/2 Other Carbohydrate, 1 1/2 Fat
Carbohydrate Choices: 1/2

KITCHEN TIPS

✿ Use your favorite juice flavors, or try a more unusual blend such as guava-pineapple, in this refreshing mixture of wine and sparkling water.

✿ Pour this sparkling beverage into crystal glasses or goblets for an elegant presentation.

Berry Smoothies

- 1 cup Cascadian Farm® frozen organic unsweetened blueberries or raspberries
- 1¼ cups 8th Continent® vanilla soy milk
- 1 container (6 ounces) Yoplait Original 99% Fat Free French vanilla yogurt
  Honey, if desired

1. In blender or food processor, place blueberries, soy milk and yogurt. Cover; blend on high speed about 1 minute or until smooth. Sweeten to taste with honey.

2. Pour into 2 glasses. Serve immediately.

2 servings
1 Serving: Calories 210 (Calories from Fat 30); Total Fat 3.5g (Saturated Fat 1g; Trans Fat 0g); Cholesterol 5mg; Sodium 150mg; Total Carbohydrate 37g (Dietary Fiber 3g; Sugars 29g); Protein 6g
% Daily Value: Vitamin A 15%; Vitamin C 4%; Calcium 30%; Iron 4%
Exchanges: ½ Fruit, 1 Other Carbohydrate, 1 Skim Milk, ½ Fat
Carbohydrate Choices: 2½

KITCHEN TIPS

✿ Chill glasses in advance to keep this drink cold longer on a warm day.

Pumpkin Smoothies

- 1¼ cups 8th Continent vanilla soy milk
- ¼ cup cold canned pumpkin (not pumpkin pie mix)
- 1 container (6 ounces) Yoplait Original 99% Fat Free French vanilla yogurt
- 1 tablespoon honey
- ½ teaspoon pumpkin pie spice
- ¼ teaspoon vanilla

1. Place all ingredients in blender or food processor. Cover; blend on high speed about 1 minute or until smooth.

2. Pour into 2 glasses. Serve immediately.

2 servings
1 Serving: Calories 190 (Calories from Fat 25); Total Fat 3g (Saturated Fat 1g; Trans Fat 0g); Cholesterol 5mg; Sodium 150mg; Total Carbohydrate 35g (Dietary Fiber 1g; Sugars 30g); Protein 7g
% Daily Value: Vitamin A 15%; Vitamin C 4%; Calcium 30%; Iron 4%
Exchanges: ½ Fruit, 1 Other Carbohydrate, 1 Skim Milk, ½ Fat
Carbohydrate Choices: 2

Berry Smoothies

Pumpkin Smoothies

Creamy Peach Smoothie

Prep Time: 10 min Start to Finish: 10 min

1 cup frozen sliced peaches

1 banana, thickly sliced

1½ cups orange juice

1 tablespoon honey

1 container (6 ounces) Yoplait 99% Fat Free French vanilla yogurt

1. In food processor or blender, place all ingredients except yogurt. Cover; blend on high speed about 1 minute or until smooth and creamy. Pour about ¼ cup mixture into each of 3 glasses; add 1 tablespoon yogurt to each. Repeat layers 2 more times. Swirl yogurt into peach mixture with knife.

3 servings
1 Serving: Calories 200 (Calories from Fat 5); Total Fat 1g (Saturated Fat 0g; Trans Fat 0g); Cholesterol 0mg; Sodium 35mg; Total Carbohydrate 44g (Dietary Fiber 2g; Sugars 37g); Protein 3g
% Daily Value: Vitamin A 15%; Vitamin C 220%; Calcium 8%; Iron 2%
Exchanges: 1 Starch, 2 Fruit
Carbohydrate Choices: 3

KITCHEN TIPS

✺ If your blender doesn't handle frozen fruit very well, thaw the peaches slightly before adding them to the blender.

✺ Instead of swirling the yogurt into the drink, you can add the yogurt to the other ingredients in the blender and blend everything together.

Quick

Chicken-Filled Lettuce Wraps

Prep Time: 30 min Start to Finish: 30 min

⅓ cup orange marmalade

1 tablespoon fresh lime juice

1 tablespoon soy sauce

½ teaspoon grated gingerroot

⅓ cup Thai peanut sauce

2 cups bite-size strips cooked chicken breast

12 leaves Boston lettuce (about 1½ heads)

1 cup diced fresh mango (about 1 mango)

1 medium red bell pepper, cut into bite-size strips (about 1 cup)

1 cup diagonally sliced fresh snow (Chinese) pea pods (strings removed)

½ cup coarsely chopped peanuts

1. In small bowl, mix marmalade, lime juice, soy sauce and gingerroot; set aside.

2. In medium bowl, mix peanut sauce and 1 tablespoon of the marmalade mixture. Stir in chicken until coated.

3. Spoon about 2 tablespoons chicken mixture onto center of each lettuce leaf. Top with mango, bell pepper, pea pods, peanuts and marmalade mixture. To eat, wrap lettuce around chicken mixture and toppings.

12 appetizers
1 Appetizer (1 wrap and ¹⁄₁₂ of toppings each): Calories 140 (Calories from Fat 50); Total Fat 6g (Saturated Fat 1g; Trans Fat 0g); Cholesterol 20mg; Sodium 130mg; Total Carbohydrate 12g (Dietary Fiber 1g; Sugars 7g); Protein 10g
% Daily Value: Vitamin A 20%; Vitamin C 35%; Calcium 2%; Iron 4%
Exchanges: 1 Other Carbohydrate, 1½ Lean Meat
Carbohydrate Choices: 1

KITCHEN TIPS

✿ Look for Thai or Asian peanut sauce in the ethnic-foods section of the grocery store.

✿ Other tender leaf lettuce can be used in this recipe. Or use small piece of iceberg lettuce to make lettuce cups instead of wraps.

✿ Rotisserie chicken or refrigerated cooked chicken breast strips, cut into small strips, work well in this recipe, too.

Low Fat

Green Beans with Peanut-Ginger Dip

Prep Time: 20 min   Start to Finish: 50 min

1 pound fresh green beans, trimmed
¼ cup creamy peanut butter
1 tablespoon sugar
2 tablespoons rice vinegar
2 tablespoons soy sauce
1 tablespoon vegetable oil
¼ teaspoon crushed red pepper flakes
1 piece (1 inch) gingerroot, peeled, finely chopped (2 tablespoons)
1 clove garlic, finely chopped
   Chopped peanuts, if desired

1. In 3-quart saucepan, heat 6 cups water to boiling over high heat. Add beans to boiling water. Cook 4 to 6 minutes or until crisp-tender; drain. Rinse with cold water; drain. Cover; refrigerate while making dip.

2. In medium bowl, beat remaining ingredients except peanuts with wire whisk until smooth. Cover; refrigerate at least 30 minutes to blend flavors. Stir before serving. Garnish with peanuts. Serve beans with dip.

20 appetizers
1 Appetizer (5 beans and 1 teaspoon dip each): Calories 40 (Calories from Fat 20); Total Fat 2.5g (Saturated Fat 0g; Trans Fat 0g); Cholesterol 0mg; Sodium 105mg; Total Carbohydrate 3g (Dietary Fiber 1g; Sugars 2g); Protein 1g
% Daily Value: Vitamin A 4%; Vitamin C 4%; Calcium 0%; Iron 0%
Exchanges: ½ Vegetableetableetable, ½ Fat
Carbohydrate Choices: 0

KITCHEN TIPS

✿ Fresh gingerroot resembles a gnarled, tan-colored root. It adds a distinctive pungency and aroma to foods and is used extensively in dishes of the Far East. To prepare, use a small sharp knife to peel the tough skin and then finely chop the gingerroot into pieces.

✿ Cooking the beans in boiling water and then rinsing them in cold water will bring out their bright color.

Quick

Ham and Asparagus Rolls

Prep Time: 20 min Start to Finish: 20 min

12 fresh asparagus spears (about 1 pound)
$\frac{1}{4}$ cup mayonnaise or salad dressing
1 tablespoon Dijon mustard
1 teaspoon chopped fresh thyme leaves
6 slices ($\frac{1}{16}$ inch thick) cooked ham (from deli, about 10 ounces)

1. Fill 13 × 9-inch (3-quart) glass baking dish half full with water and ice; set aside.

2. In 12-inch skillet, heat 1 inch water to boiling over high heat. Snap or cut off tough ends of asparagus spears. Add asparagus to boiling water; cook uncovered 2 to 3 minutes or until crisp-tender. Remove asparagus from skillet; place in baking dish with ice water. Let stand 3 to 5 minutes or until chilled. Drain; pat dry with paper towels. Set aside.

3. Meanwhile, in small bowl, mix mayonnaise, mustard and thyme.

4. Spread about 1 teaspoon mayonnaise mixture over each ham slice to within 1 inch of edges. Cut each ham slice in half lengthwise. Roll 1 ham strip tightly around each asparagus spear. Store tightly covered in refrigerator.

12 appetizers
1 Appetizer: Calories 70 (Calories from Fat 45); Total Fat 5g (Saturated Fat 1g; Trans Fat 0g); Cholesterol 15mg; Sodium 340mg; Total Carbohydrate 1g (Dietary Fiber 0g; Sugars 0g); Protein 5g
% Daily Value: Vitamin A 4%; Vitamin C 0%; Calcium 0%; Iron 4%
Exchanges: $\frac{1}{2}$ Lean Meat, 1 Fat
Carbohydrate Choices: 0

KITCHEN TIPS

✿ Prosciutto can be substituted for the ham.
✿ These appetizers can be prepared a day ahead. Refrigerate them tightly covered.

Quick & Low-Fat
Greek Salad Kabobs

Prep Time: 15 min Start to Finish: 15 min

Dip

- ¾ cup plain yogurt
- 2 teaspoons honey
- 2 teaspoons chopped fresh dill weed
- 2 teaspoons chopped fresh oregano leaves
- ¼ teaspoon salt
- 1 small clove garlic, finely chopped

Kabobs

- 24 cocktail picks or toothpicks
- 24 pitted Kalamata olives
- 24 small grape tomatoes
- 12 slices (½ inch) English (seedless) cucumber, cut in half crosswise

1. In small bowl, mix dip ingredients; set aside.

2. On each cocktail pick, thread 1 olive, 1 tomato and 1 half-slice cucumber. Serve kabobs with dip.

24 appetizers
1 Appetizer (1 kabob and ½ tablespoon dip each): Calories 15 (Calories from Fat 5); Total Fat 0.5g (Saturated Fat 0g; Trans Fat 0g); Cholesterol 0mg; Sodium 70mg; Total Carbohydrate 2g (Dietary Fiber 0g; Sugars 1g); Protein 0g
% Daily Value: Vitamin A 0%; Vitamin C 2%; Calcium 2%; Iron 0%
Exchanges: Free
Carbohydrate Choices: 0

KITCHEN TIPS

✽ A regular cucumber can be substituted. If the skin is thick or has been coated with a vegetable coating, you may want to peel it.

✽ Small pitted ripe olives can be substituted but will lack some of the flavor Kalamata olives impart.

Quick
Grilled Veggie Platter with Ginger-Mustard Dip

Prep Time: 15 min Start to Finish: 45 min

- 1 small zucchini
- 8 fresh asparagus spears (about ¾ pound)
- 1 medium red bell pepper
- 1 tablespoon olive or vegetable oil
- ½ cup mayonnaise or salad dressing
- 2 tablespoons honey mustard
- 2 teaspoons finely chopped gingerroot
- 1 clove garlic, finely chopped

1. Heat gas or charcoal grill. Cut zucchini in half crosswise, then cut each half lengthwise into 4 spears. Snap or cut off tough ends of asparagus spears. Cut bell pepper into 8 strips.

2. In ungreased 15 × 10 × 1-inch pan, arrange zucchini, asparagus and bell pepper in single layer. Drizzle with oil. Shake pan to coat vegetables with oil.

3. Place vegetables carefully in single layer on grill over medium heat. Cover grill; cook 1 to 2 minutes or until lightly charred. Turn vegetables; cook 1 to 2 minutes longer or until lightly charred and just beginning to soften. Remove from grill; cover and refrigerate 30 minutes or until serving time.

4. Meanwhile, in small bowl, mix mayonnaise, honey mustard, gingerroot and garlic. Serve with cold grilled vegetables.

8 appetizers
1 Appetizer (3 Vegetableetableetables and 1 tablespoon dip each): Calories 130 (Calories from Fat 110); Total Fat 13g (Saturated Fat 2g; Trans Fat 0g); Cholesterol 5mg; Sodium 90mg; Total Carbohydrate 3g (Dietary Fiber 0g; Sugars 2g); Protein 1g
% Daily Value: Vitamin A 15%; Vitamin C 20%; Calcium 0%; Iron 4%
Exchanges: ½ Vegetableetableetableetable, 2½ Fat
Carbohydrate Choices: 0

Greek Salad Kabobs

Grilled Veggie Platter with Ginger-Mustard Dip

Curried Chicken Salad Cups

Prep Time: 15 min Start to Finish: 15 min

- 1   can (12.5 ounces) white chicken breast, drained
- $1/3$ cup diced celery
- $1/3$ cup mayonnaise or salad dressing
- $1/4$ cup chopped cashews
- 1   tablespoon mild curry paste (from 10-ounce jar)
- 24   frozen mini fillo shells (from two 2.1-ounce packages)
- 24   fresh parsley leaves

1. In medium bowl, stir together all ingredients except fillo shells and parsley.

2. Just before serving, spoon about 1 tablespoon chicken mixture into each fillo shell. Garnish with parsley.

24 appetizers
1 Appetizer: Calories 60 (Calories from Fat 35); Total Fat 4g (Saturated Fat 0g; Trans Fat 0g); Cholesterol 5mg; Sodium 85mg; Total Carbohydrate 3g (Dietary Fiber 0g; Sugars 0g); Protein 3g
% Daily Value: Vitamin A 0%; Vitamin C 2%; Calcium 0%; Iron 0%
Exchanges: $1/2$ Lean Meat, $1/2$ Fat
Carbohydrate Choices: 0

KITCHEN TIPS

✿ Curry paste is a blend of clarified butter, curry powder, vinegar and other seasonings. It can be found in the Asian-foods section of the supermarket.

✿ There's no need to thaw the fillo shells before filling them. They'll be thawed by the time you serve them.

Fresh Mozzarella in Tomato Cups

Prep Time: 15 min Start to Finish: 15 min

- 12   large cherry tomatoes
- 2   ounces fresh mozzarella cheese, cut into $1/2$-inch cubes
- $1/4$ cup Italian dressing
- 12   small basil leaves

1. Cut top off each cherry tomato. With melon baller or measuring spoon, scoop out seeds from each tomato, leaving enough for a firm shell. If necessary, cut small slice from bottom so tomato stands upright. Place tomatoes on serving plate or tray.

2. In small bowl, toss cheese and dressing. Place 1 cheese cube in each tomato; top each with basil leaf.

12 appetizers
1 Appetizer: Calories 35 (Calories from Fat 20); Total Fat 2.5g (Saturated Fat 0.5g; Trans Fat 0g); Cholesterol 0mg; Sodium 115mg; Total Carbohydrate 2g (Dietary Fiber 0g; Sugars 1g); Protein 1g
% Daily Value: Vitamin A 4%; Vitamin C 4%; Calcium 4%; Iron 0%
Exchanges: $1/2$ Fat
Carbohydrate Choices: 0

KITCHEN TIPS

✿ Fresh mozzarella is made with whole milk, is white colored and has a delicate, sweet, milky flavor. This soft cheese is packed in water or whey and is often formed into balls or slices.

✿ If tiny basil leaves are not available, shred 3 to 4 large leaves for the garnish.

Curried Chicken Salad Cups

Fresh Mozzarella in Tomato Cups

Spanish Fruit and Cheese Stacks

Prep Time: 15 min Start to Finish: 15 min

1 container (10 ounces) quince paste

6 ounces Manchego or Parmesan cheese

2 large pears

Grated peel of 4 lemons (about 3 tablespoons)

24 appetizers
1 Appetizer: Calories 50 (Calories from Fat 15); Total Fat 2g (Saturated Fat 1g; Trans Fat 0g); Cholesterol 0mg; Sodium 115mg; Total Carbohydrate 5g (Dietary Fiber 1g; Sugars 3g); Protein 2g
% Daily Value: Vitamin A 0%; Vitamin C 6%; Calcium 8%; Iron 0%
Exchanges: $1/2$ Other Carbohydrate, $1/2$ Fat
Carbohydrate Choices: $1/2$

1. Remove quince paste from container. Cut paste crosswise into 12 equal slices; cut each slice diagonally in half for total of 24 slices.

2. Cut cheese into 24 equal slices.

3. Cut each pear in half lengthwise and remove core. Cut each half into 6 equal wedges for total of 24 wedges.

4. To serve, place pear wedges on serving plate; top each wedge with cheese slice and quince paste slice. Sprinkle with lemon peel.

KITCHEN TIPS

✿ Quince is a fruit that tastes like a cross between an apple and a pear. Quince paste usually comes in cans or plastic tubs. Often you can find it near the cheese section or in the deli department of your grocery store.

✿ Next time, for a change of flavor, use apple slices instead of the pear slices.

Low Fat

Mojito Melon Kabobs

Prep Time: 20 min Start to Finish: 1 hr 20 min

- 2 limes
- 1½ pounds assorted melons, cut into 1-inch cubes (about 5 cups)
- ⅓ cup sugar
- ⅓ cup dark rum, if desired
- 3 tablespoons finely chopped fresh mint leaves
- 12 bamboo skewers (5 or 6 inch)

1. Grate 2 tablespoons peel from limes. Cut each lime in half crosswise; squeeze halves over small bowl to remove 6 tablespoons juice.

2. Place melon cubes in 1-gallon resealable plastic food-storage bag. Sprinkle lime peel and pour lime juice over melon. Add sugar, rum and mint. Seal bag; turn to coat melon.

3. Refrigerate at least 1 hour to blend flavors but no longer than 24 hours. To serve, thread 4 or 5 melon cubes on each skewer. Discard marinade.

12 appetizers
1 Appetizer: Calories 50 (Calories from Fat 0); Total Fat 0g (Saturated Fat 0g; Trans Fat 0g); Cholesterol 0mg; Sodium 10mg; Total Carbohydrate 13g (Dietary Fiber 1g; Sugars 11g); Protein 0g
% Daily Value: Vitamin A 25%; Vitamin C 35%; Calcium 0%; Iron 0%
Exchanges: 1 Other Carbohydrate
Carbohydrate Choices: 1

KITCHEN TIPS

✪ "Mojito" typically refers to a cocktail made with lime juice, sugar, mint leaves and rum. We've taken those same flavors and turned them into a refreshing appetizer.

✪ One-third cup frozen (thawed) limeade concentrate can be substituted for the rum.

Pimiento-Cheese Spread Appetizers

Creamy Salsa Dip

Quick

Pimiento-Cheese Spread Appetizers

Prep Time: 15 min Start to Finish: 15 min

- 2/3 cup small whole pimiento-stuffed green olives (from 10-ounce jar)
- 1 cup shredded Cheddar cheese (4 ounces)
- 1/4 cup mayonnaise or salad dressing
- 1 package (3 ounces) cream cheese, softened
    Dash ground red pepper (cayenne)
- 16 slices cocktail rye bread

1. Reserve 16 whole olives for garnish. Chop remaining olives; place in medium bowl. Add Cheddar cheese, mayonnaise, cream cheese and red pepper; beat with electric mixer on medium speed until well blended.

2. Spread about 2 tablespoons cheese mixture on 8 of the bread slices. Top with remaining bread slices. Cut each sandwich diagonally in half.

3. Garnish each appetizer with 1 whole olive secured with a toothpick or decorative pick.

16 appetizers
1 Appetizer: Calories 130 (Calories from Fat 80); Total Fat 8g (Saturated Fat 3.5g; Trans Fat 0g); Cholesterol 15mg; Sodium 290mg; Total Carbohydrate 9g (Dietary Fiber 1g; Sugars 0g); Protein 3g
% Daily Value: Vitamin A 4%; Vitamin C 0%; Calcium 6%; Iron 4%
Exchanges: 1/2 Starch, 2 Fat
Carbohydrate Choices: 1/2

KITCHEN TIPS

✿ To quickly soften cream cheese, use your microwave. Remove the foil wrapper and place cream cheese in a microwavable bowl. Microwave uncovered on Medium (50%) 45 to 60 seconds for a 3-ounce package of cream cheese.

✿ If cocktail rye bread isn't available, spread cheese mixture on low-fat rye crackers instead.

Quick

Creamy Salsa Dip

Prep Time: 10 min Start to Finish: 10 min

- 1/2 cup sour cream
- 1/2 cup mayonnaise or salad dressing
- 3/4 cup chipotle salsa or Old El Paso® Thick 'n Chunky salsa
- 1/4 cup lightly packed chopped fresh cilantro
- 8 ounces round tortilla chips or crackers

1. In small bowl, mix all ingredients except tortilla chips.

2. Serve immediately with tortilla chips, or cover and refrigerate 1 to 2 hours to blend flavors.

14 appetizers
1 Appetizer (2 tablespoons dip and 6 tortilla chips each):
Calories 160 (Calories from Fat 110); Total Fat 12g (Saturated Fat 2.5g; Trans Fat 0g); Cholesterol 10mg; Sodium 230mg; Total Carbohydrate 12g (Dietary Fiber 0g; Sugars 1g); Protein 1g
% Daily Value: Vitamin A 4%; Vitamin C 0%; Calcium 0%; Iron 4%
Exchanges: 1/2 Starch, 2 1/2 Fat
Carbohydrate Choices: 1

KITCHEN TIPS

✿ To make this dip more healthful, use reduced-fat sour cream and mayo, and serve it with bell pepper strips and carrot sticks as dippers.

✿ Look for chipotle salsa in the Mexican-foods section, refrigerated section or condiment section of most grocery stores.

Quick

Spicy Corn Guacamole

Prep Time: 15 min Start to Finish: 15 min

½ cup Green Giant® Niblets® frozen whole kernel corn, thawed

2 ripe avocados, pitted, peeled and diced

¼ cup diced red onion

¼ cup Old El Paso pickled jalapeño slices (from 12-ounce jar), drained, diced

2 tablespoons fresh lime juice

2 tablespoons mayonnaise or salad dressing

½ teaspoon salt

48 tortilla chips

1. In 8-inch nonstick skillet, cook corn over medium-high heat 5 to 8 minutes, stirring occasionally, until lightly toasted.

2. Meanwhile, in medium bowl, mix remaining ingredients except tortilla chips with fork, mashing avocados. Stir in corn. Serve with tortilla chips.

16 appetizers
1 Appetizer (2 tablespoons guacamole and 3 chips each): Calories 90 (Calories from Fat 60); Total Fat 6g (Saturated Fat 1g; Trans Fat 0g); Cholesterol 0mg; Sodium 170mg; Total Carbohydrate 9g (Dietary Fiber 1g; Sugars 0g); Protein 1g
% Daily Value: Vitamin A 0%; Vitamin C 4%; Calcium 0%; Iron 2%
Exchanges: ½ Starch, 1 Fat
Carbohydrate Choices: ½

KITCHEN TIPS

✿ To easily dice avocados, cut lengthwise around the pit and twist to separate halves. Hold the half with the pit in one hand. Tap pit firmly with edge of sharp knife and twist to remove pit. Score avocado flesh lengthwise and crosswise with tip of knife, making little cubes. Scoop out with a spoon.

✿ The acidic nature of lime juice prevents the avocado from darkening.

Low-Fat

Cashew-Chicken Firecrackers

Prep Time: 25 min Start to Finish: 45 min

1 cup finely chopped cooked chicken
1/2 cup red bell pepper strips (1 × 1/4 × 1/4 inch)
1/2 cup shredded carrots (2 small)
1/3 cup coarsely chopped cashews
4 medium green onions, thinly sliced (1/4 cup)
3 tablespoons orange marmalade
1 teaspoon garlic-pepper blend
1 package (16 ounces) frozen phyllo sheets (18 × 14 inches), thawed*
Olive oil cooking spray or 2 tablespoons olive oil
1/4 cup hoisin sauce
1/4 cup orange juice

1. Heat oven to 375°F. Spray cookie sheets with cooking spray. In medium bowl, mix chicken, bell pepper, carrots, cashews, onions, marmalade and garlic-pepper blend; set aside.

2. Work with 2 phyllo sheets at a time. Cover remaining sheets with plastic wrap and damp towel. On work surface, stack 2 phyllo sheets. Spray with cooking spray (2 seconds). Cut in half crosswise, forming 2 (9 × 7-inch) rectangles.

3. Spoon 1 rounded tablespoon chicken mixture on short end of each rectangle. Roll up; twist about 1 inch from each end, sealing tube and forming firecracker shape. Place seam side down on cookie sheet.

4. Repeat with remaining phyllo sheets and chicken mixture. Spray tops of appetizers with cooking spray (1 second for 2 appetizers).

5. Bake 18 to 20 minutes or until crisp and brown. Meanwhile, in small bowl, mix hoisin sauce and orange juice for dipping sauce. Serve sauce with warm "firecrackers."

20 appetizers
1 Appetizer (1 firecracker and 2 teaspoons sauce each): Calories 120 (Calories from Fat 25); Total Fat 3g (Saturated Fat 0.5g; Trans Fat 0g); Cholesterol 5mg; Sodium 140mg; Total Carbohydrate 19g (Dietary Fiber 1g; Sugars 3g); Protein 4g
% Daily Value: Vitamin A 10%; Vitamin C 6%; Calcium 0%; Iron 6%
Exchanges: 1/2 Starch, 1 Other Carbohydrate, 1/2 Fat
Carbohydrate Choices: 1

KITCHEN TIPS

✪ *Phyllo pastry sheets vary in size depending on the brand. Cut sheets so they are about the size given in the recipe.

Feta Cheese, Lemon and Chive Turnovers

Prep Time: 30 min Start to Finish: 50 min

2 ounces crumbled garlic-and-herb feta cheese

2 tablespoons thinly sliced fresh chives

2 medium green onions, sliced (2 tablespoons)

1/2 teaspoon grated lemon peel

Flour for dusting

1 sheet frozen puff pastry (from 17.3-ounce package), thawed

1. Heat oven to 400°F. In medium bowl, mash cheese with fork. Stir in chives, onions and lemon peel until well mixed.

2. On lightly floured surface, unfold pastry sheet; sprinkle lightly with flour. Roll pastry into 12-inch square. Cut pastry into 4 rows by 4 rows to make 16 squares. Spoon cheese mixture onto center of each square (about 1 rounded teaspoon each). If desired, cut small shape from one side of square.

3. Moisten edges of 1 square with fingertip dipped in water. Fold square over filling to form a triangle, gently pressing to remove air pockets around filling and pressing edges of pastry together. Use tines of fork to crimp and seal edges of turnover. Repeat with remaining squares. Using spatula, make edges of turnovers even if necessary; place, cutout side up, on ungreased cookie sheet.

4. Bake 10 to 15 minutes or until puffed and golden all over. Remove from cookie sheet to cooking rack; cool 2 to 3 minutes before serving.

16 appetizers
1 Appetizer: Calories 100 (Calories from Fat 60); Total Fat 7g (Saturated Fat 2.5g; Trans Fat 0.5g); Cholesterol 20mg; Sodium 80mg; Total Carbohydrate 7g (Dietary Fiber 0g; Sugars 0g); Protein 1g
% Daily Value: Vitamin A 0%; Vitamin C 0%; Calcium 2%; Iron 4%
Exchanges: 1/2 Starch, 1 1/2 Fat
Carbohydrate Choices: 1/2

KITCHEN TIPS

❂ Puff pastry is made of hundreds of layers of chilled butter and pastry dough. As it bakes, the moisture in the butter creates steam, causing the dough to puff and separate into hundreds of flaky layers.

❂ Turnovers can be prepared, covered and refrigerated for up to 2 hours before baking.

Grilled Spicy Chili-Glazed Riblets

Prep Time: 25 min Start to Finish: 7 hr 25 min

- 3 pounds pork baby back ribs (ask butcher to cut ribs in half horizontally)
- 1 tablespoon garlic-pepper blend
- 1/3 cup maple-flavored syrup
- 1/4 cup Dijon mustard
- 3 tablespoons hot chili paste
- 3 tablespoons molasses
- 1 tablespoon cider vinegar

1. Spray inside of 3- to 4-quart slow cooker with cooking spray. Cut ribs between bones into individual pieces. Place riblets in slow cooker. Sprinkle garlic-pepper blend over top; stir to coat evenly.

2. Cover; cook on Low heat setting 7 to 8 hours.

3. In large bowl, mix remaining ingredients. Using slotted spoon, remove riblets from slow cooker and add to maple syrup mixture. Toss riblets to coat.

4. Heat gas or charcoal grill. Spray grill basket (grill "wok") with cooking spray. Place riblets in basket; place basket on grill over medium heat. Cover grill; cook 10 to 12 minutes, stirring ribs or shaking basket after 5 minutes, until ribs are well glazed.

30 appetizers
1 Appetizer: Calories 100 (Calories from Fat 60); Total Fat 7g (Saturated Fat 2.5g; Trans Fat 0g); Cholesterol 25mg; Sodium 115mg; Total Carbohydrate 5g (Dietary Fiber 0g; Sugars 4g); Protein 6g
% Daily Value: Vitamin A 2%; Vitamin C 0%; Calcium 0%; Iron 4%
Exchanges: 1/2 Other Carbohydrate, 1 Medium-Fat Meat
Carbohydrate Choices: 1/2

KITCHEN TIPS

✿ To bake riblets, prepare as directed in steps 1 and 2.

✿ Heat oven to 450°F. Place riblets in 15 × 10 × 1-inch pan lined with aluminum foil. Bake 10 to 12 minutes, without turning, until ribs are well glazed.

✿ The heat level among brands of chili paste varies a lot. If you want spicier ribs, add 1 to 2 tablespoons more chili paste.

Low-Fat

Grilled Firecracker Chicken Drummies

Prep Time: 35 min Start to Finish: 1 hr 35 min

2 tablespoons chili powder

1½ teaspoons dried oregano leaves

1¼ teaspoons ground red pepper (cayenne)

1 teaspoon garlic salt

1 teaspoon ground cumin

1 teaspoon pepper

2 packages (1 pound each) chicken wing drummettes

Sour cream, if desired

Paprika, if desired

1. In 1-gallon resealable plastic food-storage bag, place all ingredients except chicken, sour cream and paprika. Seal bag; shake to blend seasonings. Add chicken; seal bag and shake until chicken is coated with seasonings. Refrigerate at least 1 hour to marinate but no longer than 24 hours.

2. Heat gas or charcoal grill. Place chicken in grill basket (grill "wok"). Place basket on grill over medium heat.

Cover grill; cook 20 to 25 minutes, shaking basket to turn chicken after 10 minutes, until juice of chicken is clear when thickest part is cut to bone (180°F).

3. Serve chicken with sour cream sprinkled with paprika.

20 appetizers
1 Appetizer: Calories 50 (Calories from Fat 20); Total Fat 2.5g (Saturated Fat 1g; Trans Fat 0g); Cholesterol 20mg; Sodium 70mg; Total Carbohydrate 0g (Dietary Fiber 0g; Sugars 0g); Protein 6g
% Daily Value: Vitamin A 6%; Vitamin C 0%; Calcium 0%; Iron 4%
Exchanges: 1 Lean Meat
Carbohydrate Choices: 0

KITCHEN TIPS

✿ Purchased blue cheese dressing can be served instead of the sour cream and paprika.

✿ Grill baskets (grill "woks") are available at discount stores or in kitchen specialty shops.

Low Fat

Barbecued Bacon-Chicken Skewers

Prep Time: 25 min Start to Finish: 40 min

15 bamboo skewers (6 inch)

3 large boneless, skinless chicken breasts (about 1 pound)

4 large green onions

1 package (2.1 ounces) refrigerated fully cooked bacon (15 pieces)

$1/2$ cup barbecue sauce

1. Soak skewers in water at least 30 minutes to prevent burning. Meanwhile, cut each chicken breast in half lengthwise, then cut crosswise to make 10 (about 1-inch) pieces. Cut onions into 2-inch pieces (30 pieces total). Cut bacon slices in half crosswise.

2. Heat gas or charcoal grill. Push 1 skewer through end of 1 bacon piece, then through middle of 1 chicken piece and back through other end of bacon piece; add 2 onion pieces, then repeat with another bacon piece and chicken piece. Place on large plate or tray. Repeat to make remaining kabobs.

3. Place kabobs on grill over medium heat. Cover grill; cook 5 minutes. Turn kabobs; brush with half of the barbecue sauce. Cover; cook 5 minutes. Turn kabobs; brush with remaining sauce. Cover; cook about 1 minute longer or until chicken is no longer pink in center. If desired, serve with additional barbecue sauce for dipping.

KITCHEN TIPS

❁ To bake: Heat oven to 400°F. Line large cookie sheet with aluminum foil; spray with cooking spray.

❁ Make kabobs as directed; place on cookie sheet. Drizzle or brush barbecue sauce over all sides of kabobs. Bake 10 minutes. Turn kabobs. Bake 5 to 10 minutes longer or until chicken is no longer pink in center.

❁ Keep pieces of kabob at the tip of the skewer while threading to keep bacon tight.

15 appetizers
1 Appetizer: Calories 70 (Calories from Fat 25); Total Fat 2.5g (Saturated Fat 1g; Trans Fat 0g); Cholesterol 25mg; Sodium 180mg; Total Carbohydrate 4g (Dietary Fiber 0g; Sugars 3g); Protein 8g
% Daily Value: Vitamin A 0%; Vitamin C 0%; Calcium 0%; Iron 2%
Exchanges: $1/2$ Other Carbohydrate, 1 Lean Meat
Carbohydrate Choices: 0

Tomato and Onion Tart

Prep Time: 35 min Start to Finish: 1 hr 15 min

1 tablespoon extra-virgin olive oil or vegetable oil

1 tablespoon butter or margarine

1 large sweet onion (such as Maui or Walla Walla), quartered, thinly sliced

1 Pillsbury® refrigerated pie crust (from 15-ounce box), softened as directed on box

¼ cup grated Parmesan cheese

2 medium roma (plum) tomatoes, thinly sliced

½ small zucchini, thinly sliced

¼ cup whipping cream

1 egg

¾ cup shredded Gruyère or Swiss cheese (3 ounces)

4 medium green onions, thinly sliced (¼ cup)

1. In 10-inch skillet, heat oil and butter over medium-high heat. Add onion; cook 5 minutes, stirring occasionally, until onion begins to brown. Reduce heat to medium-low; cook 20 to 25 minutes, stirring frequently, until browned and tender.

2. Meanwhile, heat oven to 450°F. Unroll pie crust on work surface. Roll pie crust with rolling pin to 12 inches in diameter. Gently press crust in bottom and up side of ungreased 10-inch tart pan with removable bottom. Trim off excess crust. Prick bottom and side of crust with fork. Bake 10 minutes. Remove from oven. Reduce oven temperature to 400°F.

3. Sprinkle bottom of partially baked crust with 2 tablespoons of the Parmesan cheese. Using slotted spoon, spoon onions evenly over bottom of crust. Top with tomatoes and zucchini, arranging a circle of tomato slices around outside edge, a circle of zucchini slices next to the tomatoes and a circle of tomato slices in the center.

4. In small bowl, beat whipping cream and egg with wire whisk. Pour over vegetables. Top with Gruyère cheese and remaining 2 tablespoons Parmesan cheese.

5. Bake at 400°F 15 minutes. Top with green onions; bake 10 to 15 minutes longer or until filling is set and crust is golden brown. Cool 5 minutes before removing side of pan.

12 appetizers
1 Appetizer: Calories 150 (Calories from Fat 100); Total Fat 11g (Saturated Fat 5g; Trans Fat 0g); Cholesterol 35mg; Sodium 135mg; Total Carbohydrate 9g (Dietary Fiber 0g; Sugars 1g); Protein 4g
% Daily Value: Vitamin A 6%; Vitamin C 2%; Calcium 10%; Iron 0%
Exchanges: ½ Other Carbohydrate, ½ High-Fat Meat, 1½ Fat
Carbohydrate Choices: ½

KITCHEN TIPS

❊ Sweet onions are available most of the year. If they are unavailable, use a large mild yellow onion.

❊ This tart is delicious either hot from the oven or cooled to room temperature before serving.

Cheesy Stars

Prep Time: 25 min Start to Finish: 40 min

- ¹/₂ cup finely chopped sweet onion (such as Maui or Walla Walla)
- ¹/₂ cup shredded Swiss cheese (2 ounces)
- ¹/₂ cup diced red bell pepper
- ¹/₂ cup mayonnaise or salad dressing
- 16 slices firm white bread

1. Heat oven to 375°F. In small bowl, stir together all ingredients except bread.

2. Spray cookie sheet with cooking spray. Cut star shape from each bread slice with 3- or 4-inch star-shaped cookie cutter. Spread about 1 tablespoon cheese mixture on each bread star; place on cookie sheet.

3. Bake 12 to 15 minutes or until cheese is melted and bottoms of bread stars are golden brown.

16 appetizers
1 Appetizer: Calories 100 (Calories from Fat 60); Total Fat 7g (Saturated Fat 1.5g; Trans Fat 0g); Cholesterol 5mg; Sodium 140mg; Total Carbohydrate 8g (Dietary Fiber 0g; Sugars 1g); Protein 2g
% Daily Value: Vitamin A 0%; Vitamin C 8%; Calcium 6%; Iron 4%
Exchanges: ¹/₂ Starch, 1¹/₄ Fat
Carbohydrate Choices: ¹/₂

KITCHEN TIPS

✿ Serve these cute canapés at your Fourth of July get-together.

Marinara Sauce with Mozzarella Cheese Dip

Prep Time: 5 min Start to Finish: 2 hr 35 min

- 2 cups chunky marinara sauce (from 26-ounce jar)
- 8 ounces mozzarella cheese, cubed
- 2 tablespoons chopped fresh basil leaves
- 2 loaves (10 ounces each) baguette-style French bread, cut into ¹⁄₂-inch slices, toasted

1. Spray 1¹⁄₂-quart slow cooker with cooking spray. Pour marinara sauce into cooker.

2. Cover; cook on low heat setting about 2 hours or until hot.

3. Stir in cheese and basil. Cover; cook on Low heat setting about 30 minutes longer or until cheese is just starting to melt. Serve with baguette slices. Dip can be kept warm on Low heat setting up to 2 hours; stir occasionally.

24 servings
1 Serving (2 tablespoons dip and 4 baguette slices): Calories 110 (Calories from Fat 30); Total Fat 3.5g (Saturated Fat 1.5g; Trans Fat 0g); Cholesterol 5mg; Sodium 290mg; Total Carbohydrate 16g (Dietary Fiber 0g; Sugars 2g); Protein 5g
% Daily Value: Vitamin A 4%; Vitamin C 0%; Calcium 10%; Iron 6%
Exchanges: 1 Starch, ¹⁄₂ Fat
Carbohydrate Choices: 1

KITCHEN TIPS

✿ For a change of flavor, try using goat cheese instead of the fresh mozzarella.
✿ Garnish the warm appetizer with fresh basil leaves.

Chili-Cheese Twists

Prep Time: 15 min Start to Finish: 40 min

- 1 sheet frozen puff pastry (from 17.3-ounce package)
- 1 egg
- 1 tablespoon water
- ¹⁄₂ cup finely shredded Cheddar cheese (2 ounces)
- 1 tablespoon chili powder

1. Thaw pastry sheet at room temperature 30 minutes. Meanwhile, in small bowl, beat egg and water until well blended; set aside. In another small bowl, mix cheese and chili powder.

2. Heat oven to 400°F. Spray large cookie sheet with cooking spray.

3. On lightly floured surface, roll thawed pastry sheet with rolling pin into 14 × 10-inch rectangle; cut in half lengthwise. Brush egg mixture over both rectangles; reserve remaining egg mixture. Spread cheese mixture evenly over 1 rectangle; top with second rectangle, egg side down. Gently press pastry to seal.

4. Cut pastry crosswise into 28 (¹⁄₂-inch) strips. Twist strips; place 2 inches apart on cookie sheet, pressing ends down. Brush with remaining egg mixture.

5. Bake 10 to 12 minutes or until golden brown. Serve warm or at room temperature.

28 appetizers
1 Appetizer: Calories 60 (Calories from Fat 40); Total Fat 4.5g (Saturated Fat 1.5g; Trans Fat 0g); Cholesterol 20mg; Sodium 40mg; Total Carbohydrate 4g (Dietary Fiber 0g; Sugars 0g); Protein 1g
% Daily Value: Vitamin A 2%; Vitamin C 0%; Calcium 0%; Iron 2%
Exchanges: 1 Fat
Carbohydrate Choices: 0

KITCHEN TIPS

✿ These cheesy twists can be made up to a month ahead and frozen until ready to bake. Increase the bake time to 15 minutes.
✿ Store the twists refrigerated in an airtight container up to one week.
✿ Serve the twists in glass tumblers to add height to the appetizer buffet table.

Chili-Cheese Twists

Marinara Sauce with Mozzarella Cheese Dip

Grilled Brie with Mango and Raspberries

Prep Time: 25 min Start to Finish: 55 min

1 untreated cedar plank (about 15 × 6 inches)
1 small round (4¹/₂ ounces) Brie cheese
¹/₂ cup diced mango
¹/₂ cup fresh raspberries
¹/₂ teaspoon kosher (coarse) salt
2 tablespoons honey
10 slices (¹/₄ inch thick) baguette French bread

1. Soak cedar plank in water at least 30 minutes. Meanwhile, heat gas or charcoal grill.

2. Remove plank from water. Place cheese (in rind) on plank. Spoon mango and raspberries over cheese. Sprinkle with salt.

3. Place plank with cheese on grill over medium heat. Cover grill; cook 15 to 20 minutes or until cheese is warm.

4. Remove plank from grill. Transfer cheese and fruits to serving plate. Drizzle honey over cheese and fruits. Serve with bread slices.

10 appetizers
1 Appetizer: Calories 80 (Calories from Fat 35); Total Fat 3.5g (Saturated Fat 2.5g; Trans Fat 0g); Cholesterol 15mg; Sodium 180mg; Total Carbohydrate 9g (Dietary Fiber 0g; Sugars 5g); Protein 3g
% Daily Value: Vitamin A 2%; Vitamin C 6%; Calcium 2%; Iron 2%
Exchanges: ¹/₂ Other Carbohydrate, ¹/₂ High-Fat Meat
Carbohydrate Choices: ¹/₂

KITCHEN TIPS

✪ Kosher salt is coarser grained than regular table salt. Look for it next to regular table salt, which by the way can be used instead of the kosher type.

Quick

Apricot-Chipotle-Cream Cheese Star

Prep Time: 15 min Start to Finish: 15 min

12 ounces cream cheese (from two 8-ounce packages), softened
1 cup shredded sharp white Cheddar cheese (4 ounces)
½ teaspoon onion powder
½ teaspoon ground mustard
½ cup chopped pecans
½ cup apricot preserves
2 teaspoons finely chopped gingerroot
2 teaspoons chopped chipotle chilies in adobo sauce (from 7-ounce can)
48 crackers

1. In food processor, place cream cheese, Cheddar cheese, onion powder and mustard. Cover; process, scraping side of bowl if necessary, until well mixed. Add pecans. Cover; process with on-and-off pulses 2 or 3 times until mixed.

2. Draw a pattern of a 5-pointed star that's approximately 6½ inches from point to point on a piece of parchment paper and cut out the star. Spoon the cheese spread evenly onto the shape, using a table knife to shape the star. Turn onto a serving plate; remove the parchment paper.

3. In small bowl, mix preserves, gingerroot and chilies. Spoon over cheese star. Serve with crackers.

16 servings
1 Serving (2 tablespoons spread and 3 crackers each): Calories 200 (Calories from Fat 130); Total Fat 15g (Saturated Fat 7g; Trans Fat 0g); Cholesterol 30mg; Sodium 190mg; Total Carbohydrate 14g (Dietary Fiber 0g; Sugars 6g); Protein 4g
% Daily Value: Vitamin A 8%; Vitamin C 0%; Calcium 6%; Iron 4%
Exchanges: ½ Starch, ½ Other Carbohydrate, 3 Fat
Carbohydrate Choices: 1

KITCHEN TIPS

❄ Chipotle chilies in adobo sauce can be found in the ethnic-foods section of the grocery store. Pour the remaining chilies and sauce into a freezer container and freeze for future use.

Quick

Spicy Chicken Nachos

Prep Time: 15 min Start to Finish: 3 hr

1 loaf (16 ounces) Mexican prepared cheese product with jalapeño peppers, cut into cubes

¾ cup Old El Paso Thick n' Chunky salsa

1 can (15 ounces) Progresso® black beans, drained, rinsed

1 package (9 ounces) frozen cooked chicken breast strips, thawed, cubed

1 container (8 ounces) sour cream

1 medium red bell pepper, chopped (1 cup)

3 medium green onions, sliced (3 tablespoons)

Large tortilla chips

1. Spray 3- to 4-quart slow cooker with cooking spray. In cooker, place cheese, salsa, beans and chicken.

2. Cover; cook on Low heat setting 2 hours, stirring once halfway through cooking.

3. Stir in sour cream, bell pepper and onions. Increase heat setting to High. Cover; cook about 45 minutes longer or until mixture is hot.

4. Serve with tortilla chips. Topping can be kept warm on Low heat setting up to 2 hours; stir occasionally.

24 servings
1 Serving (¼ cup topping and 7 chips each): Calories 200 (Calories from Fat 100); Total Fat 11g (Saturated Fat 4.5g; Trans Fat 0g); Cholesterol 25mg; Sodium 400mg; Total Carbohydrate 17g (Dietary Fiber 2g; Sugars 3g); Protein 9g
% Daily Value: Vitamin A 10%; Vitamin C 8%; Calcium 10%; Iron 6%
Exchanges: 1 Starch, 1 High-Fat Meat, ½ Fat
Carbohydrate Choices: 1

KITCHEN TIPS

✪ In place of the frozen cooked chicken, use rotisserie or deli chicken.

✪ Use flavored or multicolored tortillas for these nachos.

Quick

Mediterranean Nachos

Prep Time: 10 min Start to Finish: 10 min

2 tablespoons finely chopped Kalamata olives

2 tablespoons finely chopped sun-dried tomatoes in oil (from 7-ounce jar)

2 teaspoons oil from jar of sun-dried tomatoes

1 small roma (plum) tomato, finely chopped, drained

1 medium green onion, thinly sliced (1 tablespoon)

4 ounces restaurant-style corn tortilla chips (about 30 chips)

1 package (4 ounces) feta cheese, finely crumbled

1. In small bowl, mix olives, sun-dried tomatoes, oil, roma tomato and onion; set aside.

2. On large microwavable plate, arrange tortilla chips in single layer. Top evenly with cheese. Microwave uncovered on High 1 minute. Rotate plate ½ turn; microwave 30 to 60 seconds longer or until cheese is melted and bubbly.

3. Spoon tomato mixture evenly over chips and cheese.

6 appetizers
1 Appetizer: Calories 170 (Calories from Fat 100); Total Fat 11g (Saturated Fat 3.5g; Trans Fat 0g); Cholesterol 15mg; Sodium 360mg; Total Carbohydrate 14g (Dietary Fiber 1g; Sugars 2g); Protein 4g
% Daily Value: Vitamin A 4%; Vitamin C 6%; Calcium 10%; Iron 6%
Exchanges: 1 Starch, 2 Fat
Carbohydrate Choices: 1

KITCHEN TIPS

❁ For an extra flavor boost, look for sun-dried tomatoes in oil with herbs.

❁ Choose the unbroken chips from the bag for this appetizer. The broken chips are fine for dipping in salsa or for crumbling onto salads.

❁ Feta cheese is available plain or flavored. You can use cheese with garlic, basil, sun-dried tomato or herbs.

The Big Game Chex Mix

Prep Time: 15 min Start to Finish: 30 min

- 3 cups Corn Chex® cereal
- 3 cups Rice Chex® cereal
- 3 cups Wheat Chex® cereal
- 2 cups honey mustard flavor small pretzel twists, pieces or nuggets
- 1 cup smoked almonds
- ¼ cup butter or margarine
- 2 tablespoons yellow mustard or hot and spicy mustard
- 2 tablespoons honey
- 1 teaspoon seasoned salt

1. In large microwavable bowl, mix cereals, pretzels and almonds.

2. In microwavable cup, microwave butter, mustard, honey and seasoned salt uncovered on High 1 to 2 minutes or until butter is melted and mixture is hot; stir. Pour over cereal mixture, stirring until evenly coated. Microwave uncovered on High 5 to 6 minutes, stirring every 2 minutes, until mixture begins to brown.

3. Spread on waxed paper or aluminum foil to cool; about 15 minutes. Store in airtight container.

   Oven Directions: Heat oven to 250°F. In ungreased large roasting pan, mix cereals, pretzels and almonds. In 1-quart saucepan, heat butter, mustard, honey and seasoned salt over medium heat, stirring frequently, until butter is melted and mixture is hot. Pour over cereal mixture, stirring until evenly coated. Bake uncovered about 45 minutes, stirring every 15 minutes, until mixture begins to brown. Spread on waxed paper or foil to cool, about 15 minutes. Store in airtight container.

24 servings (½ cup each)
1 Serving: Calories 130 (Calories from Fat 45); Total Fat 5g (Saturated Fat 1.5g; Trans Fat 0g); Cholesterol 5mg; Sodium 290mg; Total Carbohydrate 18g (Dietary Fiber 2g; Sugars 3g); Protein 3g
% Daily Value: Vitamin A 6%; Vitamin C 2%; Calcium 6%; Iron 25%
Exchanges: 1 Starch, 1 Fat
Carbohydrate Choices: 1

KITCHEN TIPS

- Colorful paper cups make great holders for snack mixes. Look for them at paper and discount stores.
- Store any additional mix in an airtight container. The snack is great to serve at football watching parties.

Salads
and Soups

Lighter Fare

Spinach Pasta Salad (page 78)

Slow Cooker Meatball Stone Soup (page 94)

Creamy Fruit Salad

Prep Time: 20 min Start to Finish: 20 min

Dressing

- 1 container (6 ounces) Yoplait Original 99% Fat Free lemon burst or French vanilla yogurt
- 1 tablespoon light mayonnaise
- 1/4 teaspoon grated orange peel
- 2 tablespoons orange juice

Salad

- 2 large unpeeled red apples, cubed (about 3 cups)
- 1 medium orange, peeled, cut into bite-size pieces
- 2 tablespoons golden raisins
- 4 leaves Bibb lettuce
- 2 tablespoons coarsely chopped walnuts

1. In small bowl, mix dressing ingredients until well blended.

2. In medium bowl, mix apples, orange and raisins. Pour dressing over fruit; toss gently to coat.

3. Divide lettuce leaves among 4 serving plates. Spoon fruit mixture into lettuce leaves; sprinkle with walnuts.

4 servings (1 cup each)
1 Serving: Calories 180 (Calories from Fat 40); Total Fat 4.5g (Saturated Fat 0.5g; Trans Fat 0g); Cholesterol 0mg; Sodium 45mg; Total Carbohydrate 32g (Dietary Fiber 4g; Sugars 24g); Protein 2g
% Daily Value: Vitamin A 10%; Vitamin C 45%; Calcium 8%; Iron 2%
Exchanges: 1 Fruit, 1 Other Carbohydrate, 1/2 High-Fat Meat
Carbohydrate Choices: 2

KITCHEN TIPS

✿ Use a Microplane grater to efficiently and effortlessly grate only the colored portion of the orange peel.

Fall Fruit Medley

Prep Time: 20 min Start to Finish: 20 min

Honey–Poppy Seed Dressing

- ¼ cup vegetable oil
- 3 tablespoons honey
- 2 tablespoons lemon juice
- 1½ teaspoons poppy seed

Fruits

- 1 orange, peeled, sliced
- 1 medium pineapple, peeled, cored and cut into 1-inch pieces
- 1 small bunch seedless grapes, each cut in half (2 cups)
- 2 apples, cubed

1. In tightly covered container, shake dressing ingredients until well mixed. Shake again before pouring over fruits.

2. In large bowl, toss dressing with orange, pineapple and grapes. Cover; refrigerate up to 24 hours. Just before serving, stir in apples.

12 servings
1 Serving: Calories 120 (Calories from Fat 45); Total Fat 5g (Saturated Fat 0.5g; Trans Fat 0g); Cholesterol 0mg; Sodium 0mg; Total Carbohydrate 19g (Dietary Fiber 1g; Sugars 15g); Protein 0g
% Daily Value: Vitamin A 0%; Vitamin C 40%; Calcium 0%; Iron 0%
Exchanges: ½ Fruit, 1 Other Carbohydrate, 1 Fat
Carbohydrate Choices: 1

KITCHEN TIPS

✿ Use a mixture of red and green grapes to add color to the fruit medley.
✿ Save prep time by purchasing precut pineapple.

Quick

Apple-Gorgonzola Salad with Red Wine Vinaigrette

Prep Time: 20 min Start to Finish: 20 min

Vinaigrette

- 1/3 cup olive or vegetable oil
- 1/4 cup red wine vinegar
- 2 tablespoons sugar
- 1 teaspoon Dijon mustard
- 1 clove garlic, finely chopped

Salad

- 1 bag (10 ounces) mixed baby greens or Italian-blend salad greens
- 1 medium red or green apple, chopped (1 cup)
- 1/2 cup crumbled Gorgonzola or blue cheese (2 ounces)
- 1/3 cup chopped walnuts, toasted

1. In small bowl, beat vinaigrette ingredients with wire whisk until smooth.

2. In large bowl, toss salad ingredients with vinaigrette just before serving.

6 servings
1 Serving: Calories 230 (Calories from Fat 170); Total Fat 19g (Saturated Fat 4g; Trans Fat 0g); Cholesterol 5mg; Sodium 170mg; Total Carbohydrate 10g (Dietary Fiber 2g; Sugars 8g); Protein 4g
% Daily Value: Vitamin A 50%; Vitamin C 15%; Calcium 8%; Iron 6%
Exchanges: 1/2 Other Carbohydrate, 1/2 High-Fat Meat, 3 Fat
Carbohydrate Choices: 1/2

KITCHEN TIPS

✿ To toast nuts, bake uncovered in ungreased shallow pan in 350°F oven 6 to 10 minutes, stirring occasionally, until golden brown. Or cook in ungreased heavy skillet over medium-low heat 5 to 7 minutes, stirring frequently until browning begins, then stirring constantly until golden brown.

✿ The vinaigrette can be made up to 2 days ahead of time. Cover tightly and refrigerate until serving.

Quick

Blueberry and Orange Spinach Salad

Prep Time: 20 min Start to Finish: 25 min

- 1/4 cup coarsely chopped pecans
- 2 teaspoons real maple syrup
- 1/2 teaspoon sugar
- 2 tablespoons fresh orange juice
- 1 tablespoon white wine vinegar
- 1 tablespoon olive or vegetable oil
- 2 teaspoons sugar
- 4 cups torn fresh spinach leaves
- 1 cup fresh blueberries
- 2 medium oranges, peeled, cut into sections (about 1/2 cup)

1. Heat oven to 350°F. Line cookie sheet with aluminum foil. In small bowl, mix pecans and syrup until pecans are well coated. Spread pecans on foil. Sprinkle with 1/2 teaspoon sugar. Bake 7 to 9 minutes, stirring occasionally, until pecans are lightly toasted. Cool completely, about 15 minutes.

2. Meanwhile, in small bowl, beat orange juice, vinegar, oil and 2 teaspoons sugar with wire whisk until well blended.

3. In large bowl, toss spinach, blueberries and orange pieces. Pour dressing over salad; toss. Sprinkle with pecans. Serve immediately.

5 servings
1 Serving: Calories 140 (Calories from Fat 60); Total Fat 7g (Saturated Fat 0.5g; Trans Fat 0g); Cholesterol 0mg; Sodium 20mg; Total Carbohydrate 16g (Dietary Fiber 3g; Sugars 12g); Protein 2g
% Daily Value: Vitamin A 50%; Vitamin C 70%; Calcium 6%; Iron 6%
Exchanges: 1/2 Fruit, 1 Vegetable, 1 1/2 Fat
Carbohydrate Choices: 1

KITCHEN TIPS

✿ Blueberries are a low-fat food and a good source of fiber and vitamin C. The intense color of the blueberry comes from anthocyanins, which are potent antioxidants.

✿ Make the sugared pecans ahead and store in a resealable plastic food-storage bag until ready to use for this salad.

Apple-Gorgonzola Salad with Red Wine Vinaigrette

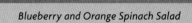

Blueberry and Orange Spinach Salad

Blueberries

Blueberries couldn't be a more effortless fruit. There's no peeling, coring or cutting—just pick and enjoy! This native North American fruit has been prized for centuries. There are two types of blueberries. Highbush, or cultivated, blueberries are grown primarily for commercial use. Lowbush, or wild, blueberries occur naturally and grow on carpetlike vines in Northern Maine and Canada. They can be grown for commercial production, but these berries are quite a bit smaller than the highbush blueberries.

Pick and Choose

When you're picking blueberries, make sure they are plump and firm and are a frosted indigo color. Blueberries do not ripen after picking, so remove any berries that aren't fully ripened. Also remove any shriveled, soft or molded blueberries, which often indicate the fruit is overripe. Although blueberries are in peak season from late May to mid-August, they extend beyond these months. Cover berries and store in the refrigerator after purchasing or picking. They will keep up to 10 days. Wash before serving. One pint of blueberries is equal to 2 cups.

A Blue Hue

Blueberries and their beautiful blue color have a weak side. If you cook the berries with an acid, such as lemon juice or vinegar, the fruit will turn reddish. Also, part of the pigment in blueberries is a yellow that when in an alkaline mix (like too much baking soda) may produce a greenish-blue color. Although the color may be affected, the taste is the same.

Frozen Blues

You can freeze fresh blueberries to use later. Do not wash blueberries before freezing. The waxy coating protects them. Spread berries on a cookie sheet and freeze. Transfer to a freezer container or a plastic freezer bag. If you're planning to use them in baked goods, the color may bleed into the batter. To prevent this, be sure the berries are frozen solid and stir them into the batter just before baking.

RECIPES:

▶ Blueberry and Orange Spinach Salad, page 66

▶ Summer Fruit-Topped Sorbet Sundae, page 335

▶ Red, White and Blueberry Sundaes, page 336

BLUEBERRIES AS "SUPER FOOD"

Don't let their small size fool you—blueberries are nutrient powerhouses.

▶ Blueberries are sometimes referred to as "brain berries" because they are a top source of antioxidant phytonutrients. Early research suggests that regular consumption of phytonutrients may support healthy brain function.

▶ According to the USDA, blueberries have some of the highest antioxidant ability among fruits.

▶ Blueberries contain anthocyanins, powerful antioxidants that are thought to prevent harmful cell damage and reduce "free radicals" in the body. These may help slow the aging process.

▶ Blueberries are a good source of vitamin C, as well as potassium, magnesium and fiber.

▶ Blueberries are lower in calories than many fruits and have zero fat.

Pineapple-Berry Salad with Honey-Mint Dressing

Prep Time: 15 min Start to Finish: 15 min

- 3 tablespoons frozen (thawed) lemonade concentrate
- 2 tablespoons honey
- 1 tablespoon chopped fresh mint leaves
- 1/2 fresh pineapple, peeled, cored and cut into chunks (about 2 cups)
- 1/4 cup fresh blueberries
- 1/4 cup fresh raspberries
- 1/4 cup sliced fresh strawberries

1. In 1-cup measuring cup, mix lemonade concentrate, honey and mint.

2. In large bowl, gently stir together remaining ingredients. Stir in lemonade mixture until fruits are coated. Serve immediately, or refrigerate up to 4 hours.

4 servings (3/4 cup each)
1 Serving: Calories 120 (Calories from Fat 0); Total Fat 0g (Saturated Fat 0g; Trans Fat 0g); Cholesterol 0mg; Sodium 0mg; Total Carbohydrate 28g (Dietary Fiber 2g; Sugars 23g); Protein 0g
% Daily Value: Vitamin A 0%; Vitamin C 70%; Calcium 0%; Iron 0%
Exchanges: 1/2 Fruit, 1 1/2 Other Carbohydrate
Carbohydrate Choices: 2

KITCHEN TIPS

✪ Go berry crazy and use 3/4 cup of any combination of your favorite berries.

✪ Pineapples don't ripen after harvest, so select fresh-looking pineapples with a sweet aroma.

Tomato and Herb Salad

Prep Time: 20 min Start to Finish: 20 min

Dressing
- 1/4 cup extra-virgin olive oil
- 3 tablespoons red wine vinegar
- 1 teaspoon salt
- 1/2 teaspoon freshly ground pepper

Salad
- 5 tomatoes (assorted varieties, including yellow and/or heirlooms), sliced or cut into wedges
- 1 cup small grape tomatoes, cut in half
- 1/4 cup thinly sliced sweet onion (such as Maui or Walla Walla)
- 2 tablespoons chopped fresh basil leaves
- 2 tablespoons chopped fresh Italian (flat-leaf) parsley
- 2 tablespoons chopped fresh oregano leaves

1. In small bowl, beat oil, vinegar, salt and pepper with wire whisk until well blended.

2. On large platter, arrange tomatoes and onion. Drizzle dressing over tomatoes and onion. Sprinkle with basil, parsley and oregano.

8 servings
1 Serving: Calories 90 (Calories from Fat 60); Total Fat 7g (Saturated Fat 1g; Trans Fat 0g); Cholesterol 0mg; Sodium 300mg; Total Carbohydrate 5g (Dietary Fiber 1g; Sugars 3g); Protein 1g
% Daily Value: Vitamin A 20%; Vitamin C 25%; Calcium 2%; Iron 4%
Exchanges: 1 Vegetable, 1 1/2 Fat
Carbohydrate Choices: 1/2

KITCHEN TIPS

✪ Make this simple, fresh salad when tomatoes are at their peak. Heirloom tomatoes provide unique flavors. They're often available at farmers' markets and many grocery stores in the summer.

✪ Curly leaf parsley can be used, but it usually has less flavor than flat-leaf parsley.

Tomato and Herb Salad

Pineapple-Berry Salad with Honey-Mint Dressing

Salads and Soups   71

Quick & Low Fat

Spinach-Mango Salad

Prep Time: 10 min Start to Finish: 10 min

1 tablespoon canola oil

2 tablespoons cider vinegar

$1/3$ cup peach or apricot preserves

$1/2$ teaspoon salt

1 bag (6 ounces) baby spinach leaves

2 mangoes, cut lengthwise in half, seed removed and cut up (2 cups)

$1/2$ cup very thinly sliced red onion

$1/2$ cup golden raisins

1. In small bowl, beat oil, vinegar, preserves and salt with wire whisk or fork until blended.

2. In large bowl, toss remaining ingredients. Pour dressing over spinach mixture, tossing gently to coat.

6 servings (1 cup each)
1 Serving: Calories 170 (Calories from Fat 25); Total Fat 2.5g (Saturated Fat 0g; Trans Fat 0g); Cholesterol 0mg; Sodium 230mg; Total Carbohydrate 36g (Dietary Fiber 2g; Sugars 25g); Protein 2g
% Daily Value: Vitamin A 60%; Vitamin C 50%; Calcium 4%; Iron 6%
Exchanges: 1 Fruit, 1 Other Carbohydrate, 1 Vegetable, $1/2$ Fat
Carbohydrate Choices: $2^1/2$

KITCHEN TIPS

❂ This light and sweet salad partners nicely with baked fish, cooked carrots and crusty whole-grain rolls.

❂ Spinach and mangoes make this recipe high in vitamins A and C. Try to get at least five or more $1/2$ cup servings of fruits and veggies per day for optimal health.

Quick

Asian Tossed Salad

Prep Time: 20 min Start to Finish: 20 min

- 3 cups shredded romaine lettuce
- 1½ cups coleslaw mix
- 1 cup fresh snap pea pods, trimmed
- ½ cup shredded carrots
- ¼ cup very thinly sliced red onion
- ¼ cup fat-free mayonnaise or salad dressing
- ¼ cup Chinese chicken salad dressing
- 1 tablespoon honey
- 2 tablespoons slivered almonds

1. In large bowl, mix lettuce, coleslaw mix, pea pods, carrots and onion.

2. In small bowl, mix mayonnaise, salad dressing and honey with wire whisk until smooth.

3. Add dressing mixture to salad; toss to mix. Sprinkle with almonds.

5 servings (1 cup each)
1 Serving: Calories 110 (Calories from Fat 50); Total Fat 6g (Saturated Fat 1g; Trans Fat 0g); Cholesterol 0mg; Sodium 240mg; Total Carbohydrate 12g (Dietary Fiber 2g; Sugars 8g); Protein 2g
% Daily Value: Vitamin A 90%; Vitamin C 35%; Calcium 4%; Iron 4%
Exchanges: ½ Other Carbohydrate, 1 Vegetable, 1 Fat
Carbohydrate Choices: 1

KITCHEN TIPS

✿ If you can't find Chinese dressing you can make your own by mixing ¼ cup reduced-fat or fat-free mayonnaise, 3 tablespoons citrus vinaigrette dressing, 1 tablespoon soy sauce and 1 tablespoon honey.

✿ For the best results, toss the dressing with the salad ingredients just before serving.

Dill-Potato Salad

Prep Time: 15 min   Start to Finish: 1 hr 50 min

Dill Dressing

- $^2/_3$ cup white vinegar
- $^1/_2$ cup olive or vegetable oil
- 2 tablespoons chopped fresh or 4 teaspoons dried dill weed
- 2 teaspoons sugar
- 1 teaspoon salt
- 1 teaspoon ground mustard
- $^1/_2$ teaspoon coarsely ground pepper
- 2 cloves garlic, finely chopped

Salad

- $1^1/_2$ pounds fresh green beans
- 3 pounds small red potatoes (20 to 24), cut into quarters
- $^1/_2$ cup chopped red onion
- 1 medium yellow bell pepper, coarsely chopped (1 cup)

1. In tightly covered container, shake dressing ingredients.

2. Cut beans in half if desired. In 4-quart Dutch oven, place beans and potatoes; add enough water just to cover vegetables. Cover; heat to boiling. Reduce heat to low; cook covered 30 to 35 minutes or until potatoes are tender. Drain.

3. In very large glass or plastic bowl, toss beans, potatoes and dressing. Add onion and bell pepper; toss. Cover; refrigerate 1 to 2 hours or until chilled before serving.

16 servings
1 Serving: Calories 150 (Calories from Fat 60); Total Fat 7g (Saturated Fat 1g; Trans Fat 0g); Cholesterol 0mg; Sodium 153mg; Total Carbohydrate 18g (Dietary Fiber 3g; Sugars 2g); Protein 2g
% Daily Value: Vitamin A 6%; Vitamin C 45%; Calcium 2%; Iron 6%
Exchanges: $1^1/_2$ Fat, 1 Starch, 1 Vegetable
Carbohydrate Choices: 1

KITCHEN TIPS

- Add strips of rotisserie chicken for a hearty dinner salad.
- Be sure not to overcook the potatoes, or they will fall apart in the salad. When the potatoes are done, you should be able to just pierce them with a fork.

Old-Fashioned Potato Salad

Prep Time: 10 min Start to Finish: 4 hr 45 min

6 medium potatoes (2 pounds), peeled
1½ cups mayonnaise or salad dressing
1 tablespoon white or cider vinegar
1 tablespoon yellow mustard
1 teaspoon salt
¼ teaspoon pepper
2 medium stalks celery, chopped (1 cup)
1 medium onion, chopped (½ cup)
4 hard-cooked eggs, chopped

1. In 3-quart saucepan, heat 1 inch water (salted if desired) to boiling. Add potatoes; cover and heat to boiling. Reduce heat; cook 30 to 35 minutes or until tender. Drain. Cool slightly; cut into cubes.

2. In large glass or plastic bowl, mix mayonnaise, vinegar, mustard, salt and pepper. Add potatoes, celery and onion; toss. Stir in eggs. Cover; refrigerate at least 4 hours until chilled.

8 servings
1 Serving: Calories 440 (Calories from Fat 320); Total Fat 35g (Saturated Fat 6g; Trans Fat 0g); Cholesterol 120mg; Sodium 600mg; Total Carbohydrate 26g (Dietary Fiber 3g; Sugars 3g); Protein 6g
% Daily Value: Vitamin A 6%; Vitamin C 15%; Calcium 4%; Iron 6%
Exchanges: 1 Starch, 1 Other Carbohydrate, ½ Medium-Fat Meat, 6 Fat
Carbohydrate Choices: 2

KITCHEN TIPS

✿ Put each potato in a bowl of cold water as you peel it. That way, the peeled potatoes won't turn brown while you're peeling the remaining ones.
✿ To decrease the amount of fat in this recipe, use reduced-fat mayonnaise or salad dressing.

Primavera Pasta Salad

Quick

Primavera Pasta Salad

Prep Time: 25 min Start to Finish: 25 min

3½ cups uncooked farfalle (bow-tie) pasta
   (9 ounces)

2 cups fresh snow (Chinese) pea pods
   (12 ounces), strings removed

2 large red bell peppers, cut into 1-inch pieces
   (2 cups)

2 medium carrots, sliced (1 cup)

½ cup chopped fresh basil leaves

½ cup shredded Parmesan cheese (2 ounces)

1 cup creamy Parmesan dressing

2 tablespoons milk

1. Cook and drain pasta as directed on package, adding pea pods for last minute of cooking. Rinse with cold water; drain.

2. In very large (4-quart) bowl, mix bell peppers, carrots, basil and cheese. In small bowl, mix dressing and milk with wire whisk. Add dressing mixture, pasta and pea pods to bell pepper mixture; toss to coat.

14 servings
1 Serving: Calories 180 (Calories from Fat 80); Total Fat 9g (Saturated Fat 1.5g; Trans Fat 0g); Cholesterol 10mg; Sodium 310mg; Total Carbohydrate 19g (Dietary Fiber 2g; Sugars 3g); Protein 5g
% Daily Value: Vitamin A 50%; Vitamin C 80%; Calcium 8%; Iron 6%
Exchanges: 1 Starch, 1 Vegetable, 1½ Fat
Carbohydrate Choices: 1

KITCHEN TIPS

✪ Look for low-fat or fat-free salad dressing. If you can't find the Parmesan flavor with less fat, look for low-fat creamy Italian.

✪ Any medium-size pasta shape can be substituted for the bow-tie pasta.

Quick

Spinach Pasta Salad

Prep Time: 20 min Start to Finish: 35 min

3 cups uncooked farfalle (bow-tie) pasta (6 ounces)

1 small tomato, cut into fourths

½ cup basil pesto

¼ teaspoon salt

¼ teaspoon pepper

4 cups bite-size pieces spinach leaves

2 medium carrots, thinly sliced (1 cup)

1 small red onion, thinly sliced

1 can (14 ounces) quartered artichoke hearts, drained, rinsed

1. Cook and drain pasta as directed on package. Rinse with cold water; drain.

2. While pasta is cooking, place tomato, pesto, salt and pepper in food processor or blender. Cover; process 30 seconds.

3. Toss pasta, pesto mixture and remaining ingredients.

6 servings
1 Serving: Calories 290 (Calories from Fat 110); Total Fat 12g (Saturated Fat 2.5g; Trans Fat 0g); Cholesterol 0mg; Sodium 560mg; Total Carbohydrate 35g (Dietary Fiber 6g; Sugars 3g); Protein 9g
% Daily Value: Vitamin A 110%; Vitamin C 25%; Calcium 15%; Iron 15%
Exchanges: 1½ Starch, ½ Other Carbohydrate, 1 Vegetable, 2½ Fat
Carbohydrate Choices: 2

KITCHEN TIPS

✿ Use the packaged already-cleaned spinach found in the salad section of the produce department.

✿ No bow-tie pasta in the pantry? Other medium-size pasta shapes, such as shells, rotini or fusilli, work too.

Quick & Low Fat

Gingered Chicken and Fruit Salad

Prep Time: 25 min Start to Finish: 25 min

Dressing

- ½ teaspoon grated lime peel
- 2 tablespoons fresh lime juice
- 2 tablespoons canola oil
- 1 tablespoon water
- 2 teaspoons honey
- ½ teaspoon ground ginger

Salad

- 6 cups fresh baby spinach leaves
- 2 cups cubed cooked chicken breast
- 1 ripe medium mango, seed removed, peeled and cubed
- 1 cup red seedless grapes, halved
- 2 medium green onions, sliced (2 tablespoons)
- 2 tablespoons coarsely chopped pecans, toasted

1. In container with tight-fitting lid, shake dressing ingredients until well mixed.

2. Divide spinach leaves among 4 serving plates. Top each with chicken, mango, grapes, onions and pecans. Drizzle with dressing.

4 servings
1 Serving: Calories 290 (Calories from Fat 110); Total Fat 13g (Saturated Fat 1.5g; Trans Fat 0g); Cholesterol 55mg; Sodium 90mg; Total Carbohydrate 22g (Dietary Fiber 3g; Sugars 16g); Protein 23g
% Daily Value: Vitamin A 90%; Vitamin C 60%; Calcium 8%; Iron 15%
Exchanges: ½ Fruit, 1 Other Carbohydrate, 3 Lean Meat, 1 Fat
Carbohydrate Choices: 1½

KITCHEN TIPS

✿ Fresh is best! Fresh lime juice has a brighter flavor than bottled. You'll need 1 medium lime for the 2 tablespoons lime juice called for here.

✿ If you poach your own chicken breasts in reduced-sodium chicken broth instead of using packaged cooked cubed chicken, you'll reduce the overall sodium in this recipe.

Quick

Tropical Chicken Salad

Prep Time: 25 min Start to Finish: 25 min

1 pound boneless, skinless chicken breasts, cut into ½-inch strips

2 tablespoons blackened seasoning blend

1 tablespoon canola oil

1 bag (5.5 ounces) mixed baby salad greens (4 cups)

1 medium mango, seed removed, peeled and diced (1 cup)

½ medium red onion, sliced (¾ cup)

1 small red bell pepper, chopped (½ cup)

⅔ cup raspberry vinaigrette

1. Place chicken in heavy-duty resealable plastic food-storage bag. Sprinkle seasoning blend over chicken; seal bag and shake until chicken is evenly coated.

2. Heat oil in 10-inch nonstick skillet over medium-high heat. Cook chicken in oil 7 to 10 minutes, stirring frequently, until no longer pink in center. Remove chicken from skillet; drain on paper towels.

3. In large bowl, toss salad greens, mango, onion and bell pepper; divide among 4 plates. Top with chicken. Drizzle with vinaigrette.

4 servings
1 Serving: Calories 280 (Calories from Fat 70); Total Fat 7g (Saturated Fat 1.5g; Trans Fat 0g); Cholesterol 70mg; Sodium 560mg; Total Carbohydrate 26g (Dietary Fiber 3g; Sugars 14g); Protein 26g
% Daily Value: Vitamin A 70%; Vitamin C 100%; Calcium 6%; Iron 10%
Exchanges: 1½ Other Carbohydrate, 1 Vegetable, 3½ Very Lean Meat, 1 Fat
Carbohydrate Choices: 2

KITCHEN TIPS

❂ The mango and bell pepper in this salad make it a tasty source of vitamins A and C. Vitamin A is vital for proper eyesight and healthy hair and skin; vitamin C helps promote healthy gums, blood vessels, bones and teeth.

Quick

Summer Layered Chicken Salad

Prep Time: 15 min Start to Finish: 15 min

Salad

- 7 cups torn romaine lettuce (from 1 head)
- 2 packages (9 ounces each) frozen fully cooked chicken breast strips (not breaded), thawed (4 cups)
- 1 cup crumbled Gorgonzola cheese (about 4 ounces)
- 1 cup pecan halves (4 ounces)
- 1 quart fresh strawberries, quartered (3 cups)

Dressing

- 1/3 cup olive or vegetable oil
- 2 tablespoons sugar
- 1/2 teaspoon salt
- 3 tablespoons red wine vinegar
- 1 teaspoon Dijon mustard
- 1 clove garlic, finely chopped

1. In deep 3-quart salad bowl, place half of the lettuce. Layer with chicken, cheese, pecan halves, remaining lettuce and strawberries.

2. In small bowl or glass measuring cup, mix dressing ingredients with wire whisk until well blended. Just before serving, pour dressing over salad.

6 servings
1 Serving: Calories 490 (Calories from Fat 320); Total Fat 35g (Saturated Fat 7g; Trans Fat 0g); Cholesterol 75mg; Sodium 990mg; Total Carbohydrate 17g (Dietary Fiber 4g; Sugars 10g); Protein 28g
% Daily Value: Vitamin A 70%; Vitamin C 100%; Calcium 15%; Iron 8%
Exchanges: 1/2 Fruit, 1/2 Other Carbohydrate, 4 Lean Meat, 4 1/2 Fat
Carbohydrate Choices: 1

KITCHEN TIPS

✿ Make the salad and the dressing ahead. Cover each with plastic wrap and refrigerate up to 4 hours before serving.
✿ Purchased red wine vinaigrette dressing can be substituted for the homemade dressing.

Chicken-Gorgonzola Pasta Salad

Prep Time: 20 min Start to Finish: 20 min

7 cups uncooked radiatore (nuggets) pasta (about 19 ounces)

4½ cups cubed cooked chicken breast (about 20 ounces)

1 package (2.1 ounces) refrigerated precooked bacon (about 15 slices), cut into small pieces

1 can (14.5 ounces) Muir Glen® organic fire-roasted diced tomatoes, drained

2 cups lightly packed fresh baby spinach leaves

1 jar (16 ounces) refrigerated ranch dressing

1 cup crumbled Gorgonzola cheese (4 ounces)
    Bibb lettuce, if desired

12 servings
1 Serving: Calories 530 (Calories from Fat 250); Total Fat 28g (Saturated Fat 7g; Trans Fat 0g); Cholesterol 70mg; Sodium 790mg; Total Carbohydrate 42g (Dietary Fiber 3g; Sugars 3g); Protein 28g
% Daily Value: Vitamin A 10%; Vitamin C 10%; Calcium 10%; Iron 15%
Exchanges: 2 Starch, 1 Other Carbohydrate, 3 Lean Meat, 3½ Fat
Carbohydrate Choices: 3

KITCHEN TIPS

✿ Use cut-up cooked rotisserie or deli chicken for the cooked chicken breast.

✿ If you'd prefer, you can cook 15 slices of raw bacon until crisp and then crumble it instead of using the precooked bacon.

1. Cook and drain pasta as directed on package.

2. In large bowl, mix cooked pasta, chicken, bacon, tomatoes and spinach. Pour dressing over pasta mixture; toss until coated. Fold in cheese. Cover and refrigerate until serving. To serve, line bowl with lettuce and spoon in salad.

Low Fat

Fire-Roasted Tomato Gazpacho

Prep Time: 15 min Start to Finish: 1 hr 15 min

1 can (14.5 ounces) fire-roasted diced tomatoes, undrained

1½ cups tomato juice

1 small cucumber, peeled, chopped (1 cup)

¼ cup finely chopped red bell pepper

2 tablespoons finely chopped red onion

2 tablespoons finely chopped fresh cilantro

2 teaspoons white wine vinegar

1. In food processor, place all ingredients. Cover; process with quick on-and-off motions until mixture is coarsely pureed.

2. Cover; refrigerate at least 1 hour to blend flavors before serving.

4 servings
1 Serving: Calories 50 (Calories from Fat 0); Total Fat 0g (Saturated Fat 0g; Trans Fat 0g); Cholesterol 0mg; Sodium 380mg; Total Carbohydrate 10g (Dietary Fiber 2g; Sugars 7g); Protein 2g
% Daily Value: Vitamin A 20%; Vitamin C 80%; Calcium 4%; Iron 8%
Exchanges: 2 Vegetable
Carbohydrate Choices: ½

KITCHEN TIPS

❂ Lycopene, an important antioxidant, is the nutrient that gives tomatoes their color. Tomatoes, especially those that are cooked, are one of the richest sources of lycopene.

❂ Gazpacho is often served as a first course on a hot summer day.

Quick

Chicken and Barley Soup

Prep Time: 35 min Start to Finish: 35 min

1 carton (32 ounces) chicken broth

1 can (14.5 ounces) diced tomatoes, undrained

2 medium carrots, sliced (1 cup)

2 medium stalks celery, sliced (1 cup)

1 cup sliced fresh mushrooms (about 3 ounces)

⅓ cup uncooked quick-cooking barley

1 teaspoon dried minced onion

2 cups chopped deli rotisserie chicken (from 2- to 2½-pound chicken)

1. In 3-quart saucepan, mix all ingredients except chicken. Heat to boiling over medium-high heat. Reduce heat to medium. Cover; simmer 15 to 20 minutes or until barley is tender.

2. Add chicken. Cover; cook about 3 minutes or until chicken is hot.

6 servings (1⅓ cups each)
1 Serving: Calories 170 (Calories from Fat 28); Total Fat 3.1g (Saturated Fat 1g; Trans Fat 0g); Cholesterol 40mg; Sodium 1138mg; Total Carbohydrate 15g (Dietary Fiber 3g; Sugars 4g); Protein 21g
% Daily Value: Vitamin A 0%; Vitamin C 20%; Calcium 2%; Iron 4%
Exchanges: ½ Starch, 2 Meat, 1 Vegetable
Carbohydrate Choices: 1

KITCHEN TIPS

✿ Add ½ teaspoon dried thyme leaves to the soup for a savory flavor.

✿ Be sure to use quick-cooking barley because the regular type needs to cook longer than this recipe allows.

Noodle and Chicken Bowl

Prep Time: 15 min Start to Finish: 15 min

4 cups water

2 packages (3 ounces each) Oriental-flavor ramen noodle soup mix

1 cup fresh spinach leaves, torn into bite-size pieces

2 ounces fresh snow (Chinese) pea pods, strings removed, cut in half crosswise (1/2 cup)

1/2 cup shredded or julienne-cut carrots

1 can (8 ounces) sliced water chestnuts, drained

1 teaspoon sesame oil

1 1/2 cups chopped deli rotisserie chicken (from 2- to 2 1/2-pound chicken)

2 medium green onions, chopped (2 tablespoons)

1. In 3-quart saucepan, heat water to boiling over medium-high heat. Add noodles (breaking apart if desired), spinach, pea pods, carrots and water chestnuts. Cook 3 minutes, stirring occasionally.

2. Stir in seasoning packets from soup mixes, sesame oil, chicken and onions. Cook 1 to 2 minutes or until chicken is hot.

4 servings (1 1/2 cups each)
1 Serving: Calories 290 (Calories from Fat 43); Total Fat 5g (Saturated Fat 1g; Trans Fat 0g); Cholesterol 52mg; Sodium 1020mg; Total Carbohydrate 39g (Dietary Fiber 6g; Sugars 4g); Protein 26g
% Daily Value: Vitamin A 70%; Vitamin C 20%; Calcium 4%; Iron 10%
Exchanges: 1/2 Fat, 2 Starch, 1 1/2 Vegetable, 2 1/2 Meat
Carbohydrate Choices: 3

KITCHEN TIPS

❀ Scatter chopped fresh basil, mint or cilantro over the soup just before serving for a fresh taste reminiscent of Vietnamese pho noodle bowls.

❀ Look for stringless snow pea pods. If they are not available, peel the string from each pod before using.

Chicken Vegetable Potpie Soup

Prep Time: 20 min Start to Finish: 1 hr

1 sheet frozen puff pastry (from 17.3-ounce package), thawed

2 tablespoons butter or margarine

6 small red potatoes, cut into eighths

1 medium stalk celery, coarsely chopped ($\frac{1}{2}$ cup)

1 medium carrot, coarsely chopped ($\frac{1}{2}$ cup)

1 small onion, coarsely chopped ($\frac{1}{4}$ cup)

5 cups chicken broth

$\frac{1}{4}$ cup Gold Medal Wondra® quick-mixing flour

1 teaspoon poultry seasoning

$\frac{1}{4}$ teaspoon salt

$\frac{1}{8}$ teaspoon pepper

$2\frac{1}{2}$ cups 1-inch pieces deli rotisserie chicken (from 2- to $2\frac{1}{2}$-pound chicken)

1 cup Green Giant frozen sweet peas

$\frac{1}{4}$ cup whipping cream

1. Heat oven to 400°F. Cut 6 rounds from puff pastry with 3-inch round cutter. Place on ungreased cookie sheet. Bake 12 to 15 minutes or until puffed and golden brown. Keep warm.

2. Meanwhile, in $4\frac{1}{2}$- to 5-quart Dutch oven, melt butter over medium-high heat. Cook potatoes, celery, carrot and onion in butter 5 to 6 minutes, stirring frequently, until onion is softened.

3. Beat broth, flour, poultry seasoning, salt and pepper into potato mixture with wire whisk. Heat to boiling; reduce heat to medium-low. Cover; cook 15 to 20 minutes, stirring occasionally, until potatoes are tender and soup is slightly thickened.

4. Stir in remaining ingredients. Cover; cook 5 to 6 minutes, stirring occasionally, until chicken and peas are hot. Ladle soup into bowls; top each serving with pastry.

6 servings ($1\frac{1}{3}$ cups each)
1 Serving: Calories 295 (Calories from Fat 113); Total Fat 13g (Saturated Fat 6g; Trans Fat 0g); Cholesterol 70mg; Sodium 1250mg; Total Carbohydrate 25g (Dietary Fiber 4g; Sugars 4g); Protein 23g
% Daily Value: Vitamin A 49%; Vitamin C 20%; Calcium 2%; Iron 8%
Exchanges: 2 Fat, $\frac{1}{2}$ Vegetable, 2 Meat, 1 Starch
Carbohydrate Choices: 2

KITCHEN TIPS

✿ An easy way to add layers of flavor is to use poultry seasoning. A blend of sage, thyme, marjoram, rosemary, black pepper and nutmeg, this seasoning lends a subtle savory note to chicken and turkey dishes.

Chicken Vegetable Potpie Soup

Quick & Low Fat
Chicken Creole Soup

Prep Time: 35 min Start to Finish: 55 min

- 2 tablespoons butter or margarine
- 2 medium onions, coarsely chopped (1 cup)
- 2 medium stalks celery, coarsely chopped (1 cup)
- 1 medium green bell pepper, coarsely chopped (1 cup)
- 2 teaspoons finely chopped garlic
- 2½ pounds boneless, skinless chicken breasts or thighs, cut into 1-inch pieces
- ¼ cup Gold Medal all-purpose flour
- 2 cans (14.5 ounces each) diced tomatoes, undrained
- 4 cups reduced-sodium chicken broth
- 2 cups water
- 1 cup uncooked regular long-grain white rice
- 1 teaspoon salt
- ¼ teaspoon ground red pepper (cayenne)
- 2 dried bay leaves

1. In 5- to 6-quart Dutch oven, melt butter over medium-high heat. Add onions, celery, bell pepper, garlic and chicken; cook 7 to 9 minutes, stirring frequently, until onion is softened.

2. Stir in flour. Cook 5 to 6 minutes, stirring constantly, until flour is light brown.

3. Stir in remaining ingredients. Heat to boiling. Reduce heat to medium-low. Cover; cook 15 to 20 minutes, stirring occasionally, until rice is tender and chicken is no longer pink in center. Remove bay leaves.

8 servings (1½ cups each)
1 Serving: Calories 323 (Calories from Fat 45); Total Fat 5g (Saturated Fat 2.3g; Trans Fat 0g); Cholesterol 90mg; Sodium 881mg; Total Carbohydrate 29g (Dietary Fiber 2g; Sugars 4g); Protein 37g
% Daily Value: Vitamin A 15%; Vitamin C 45%; Calcium 4%; Iron 15%
Exchanges: 1 Fat, 1 Starch, 1½ Vegetable, 3½ Meat
Carbohydrate Choices: 2

Thai-Style Chicken Curry Soup

Prep Time: 15 min Start to Finish: 15 min

1 carton (32 ounces) chicken broth

3 tablespoons packed brown sugar

2 tablespoons soy sauce

2 tablespoons rice vinegar

2 teaspoons curry powder

1 small red bell pepper, coarsely chopped (½ cup)

1 small jalapeño chili, seeded and finely chopped (1 tablespoon)

2 cups chopped deli rotisserie chicken (from 2- to 2½-pound chicken)

2 tablespoons chopped fresh cilantro, if desired

1. In 3-quart saucepan, stir all ingredients except chicken and cilantro. Heat to boiling over medium-high heat. Reduce heat to medium. Simmer uncovered 3 to 5 minutes or until bell pepper is crisp-tender.

2. Stir in chicken. Cook 1 to 2 minutes or until chicken is hot. Just before serving, add cilantro.

4 servings (1½ cups each)
1 Serving: Calories 210 (Calories from Fat 60); Total Fat 7g (Saturated Fat 2g; Trans Fat 0g); Cholesterol 77mg; Sodium 2031mg; Total Carbohydrate 14g (Dietary Fiber 1g; Sugars 13g); Protein 22g
% Daily Value: Vitamin A 10%; Vitamin C 40%; Calcium 2%; Iron 2%
Exchanges: ½ Fat, ½ Starch, 2½ Meat
Carbohydrate Choices: 1

KITCHEN TIPS

✿ Brown sugar, soy sauce and rice vinegar mimic the flavors of the fish sauce typically used in Thai cooking.

✿ Like spicy food? Add an additional tablespoon of finely chopped jalapeño chili.

Homemade Turkey Soup

Prep Time: 30 min Start to Finish: 2 hr 55 min

Carcass from cooked 10- to 12-pound turkey
3 quarts (12 cups) water
1 teaspoon salt
$\frac{1}{2}$ teaspoon pepper
$\frac{1}{4}$ teaspoon poultry seasoning or dried sage leaves
1 dried bay leaf
$\frac{1}{2}$ cup uncooked pearl barley
3 medium carrots, sliced ($1\frac{1}{2}$ cups)
1 large onion, chopped (1 cup)
2 medium stalks celery, sliced (1 cup)
3 cups cut-up cooked turkey
2 tablespoons chopped fresh parsley, if desired

1. Break up turkey carcass to fit 6-quart Dutch oven. Add water, salt, pepper, poultry seasoning and bay leaf. Heat to boiling over high heat; reduce heat to low. Cover; simmer 1 hour 30 minutes.

2. Skim off any residue that rises to the surface. Remove bones, meat and bay leaf from broth; cool. When cool enough to handle, remove meat from bones and cut into bite-size pieces; set aside. Discard bones and bay leaf.

3. Skim fat from broth; discard. Add turkey meat cut from bones to broth; stir in barley. Heat to boiling; reduce heat to low. Cover; simmer 30 minutes, stirring occasionally.

4. Stir in carrots, onion, celery and 3 cups cooked turkey. Simmer uncovered 20 to 25 minutes longer, stirring occasionally, until vegetables and barley are tender. Stir in parsley.

10 servings
1 Serving: Calories 140 (Calories from Fat 30); Total Fat 3.5g (Saturated Fat 1g; Trans Fat 0g); Cholesterol 40mg; Sodium 330mg; Total Carbohydrate 13g (Dietary Fiber 3g; Sugars 2g); Protein 15g
% Daily Value: Vitamin A 70%; Vitamin C 4%; Calcium 4%; Iron 6%
Exchanges: 1 Starch, 2 Very Lean Meat
Carbohydrate Choices: 1

KITCHEN TIPS

❀ Turn this into Homemade Turkey-Vegetable Soup by adding up to 3 cups raw or cooked vegetables, such as whole kernel corn, green peas, diced potatoes, sliced zucchini, sliced mushrooms or any combination, along with the carrots, onion and celery.

❀ An easy way to add layers of flavor is to use poultry seasoning. A blend of sage, thyme, marjoram, rosemary, black pepper and nutmeg, this seasoning lends a subtle savory note to chicken and turkey dishes.

Southwestern Pork Soup

Prep Time: 25 min Start to Finish: 35 min

2 teaspoons vegetable oil

1 pound boneless pork loin, trimmed of fat, cut into $1/2$-inch cubes

4 medium green onions, sliced ($1/4$ cup)

1 small jalapeño chili, seeded, finely chopped (1 tablespoon)

1 clove garlic, finely chopped

2 cans (14 ounces each) reduced-sodium chicken broth

2 cans (15 to 16 ounces each) great northern beans, rinsed, drained

$1/2$ cup loosely packed chopped fresh cilantro

$1/4$ cup loosely packed chopped fresh parsley

1. In 3-quart nonstick saucepan, heat oil over medium-high heat. Add pork; cook 3 to 5 minutes, stirring occasionally, until browned. Add onions, chili and garlic; cook and stir 1 minute.

2. Add broth and beans. Heat to boiling; reduce heat. Cover; simmer about 10 minutes or until pork is no longer pink in center. Stir in cilantro and parsley; cook until heated through.

5 servings (1$1/4$ cups each)
1 Serving: Calories 214 (Calories from Fat 47); Total Fat 5g (Saturated Fat 1g; Trans Fat 0g); Cholesterol 60mg; Sodium 920mg; Total Carbohydrate 19g (Dietary Fiber 7g; Sugars 4g); Protein 27g
% Daily Value: Vitamin A 10%; Vitamin C 15%; Calcium 8%; Iron 15%
Exchanges: $1/2$ Fat, 1 Starch, 2$1/2$ Meat
Carbohydrate Choices: 1

Smoked Sausage and Bean Soup

Slow Cooker Tuscan Bean Soup

Low Fat
Smoked Sausage and Bean Soup

Prep Time: 15 min Start to Finish: 8 hr 45 min

1 pound small red potatoes, each cut into 8 pieces (about 3 cups)
4 medium carrots, sliced (2 cups)
1 medium onion, chopped (1/2 cup)
1 medium stalk celery, sliced (1/2 cup)
2 cans (15 ounces each) navy or cannellini beans, drained, rinsed
2 cans (14 ounces each) chicken broth
1 teaspoon dried thyme leaves
1/2 teaspoon seasoned salt
1 pound fully cooked kielbasa sausage, cut in half lengthwise, then into 1/4-inch slices
2 tablespoons chopped fresh parsley

1. Spray 3- to 4-quart slow cooker with cooking spray. In cooker, mix all ingredients except sausage and parsley.

2. Cover; cook on Low heat setting 8 to 9 hours.

3. Stir in sausage and parsley. Cover; cook on Low heat setting 30 minutes longer or until sausage is hot.

7 servings (1 1/2 cups each)
1 Serving: Calories 440 (Calories from Fat 170); Total Fat 19g (Saturated Fat 7g; Trans Fat 0.5g); Cholesterol 40mg; Sodium 1220mg; Total Carbohydrate 47g (Dietary Fiber 14g; Sugars 5g); Protein 20g
% Daily Value: Vitamin A 120%; Vitamin C 10%; Calcium 10%; Iron 25%
Exchanges: 2 1/2 Starch, 1 Vegetable, 1 1/2 High-Fat Meat, 1 Fat
Carbohydrate Choices: 3

KITCHEN TIPS

✿ If the red potatoes are very small, cut them in half to prevent overcooking.
✿ Diced cooked ham can be used in place of the sausage.

Slow Cooker Tuscan Bean Soup

Prep Time: 25 min Start to Finish: 8 hr 25 min

1 pound small red potatoes, cut into quarters (about 3 cups)
4 medium carrots, sliced (2 cups)
1 medium onion, chopped (1/2 cup)
2 cloves garlic, finely chopped
2 cans (15 to 16 ounces each) great northern beans, drained, rinsed
2 cans (14 ounces each) chicken broth
2 cups diced fully cooked ham
1 teaspoon Italian seasoning
1/2 teaspoon salt
2 tablespoons chopped fresh parsley
1 tablespoon olive or vegetable oil

1. In 3- to 4-quart slow cooker, mix all ingredients except parsley and oil.

2. Cover; cook on Low heat setting 8 to 10 hours.

3. Stir in parsley and oil before serving.

6 servings (1 1/2 cups each)
1 Serving: Calories 275 (Calories from Fat 80); Total Fat 9g (Saturated Fat 3g; Trans Fat 0g); Cholesterol 43mg; Sodium 975mg; Total Carbohydrate 33g (Dietary Fiber 8g; Sugars 6g); Protein 27g
% Daily Value: Vitamin A 140%; Vitamin C 20%; Calcium 6%; Iron 15%
Exchanges: 1 Fat, 1 1/2 Starch, 1 Vegetable, 2 Meat
Carbohydrate Choices: 2

KITCHEN TIPS

✿ Sliced cooked sausage can be used in place of the ham.
✿ Although you can purchase deli ham and dice it at home, you can also purchase a package of diced ham as a great time-saver.
✿ This fragrant bean soup is perfect fare for a chilly winter evening. Serve with slices of crusty French baguette and a warm apple crisp for dessert.

Slow Cooker Steak and Pasta Soup

Prep Time: 10 min Start to Finish: 8 hr 40 min

1 pound boneless beef round steak, cut into $1/2$-inch cubes

1 jar (26 to 28 ounces) marinara sauce

$2^1/2$ cups water

1 package (9 ounces) refrigerated cheese-filled ravioli

$1/2$ cup grated Parmesan cheese

1. In $3^1/2$- to 4-quart slow cooker, mix beef, marinara sauce and water.

2. Cover; cook on Low heat setting 8 to 10 hours.

3. Stir in ravioli. Increase heat setting to High. Cover; cook 20 to 30 minutes until ravioli are tender. Sprinkle individual servings with cheese.

5 servings ($1^1/2$ cups each)
1 Serving: Calories 324 (Calories from Fat 121); Total Fat 13g (Saturated Fat 5g; Trans Fat 0g); Cholesterol 52mg; Sodium 898mg; Total Carbohydrate 36g (Dietary Fiber 2g; Sugars 0g); Protein 30g
% Daily Value: Vitamin A 15%; Vitamin C 25%; Calcium 20%; Iron 15%
Exchanges: 1 Fat, $3^1/2$ Meat, $2^1/2$ Starch
Carbohydrate Choices: 2

KITCHEN TIPS

✿ For quick morning preparation, cut up the beef the night before and refrigerate.

Slow Cooker Meatball Stone Soup

Prep Time: 10 min Start to Finish: 10 hr 10 min

1 bag (16 ounces) frozen cooked Italian-style meatballs

2 cans (14 ounces each) beef broth

2 cans (14.5 ounces each) diced tomatoes with Italian herbs, undrained

1 medium potato, chopped (1 cup)

1 medium onion, chopped (1 cup)

$1/4$ teaspoon garlic-pepper blend

1 bag (1 pound) frozen mixed vegetables

1. In $3^1/2$- to 4-quart slow cooker, mix frozen meatballs, broth, tomatoes, potato, onion and garlic-pepper blend.

2. Cover; cook on Low heat setting 9 to 11 hours or until vegetables are tender.

3. Stir in frozen mixed vegetables. Cover; cook on High heat setting 1 hour.

6 servings
1 Serving: Calories 272 (Calories from Fat 81); Total Fat 9g (Saturated Fat 3g; Trans Fat 0g); Cholesterol 61mg; Sodium 1026mg; Total Carbohydrate 26g (Dietary Fiber 4g; Sugars 8g); Protein 19g
% Daily Value: Vitamin A 30%; Vitamin C 45%; Calcium 6%; Iron 25%
Exchanges: 1 Fat, $1^1/2$ Meat, 1 Starch, 1 Vegetable
Carbohydrate Choices: 2

KITCHEN TIPS

✿ Make this hot and hearty soup the main course of a simple meal. Serve with whole-grain rolls or bread, or assorted crackers.
✿ Sprinkle with freshly grated Parmesan or Romano cheese.

Slow Cooker Steak and Pasta Soup

Slow Cooker Meatball Stone Soup

Slow Cooker Hearty Steak and Tater Soup

Prep Time: 20 min Start to Finish: 8 hr 50 min

1 pound boneless beef round steak

1 pound small red potatoes, cut into ¼-inch slices (4 cups)

2 medium stalks celery, chopped (1 cup)

2 medium carrots, chopped (1 cup)

1 medium onion, chopped (½ cup)

2 cloves garlic, finely chopped

1 tablespoon beef bouillon granules

½ teaspoon pepper

4 cans (14 ounces each) beef broth

1 jar (6 ounce) Green Giant sliced mushrooms, undrained

½ cup water

½ cup Gold Medal all-purpose flour

1. Cut beef into 1 × ¼-inch pieces. In 5-quart slow cooker, mix beef and remaining ingredients except water and flour.

2. Cover; cook on Low heat setting 8 to 9 hours.

3. Mix water and flour in small bowl; gradually stir into soup until blended. Increase heat setting to High. Cover; cook about 30 minutes or until slightly thickened.

9 servings (1½ cups each)
1 Serving: Calories 185 (Calories from Fat 46); Total Fat 5g (Saturated Fat 2g; Trans Fat 0g); Cholesterol 20mg; Sodium 964mg; Total Carbohydrate 17g (Dietary Fiber 2g; Sugars 2g); Protein 17g
% Daily Value: Vitamin A 45%; Vitamin C 10%; Calcium 4%; Iron 25%
Exchanges: ½ Fat, 1 Starch, 1 Vegetable, 1½ Meat
Carbohydrate Choices: 1

KITCHEN TIPS

✿ For accurate cooking times and proper doneness, cut all meats and vegetables into the sizes specified in a recipe.

Low Fat

Beef and Barley Soup

Prep Time: 20 min Start to Finish: 9 hr 50 min

1½ pounds beef stew meat

3 medium carrots, sliced (1½ cups)

1 large onion, chopped (1 cup)

2 cloves garlic, finely chopped

⅔ cup Green Giant Niblets frozen whole kernel corn, thawed

⅔ cup uncooked pearl barley

½ teaspoon salt

½ teaspoon pepper

1 can (14.5 ounces) diced tomatoes, undrained

3 cans (14 ounces each) beef broth

1 cup Green Giant frozen sweet peas, thawed

1. Spray 5- to 6-quart slow cooker with cooking spray. In cooker, mix all ingredients except peas.

2. Cover; cook on Low heat setting 9 to 10 hours.

3. Stir in peas. Increase heat setting to High. Cover; cook 20 to 30 minutes longer or until peas are tender.

8 servings (1½ cups each)
1 Serving: Calories 280 (Calories from Fat 100); Total Fat 11g (Saturated Fat 4g; Trans Fat 0g); Cholesterol 50mg; Sodium 930mg; Total Carbohydrate 25g (Dietary Fiber 5g; Sugars 5g); Protein 21g
% Daily Value: Vitamin A 90%; Vitamin C 8%; Calcium 6%; Iron 20%
Exchanges: 1 Starch, ½ Other Carbohydrate, 1 Vegetable, 2 Medium-Fat Meat
Carbohydrate Choices: 1½

KITCHEN TIPS

✿ Pearl barley, which is the most common form, is the perfect grain to cook in the slow cooker. The long, slow cooking produces barley that is tender but not gummy.

✿ Select lean beef to avoid having to trim excess fat before adding beef to the soup.

Quick

Asian Beef and Noodle Soup

Prep Time: 45 min Start to Finish: 1 hr 10 min

3	ounces uncooked cellophane noodles
1	tablespoon dark sesame oil
1½	pounds boneless beef top sirloin steak, cut into bite-size strips
2	teaspoons finely chopped garlic
2	packages (about 3.5 ounces each) fresh shiitake or button mushrooms, sliced
6	cups reduced-sodium beef broth
2	cups finely sliced bok choy
1	cup julienne (matchstick-size) carrots
½	teaspoon ground ginger
⅛	teaspoon pepper
2	medium green onions, sliced (2 tablespoons)

1. In medium bowl, soak bundle of cellophane noodles in warm water 10 to 15 minutes or until softened; drain. Cut noodle bundle into thirds. Cover and set aside.

2. In 5- to 6-quart Dutch oven, heat oil over medium-high heat. Cook beef, garlic and mushrooms in oil 5 to 6 minutes, stirring occasionally, just until beef is no longer pink.

3. Stir in remaining ingredients except noodles and onions. Heat to boiling; reduce heat to medium-low. Cover; cook 14 to 15 minutes, stirring occasionally, until beef is tender.

4. Stir in noodles. Cover; cook 2 to 3 minutes or until noodles are hot. Sprinkle with onions.

6 servings (1½ cups each)
1 Serving: Calories 262 (Calories from Fat 72); Total Fat 8g (Saturated Fat 2g; Trans Fat 0g); Cholesterol 53mg; Sodium 250mg; Total Carbohydrate 16g (Dietary Fiber 1g; Sugars 2g); Protein 30g
% Daily Value: Vitamin A 90%; Vitamin C 20%; Calcium 6%; Iron 15%
Exchanges: ½ Fat, 1 Starch, 1 Vegetable, 3½ Meat
Carbohydrate Choices: 1

KITCHEN TIPS

✿ If you can't find cellophane noodles, you can use vermicelli instead. Simply cook and drain 3 ounces vermicelli as directed on package, and stir into soup in step 4.

Pizzas, Sandwiches and Burgers

Hearty Handheld Delights

Caesar Chicken Subs (page 106)

Chipotle Pulled-Pork Sandwiches (page 110)

Turkey Taco Pizza

Prep Time: 20 min Start to Finish: 30 min

- 1 package (10 ounces) prebaked thin Italian pizza crust (12 inch)
- 1/2 cup Old El Paso taco sauce
- 2 cups chopped cooked turkey
- 1 1/2 cups shredded mozzarella and Cheddar cheese blend (6 ounces)
- 1/2 cup sour cream
- 1 cup shredded lettuce
- 1 medium tomato, seeded, chopped (3/4 cup)
- 1/2 cup crushed nacho-flavored tortilla chips

1. Heat oven to 450°F. On cookie sheet, place pizza crust. In small bowl, stir taco sauce and turkey.

2. Spread turkey mixture over pizza crust, leaving 1-inch border. Top with cheese. Bake 8 to 10 minutes or until cheese is melted and pizza is thoroughly heated.

3. Drop sour cream by teaspoonfuls over pizza. Top with lettuce, tomato and tortilla chips. Cut into 8 wedges.

4 servings
1 Serving: Calories 580 (Calories from Fat 260); Total Fat 29g (Saturated Fat 14g; Trans Fat 1g); Cholesterol 125mg; Sodium 960mg; Total Carbohydrate 43g (Dietary Fiber 2g; Sugars 3g); Protein 38g
% Daily Value: Vitamin A 20%; Vitamin C 8%; Calcium 30%; Iron 20%
Exchanges: 2 1/2 Starch, 1/2 Other Carbohydrate, 4 Lean Meat, 3 Fat
Carbohydrate Choices: 3

KITCHEN TIPS

✪ Make this pizza your own by topping it with your favorite taco toppers. Try sliced olives, chopped avocado, fresh cilantro or pickled jalapeño slices.

✪ Instead of the shredded mozzarella and Cheddar cheese blend, try making this pizza with shredded taco cheese.

Quick

Barbecue Pizza Wedges

Prep Time: 10 min Start to Finish: 20 min

1 package (10 ounces) prebaked Italian pizza
 crust (two 6-inch crusts)
¼ cup barbecue sauce
½ cup chopped cooked chicken
1 tablespoon chopped red onion
1 cup finely shredded mozzarella cheese
 (4 ounces)
6 cherry tomatoes, chopped (⅓ cup)

1. Heat gas or charcoal grill for indirect cooking as
 directed by manufacturer. Top pizza crusts with
 remaining ingredients in order given.

2. Place pizzas on grill for indirect cooking over
 medium heat. Cover grill; cook 8 to 10 minutes,
 rotating pizzas occasionally, until cheese is melted
 and pizzas are hot. Cut each into 6 wedges.

4 servings (3 wedges each)
1 Serving: Calories 340 (Calories from Fat 100); Total Fat 11g
(Saturated Fat 6g; Trans Fat 0g); Cholesterol 40mg; Sodium 690mg;
Total Carbohydrate 40g (Dietary Fiber 2g; Sugars 6g); Protein 20g
% Daily Value: Vitamin A 10%; Vitamin C 4%; Calcium 25%; Iron 15%
Exchanges: 2 Starch, ½ Other Carbohydrate, 2 Lean Meat, 1 Fat
Carbohydrate Choices: 2½

KITCHEN TIPS

❂ If you prefer, you can bake these pizzas on a cookie sheet
 in a 450°F oven about 6 minutes.
❂ The crusts for these pizza wedges are the individual size.
 They make small wedges that are easy to handle.

Grilled Bacon and Tomato Pizza Wedges

Prep Time: 15 min Start to Finish: 25 min

5	slices bacon, cut into $1/2$-inch pieces
$1/2$	cup garlic-and-herb spreadable cheese (from 6.5-ounce container)
1	package (10 ounces) prebaked Italian pizza crust (two 8-inch crusts)
1	large roma (plum) tomato, cut into 10 thin slices
1	tablespoon extra-virgin olive oil
$1/4$	cup chopped fresh basil leaves

1. Heat gas or charcoal grill. In 10-inch skillet, cook bacon over medium heat, stirring frequently, until crisp. Drain on paper towel; set aside.

2. Spread cheese evenly on pizza crusts. Top with tomato and bacon. Drizzle with oil.

3. Place pizzas on grill over low heat. Cover grill; cook 4 to 8 minutes or until bottoms are deep golden brown and toppings are warm. Sprinkle basil over pizzas. Cut each into 8 wedges.

16 appetizers
1 Appetizer: Calories 90 (Calories from Fat 50); Total Fat 5g (Saturated Fat 2.5g; Trans Fat 0g); Cholesterol 10mg; Sodium 170mg; Total Carbohydrate 8g (Dietary Fiber 0g; Sugars 0g); Protein 3g
% Daily Value: Vitamin A 4%; Vitamin C 0%; Calcium 0%; Iron 4%
Exchanges: $1/2$ Starch, 1 Fat
Carbohydrate Choices: $1/2$

KITCHEN TIPS

✪ Watch pizzas carefully. Each grill heats and cooks differently. If the lowest setting of your grill seems too hot, move pizzas to a cooler part of the grill. You can also turn off a burner if your grill has more than one burner.

✪ To bake pizzas, heat oven to 375°F. Place pizzas on cookie sheet. Bake 6 to 8 minutes or until toppings are warm. Sprinkle basil over pizzas.

✪ Use a kitchen scissors to easily cut the fresh basil leaves.

Mascarpone and Pistachio Toasts

Prep Time: 10 min Start to Finish: 25 min

4	ounces mascarpone cheese (about $1/2$ cup), softened
18	slices ($1/4$ inch thick) baguette French bread
$1/3$	cup pistachio nuts (about 2 ounces), coarsely chopped
2	tablespoons honey
2	tablespoons thinly sliced fresh basil leaves

1. Heat oven to 350°F. Spread cheese on each bread slice. Place a single layer of bread slices in ungreased 15 × 10 × 1-inch pan. Sprinkle nuts over cheese.

2. Bake 10 to 12 minutes or until edges of bread are light golden.

3. Drizzle honey over top of each toast. Garnish with basil.

18 appetizers
1 Appetizer: Calories 60 (Calories from Fat 30); Total Fat 3g (Saturated Fat 1.5g; Trans Fat 0g); Cholesterol 5mg; Sodium 40mg; Total Carbohydrate 7g (Dietary Fiber 0g; Sugars 3g); Protein 1g
% Daily Value: Vitamin A 0%; Vitamin C 0%; Calcium 0%; Iron 0%
Exchanges: $1/2$ Starch, $1/2$ Fat
Carbohydrate Choices: $1/2$

KITCHEN TIPS

✪ If mascarpone isn't available, you can still make these tasty toasts. Use 4 ounces of cream cheese, softened, instead.

✪ Spray your tablespoon with cooking spray to keep the honey from sticking when you measure it.

Mascarpone and Pistachio Toasts

Grilled Bacon and Tomato Pizza Wedges

Mushroom-Pepper–Whole Wheat Sandwich

Hummus and Cucumber Bites

Hummus and Cucumber Bites

Prep Time: 15 min Start to Finish: 15 min

- 2 pita (pocket) breads (6 inch)
- 2/3 cup roasted red pepper hummus (from 7-ounce container)
- 1/3 English (seedless) cucumber (about 4 inches)
- 1/2 teaspoon smoked Spanish paprika
- 16 fresh dill weed sprigs

1. Cut each pita bread into 8 wedges. Spread about 1 teaspoon hummus on each wedge.

2. Score cucumber peel lengthwise with tines of fork. Cut cucumber in half lengthwise. Cut each half crosswise into 16 thin slices. Place 2 half-slices cucumber on hummus on each bite.

3. Sprinkle with paprika. Garnish with dill weed.

16 appetizers
1 Appetizer: Calories 40 (Calories from Fat 10); Total Fat 1g (Saturated Fat 0g; Trans Fat 0g); Cholesterol 0mg; Sodium 70mg; Total Carbohydrate 6g (Dietary Fiber 0g; Sugars 0g); Protein 1g
% Daily Value: Vitamin A 0%; Vitamin C 0%; Calcium 0%; Iron 4%
Exchanges: 1/2 Starch
Carbohydrate Choices: 1/2

KITCHEN TIPS

✿ Smoked Spanish paprika has a smoky, spicy flavor. Regular paprika can be substituted for it, if you like.

✿ Hummus comes in a variety of flavors; try these bites with your favorite.

Mushroom-Pepper-Whole Wheat Sandwich

Prep Time: 30 min Start to Finish: 30 min

- 4 medium fresh portabella mushroom caps (3 1/2 to 4 inches)
- 4 slices red onion, 1/2 inch thick
- 2 tablespoons reduced-fat mayonnaise or salad dressing
- 2 teaspoons reduced-fat balsamic vinaigrette
- 8 slices whole wheat bread
- 4 slices (3/4 ounce each) reduced-fat mozzarella cheese
- 8 strips (2 × 1 inch) roasted red bell pepper (from 7-ounce jar), patted dry
- 8 large basil leaves

1. Heat closed medium-size contact grill for 5 minutes.

2. Place mushrooms on grill. Close grill; cook 4 to 5 minutes or until slightly softened. Remove mushrooms from grill. Place onion on grill. Close grill; cook 4 to 5 minutes or until slightly softened. Remove onion from grill.

3. In small bowl, mix mayonnaise and vinaigrette; spread over bread slices. Top 4 bread slices with mushrooms, cheese, onion, bell pepper and basil. Top with remaining bread, mayonnaise sides down.

4. Place 2 sandwiches on grill. Close grill; cook 2 to 3 minutes or until sandwiches are golden brown and toasted. Repeat with remaining 2 sandwiches.

4 sandwiches
1 Sandwich: Calories 280 (Calories from Fat 70); Total Fat 7g (Saturated Fat 2.5g; Trans Fat 0g); Cholesterol 10mg; Sodium 490mg; Total Carbohydrate 38g (Dietary Fiber 6g; Sugars 15g); Protein 15g
% Daily Value: Vitamin A 90%; Vitamin C 110%; Calcium 25%; Iron 10%
Exchanges: 2 Starch, 1/2 Other Carbohydrate, 1 1/2 Lean Meat
Carbohydrate Choices: 2 1/2

Quick
Caesar Chicken Subs

Prep Time: 15 min Start to Finish: 15 min

- 4 submarine sandwich rolls (about 6 inch) or 1 baguette (8 ounce)
- 1/3 cup Caesar dressing
- 1/2 package (3.5-ounce size) sandwich sliced pepperoni
- 3/4 pound deli rotisserie chicken (from 2- to 2 1/2-pound chicken), cut into about 1/4-inch slices
- 4 slices (1 ounce each) Colby-Monterey Jack cheese blend
- 4 slices tomato, cut in half
- 4 lettuce leaves
- 1/2 medium red onion, thinly sliced

1. Cut rolls horizontally in half (if using baguette, first cut into 4 equal pieces). Spread dressing over cut sides of rolls.

2. Layer bottom halves of rolls with pepperoni, chicken, cheese, tomato, lettuce and onion. Top with roll tops, press gently. Secure with toothpicks. Cut each sandwich diagonally in half.

4 sandwiches
1 Sandwich: Calories 616 (Calories from Fat 340); Total Fat 38g (Saturated Fat 12g; Trans Fat 0g); Cholesterol 120mg; Sodium 1413mg; Total Carbohydrate 37g (Dietary Fiber 3g; Sugars 0g); Protein 40g
% Daily Value: Vitamin A 20%; Vitamin C 10%; Calcium 30%; Iron 10%
Exchanges: 4 Fat, 2 Starch, 1/2 Vegetable, 4 Meat
Carbohydrate Choices: 2 1/2

KITCHEN TIPS

✿ These sandwiches are perfect to wrap and tote for any type of outing.
✿ You could use ranch dressing instead of the Caesar.

Quick
Turkey Salad Sandwiches

Prep Time: 20 min Start to Finish: 20 min

- 1 1/2 cups diced cooked turkey
- 1/2 cup diced unpeeled apple
- 1/2 cup mayonnaise or salad dressing
- 1 1/2 teaspoons curry powder
- 1/4 teaspoon ground ginger
- 1/4 teaspoon pepper
- 1 medium stalk celery, chopped (1/2 cup)
- 2 green onions, chopped (2 tablespoons)
- 8 slices whole grain bread

1. In medium bowl, mix all ingredients except bread.

2. Spread turkey mixture on 4 slices bread. Top with remaining bread.

4 sandwiches
1 Sandwich: Calories 460 (Calories from Fat 250); Total Fat 28g (Saturated Fat 5g; Trans Fat 0.5g); Cholesterol 55mg; Sodium 510mg; Total Carbohydrate 31g (Dietary Fiber 5g; Sugars 9g); Protein 21g
% Daily Value: Vitamin A 4%; Vitamin C 4%; Calcium 6%; Iron 15%
Exchanges: 2 Starch, 2 Lean Meat, 4 Fat
Carbohydrate Choices: 2

KITCHEN TIPS

✿ Skip the bread and serve this turkey salad on a lettuce-lined plate with cut-up fresh vegetables or fruits.
✿ For less fat per serving, use fat-free or reduced-fat mayonnaise.

Caesar Chicken Subs

Turkey Salad Sandwiches

Quick

Turkey and Roasted Red Pepper Sandwich

Prep Time: 25 min   Start to Finish: 25 min

1 loaf (16 ounces) French bread
1 pound thinly sliced cooked turkey
1 jar (7 ounces) roasted red bell peppers, drained
8 slices (about 1 ounce each) Monterey Jack cheese with jalapeño peppers

1. Heat gas or charcoal grill. Cut 30 × 18-inch sheet of heavy-duty aluminum foil. Cut bread in half horizontally. Layer turkey, peppers and cheese on bottom half of bread. Cover with top half. Place sandwich on center of foil.

2. Bring up 2 sides of foil over sandwich so edges meet. Seal edges, making tight 1/2-inch fold; fold again, allowing space for heat circulation and expansion. Fold other sides to seal.

3. Place packet on grill over low heat. Cover grill; cook 10 to 13 minutes, rotating packet 1/2 turn after 5 minutes, until sandwich is toasted and cheese is melted.

4. To serve, carefully fold back foil to allow steam to escape. Cut sandwich into 6 pieces.

6 servings
1 Serving: Calories 470 (Calories from Fat 160); Total Fat 18g (Saturated Fat 8g; Trans Fat 1g); Cholesterol 100mg; Sodium 780mg; Total Carbohydrate 41g (Dietary Fiber 2g; Sugars 3g); Protein 37g
% Daily Value: Vitamin A 40%; Vitamin C 40%; Calcium 30%; Iron 20%
Exchanges: 2 1/2 Starch, 4 Lean Meat, 1 Fat
Carbohydrate Choices: 3

KITCHEN TIPS

✪ You can also bake this flavorful sandwich at 350°F for 10 to 13 minutes or until the cheese is melted.

✪ For a milder cheese flavor, use Swiss or provolone cheese instead of the pepper Jack.

Pork Fajita Wraps

Prep Time: 20 min Start to Finish: 35 min

¼ cup lime juice

1½ teaspoons ground cumin

¾ teaspoon salt

4 cloves garlic, finely chopped

½ pound pork tenderloin, cut into very thin slices

1 large onion, thinly sliced

3 medium bell peppers, thinly sliced

4 flour tortillas (8 inch)

1. In shallow glass or plastic dish, mix lime juice, cumin, salt and garlic. Stir in pork. Cover; refrigerate, stirring occasionally, at least 15 minutes but no longer than 24 hours.

2. Remove pork from marinade; reserve marinade. Heat 12-inch nonstick skillet over medium-high heat. Add pork; cook 3 minutes, stirring once. Stir in onion, bell peppers and marinade. Cook 5 to 8 minutes longer, stirring frequently, until onion and peppers are crisp-tender.

3. Place one-fourth of pork mixture on center of each tortilla. Fold one end of tortilla up about 1 inch over pork mixture; fold right and left sides over folded portion.

4 servings
1 Serving: Calories 260 (Calories from Fat 60); Total Fat 6g (Saturated Fat 1.5g; Trans Fat 0.5g); Cholesterol 35mg; Sodium 0mg; Total Carbohydrate 34g (Dietary Fiber 3g; Sugars 5g); Protein 0g
% Daily Value: Vitamin A 6%; Vitamin C 70%; Calcium 10%; Iron 0%
Exchanges: 2 Starch, 1 Vegetableetable, 1½ Lean Meat
Carbohydrate Choices: 2

KITCHEN TIPS

✿ One bell pepper packs a nutritional punch. It contains one and one-half times the vitamin C your body needs daily.

Chipotle Pulled-Pork Sandwiches

Prep Time: 15 min Start to Finish: 7 hr 45 min

- 1 tablespoon packed brown sugar
- 2 teaspoons salt
- 2 teaspoons garlic powder
- 1½ teaspoons ground mustard
- 3 teaspoons chili powder
- 1 boneless pork shoulder (3 pounds), trimmed of fat
- 1 can (8 ounces) tomato sauce
- 2 canned chipotle chilies, finely chopped
- 1 tablespoon adobo sauce from canned chipotle chilies
- 20 burger buns, split
- 5 medium avocados, pitted, peeled and thinly sliced

1. Spray 4- to 5-quart slow cooker with cooking spray. In small bowl, mix brown sugar, salt, garlic powder, mustard and chili powder. Rub seasoning mixture over pork. Place pork in cooker. Sprinkle any remaining seasoning mixture that doesn't stick to pork over top of pork in cooker.

2. Cover; cook on Low heat setting 7 to 8 hours.

3. Remove pork from cooker; place on cutting board. Remove liquid from cooker; skim fat from liquid and reserve liquid. Cool pork slightly. With 2 forks, shred pork. Return to cooker. Stir tomato sauce, chipotle chilies and adobo sauce into shredded pork. If desired, stir in some of the reserved cooking liquid for desired moistness.

4. Increase heat setting to High. Cover; cook 15 to 30 minutes longer or until hot. Spoon about ⅓ cup pork mixture into each bun. Place a few slices of avocado over pork in each bun. Pork mixture can be kept warm on Low heat setting up to 2 hours; stir occasionally.

20 sandwiches
1 Sandwich: Calories 340 (Calories from Fat 150); Total Fat 17g (Saturated Fat 4.5g; Trans Fat 0g); Cholesterol 45mg; Sodium 550mg; Total Carbohydrate 27g (Dietary Fiber 4g; Sugars 4g); Protein 20g
% Daily Value: Vitamin A 4%; Vitamin C 4%; Calcium 8%; Iron 15%
Exchanges: 1 Starch, ½ Other Carbohydrate, 2½ Lean Meat, 2 Fat
Carbohydrate Choices: 2

KITCHEN TIPS

- Complete this meal with carrot sticks and corn chips.
- Leftover pork makes a tasty burrito filling or tostada topping.
- Chipotle chilies are canned in adobo sauce. Remove the chilies from the sauce to chop.

Southwestern Pork Burritos

Prep Time: 10 min Start to Finish: 8 hr 10 min

1 boneless pork shoulder roast (2½ pounds), trimmed of fat

1 can (10 ounces) diced tomatoes and green chilies, undrained

3 tablespoons tomato paste

1 tablespoon honey

3 cloves garlic, finely chopped

1 tablespoon chili powder

¼ teaspoon salt

12 Old El Paso flour tortillas for burritos (8 inch; from two 11.5-ounce packages)

Assorted toppings (such as shredded Cheddar cheese, sour cream, chopped fresh cilantro, shredded lettuce, diced tomatoes), if desired

1. Spray 3- to 4-quart slow cooker with cooking spray. Place pork in center.

2. In blender, place tomatoes, tomato paste, honey, garlic, chili powder and salt. Cover; blend on medium-high speed 10 seconds, stopping blender frequently to scrape sides. Pour over pork.

3. Cover; cook on Low heat setting 8 to 10 hours.

4. Remove pork from cooker; place on cutting board. Shred pork with 2 forks; return to cooker and mix well.

5. Serve pork mixture on tortillas with toppings; roll up. Pork mixture will hold on Low heat setting up to 2 hours.

12 burritos
1 Burrito: Calories 330 (Calories from Fat 140); Total Fat 15g (Saturated Fat 5g; Trans Fat 1g); Cholesterol 60mg; Sodium 490mg; Total Carbohydrate 24g (Dietary Fiber 0g; Sugars 3g); Protein 24g
% Daily Value: Vitamin A 6%; Vitamin C 2%; Calcium 8%; Iron 10%
Exchanges: 1 Starch, ½ Other Carbohydrate, 3 Lean Meat, 1 Fat
Carbohydrate Choices: 1½

KITCHEN TIPS

✪ This tasty pork filling also makes great sandwiches. Spoon the filling on top of toasted bread slices. Top with shredded lettuce and shredded Monterey Jack or Cheddar cheese.

✪ To warm tortillas, wrap them in aluminum foil and heat in 325°F oven for about 15 minutes. Or place on a microwavable paper towel and microwave on High for 30 seconds.

Quick

Reuben Brats

Prep Time: 30 min Start to Finish: 30 min

1 can or bottle (12 ounces) beer or nonalcoholic beer

4 uncooked fresh bratwurst links (about 1 pound)

2 tablespoons Thousand Island dressing

4 rye or whole wheat bratwurst buns, split

½ cup shredded Swiss cheese (2 ounces)

1 cup sauerkraut, drained, heated if desired

1. Heat gas or charcoal grill. In 2-quart saucepan, heat beer to boiling. Add bratwurst; reduce heat to low. Cover; simmer 15 minutes.

2. Drain bratwurst. Place on grill over medium heat. Cover grill; cook 5 to 10 minutes, turning once, until brown.

3. Spread dressing on cut sides of buns. Place bratwurst in buns, top with cheese, bratwurst and sauerkraut.

Broil Directions: Set oven control to broil. Place bratwurst on rack in broiler pan. Broil with tops 4 to 6 inches from heat 5 to 10 minutes, turning once, until brown.

4 servings
1 Serving: Calories 480 (Calories from Fat 280); Total Fat 32g (Saturated Fat 12g; Trans Fat 1g); Cholesterol 65mg; Sodium 1670mg; Total Carbohydrate 28g (Dietary Fiber 3g; Sugars 4g); Protein 18g
% Daily Value: Vitamin A 2%; Vitamin C 8%; Calcium 20%; Iron 15%
Exchanges: 1½ Starch, ½ Other Carbohydrate, 2 High-Fat Meat, 3 Fat
Carbohydrate Choices: 2

KITCHEN TIPS

✿ Simmering the brats in beer makes them moist and flavorful, and it shortens the grilling time.

✿ To cut fat and calories, use fat-free Thousand Island dressing and chicken or turkey brats.

Philly Cheese Steak Sandwiches

Prep Time: 15 min Start to Finish: 6 hr 15 min

1 boneless beef round steak, 1 inch thick (2 pounds), trimmed of fat, cut into bite-size strips

2 medium onions, sliced

1 tablespoon garlic-pepper blend

2 tablespoons water

1 tablespoon beef bouillon granules

2 large green bell peppers, cut into bite-size strips

6 slices (¾ ounces each) American cheese, cut in half

6 hoagie buns, split

1. Spray 3- to 4-quart slow cooker with cooking spray. In medium bowl, sprinkle beef and onions with garlic-pepper blend; stir to coat evenly. Spoon mixture into cooker.

2. In measuring cup, stir water and bouillon granules until dissolved. Pour over mixture in cooker.

3. Cover; cook on Low heat setting 6 to 8 hours. About 20 minutes before serving, stir in bell peppers.

4. Place 2 cheese pieces on bottom of each bun. Using slotted spoon, spoon beef mixture over cheese. Cover with tops of buns. Beef mixture can be kept warm on Low heat setting up to 2 hours.

6 sandwiches
1 Sandwich: Calories 550 (Calories from Fat 130); Total Fat 14g (Saturated Fat 7g; Trans Fat 1g); Cholesterol 105mg; Sodium 1360mg; Total Carbohydrate 56g (Dietary Fiber 4g; Sugars 11g); Protein 49g
% Daily Value: Vitamin A 8%; Vitamin C 40%; Calcium 20%; Iron 35%
Exchanges: 2 Starch, 1 Other Carbohydrate, 1 Vegetableetable, 6 Very Lean Meat, 2 Fat
Carbohydrate Choices: 4

KITCHEN TIPS

❂ Cheddar or mozzarella cheese can be used in place of the American cheese.

❂ If you don't have hoagie buns, use crusty French or Kaiser rolls instead.

Easy French Dip Sandwiches

Prep Time: 10 min Start to Finish: 8 hr 10 min

- 1 fresh beef brisket (not corned beef) (3 pounds)
- 1 package (1 ounce) onion recipe and dip soup mix (from 2-ounce box)
- 1 can (10 1/2 ounces) condensed beef broth
- 8 mini baguettes or sandwich buns

1. Spray 3- to 4-quart slow cooker with cooking spray. Place beef in cooker. In small bowl, mix dry soup mix and broth; pour over beef.

2. Cover; cook on Low heat setting 8 to 10 hours.

3. Skim fat from liquid in cooker. Remove beef from cooker; place on cutting board. Cut beef across grain into thin slices or shred beef.

4. To serve, cut each baguette in half horizontally. Fill baguettes with beef; cut crosswise in half. Serve with broth for dipping. Beef mixture will hold on Low heat setting up to 2 hours; stir occasionally.

8 sandwiches
1 Sandwich: Calories 480 (Calories from Fat 130); Total Fat 14g (Saturated Fat 5g; Trans Fat 1g); Cholesterol 75mg; Sodium 1000mg; Total Carbohydrate 41g (Dietary Fiber 2g; Sugars 2g); Protein 48g
% Daily Value: Vitamin A 0%; Vitamin C 0%; Calcium 8%; Iron 30%
Exchanges: 2 Starch, 1/2 Other Carbohydrate, 6 Very Lean Meat, 2 Fat
Carbohydrate Choices: 3

KITCHEN TIPS

✺ Make this recipe the day ahead; cover and refrigerate. Reheat in the microwave or on the stovetop just before serving.

✺ Complete your menu with warm Old-Fashioned Potato Salad, page 75.

Quick & Low-Fat
Mushroom-Swiss Veggie Burger

Prep Time: 20 min Start to Finish: 20 min

- 4 frozen vegetable burgers
- 1 jar (4.5 ounces) Green Giant sliced mushrooms, drained
- 4 slices (about 1 ounce each) reduced-fat Swiss cheese
- 1/4 cup fat-free mayonnaise
- 4 whole-grain hamburger buns
- 4 tomato slices
- 4 lettuce leaves
- Ketchup and mustard, if desired

1. Heat gas or charcoal grill. Place vegetable burger on grill over medium heat. Cover grill; cook 6 to 9 minutes, turning once, until thoroughly heated.

2. Divide mushrooms evenly onto patties; top with cheese. Cover grill; cook 1 to 2 minutes longer or until cheese is melted. Spread 1 tablespoon mayonnaise on each bun. Serve patties in buns with tomatoes, lettuce, ketchup and mustard.

4 servings
1 Serving: Calories 300 (Calories from Fat 70); Total Fat 8g (Saturated Fat 2.5g; Trans Fat 0g); Cholesterol 15mg; Sodium 930mg; Total Carbohydrate 32g (Dietary Fiber 8g; Sugars 8g); Protein 25g
% Daily Value: Vitamin A 10%; Vitamin C 4%; Calcium 40%; Iron 20%
Exchanges: 1 1/2 Starch, 1/2 Other Carbohydrate, 3 Very Lean Meat, 1 Fat
Carbohydrate Choices: 2

KITCHEN TIPS

✺ If you haven't had veggie burgers for a while, you're in for a treat! They come in many flavors, from Cajun-spiced to classic grilled. Choose your favorite version.

✺ Team these burgers with classic picnic fare: Carrot and celery sticks, fresh-cut melon and lemonade.

Easy French Dip Sandwiches

Mushroom-Swiss Veggie Burger

Greek Turkey Burgers with Yogurt Sauce

Prep Time: 20 min Start to Finish: 20 min

Yogurt Sauce

- 1/2 cup plain fat-free yogurt
- 1/4 cup chopped red onion
- 1/4 cup chopped cucumber

Burgers

- 1 pound lean ground turkey
- 1/2 cup plain fat-free yogurt
- 1 teaspoon dried oregano leaves
- 1/2 teaspoon garlic powder
- 1/2 teaspoon salt
- 1/2 teaspoon pepper
- 4 whole wheat hamburger buns

1. In small bowl, mix all sauce ingredients; refrigerate until ready to serve.

2. Set oven control to broil. In medium bowl, mix all burger ingredients except buns. Shape mixture into 4 patties, each about 1/2 inch thick and 5 inches in diameter. Place on rack in broiler pan.

3. Broil burgers with tops about 6 inches from heat 8 to 10 minutes, turning after 5 minutes, until thermometer inserted in center reads 165°F. Place burgers on buns. Serve with sauce.

4 servings
1 Serving: Calories 310 (Calories from Fat 70); Total Fat 8g (Saturated Fat 2g; Trans Fat 0.5g); Cholesterol 75mg; Sodium 640mg; Total Carbohydrate 26g (Dietary Fiber 3g; Sugars 8g); Protein 33g
% Daily Value: Vitamin A 0%; Vitamin C 0%; Calcium 15%; Iron 15%
Exchanges: 1 1/2 Starch, 4 Very Lean Meat, 1 Fat
Carbohydrate Choices: 2

KITCHEN TIPS

✿ This flavorful yogurt sauce also tastes great on pita bread wedges, or use it as a dip for veggies.

Quick

Grilled Blue Cheese Burgers

Prep Time: 25 min Start to Finish: 25 min

2 cloves garlic, finely chopped
$1/4$ cup butter or margarine
2 teaspoons Worcestershire sauce
3 pounds lean (at least 85%) ground beef
2 tablespoons Montreal steak grill seasoning
1 cup blue cheese crumbles (4 ounces)
8 diagonal slices ($1/2$ to 1 inch thick) French bread
2 cups loosely packed baby salad greens

1. In 8-inch skillet, cook garlic in butter over low heat 2 to 3 minutes, stirring occasionally, until garlic is tender. Stir in Worcestershire sauce. Remove from heat.

2. Heat gas or charcoal grill. In large bowl, mix beef and grill seasoning. Shape mixture into 8 oval patties, $1/2$ inch thick.

3. Place patties on grill over medium heat. Cover grill, cook 10 to 12 minutes, turning once, until meat thermometer inserted in center of patties reads 165°F. Remove from grill to platter; top with cheese. Place bread on grill. Cover; cook 2 to 4 minutes, turning once, until lightly toasted.

4. Spread one side of each toasted bread slice with butter mixture. Top bread slices with salad greens and burgers.

8 servings
1 Serving: Calories 480 (Calories from Fat 250); Total Fat 27g (Saturated Fat 13g; Trans Fat 1.5g); Cholesterol 135mg; Sodium 1070mg; Total Carbohydrate 21g (Dietary Fiber 1g; Sugars 3g); Protein 38g
% Daily Value: Vitamin A 20%; Vitamin C 2%; Calcium 10%; Iron 25%
Exchanges: $1^1/2$ Starch, $4^1/4$ Medium-Fat Meat, $1/2$ Fat
Carbohydrate Choices: $1^1/2$

KITCHEN TIPS

❂ Shape the oval burgers slightly larger than the slices of French bread. They tend to shrink slightly as they cook.

❂ Use your favorite small salad greens. Baby arugula or spinach provides a slightly bitter flavor that goes well with the grill flavor and blue cheese.

❂ Grill seasonings are found with the other spices in the baking section of the grocery store. They are salt and pepper mixtures with other herbs and spices added.

Quick & Low Fat

Grilled Barbecued Beef and Bean Burgers

Prep Time: 25 min Start to Finish: 25 min

½ pound extra-lean (at least 90%) ground beef

1 can (15 to 16 ounces) great northern beans, drained, rinsed

¼ cup finely crushed saltine crackers (about 7 squares)

2 tablespoons barbecue sauce

¼ teaspoon pepper

1 egg

5 teaspoons barbecue sauce

5 whole-grain hamburger buns, split

Leaf lettuce, sliced tomatoes and sliced onions, if desired

1. Heat gas or charcoal grill. In large bowl, mix beef, beans, cracker crumbs, 2 tablespoons barbecue sauce, the pepper and egg. Shape mixture into 5 patties, about ½ inch thick.

2. Carefully brush grill rack with oil. Place patties on grill over medium heat. Cover grill; cook 5 minutes. Turn patties; spread each patty with 1 teaspoon barbecue sauce. Cook 6 to 8 minutes longer or until meat thermometer inserted in center of patties reads 160°F.

3. Fill buns with lettuce, patties, tomatoes and onion.

5 servings
1 Serving: Calories 320 (Calories from Fat 60); Total Fat 7g (Saturated Fat 2.5g; Trans Fat 0.5g); Cholesterol 70mg; Sodium 390mg; Total Carbohydrate 43g (Dietary Fiber 7g; Sugars 8g); Protein 21g
% Daily Value: Vitamin A 0%; Vitamin C 0%; Calcium 10%; Iron 30%
Exchanges: 2 Starch, 1 Other Carbohydrate, 2 Lean Meat
Carbohydrate Choices: 3

KITCHEN TIPS

✿ Top these delicious burgers with your favorites: grilled onions, lettuce and tomato, relish or any veggies.

Quick & Low Fat
Large Crowd Sloppy Joes

Prep Time: 20 min Start to Finish: 7 hr 20 min

3	pounds lean (at least 80%) ground beef
1	large onion, coarsely chopped (1 cup)
1½	medium stalks celery, chopped (¾ cup)
1	cup barbecue sauce
1	can (26.5 ounces) sloppy joe sauce
24	sandwich buns, split

1. In 4-quart Dutch oven, cook beef and onion over medium-high heat 5 to 7 minutes, stirring occasionally, until beef is thoroughly cooked; drain.

2. Mix beef mixture and remaining ingredients except buns in 3- to 4-quart slow cooker.

3. Cover; cook on Low heat setting 7 to 9 hours.

4. Stir well before serving. To serve, fill each bun with about ⅓ cup beef mixture. Beef mixture will hold on Low heat setting up to 2 hours; stir occasionally.

24 sandwiches
1 Sandwich: Calories 305 (Calories from Fat 104); Total Fat 12g (Saturated Fat 4g; Trans Fat 0.5g); Cholesterol 39mg; Sodium 708mg; Total Carbohydrate 34g (Dietary Fiber 1g; Sugars 12g); Protein 16g
% Daily Value: Vitamin A 10%; Vitamin C 2%; Calcium 6%; Iron 15%
Exchanges: 1½ Meat, 1½ Starch, 1 Other Carbohydrate
Carbohydrate Choices: 2

KITCHEN TIPS

✪ Set out bowls of shredded mozzarella, sharp Cheddar and Monterey Jack cheese with jalapeño peppers for topping off the sandwiches.

✪ A bold or zesty barbecue sauce would boost the flavor of these crowd-pleasing sandwiches.

Meatball Mini Burgers

Prep Time: 45 min Start to Finish: 45 min

Tiny Buns

1   can (16.3 ounces) Pillsbury Grands!® Flaky Layers refrigerated buttermilk or original biscuits (8 biscuits)

1   egg

1   tablespoon water

2   tablespoons sesame seed

Meatballs

2   teaspoons vegetable oil

1   medium onion, chopped ($\frac{1}{2}$ cup)

$\frac{3}{4}$ cup chili sauce

$\frac{1}{4}$ cup water

$\frac{1}{4}$ cup yellow mustard

2   teaspoons chili powder

32   frozen plain meatballs (from 28-ounce package; about 3 cups), thawed

8   slices ($\frac{3}{4}$ ounce each) American cheese, cut into quarters

1. Heat oven to 350°F. On ungreased cookie sheet, place biscuits 1 to 2 inches apart. Cut each biscuit into quarters, but do not separate pieces. In small bowl, beat egg and 1 tablespoon water. Brush egg mixture over tops of biscuits; sprinkle with sesame seed.

2. Bake 14 to 17 minutes or until golden brown. Cool slightly; separate biscuit quarters.

3. Meanwhile, in 2-quart saucepan, heat oil over medium-high heat. Add onion; cook, stirring frequently, until onion is tender. Stir in chili sauce, $\frac{1}{4}$ cup water, the mustard and chili powder. Cook 3 to 5 minutes, stirring frequently, until slightly thickened.

4. Add meatballs to chili sauce mixture. Cover; cook over medium heat 8 to 10 minutes, stirring occasionally, until meatballs are hot.

5. Split each biscuit quarter to make tiny bun. Fill each bun with 1 meatball, some of the sauce and 1 cheese piece. Secure with toothpick.

32 appetizers
1 Appetizer: Calories 150 (Calories from Fat 70); Total Fat 8g (Saturated Fat 3g; Trans Fat 1g); Cholesterol 40mg; Sodium 470mg; Total Carbohydrate 11g (Dietary Fiber 1g; Sugars 3g); Protein 8g
% Daily Value: Vitamin A 4%; Vitamin C 0%; Calcium 6%; Iron 6%
Exchanges: $\frac{1}{2}$ Starch, 1 High-Fat Meat
Carbohydrate Choices: 1

KITCHEN TIPS

✪ Experiment with different cheeses, such as Cheddar, Gouda or Monterey Jack with jalapeño peppers, to create a new taste sensation.

✪ To save time, purchase small dinner rolls or dollar buns instead of making your own.

Meatless Meals

Wholesome Goodness

Hearty Soybean and Cheddar Pasta Salad (page 126)

Bean and Vegetable Stew with Polenta (page 132)

Picnic Taco Nachos

Prep Time: 15 min Start to Finish: 15 min

- 5 cups tortilla chips
- 1 can (15 ounces) Progresso black beans, rinsed and mashed
- 1 can (4.5 ounces) Old El Paso chopped green chilies, drained
- 2 teaspoons Old El Paso taco seasoning mix (from 1.25-ounce package)
- 2 roma (plum) tomatoes, chopped
- 2 medium green onions, sliced (2 tablespoons)
- 2 cups finely shredded Colby-Monterey Jack cheese blend (8 ounces)

1. Heat gas or charcoal grill. Spray 12 × 18-inch foil pan with cooking spray. Spread tortilla chips in pan.

2. In medium bowl, mix beans, chilies and taco seasoning mix; spoon evenly over tortilla chips. Top with tomatoes and onions. Sprinkle with cheese. Cover pan with aluminum foil.

3. Place foil pan on grill over medium heat. Cover grill; cook 8 to 10 minutes or until cheese is melted. Carefully remove foil.

4 servings
1 Serving: Calories 570 (Calories from Fat 260); Total Fat 29g (Saturated Fat 13g; Trans Fat 0.5g); Cholesterol 55mg; Sodium 1180mg; Total Carbohydrate 54g (Dietary Fiber 12g; Sugars 3g); Protein 25g
% Daily Value: Vitamin A 25%; Vitamin C 6%; Calcium 50%; Iron 25%
Exchanges: 3$\frac{1}{2}$ Starch, 2 High-Fat Meat, 2 Fat
Carbohydrate Choices: 3$\frac{1}{2}$

KITCHEN TIPS

✿ To reduce the calories to 470 and the fat to 12 grams per serving, make these nachos with baked tortilla chips and reduced-fat Monterey Jack cheese.

✿ Foil pans can bend or buckle when you lift them. Slide the pan onto a cutting board to give it more stability.

Low Fat

Red Beans-and-Rice Cakes

Prep Time: 20 min Start to Finish: 45 min

$^1/_2$ cup uncooked regular long-grain white rice

1 cup water

1 cup original Fiber One cereal

2 cans (15 to 16 ounces each) red or kidney beans, drained, rinsed

1 small onion, finely chopped

$^1/_4$ cup diced green bell pepper

1 egg or 2 egg whites, beaten

1 tablespoon chili powder

1 teaspoon ground cumin

$^1/_4$ teaspoon ground red pepper (cayenne) Salad greens, if desired

$^1/_2$ cup Old El Paso Thick n' Chunky salsa

1. Cook rice in water as directed on package. Meanwhile, place cereal in resealable plastic food-storage plastic bag; seal bag and crush with rolling pin or meat mallet (or crush in food processor).

2. In large bowl, place beans; mash with potato masher or fork. Stir in onion, bell pepper, cooked rice, egg, 2 tablespoons of the cereal, the chili powder, cumin and red pepper. Shape into 8 patties; coat patties completely with remaining cereal.

3. Spray 10-inch skillet with cooking spray. Cook 4 patties in skillet over medium heat about 10 minutes, turning once, until brown. Remove patties from skillet. Cover and keep warm while cooking remaining patties.

4. Serve patties on salad greens; top with salsa.

8 servings
1 Serving: Calories 210 (Calories from Fat 15); Total Fat 1.5g (Saturated Fat 0g; Trans Fat 0g); Cholesterol 25mg; Sodium 300mg; Total Carbohydrate 40g (Dietary Fiber 10g; Sugars 2g); Protein 10g
% Daily Value: Vitamin A 10%; Vitamin C 6%; Calcium 8%; Iron 20%
Exchanges: 2 Starch, $^1/_2$ Other Carbohydrate, $^1/_2$ Very Lean Meat
Carbohydrate Choices: 2$^1/_2$

KITCHEN TIPS

✪ Potassium can minimize the effects of salt on blood pressure. This recipe supplies an excellent source of potassium.

✪ Make a meatless main dish that's high in flavor and fiber. Chili powder, cumin, cayenne and salsa elevate the flavor, while cereal adds crunch and fiber.

Quick & Low-Fat
Black Beans and Greens

Prep Time: 10 min Start to Finish: 10 min

- 3 tablespoons fat-free Italian dressing
- ½ teaspoon grated lime peel
- 1 tablespoon lime juice
- 1 tablespoon chopped fresh cilantro
- 1 can (15 ounces) black beans, drained, rinsed
- 3½ cups mixed salad greens (about half of 10-ounce bag)
- 1 medium tomato, cut into wedges
- ½ avocado, pitted, peeled and chopped (⅓ cup)

1. In 1-cup measuring cup, mix dressing, lime peel, lime juice and cilantro.

2. In large bowl, toss beans, salad greens and tomato. Stir in dressing mixture until salad is coated. Top with avocado.

6 servings (about 1 cup each)
1 Serving: Calories 130 (Calories from Fat 25); Total Fat 3g (Saturated Fat 0g; Trans Fat 0g); Cholesterol 0mg; Sodium 95mg; Total Carbohydrate 20g (Dietary Fiber 8g; Sugars 2g); Protein 6g
% Daily Value: Vitamin A 35%; Vitamin C 15%; Calcium 6%; Iron 10%
Exchanges: 1 Starch, 1 Vegetableetable, ½ Fat
Carbohydrate Choices: 1

KITCHEN TIPS

✿ For added crunch, divide salad among six plates and arrange baked tortilla chips around the edge of each plate.

✿ Avocados contain vitamin E, an antioxidant thought to help protect against heart disease and some types of cancer.

Quick
Crunchy Oriental "Chicken" Salad

Prep Time: 25 min Start to Finish: 25 min

Dressing
- ⅓ cup fat-free mayonnaise or salad dressing
- ¼ cup Asian sesame dressing and marinade

Salad
- 1 package (10 or 10.5 ounces) frozen chicken-style breaded soy-protein nuggets
- 8 cups torn mixed salad greens
- 2 cups shredded red cabbage
- 2 cups shredded carrots (3 medium)
- 4 medium green onions, sliced (¼ cup)
- ½ cup wide chow mein noodles

1. In small bowl, mix dressing ingredients with wire whisk until creamy.

2. Heat nuggets as directed on package.

3. Divide salad greens, cabbage, carrots and onions among 4 serving plates or shallow bowls. Top with nuggets; sprinkle with noodles. Drizzle with dressing.

5 servings
1 Serving: Calories 260 (Calories from Fat 100); Total Fat 12g (Saturated Fat 2.5g; Trans Fat 0g); Cholesterol 0mg; Sodium 660mg; Total Carbohydrate 27g (Dietary Fiber 5g; Sugars 9g); Protein 13g
% Daily Value: Vitamin A 250%; Vitamin C 60%; Calcium 15%; Iron 15%
Exchanges: 1 Starch, ½ Other Carbohydrate, 1 Vegetableetable, 1 Medium-Fat Meat, 1 Fat
Carbohydrate Choices: 2

KITCHEN TIPS

✿ The produce department is loaded with convenience items; look for preshredded carrots to save time.

✿ Toasted sliced almonds would add another layer of flavor to this salad. To toast them, place ¼ cup in an ungreased heavy skillet and cook over medium-low heat about 5 minutes, stirring frequently until they begin to brown, then stirring constantly until golden brown.

Crunchy Oriental "Chicken" Salad

Black Beans and Greens

Hearty Soybean and Cheddar Pasta Salad

Prep Time: 20 min Start to Finish: 1 hr 30 min

Dressing

3	tablespoons canola or olive oil
¼	cup red wine vinegar
1	teaspoon Italian seasoning
½	teaspoon salt
¼	teaspoon pepper
¼	teaspoon garlic powder

Salad

1	cup uncooked penne pasta (3 ounces)
1	box (10 ounces) frozen shelled edamame (green) soybeans
2	large tomatoes, coarsely chopped (2 cups)
1	medium cucumber, coarsely chopped (1 cup)
2	small yellow bell peppers, coarsely chopped (1 cup)
3	ounces Cheddar cheese, cut into ½-inch cubes (¾ cup)

1. In small bowl, beat all dressing ingredients with wire whisk until well mixed.

2. Cook and drain pasta as directed on package. Rinse with cold water; drain.

3. Meanwhile, cook soybeans as directed on package. Rinse with cold water; drain.

4. In large bowl, toss pasta, soybeans, remaining salad ingredients and dressing. Cover and refrigerate at least 1 hour before serving.

6 servings
1 Serving: Calories 270 (Calories from Fat 130); Total Fat 15g (Saturated Fat 4g; Trans Fat 0g); Cholesterol 15mg; Sodium 350mg; Total Carbohydrate 22g (Dietary Fiber 4g; Sugars 5g); Protein 12g
% Daily Value: Vitamin A 15%; Vitamin C 90%; Calcium 10%; Iron 10%
Exchanges: 1 Starch, 1 Vegetableetable, 1 Medium-Fat Meat, 2 Fat
Carbohydrate Choices: 1½

KITCHEN TIPS

❂ Edamame is the Japanese name for fresh green soybeans, tasty little, bright green gems that are high in protein and easily digested. The soybeans are picked before they are completely mature and are often sold in their fuzzy green pods. Fresh edamame is available spring through fall in raw or ready-to-eat forms at co-ops, natural-foods stores or large supermarkets. Raw beans should be steamed 20 minutes before eating and are usually served chilled. They're also available frozen in boxes or bags. Once cooked, edamame can be served right in the pods as a fun appetizer or snack, and it can be shelled and used in salads or other cold or hot side dishes.

Noodles and Peanut Sauce Salad Bowl

Prep Time: 25 min Start to Finish: 25 min

8 ounces uncooked whole wheat linguine, broken in half

2 cups fresh broccoli florets

1 cup julienne-cut carrots (from 10-ounce bag)

1 medium bell pepper, cut into bite-size pieces

1/4 cup peanut butter

2 tablespoons water

2 teaspoons canola oil

2 tablespoons rice vinegar or white vinegar

2 tablespoons reduced-sodium soy sauce

1/2 teaspoon ground ginger

1/8 teaspoon ground red pepper (cayenne)

3 medium green onions, chopped (3 tablespoons)

3 tablespoons chopped fresh cilantro

1. Cook linguine as directed on package, adding broccoli, carrots and bell pepper during last minute of cooking; drain pasta and vegetables. Rinse with cold water until pasta and vegetables are cool; drain.

2. Place peanut butter in small bowl. With wire whisk, gradually beat water and oil into peanut butter until smooth. Beat in vinegar, soy sauce, ginger and ground red pepper.

3. In large serving bowl, stir together pasta mixture, peanut sauce, onions and cilantro until well mixed.

4 servings (1³⁄₄ cups each)
1 Serving: Calories 370 (Calories from Fat 100); Total Fat 12g (Saturated Fat 2g; Trans Fat 0g); Cholesterol 0mg; Sodium 570mg; Total Carbohydrate 51g (Dietary Fiber 8g; Sugars 6g); Protein 14g
% Daily Value: Vitamin A 120%; Vitamin C 110%; Calcium 8%; Iron 15%
Exchanges: 2 Starch, 1 Other Carbohydrate, 1 Vegetableetable, 1 High-Fat Meat, 1/2 Fat
Carbohydrate Choices: 3¹⁄₂

KITCHEN TIPS

✿ This recipe is an all-in-one. It's packed with all the nutrients you need for a meal (and more!); just add a glass of sparkling water flavored with fresh lemon or lime slices.

Mediterranean Quinoa Salad

Farmers' Market Barley Risotto

Farmers' Market Barley Risotto

Prep Time: 1 hr 15 min Start to Finish: 1 hr 15 min

- 1 tablespoon olive oil
- 1 medium onion, chopped ($\frac{1}{2}$ cup)
- 1 medium bell pepper, coarsely chopped (1 cup)
- 2 cups chopped fresh mushrooms (4 ounces)
- 1 cup Green Giant Niblets frozen whole kernel corn (from 1-pound bag)
- 1 cup uncooked pearl barley
- $\frac{1}{4}$ cup dry white wine or chicken broth
- 2 cups roasted vegetable stock or chicken broth
- 3 cups water
- $1\frac{1}{2}$ cups grape tomatoes, cut in half (if large, cut into quarters)
- $\frac{2}{3}$ cup shredded Parmesan cheese
- 3 tablespoons chopped fresh or 1 teaspoon dried basil leaves
- $\frac{1}{2}$ teaspoon pepper

1. In 4-quart Dutch oven, heat oil over medium heat. Cook onion, bell pepper, mushrooms and corn in oil about 5 minutes, stirring frequently, until onion is crisp-tender. Add barley, stirring about 1 minute to coat.

2. Stir in wine and $\frac{1}{2}$ cup of the vegetable stock. Cook 5 minutes, stirring frequently, until liquid is almost absorbed. Repeat with remaining stock and 3 cups water, adding $\frac{1}{2}$ to $\frac{3}{4}$ cup of stock or water at a time and stirring frequently, until absorbed.

3. Stir in tomatoes, $\frac{1}{3}$ cup of the cheese, the basil and pepper. Cook until hot. Sprinkle with remaining $\frac{1}{3}$ cup cheese.

4 servings ($1\frac{1}{2}$ cups each)
1 Serving: Calories 370 (Calories from Fat 90); Total Fat 9g (Saturated Fat 4g; Trans Fat 0g); Cholesterol 15mg; Sodium 820mg; Total Carbohydrate 56g (Dietary Fiber 11g; Sugars 8g); Protein 15g
% Daily Value: Vitamin A 30%; Vitamin C 35%; Calcium 25%; Iron 15%
Exchanges: $2\frac{1}{2}$ Starch, $\frac{1}{2}$ Other Carbohydrate, 2 Vegetableetables, $\frac{1}{2}$ Medium-Fat Meat, 1 Fat
Carbohydrate Choices: 4

Low Fat

Mediterranean Quinoa Salad

Prep Time: 30 min Start to Finish: 1 hr 35 min

- 1 cup uncooked quinoa
- 2 cups cooked broth with roasted garlic (from two 14-ounce cans)
- $\frac{1}{2}$ cup chopped drained roasted red bell peppers (from 7-ounce jar)
- $\frac{1}{2}$ cup cubed reduced-fat provolone cheese
- $\frac{1}{4}$ cup chopped Kalamata olives
- 2 tablespoons chopped fresh basil leaves
- 2 tablespoons fat-free Italian dressing

1. Rinse quinoa under cold water 1 minute; drain. In 2-quart saucepan, heat quinoa and broth to boiling. Reduce heat; cover and simmer 15 to 20 minutes or until quinoa is tender; drain. Cool completely, about 45 minutes.

2. In large serving bowl, toss quinoa and remaining ingredients. Serve immediately, or refrigerate 1 to 2 hours before serving.

4 servings ($\frac{3}{4}$ cup each)
1 Serving: Calories 250 (Calories from Fat 60); Total Fat 7g (Saturated Fat 2g; Trans Fat 0g); Cholesterol 0mg; Sodium 740mg; Total Carbohydrate 33g (Dietary Fiber 3g; Sugars 5g); Protein 13g
% Daily Value: Vitamin A 30%; Vitamin C 70%; Calcium 15%; Iron 25%
Exchanges: 2 Starch, 1 Lean Meat, $\frac{1}{2}$ Fat
Carbohydrate Choices: 2

KITCHEN TIPS

✿ Quinoa is an authentic grain from Peru that's becoming more popular because it's high in protein, cooks quickly and tastes great!

Veggies and Kasha with Balsamic Vinaigrette

Prep Time: 15 min Start to Finish: 2 hr 20 min

Salad

- 1 cup water
- ½ cup uncooked kasha (roasted buckwheat groats)
- 4 medium green onions, thinly sliced (¼ cup)
- 2 medium tomatoes, seeded, coarsely chopped (1½ cups)
- 1 medium unpeeled cucumber, seeded, chopped (1¼ cups)

Vinaigrette

- 2 tablespoons balsamic or red wine vinegar
- 1 tablespoon olive oil
- 2 teaspoons sugar
- ½ teaspoon salt
- ¼ teaspoon pepper
- 1 clove garlic, finely chopped

1. In 8-inch skillet, heat water to boiling. Add kasha; cook over medium-high heat 7 to 8 minutes, stirring occasionally, until tender. Drain if necessary.

2. In large bowl, mix kasha and remaining salad ingredients.

3. In container with tight-fitting lid, shake vinaigrette ingredients until well mixed. Pour vinaigrette over kasha mixture; toss. Cover; refrigerate 1 to 2 hours to blend flavors.

4 servings (1 cup each)
1 Serving: Calories 120 (Calories from Fat 35); Total Fat 4g (Saturated Fat 0.5g; Trans Fat 0g); Cholesterol 0mg; Sodium 310mg; Total Carbohydrate 19g (Dietary Fiber 3g; Sugars 6g); Protein 2g
% Daily Value: Vitamin A 15%; Vitamin C 10%; Calcium 2%; Iron 4%
Exchanges: ½ Starch, ½ Other Carbohydrate, 1 Vegetableetable, ½ Fat
Carbohydrate Choices: 1

Low-Fat

Slow Cooker Zesty Black Bean Soup

Prep Time: 25 min Start to Finish: 11 hr 25 min

- 2 cups dried black beans (1 pound), sorted, rinsed
- 10 cups water
- 8 cups vegetable broth
- 2 cans (14.5 ounces each) no-salt-added stewed tomatoes, undrained
- 2 medium carrots, coarsely chopped (1 cup)
- 2 medium onions, coarsely chopped (1 cup)
- ¼ cup chopped fresh cilantro
- 2 teaspoons finely chopped garlic
- ¼ teaspoon pepper
- ⅛ teaspoon ground red pepper (cayenne)
  Reduced-fat sour cream, if desired
  Additional chopped fresh cilantro, if desired

1. In 4-quart Dutch oven, heat beans and water to boiling; reduce heat. Simmer uncovered 10 minutes; remove from heat. Cover; let stand 1 hour.

2. Drain beans. In 6-quart slow cooker, place beans and remaining ingredients except sour cream and additional cilantro.

3. Cover; cook on Low heat setting 10 to 12 hours.

4. Serve soup topped with sour cream and additional cilantro.

9 servings (1⅓ cups each)
1 Serving: Calories 214 (Calories from Fat 6); Total Fat 0.5g (Saturated Fat 0g; Trans Fat 0g); Cholesterol 0mg; Sodium 438mg; Total Carbohydrate 41g (Dietary Fiber 7g; Sugars 12g); Protein 13g
% Daily Value: Vitamin A 70%; Vitamin C 20%; Calcium 6%; Iron 20%
Exchanges: 2 Starch, 2 Vegetableetable
Carbohydrate Choices: 3

KITCHEN TIPS

✿ Black beans, also called turtle beans, have long been popular in Latin American and Caribbean cooking. Black on the outside and a creamy color inside, these beans have a sweet flavor.

Slow Cooker Zesty Black Bean Soup

Veggies and Kasha with Balsamic Vinaigrette

Bean and Vegetable Stew with Polenta

Prep Time: 1 hr 15 min Start to Finish: 1 hr 15 min

1 tablespoon olive or vegetable oil

1 medium yellow or green bell pepper, coarsely chopped (1 cup)

1 medium onion, coarsely chopped ($^1/_2$ cup)

2 teaspoons finely chopped garlic

2 medium carrots, cut into $^1/_4$-inch slices (1 cup)

2 cans (14.5 ounces each) diced tomatoes with basil, garlic and oregano, undrained

1 can (15 to 16 ounces) black-eyed peas, drained, rinsed

1 can (19 ounces) Progresso cannellini beans, drained, rinsed

1 cup water

1 teaspoon Italian seasoning

$^1/_2$ teaspoon salt

$^1/_4$ teaspoon pepper

1 tube (16 ounces) refrigerated polenta

1 cup Green Giant frozen cut green beans

1. In $4^1/_2$- to 5-quart Dutch oven, heat oil over medium heat. Add bell pepper, onion and garlic; cook 5 to 6 minutes, stirring frequently, until onion is softened.

2. Stir in remaining ingredients except polenta and green beans. Heat to boiling. Reduce heat to medium-low. Cover; cook 35 to 40 minutes, stirring occasionally, until carrots are tender and stew is hot.

3. Meanwhile, cook polenta as directed on package; keep warm.

4. Stir green beans into stew. Cover; cook 5 to 6 minutes, stirring occasionally, until beans are hot. Serve stew over polenta.

4 servings ($1^1/_2$ cups each)
1 Serving: Calories 311 (Calories from Fat 45); Total Fat 5g (Saturated Fat 0.5g; Trans Fat 0g); Cholesterol 0mg; Sodium 1418mg; Total Carbohydrate 52g (Dietary Fiber 10g; Sugars 3g); Protein 12g
% Daily Value: Vitamin A 120%; Vitamin C 140%; Calcium 8%; Iron 20%
Exchanges: 1 Fat, $2^1/_2$ Starch, 3 Vegetable
Carbohydrate Choices: $3^1/_2$

KITCHEN TIPS

✿ Toss together a Caesar salad and pick up some rolls and cannoli from your favorite bakery.

✿ For an extra-special touch, sprinkle each serving with chopped fresh basil and freshly shredded or shaved Parmesan cheese.

Bean and Vegetable Stew with Polenta

Three-Bean Chili

Prep Time: 20 min Start to Finish: 55 min

1 can (28 ounces) whole tomatoes, undrained

1 can (15 ounces) Progresso dark red kidney beans, drained

1 can (15 to 16 ounces) garbanzo beans, drained

1 can (15 to 16 ounces) butter beans, drained

1 can (15 ounces) tomato sauce

3 small red, orange or yellow bell peppers, cut into 1-inch pieces

1 Anaheim or jalapeño chili, seeded, chopped

1 to 2 tablespoons chili powder

2 teaspoons ground cumin

¼ teaspoon pepper

½ cup sour cream

3 tablespoons Old El Paso Thick n' Chunky salsa

Chopped fresh cilantro, if desired

1. Into 4-quart Dutch oven, pour can of tomatoes; break up tomatoes with spoon. Stir in remaining ingredients except sour cream, salsa and cilantro. Heat to boiling; reduce heat. Cover; simmer 30 to 35 minutes or until bell peppers are tender.

2. In small bowl, mix sour cream and salsa. Serve chili with sour cream mixture. Sprinkle with cilantro.

6 servings (1¼ cups each)
1 Serving: Calories 227 (Calories from Fat 40); Total Fat 4.5g (Saturated Fat 2.5g; Trans Fat 0g); Cholesterol 13mg; Sodium 1085mg; Total Carbohydrate 39g (Dietary Fiber 10g; Sugars 10g); Protein 11g
% Daily Value: Vitamin A 40%; Vitamin C 110%; Calcium 15%; Iron 25%
Exchanges: 1 Fat, 1½ Starch, 2 Vegetable
Carbohydrate Choices: 2½

Tempeh Stir-Fry with Yogurt-Peanut Sauce

Prep Time: 40 min Start to Finish: 40 min

$^1/_2$ cup uncooked regular long-grain white rice

1 cup water

$^1/_4$ cup creamy peanut butter

$^1/_4$ cup vanilla low-fat yogurt

3 tablespoons teriyaki marinade (from 12-ounce bottle)

1 tablespoon honey

2 tablespoons vegetable oil

1 package (8 ounces) tempeh, cut into 2 × $^1/_4$ × $^1/_4$-inch strips

1 medium onion, cut into thin wedges

4 medium carrots, cut into 2 × $^1/_4$ × $^1/_4$-inch strips (2 cups)

12 ounces fresh green beans, cut in half crosswise (2 cups)

$^1/_4$ cup water

1 medium red bell pepper, cut into thin bite-size strips

$^1/_4$ cup chopped fresh cilantro

1. In 2-quart saucepan, heat rice and water to boiling. Reduce heat to low; cover and simmer 15 minutes. Meanwhile, in small bowl, beat peanut butter, yogurt, teriyaki marinade and honey with wire whisk until smooth; set aside.

2. In 12-inch skillet, heat 1 tablespoon of the oil over medium heat. Add tempeh; cook 5 to 6 minutes, turning frequently, until light golden brown. Remove tempeh from skillet; set aside.

3. To same skillet, add remaining tablespoon oil and the onion; cook 1 minute, stirring occasionally. Stir in carrots, green beans and water. Cover; cook 5 minutes. Stir in bell pepper. Cook 2 to 3 minutes, stirring occasionally, until vegetables are crisp-tender.

4. Stir in tempeh and peanut butter mixture until well mixed. Cook 1 to 2 minutes, stirring occasionally, until hot. Sprinkle with cilantro. Serve over rice.

4 servings
1 Serving: Calories 490 (Calories from Fat 200); Total Fat 22g (Saturated Fat 4g; Trans Fat 0g); Cholesterol 0mg; Sodium 600mg; Total Carbohydrate 52g (Dietary Fiber 8g; Sugars 17g); Protein 20g
% Daily Value: Vitamin A 240%; Vitamin C 40%; Calcium 15%; Iron 20%
Exchanges: 1$^1/_2$ Starch, 1$^1/_2$ Other Carbohydrate, 2 Vegetableetable, 1$^1/_2$ Medium-Fat Meat, 2$^1/_2$ Fat
Carbohydrate Choices: 3$^1/_2$

KITCHEN TIPS

❂ If you don't care for cilantro, feel free to leave it out.

❂ Tempeh, pronounced TEHM-pay and also spelled tempe, is a fermented, high-protein soybean cake with a chewy texture and slightly nutty flavor. If you can't find this tasty ingredient in your supermarket, check in a health food store.

Marinara Sauce with Spaghetti

Prep Time: 25 min Start to Finish: 8 hr 25 min

- 2 cans (28 ounces each) Progresso diced tomatoes with Italian herbs, undrained
- 1 can (6 ounces) tomato paste
- 1 large onion, chopped (1 cup)
- 8 cloves garlic, finely chopped
- 1 tablespoon olive or vegetable oil
- 2 teaspoons sugar
- 2 teaspoons dried basil leaves
- 1 teaspoon dried oregano leaves
- 1 teaspoon salt
- 1 teaspoon pepper
- 24 ounces uncooked spaghetti
  Shredded Parmesan cheese, if desired

1. Spray 3- to 4-quart slow cooker with cooking spray. In cooker, mix all ingredients except spaghetti and cheese.

2. Cover; cook on Low heat setting 8 to 10 hours.

3. Cook and drain spaghetti as directed on package. Serve sauce over spaghetti. Sprinkle with cheese.

12 servings
1 Serving: Calories 320 (Calories from Fat 25); Total Fat 2.5g (Saturated Fat 0g; Trans Fat 0g); Cholesterol 0mg; Sodium 890mg; Total Carbohydrate 63g (Dietary Fiber 5g; Sugars 10g); Protein 11g
% Daily Value: Vitamin A 20%; Vitamin C 20%; Calcium 6%; Iron 20%
Exchanges: 2½ Starch, 1 Other Carbohydrate, 1½ Vegetableetable, ½ Fat
Carbohydrate Choices: 4

KITCHEN TIPS

✿ This all-purpose sauce is so easy to make that you'll want to make it often and keep a few extra containers in the freezer. Ladle the cooked sauce into airtight freezer containers; cover and freeze up to 1 month.

✿ Try serving this sauce with penne, rotini or your family's favorite pasta.

Edamame Stir-Fry Salad

Prep Time: 20 min Start to Finish: 20 min

- 1 bag (1 pound 5 ounces) Create a Meal!® frozen stir-fry sesame meal starter
- 1 bag (12 ounces) frozen shelled edamame (green) soybeans
- 2 tablespoons rice vinegar
- 4 cups thinly sliced Chinese (napa) cabbage
- 2 tablespoons chopped fresh cilantro
- ¼ cup salted soy nuts (roasted soybeans)

1. Cut large slit in frozen sesame sauce packet from meal starter. Microwave on High 30 to 60 seconds. In large bowl, reserve ¼ cup sesame sauce.

2. Spray 12-inch skillet with cooking spray; heat over medium-high heat. Add soybeans, remaining sesame sauce and frozen vegetables from meal starter. Cover; cook 5 to 7 minutes, stirring frequently, just until vegetables are crisp-tender. Remove from heat.

3. To sesame sauce in bowl, stir in vinegar. Add cabbage, cilantro and cooked vegetable mixture; toss to mix. Top with soy nuts. Serve immediately.

6 servings
1 Serving: Calories 160 (Calories from Fat 60); Total Fat 7g (Saturated Fat 1g; Trans Fat 0g); Cholesterol 0mg; Sodium 550mg; Total Carbohydrate 14g (Dietary Fiber 5g; Sugars 4g); Protein 10g
% Daily Value: Vitamin A 60%; Vitamin C 45%; Calcium 15%; Iron 10%
Exchanges: ½ Other Carbohydrate, 1 Vegetableetable, 1 High-Fat Meat
Carbohydrate Choices: 1

KITCHEN TIPS

✿ Rice vinegar is less acidic than cider, white or wine vinegar. Look for it near the other vinegars in the grocery store.

Edamame Stir-Fry Salad

Marinara Sauce with Spaghetti

Quick & Low-Fat
Corn, Cheddar and Tomato Quiche

Prep Time: 10 min Start to Finish: 45 min

1	cup 8th Continent original soy milk
1	cup fat-free egg product or 4 eggs
¼	cup chopped fresh cilantro
½	teaspoon chili powder
¼	teaspoon salt
¼	teaspoon pepper
1	cup Green Giant Niblets frozen whole kernel corn, thawed
¾	cup shredded reduced-fat Cheddar cheese (3 ounces)
1	medium tomato, seeded, chopped (¾ cup)

1. Heat oven to 350°F. Spray 9-inch glass pie plate with cooking spray. In medium bowl, stir together all ingredients except corn, cheese and tomato until blended. Stir in remaining ingredients; pour into pie plate.

2. Bake 30 to 35 minutes or until knife inserted in center comes out clean. Let stand 10 minutes before cutting.

4 servings
1 Serving: Calories 130 (Calories from Fat 25); Total Fat 3g (Saturated Fat 1g; Trans Fat 0g); Cholesterol 0mg; Sodium 510mg; Total Carbohydrate 13g (Dietary Fiber 2g; Sugars 5g); Protein 15g
% Daily Value: Vitamin A 20%; Vitamin C 6%; Calcium 25%; Iron 10%
Exchanges: 1 Other Carbohydrate, 2 Very Lean Meat
Carbohydrate Choices: 1

KITCHEN TIPS

✿ Green Giant Mexicorn®—whole kernel corn with red and green peppers—makes a colorful and easy substitute for the frozen corn and roasted peppers.

✿ If you haven't tried soy milk lately, you're in for a tasty surprise! It's also an easy recipe ingredient and contains as much calcium as cow's milk.

Quick

Confetti Egg Bake

Prep Time: 15 min Start to Finish: 55 min

1 bag (20 ounces) refrigerated cooked shredded hash brown potatoes

1 tablespoon butter or margarine

2 medium green onions, sliced (2 tablespoons)

1 package (8 ounces) sliced fresh mushrooms (3 cups)

1 cup Green Giant frozen mixed vegetables, thawed

12 eggs

2 cups shredded Cheddar cheese (8 ounces)

1/2 cup milk

1 teaspoon salt

1/4 teaspoon pepper

1. Heat oven to 350°F. Spray 13 × 9-inch (3-quart) glass baking dish with cooking spray. Pat hash brown potatoes in bottom of baking dish.

2. In 10-inch skillet, melt butter over medium heat. Add onions and mushrooms; cook 5 to 7 minutes, stirring occasionally, until mushrooms are tender. Stir in mixed vegetables.

3. In large bowl, beat eggs, cheese, milk, salt and pepper with wire whisk until well mixed. Stir in mushroom mixture. Carefully pour into baking dish.

4. Bake uncovered about 40 minutes or until eggs are set in center.

12 servings
1 Serving: Calories 213 (Calories from Fat 115); Total Fat 13g (Saturated Fat 6g; Trans Fat 0g); Cholesterol 235mg; Sodium 405mg; Total Carbohydrate 12g (Dietary Fiber 1g; Sugars 2g); Protein 13g
% Daily Value: Vitamin A 10%; Vitamin C 8%; Calcium 20%; Iron 10%
Exchanges: 1/2 Fat, 1 1/2 Meat, 1 Vegetable
Carbohydrate Choices: 1

KITCHEN TIPS

✿ Other types of cheese can be used in place of the Cheddar. Monterey Jack, Colby, Havarti and Gruyère are good choices.

✿ You can remove the 1 cup of frozen vegetables from the bag the night before, and cover and thaw in the refrigerator, or you can quickly thaw frozen vegetables under cool running water.

Quick

Potato, Egg and Sausage Frittata

Prep Time: 30 min Start to Finish: 30 min

4 eggs or 8 egg whites

¼ cup fat-free (skim) milk

1 teaspoon olive oil

2 cups frozen country-style shredded hash brown potatoes (from 30-ounce bag)

4 frozen soy-protein breakfast sausage links (from 8-ounce box), cut into eighths

¼ teaspoon salt

⅛ teaspoon dried basil leaves

⅛ teaspoon dried oregano leaves

1½ cups chopped roma (plum) tomatoes (4 medium)

½ cup shredded mozzarella and Asiago cheese blend with garlic (2 ounces)

Freshly ground pepper, if desired

1. In small bowl, beat eggs and milk with fork or wire whisk until well blended; set aside.

2. Coat 10-inch nonstick skillet with oil; heat over medium heat. Cook potatoes and breakfast links in oil 6 to 8 minutes, stirring occasionally, until potatoes are golden brown.

3. Pour egg mixture over potato mixture. Cook uncovered over medium-low heat about 5 minutes; as mixture begins to set on bottom and side, gently lift cooked portions with spatula so that thin, uncooked portion can flow to bottom. Cook until eggs are thickened throughout but still moist; avoid constant stirring.

4. Sprinkle with salt, basil, oregano, tomatoes and cheese. Reduce heat to low; cover and cook about 5 minutes or until center is set and cheese is melted. Sprinkle with pepper.

4 servings
1 Serving: Calories 280 (Calories from Fat 110); Total Fat 12g (Saturated Fat 4.5g; Trans Fat 0g); Cholesterol 220mg; Sodium 590mg; Total Carbohydrate 26g (Dietary Fiber 3g; Sugars 5g); Protein 17g
% Daily Value: Vitamin A 20%; Vitamin C 15%; Calcium 20%; Iron 10%
Exchanges: 1½ Starch, 2 Medium-Fat Meat
Carbohydrate Choices: 2

KITCHEN TIPS

✹ If you haven't tried the newest soy products lately, you're in for a pleasant surprise. Soy sausage is a tasty alternative to higher-fat regular sausage and an easy addition to this fresh-tasting frittata.

Shellfish and Fish

Flavor from the Sea

Tuna with Avocado-Kiwi Salsa (page 156)

Salmon-Pasta Toss (page 160)

Smoked Salmon Pâté

Prep Time: 15 min Start to Finish: 15 min

4	ounces smoked salmon (lox)
1	container (8 ounces) chives-and-onion cream cheese spread
¼	cup finely chopped red bell pepper
1½	teaspoons lemon-pepper seasoning
1	teaspoon chopped fresh dill weed
3	tablespoons chopped fresh parsley
24	slices cocktail pumpernickel bread

24 appetizers
1 Appetizer (1 tablespoon pâté and 1 bread slice each): Calories 50 (Calories from Fat 30); Total Fat 3g (Saturated Fat 2g; Trans Fat 0g); Cholesterol 10mg; Sodium 170mg; Total Carbohydrate 4g (Dietary Fiber 0g; Sugars 0g); Protein 2g
% Daily Value: Vitamin A 4%; Vitamin C 4%; Calcium 0%; Iron 2%
Exchanges: ½ High-Fat Meat
Carbohydrate Choices: 0

KITCHEN TIPS

✿ Lox is salmon that is brine-cured, then cold-smoked.

1. Line 2-cup bowl with plastic wrap. In medium bowl, beat all ingredients except parsley and bread with electric mixer on medium speed until smooth. Spoon into lined bowl; press with rubber spatula. Cover; refrigerate until ready to serve.

2. To unmold, place 8-inch plate upside down on bowl, then turn plate and bowl over; remove bowl and plastic wrap. Sprinkle parsley over top of pâté and on rim of plate. Serve with bread.

Quick & Low Fat

Crab Gazpacho Cocktails

Prep Time: 15 min Start to Finish: 15 min

- 1 can (14.5 ounces) Muir Glen organic fire-roasted diced tomatoes, undrained
- 1/2 cup tomato juice
- 1 slice (1/4 inch thick) red onion
- 1 tablespoon cider vinegar
- 1 tablespoon olive or vegetable oil
- 1/2 teaspoon salt
- 3 drops red pepper sauce
- 1 small cucumber, peeled, diced (3/4 cup)
- 1 can (6 1/2 ounces) special white crabmeat, drained (about 1 cup)
- 2 teaspoons coarsely chopped fresh dill weed

1. In food processor, place all ingredients except cucumber, crabmeat and dill weed. Cover; process with on-and-off pulses until mixture is coarsely pureed. Stir in cucumber.

2. Spoon about 1/3 cup tomato mixture into each of 8 martini or wine glasses. Spoon about 1 heaping tablespoon crabmeat onto center of each cocktail. Sprinkle dill weed over top.

8 appetizers
1 Appetizer: Calories 50 (Calories from Fat 20); Total Fat 2g (Saturated Fat 0g; Trans Fat 0g); Cholesterol 15mg; Sodium 320mg; Total Carbohydrate 3g (Dietary Fiber 0g; Sugars 2g); Protein 4g
% Daily Value: Vitamin A 2%; Vitamin C 15%; Calcium 4%; Iron 4%
Exchanges: 1/2 Other Carbohydrate, 1/2 Lean Meat
Carbohydrate Choices: 0

KITCHEN TIPS

✿ Canned crabmeat comes in different styles and varieties, including lump (most expensive), white and claw (least expensive). We chose the white for the best appearance in this elegant appetizer. Frozen crabmeat can be used instead of the canned, if desired.

✿ Nothing is more refreshing than chilled gazpacho on a hot summer evening! If desired, chill the tomato-cucumber mixture up to 1 hour before spooning into glasses. A bonus is the flavors will have blended more.

Layered Mediterranean Tuna Spread

Prep Time: 15 min Start to Finish: 15 min

- 1 container (8 ounces) chives-and-onion cream cheese spread
- 1 shallot, finely chopped
- 1 teaspoon Italian seasoning
- 1/2 cup pitted niçoise or Kalamata olives, cut in half
- 1 can (6 ounces) albacore tuna, well drained, broken into chunks
- 1 medium tomato, seeded, coarsely chopped
- 1 hard-cooked egg, finely chopped
- 1 tablespoon chopped fresh parsley
- 48 crackers

1. In small bowl, mix cream cheese, shallot and Italian seasoning until well blended. Spread in 8-inch circle on serving plate.

2. Top with olives, tuna, tomato, egg and parsley. Serve with crackers.

16 appetizers
1 Appetizer (1/4 cup spread and 3 crackers each): Calories 110 (Calories from Fat 60); Total Fat 7g (Saturated Fat 3g; Trans Fat 0g); Cholesterol 30mg; Sodium 220mg; Total Carbohydrate 7g (Dietary Fiber 0g; Sugars 0g); Protein 5g
% Daily Value: Vitamin A 6%; Vitamin C 2%; Calcium 2%; Iron 6%
Exchanges: 1/2 Starch, 1/2 Lean Meat, 1 Fat
Carbohydrate Choices: 1/2

KITCHEN TIPS

✿ Save time by purchasing the hard-cooked egg from your grocery store's deli.

✿ Herbes de Provence can be substituted for the Italian seasoning.

Quick
Chardonnay Shrimp Spread

Prep Time: 15 min Start to Finish: 1 hr 15 min

- 2 cups frozen cooked salad shrimp (about 7 ounces), thawed, drained
- 1/2 cup Chardonnay wine or nonalcoholic white wine
- 1 package (8 ounces) cream cheese, softened
- 3 tablespoons mayonnaise or salad dressing
- 3 medium green onions, finely chopped (3 tablespoons)
- 1 teaspoon Dijon mustard
  Bibb lettuce, if desired
- 48 crackers

1. Coarsely chop shrimp; place in small glass bowl. Pour wine over shrimp; toss to coat. Cover; refrigerate at least 1 hour to blend flavors. Drain shrimp, reserving wine.

2. In another small bowl, mix cream cheese, mayonnaise, 2 tablespoons of the onions and the mustard with spoon. Fold in shrimp. If a thinner consistency is desired, stir in small amount of reserved wine.

3. Line small serving bowl with Bibb lettuce. Spoon shrimp spread into bowl. Sprinkle remaining 1 tablespoon onion over top. Serve with crackers.

24 appetizers
1 Appetizer (4 teaspoons spread and 2 crackers each): Calories 90 (Calories from Fat 60); Total Fat 6g (Saturated Fat 2.5g; Trans Fat 0g); Cholesterol 35mg; Sodium 120mg; Total Carbohydrate 4g (Dietary Fiber 0g; Sugars 0g); Protein 3g
% Daily Value: Vitamin A 4%; Vitamin C 0%; Calcium 0%; Iron 4%
Exchanges: 1/2 Starch, 1 Fat
Carbohydrate Choices: 0

KITCHEN TIPS

✿ Do some taste-testing of various brands of Dijon mustard. Not only do they vary in color, from bright yellow to brownish yellow, but their flavors vary as well.

✿ Thaw shrimp in a colander under cold running water.

Layered Mediterranean Tuna Spread

Chardonnay Shrimp Spread

Quick & Low Fat

Shrimp Summer Rolls with Dipping Sauce

Prep Time: 40 min Start to Finish: 40 min

Dipping Sauce

- 1 jar (7.25 ounces) hoisin sauce ($^3/_4$ cup)
- 1 cup water
- 2 teaspoons roasted red chili paste (from 4-ounce jar)
- $^1/_2$ teaspoon crushed red pepper flakes

Summer Rolls

- 4 ounces dried thin rice noodles or rice vermicelli (from 8.8-ounce package)
- 2 cups shredded romaine lettuce
- $^1/_2$ cup fresh cilantro leaves
- $^1/_2$ cup shredded carrot (about 1 medium)
- 10 ounces frozen cooked salad shrimp (about $1^3/_4$ cups), thawed, drained
- 12 round rice paper wrappers (about 8 inch; from 12-ounce package)

1. In medium bowl, mix dipping sauce ingredients. Cover; refrigerate while continuing with recipe.

2. Cook and drain noodles as directed on package. Meanwhile, in large bowl, mix lettuce, cilantro, carrot and shrimp.

3. Sprinkle water over 1 paper towel; place on cutting board. Fill a 10-inch pie plate with water. Place 1 rice paper wrapper in water 45 to 60 seconds or until pliable but not completely softened. Gently remove wrapper from water, shaking to drain excess water; place on damp paper towel.

4. Starting close to one edge of wrapper, form a row of about $^1/_4$ cup noodles. On noodles, arrange about $^1/_3$ cup of the lettuce mixture. Starting with edge covered with fillings, roll up wrapper over fillings, stopping after first turn to tuck in sides. Continue to roll up, tucking in sides. Repeat with remaining wrappers.

5. Place rolls, seam sides down and without touching, on platter. (If rolls touch, they will stick together.) Serve immediately with sauce, or cover with moist paper towels and refrigerate up to 2 hours. To serve, cut each roll in half.

24 appetizers
1 Appetizer: Calories 70 (Calories from Fat 0); Total Fat 0g (Saturated Fat 0g; Trans Fat 0g); Cholesterol 25mg; Sodium 230mg; Total Carbohydrate 12g (Dietary Fiber 0g; Sugars 0g); Protein 3g
% Daily Value: Vitamin A 15%; Vitamin C 2%; Calcium 0%; Iron 2%
Exchanges: $^1/_2$ Starch, $^1/_2$ Other Carbohydrate
Carbohydrate Choices: 2

KITCHEN TIPS

❂ Rice paper, an edible sheet, is made from a dough of rice flour, water and salt. It's great to have on hand for wrapping a variety of fillings. Look for rice paper in the Asian section of the supermarket or at Asian grocery stores.

❂ Chili paste is not the same thing as chili sauce. Chili paste, used in Asian cooking, is made of fermented fava beans, flour, red chilies and sometimes garlic. You can find it in the Asian-foods section of supermarkets.

Low Fat

Easy Italian Marinated Shrimp

Prep Time: 15 min Start to Finish: 2 hr 15 min

¼ cup chopped fresh basil leaves
2 cloves garlic, finely chopped
1 tablespoon chopped fresh rosemary leaves
2 teaspoons grated fresh lemon peel
¼ teaspoon salt
⅓ cup olive or vegetable oil
3 tablespoons red wine vinegar
1 pound cooked peeled deveined medium shrimp with tails (31 to 35 count)
Lettuce, if desired

1. In medium bowl, mix all ingredients except lettuce. Cover; refrigerate at least 2 hours but no longer than 24 hours to marinate and blend flavors.

2. Just before serving, stir shrimp. Drain; serve on lettuce-lined serving plate. Store in refrigerator.

10 servings
1 Serving: Calories 60 (Calories from Fat 25); Total Fat 2.5g (Saturated Fat 0g; Trans Fat 0g); Cholesterol 90mg; Sodium 130mg; Total Carbohydrate 0g (Dietary Fiber 0g; Sugars 0g); Protein 10g
% Daily Value: Vitamin A 4%; Vitamin C 4%; Calcium 2%; Iron 8%
Exchanges: 1½ Very Lean Meat, ½ Fat
Carbohydrate Choices: 0

KITCHEN TIPS

❀ The marinade may turn cloudy in the refrigerator as the oil solidifies, so let the shrimp stand at room temperature for 10 minutes before serving.

❀ There is no need to thaw the shrimp if you purchase them frozen; they will thaw while marinating.

Sesame Shrimp Stir-Fry

Margarita Shrimp Kabobs

Quick

Margarita Shrimp Kabobs

Prep Time: 25 min Start to Finish: 25 min

- 1 teaspoon grated lime peel
- ¼ cup lime juice
- 2 cloves garlic, finely chopped
- 2 tablespoons tequila, if desired
- ¼ teaspoon salt
- 1 pound uncooked peeled deveined large shrimp (about 24), thawed if frozen, tails removed
- 1 medium zucchini, cut into ½-inch slices
- 1 large red bell pepper, cut into bite-size pieces
- 1 tablespoon olive or vegetable oil

1. Heat gas or charcoal grill. In large resealable plastic food-storage bag, mix lime peel, lime juice, garlic, tequila and salt; add shrimp. Seal bag, squeezing out air; turn to coat shrimp. Let stand 10 minutes to marinate. Drain shrimp; discard marinade.

2. On each of 8 (12-inch) metal skewers, alternately thread shrimp, zucchini and bell pepper, leaving ¼-inch space between each piece. Brush with 1 tablespoon oil.

3. Carefully brush grill rack with additional oil. Place kabobs on grill over medium-high heat. Cover grill; cook 5 to 6 minutes, turning once, until shrimp are pink and vegetables are crisp-tender.

4 servings
1 Serving: Calories 140 (Calories from Fat 40); Total Fat 4.5g (Saturated Fat 1g; Trans Fat 0g); Cholesterol 160mg; Sodium 340mg; Total Carbohydrate 6g (Dietary Fiber 1g; Sugars 3g); Protein 18g
% Daily Value: Vitamin A 30%; Vitamin C 80%; Calcium 4%; Iron 15%
Exchanges: 1 Vegetableetable, 2½ Very Lean Meat, ½ Fat
Carbohydrate Choices: ½

KITCHEN TIPS

☸ Don't slice the zucchini too thickly or it won't be cooked through when the shrimp are ready.

☸ Serve the kabobs with warm whole wheat pita bread and a garden salad on the side.

Low-Fat

Sesame Shrimp Stir-Fry

Prep Time: 25 min Start to Finish: 1 hr 25 min

- 12 ounces uncooked peeled deveined large shrimp, thawed if frozen, tails removed
- ¼ cup teriyaki marinade
- 1½ cups uncooked quinoa
- ½ cup water
- 1 tablespoon cornstarch
- 1 tablespoon canola oil
- 1 medium carrot, sliced (½ cup)
- 2 cups fresh snow (Chinese) pea pods, strings removed, cut in half
- 2 cups sliced fresh mushrooms (about 5 ounces)
- 1 tablespoon sesame seed, toasted

1. In 8-inch square (2-quart) glass baking dish, place shrimp. Pour teriyaki marinade over shrimp. Cover and refrigerate at least 1 hour but no longer than 2 hours.

2. Rinse quinoa under cold water 1 minute; drain. Cook quinoa as directed on package.

3. Meanwhile, remove shrimp from marinade; reserve marinade. Stir water and cornstarch into remaining marinade; set aside.

4. Heat wok or 10-inch nonstick skillet over medium-high heat. Add oil; rotate wok to coat side. Add carrot; cook and stir 1 minute. Add shrimp, pea pods and mushrooms; cook and stir 3 to 5 minutes or until shrimp are pink and vegetables are crisp-tender.

5. Stir marinade mixture into shrimp mixture; heat to boiling. Cook and stir until sauce is thickened. Sprinkle with sesame seed. Serve with quinoa.

4 servings
1 Serving: Calories 400 (Calories from Fat 80); Total Fat 9g (Saturated Fat 1g; Trans Fat 0g); Cholesterol 120mg; Sodium 780mg; Total Carbohydrate 53g (Dietary Fiber 5g; Sugars 8g); Protein 25g
% Daily Value: Vitamin A 60%; Vitamin C 20%; Calcium 8%; Iron 50%
Exchanges: 2 Starch, 1 Other Carbohydrate, 1 Vegetableetable, 2½ Very Lean Meat, 1½ Fat
Carbohydrate Choices: 3½

Fire Roasted Tomato-Shrimp Veracruz with Couscous

Prep Time: 15 min Start to Finish: 15 min

- 1 tablespoon olive or canola oil
- 1 pound uncooked peeled deveined medium shrimp, thawed if frozen, tails removed
- 4 medium green onions, sliced (¼ cup)
- 1 medium fresh jalapeño or serrano chili, seeded and finely chopped
- 1 teaspoon grated orange peel
- 1 teaspoon chopped fresh or ½ teaspoon dried thyme leaves
- 1 can (14.5 ounces) Muir Glen organic fire-roasted diced tomatoes, undrained
- 1½ cups uncooked whole wheat couscous

1. In 12-inch skillet, heat oil over medium-high heat. Cook shrimp, onions, chili, orange peel and thyme in oil 1 minute, stirring frequently.

2. Stir in tomatoes. Heat to boiling. Reduce heat; simmer uncovered about 5 minutes, stirring occasionally, until shrimp are pink and sauce is slightly thickened.

3. Meanwhile, make couscous as directed on package, omitting butter and salt. Serve shrimp mixture over couscous.

4 servings
1 Serving: Calories 390 (Calories from Fat 50); Total Fat 5g (Saturated Fat 0.5g; Trans Fat 0g); Cholesterol 160mg; Sodium 420mg; Total Carbohydrate 58g (Dietary Fiber 7g; Sugars 4g); Protein 27g
% Daily Value: Vitamin A 20%; Vitamin C 20%; Calcium 8%; Iron 30%
Exchanges: 2½ Starch, 1 Other Carbohydrate, 1 Vegetableetable, 2½ Very Lean Meat, ½ Fat
Carbohydrate Choices: 4

KITCHEN TIPS

✪ Great news! Now you can buy whole wheat couscous, which contains all parts of the grain, making it a wonderful whole-grain accompaniment to any main dish.

Quick

Crispy Herbed Fish Fillets

Prep Time: 25 min Start to Finish: 25 min

1 pound flounder fillets (about ¹/₂ inch thick), cut into 4 serving pieces

2 eggs

1¹/₄ cups Progresso panko crispy bread crumbs

1 teaspoon grated lemon peel

1 teaspoon dried marjoram leaves

¹/₂ teaspoon salt

¹/₄ teaspoon pepper

¹/₄ cup olive or vegetable oil

1. Dry fish well on paper towels. In shallow dish, beat eggs with fork or wire whisk until well mixed. In another shallow dish, mix bread crumbs, lemon peel, marjoram, salt and pepper.

2. In 12-inch nonstick skillet, heat 2 tablespoons of the oil over medium heat. Dip fish in eggs, then coat well with crumb mixture. Add about half of the fish in single layer to oil. Cook 3 to 4 minutes, carefully turning once, until outside is browned and crisp and fish flakes easily with fork.

3. Remove cooked fish from skillet to plate; cover to keep warm. Repeat with remaining oil and fish.

4 servings
1 Serving: Calories 328 (Calories from Fat 160); Total Fat 18g (Saturated Fat 3g; Trans Fat 0g); Cholesterol 160mg; Sodium 471mg; Total Carbohydrate 13g (Dietary Fiber 1g; Sugars 1g); Protein 27g
% Daily Value: Vitamin A 4%; Vitamin C 4%; Calcium 4%; Iron 6%
Exchanges: 3 Fat, 3 Meat
Carbohydrate Choices: 1

KITCHEN TIPS

✿ Panko, or Japanese bread crumbs, are coarser in texture than regular dry bread crumbs available in supermarkets. Once you try Progresso panko crispy bread crumbs, you'll be hooked—they're crunchier and make a more attractive coating!

Quick

Tilapia with Cucumber Salad

Prep Time: 25 min Start to Finish: 25 min

Dressing

- 1 tablespoon honey
- 1 tablespoon rice vinegar
- 2 teaspoons grated gingerroot
- 1/2 teaspoon salt

Salad

- 1/2 medium cucumber, cut in half lengthwise, thinly sliced
- 1/4 red bell pepper, diced
- 3 green onions, thinly sliced
- 1 teaspoon chopped fresh cilantro

Fish

- 2 tablespoons Gold Medal all-purpose flour
- 1 teaspoon lemon-pepper seasoning
- 1 cup Progresso panko bread crumbs
- 1 egg
- 4 tilapia or other white fish fillets (6 ounces each)
- 4 tablespoons vegetable oil

1. In medium bowl, mix dressing ingredients. Stir in salad ingredients to coat.

2. On plate, mix flour and lemon-pepper seasoning. On second plate, place bread crumbs. In medium bowl, beat egg with fork. Coat top and sides of fish with flour mixture. Dip fish into egg; drain over bowl. Coat well with bread crumbs.

3. In 10-inch nonstick skillet, heat 2 tablespoons of the oil over medium-high heat. Add 2 fish fillets; cook 3 minutes. Carefully turn fish over. Reduce heat to medium; cook about 3 minutes longer or until fish flakes easily with fork. Repeat with remaining oil and fish. Serve fish topped with salad.

4 servings
1 Serving: Calories 440 (Calories from Fat 180); Total Fat 20g (Saturated Fat 3g; Trans Fat 0g); Cholesterol 145mg; Sodium 590mg; Total Carbohydrate 29g (Dietary Fiber 0g; Sugars 7g); Protein 37g
% Daily Value: Vitamin A 10%; Vitamin C 30%; Calcium 4%; Iron 8%
Exchanges: 1 Starch, 1 Other Carbohydrate, 5 Very Lean Meat, 3 Fat
Carbohydrate Choices: 2

KITCHEN TIPS

- For even more crunch and color, add 1/4 cup shredded carrots to the cucumber salad.
- Tilapia is a fine-textured fish that can be pan-fried, broiled, grilled or baked.

Quick

Graham-Crusted Tilapia

Prep Time: 15 min Start to Finish: 25 min

1 pound tilapia, cod, haddock or other medium-firm fish fillets, about ¾ inch thick

½ cup graham cracker crumbs (about 8 squares)

1 teaspoon grated lemon peel

¼ teaspoon salt

⅛ teaspoon pepper

¼ cup fat-free (skim) milk

2 tablespoons canola oil

2 tablespoons chopped toasted pecans

1. Move oven rack to position slightly above middle of oven. Heat oven to 500°F.

2. Cut fish fillets crosswise into 2-inch-wide pieces. In shallow dish, mix cracker crumbs, lemon peel, salt and pepper. Place milk in another shallow dish.

3. Dip fish into milk, then coat with cracker mixture. Place in ungreased 13 × 9-inch pan. Drizzle oil over fish; sprinkle with pecans.

4. Bake about 10 minutes or until fish flakes easily with fork.

4 servings
1 Serving: Calories 230 (Calories from Fat 100); Total Fat 12g (Saturated Fat 1.5g; Trans Fat 0g); Cholesterol 60mg; Sodium 300mg; Total Carbohydrate 9g (Dietary Fiber 0g; Sugars 5g); Protein 23g
% Daily Value: Vitamin A 0%; Vitamin C 0%; Calcium 4%; Iron 4%
Exchanges: ½ Starch, 3 Lean Meat, ½ Fat
Carbohydrate Choices: ½

KITCHEN TIPS

✿ Toasting nuts adds a lot of great flavor. To toast nuts, bake uncovered in ungreased shallow pan in 350°F oven 6 to 10 minutes, stirring occasionally, until golden brown. Or cook in ungreased heavy skillet over medium-low heat 5 to 7 minutes, stirring frequently until browning begins, then stirring constantly until golden brown.

Shellfish and Fish   153

Halibut with Potato Succotash

Prep Time: 20 min Start to Finish: 45 min

- 1 halibut fillet (1 to 1½ pounds)
- 1 tablespoon butter or margarine, melted
- 1 tablespoon canola oil
- 2 cups frozen diced potatoes O'Brien (from 32-ounce bag)
- 1 box (9 ounces) Green Giant frozen baby lima beans
- 1 cup Green Giant Niblets frozen whole kernel corn
- ½ teaspoon garlic-pepper blend
- ½ teaspoon seasoned salt
- ½ teaspoon dried thyme leaves
- ⅛ teaspoon ground red pepper (cayenne)

1. Heat oven to 425°F. Spray 11 × 7-inch (2-quart) glass baking dish with cooking spray. Cut halibut into 4 serving-size pieces. Place halibut in baking dish. Brush butter over halibut.

2. In 10-inch nonstick skillet, heat oil over medium-high heat. Cook potatoes in oil 5 minutes, stirring occasionally. Stir in lima beans and corn. Cook 3 to 5 minutes or until vegetables are crisp-tender. Spoon mixture around halibut in baking dish. Sprinkle halibut and vegetables with remaining ingredients; stir vegetables slightly.

3. Bake 20 to 25 minutes or until halibut flakes easily with fork and vegetables are tender.

4 servings
1 Serving: Calories 300 (Calories from Fat 70); Total Fat 8g (Saturated Fat 2.5g; Trans Fat 0g); Cholesterol 70mg; Sodium 340mg; Total Carbohydrate 30g (Dietary Fiber 5g; Sugars 3g); Protein 27g
% Daily Value: Vitamin A 8%; Vitamin C 10%; Calcium 4%; Iron 10%
Exchanges: 2 Starch, 3 Very Lean Meat, 1 Fat
Carbohydrate Choices: 2

KITCHEN TIPS

❀ Try this colorful dish with swordfish or salmon instead of halibut.
❀ It's easier if you cook the halibut with the skin on. When it's done, the fish separates easily from the skin and you can discard it.

Tuna with Mediterranean Vegetables

Prep Time: 20 min Start to Finish: 20 min

1 tablespoon olive or canola oil

3 cloves garlic, finely chopped

3 cups sliced fresh mushrooms

3 medium yellow summer squash or zucchini, cut into ¼-inch slices (4 cups)

1½ cups cherry tomatoes, cut in half

¼ cup sliced ripe olives

1 tablespoon chopped fresh or 1 teaspoon dried basil leaves

½ teaspoon salt

¼ teaspoon pepper

1 tablespoon olive or canola oil

6 tuna steaks, ½ inch thick (5 ounces each)

1 tablespoon chopped fresh or 1 teaspoon dried oregano leaves

1. In 12-inch nonstick skillet, heat 1 tablespoon oil over medium-high heat. Cook garlic, mushrooms and squash in oil 2 to 3 minutes, stirring frequently. Stir in tomatoes, olives, basil, salt and pepper. Cook 2 to 4 minutes, stirring frequently, until vegetables are tender. Remove from heat; cover to keep warm.

2. Brush grill rack with oil. Heat gas or charcoal grill. Rub 1 tablespoon oil over both sides of tuna steaks. Place on grill over medium heat. Cover grill; cook 2 minutes; turn. Sprinkle tuna with oregano. Cover and grill 1 to 3 minutes longer or until tuna flakes easily with fork and is slightly pink in center. Serve tuna with vegetables.

6 servings
1 Serving: Calories 260 (Calories from Fat 110); Total Fat 13g (Saturated Fat 3g; Trans Fat 0g); Cholesterol 85mg; Sodium 330mg; Total Carbohydrate 6g (Dietary Fiber 2g; Sugars 3g); Protein 29g
% Daily Value: Vitamin A 15%; Vitamin C 20%; Calcium 4%; Iron 10%
Exchanges: 1 Vegetableeetable, 4 Lean Meat
Carbohydrate Choices: ½

KITCHEN TIPS

✿ Instead of tuna, try other fish, such as swordfish steaks or tilapia fillets. Grill until fish flakes easily with a fork.

✿ Serve with Italian bread and fettuccine topped with Parmesan cheese.

Tuna with Avocado-Kiwi Salsa

Prep Time: 40 min   Start to Finish: 1 hr 10 min

Tuna

1½	pound tuna steaks, ¾ to 1 inch thick
¼	cup lime juice
2	teaspoons chili oil
2	tablespoons finely chopped fresh cilantro
1	clove garlic, finely chopped
½	teaspoon salt

Salsa

1	small avocado, pitted, peeled and coarsely chopped (1 cup)
1	kiwifruit, peeled and chopped (½ cup)
3	medium green onions, chopped (3 tablespoons)
1	small jalapeño chili, seeded and finely chopped (1 tablespoon)
2	tablespoons lime juice
2	tablespoons chopped fresh cilantro
¼	teaspoon salt

1. If tuna steaks are large, cut into 6 serving pieces. In shallow glass or plastic dish, mix remaining tuna ingredients. Add tuna; turn to coat with marinade. Cover; refrigerate, turning once, at least 30 minutes but no longer than 2 hours to marinate.

2. Meanwhile, in medium bowl, mix all salsa ingredients; refrigerate.

3. Spray grill rack with cooking spray. Heat gas or charcoal grill. Remove tuna from marinade; reserve marinade. Place tuna on grill. Cover grill; cook over medium heat 11 to 16 minutes, brushing 2 or 3 times with marinade and turning once, until tuna flakes easily with fork and is slightly pink in center. Discard any remaining marinade. Top tuna with salsa.

6 servings
1 Serving: Calories 220 (Calories from Fat 100); Total Fat 11g (Saturated Fat 2.5g; Trans Fat 0g); Cholesterol 65mg; Sodium 360mg; Total Carbohydrate 6g (Dietary Fiber 2g; Sugars 2g); Protein 23g
% Daily Value: Vitamin A 4%; Vitamin C 40%; Calcium 2%; Iron 6%
Exchanges: ½ Other Carbohydrate, 3½ Lean Meat
Carbohydrate Choices: ½

Low Fat

Grilled Salmon with Fresh Lime Cream

Prep Time: 30 min Start to Finish: 1 hr

Salmon

1	teaspoon grated lime peel
¼	cup lime juice
2	tablespoons honey
1	tablespoon chopped fresh or 1 teaspoon dried dill weed
2	teaspoons canola oil
1½	pounds salmon fillets, cut into 6 serving pieces
½	teaspoon salt

Lime Cream

⅓	cup fat-free mayonnaise
1	teaspoon grated lime peel
2	teaspoons lime juice

1. In small bowl, mix 1 teaspoon lime peel, ¼ cup lime juice, the honey, dill weed and oil.

2. In 8-inch square (2-quart) glass baking dish, arrange salmon pieces, skin sides up, in single layer. Pour marinade over salmon; turn in marinade to cover all sides. Cover with plastic wrap and refrigerate 20 to 30 minutes.

3. Heat gas or charcoal grill. Carefully brush grill rack with oil. Remove salmon from marinade; discard marinade. Sprinkle salmon with salt. Place skin side down on grill over medium heat. Cover grill; cook 10 to 15 minutes or until salmon flakes easily with fork.

4. Meanwhile, in small bowl, mix Lime Cream ingredients with wire whisk. Serve with salmon.

6 servings
1 Serving: Calories 180 (Calories from Fat 70); Total Fat 7g (Saturated Fat 2g; Trans Fat 0g); Cholesterol 75mg; Sodium 370mg; Total Carbohydrate 4g (Dietary Fiber 0g; Sugars 3g); Protein 24g
% Daily Value: Vitamin A 2%; Vitamin C 2%; Calcium 0%; Iron 4%
Exchanges: 3½ Lean Meat
Carbohydrate Choices: 0

KITCHEN TIPS

❀ Get in the habit of serving fish at least once a week. Salmon is high in heart-friendly omega-3 fatty acids, plus it's tasty!

❀ Serve this salmon with pasta or rice and Spinach-Mango Salad, page 72.

Grilled Ginger Salmon Fillets

Prep Time: 25 min Start to Finish: 25 min

2 tablespoons honey

2 tablespoons ketchup

2 tablespoons finely chopped gingerroot

¼ teaspoon salt

¼ teaspoon red pepper sauce

1½ pounds salmon fillets

1. Heat gas or charcoal grill. In small bowl, mix all ingredients except salmon.

2. Carefully brush grill rack with vegetable oil. Place salmon skin side down and crosswise on grill over medium heat. Cover grill; cook 8 minutes.

3. Brush all of honey mixture over salmon. Cover grill; cook 3 to 6 minutes longer or until salmon flakes easily with fork.

4 servings
1 Serving: Calories 240 (Calories from Fat 70); Total Fat 8g (Saturated Fat 2.5g; Trans Fat 0g); Cholesterol 95mg; Sodium 320mg; Total Carbohydrate 11g (Dietary Fiber 0g; Sugars 10g); Protein 31g
% Daily Value: Vitamin A 4%; Vitamin C 2%; Calcium 0%; Iron 6%
Exchanges: ½ Other Carbohydrate, 4½ Very Lean Meat, 1 Fat
Carbohydrate Choices: 1

KITCHEN TIPS

✿ To broil salmon, place skin side down on rack in broiler pan. Broil with tops 6 to 8 inches from heat using times above as guide.

✿ Barbecue sauce can be substituted for the ketchup.

✿ Peel the gingerroot before chopping or slicing.

Quick

Quinoa Pilaf with Salmon and Asparagus

Prep Time: 30 min Start to Finish: 30 min

1 cup uncooked quinoa

6 cups water

1 vegetable bouillon cube

1 pound salmon fillets

2 tablespoons butter or margarine

20 stalks fresh asparagus, cut diagonally into 2-inch pieces (2 cups)

4 medium green onions, sliced (¼ cup)

1 cup Green Giant frozen sweet peas (from 1-pound bag), thawed

½ cup grape tomatoes, cut in half

½ cup vegetable or chicken broth

1 teaspoon lemon-pepper seasoning

2 teaspoons chopped fresh or ½ teaspoon dried dill weed

1. Rinse quinoa thoroughly by placing in a fine-mesh strainer and holding under cold running water until water runs clear; drain well.

2. In 2-quart saucepan, heat 2 cups of the water to boiling over high heat. Add quinoa; reduce heat to low. Cover; simmer 10 to 12 minutes or until water is absorbed.

3. Meanwhile, in 12-inch skillet, heat remaining 4 cups water and bouillon cube to boiling over high heat. Add salmon, skin side up; reduce heat to low. Cover; simmer 10 to 12 minutes or until fish flakes easily with fork. Remove with slotted spoon to plate; let cool. Discard water. Remove skin from salmon; break into large pieces.

4. Meanwhile, rinse and dry skillet. Melt butter in skillet over medium heat. Add asparagus; cook 5 minutes, stirring frequently. Stir in onions, cook 1 minute, stirring frequently. Stir in peas, tomatoes and broth; cook 1 minute.

5. Gently stir quinoa, salmon, lemon-pepper seasoning and dill weed into asparagus mixture. Cover; cook about 2 minutes or until hot.

4 servings (¾ cup each)
1 Serving: Calories 420 (Calories from Fat 130); Total Fat 15g (Saturated Fat 6g; Trans Fat 0g); Cholesterol 90mg; Sodium 650mg; Total Carbohydrate 39g (Dietary Fiber 5g; Sugars 7g); Protein 33g
% Daily Value: Vitamin A 35%; Vitamin C 10%; Calcium 8%; Iron 40%
Exchanges: 1½ Starch, 1 Other Carbohydrate, 1 Vegetableetable, 3½ Lean Meat, ½ Fat
Carbohydrate Choices: 2½

Quick
Salmon-Pasta Toss

Prep Time: 25 min Start to Finish: 25 min

8	ounces uncooked linguine
1	tablespoon olive oil
12	ounces skinless salmon fillets, cut into 1-inch pieces
1	cup sliced fresh mushrooms
12	asparagus spears, cut into 1-inch pieces
2	cloves garlic, finely chopped
1/4	cup chopped fresh or 2 teaspoons dried basil leaves
12	grape tomatoes
2	medium green onions, sliced (2 tablespoons)
4	teaspoons cornstarch
1	cup chicken broth
1/4	cup shredded Parmesan cheese

1. Cook and drain linguine as directed on package, omitting salt.

2. Meanwhile, in 12-inch nonstick skillet, heat oil over medium heat. Cook salmon in oil 4 to 5 minutes, stirring gently and frequently, until salmon flakes easily with fork (salmon may break apart). Remove from skillet.

3. Increase heat to medium-high. Add mushrooms, asparagus and garlic to skillet; cook and stir 2 minutes. Stir in basil, tomatoes and onions; cook and stir 1 minute longer.

4. In 2-cup glass measuring cup, stir cornstarch into broth. Add to vegetable mixture. Cook and stir 1 to 2 minutes or until sauce is thickened and bubbly. Stir in salmon. Serve over linguine. Sprinkle with cheese.

4 servings
1 Serving: Calories 470 (Calories from Fat 110); Total Fat 12g (Saturated Fat 3.5g; Trans Fat 0g); Cholesterol 60mg; Sodium 430mg; Total Carbohydrate 58g (Dietary Fiber 5g; Sugars 4g); Protein 33g
% Daily Value: Vitamin A 20%; Vitamin C 10%; Calcium 15%; Iron 25%
Exchanges: 3 Starch, 1/2 Other Carbohydrate, 1 Vegetableetable, 3 Lean Meat
Carbohydrate Choices: 4

KITCHEN TIPS

✿ If the salmon you purchased has skin, remove the skin before cutting the salmon into pieces. Place the fillet, skin side down, on a cutting board. Using a sharp knife, cut between the flesh and skin, angling knife down toward the skin and using a sawing motion. Grip the skin tightly with the other hand after a small portion has been removed.

Chicken and Turkey Dishes

Perfect Poultry Plates

Southwestern Chicken Scallopini (page 165)

Chicken Alfredo Stew (page 180)

Quick

Dijon Chicken Smothered in Mushrooms

Prep Time: 20 min Start to Finish: 20 min

4 boneless, skinless chicken breasts (about 1¼ pounds)

¼ cup Gold Medal all-purpose flour

½ teaspoon salt

¼ teaspoon pepper

2 tablespoons olive or canola oil

½ cup roasted garlic-seasoned chicken broth (from 14-ounce can)

1 jar (4.5 ounces) Green Giant sliced mushrooms, drained

1½ tablespoons Dijon mustard

Chopped fresh thyme, if desired

1. Between pieces of plastic wrap or waxed paper, place chicken breast half with smooth side down; gently pound with flat side of meat mallet or rolling pin until about ¼ inch thick. Repeat with remaining chicken. In shallow pan, stir together flour, salt and pepper.

2. Heat oil in 12-inch nonstick skillet over medium-high heat. Coat both sides of chicken with flour mixture. Cook chicken in hot oil 6 to 8 minutes, turning once, until chicken is no longer pink in center. Remove chicken to serving plate; cover to keep warm.

3. Stir broth into skillet. Heat to boiling over medium-high heat. Stir in mushrooms and mustard. Cook 2 to 3 minutes, stirring frequently, until slightly thickened. Spoon sauce over chicken. Sprinkle with thyme.

4 servings
1 Serving: Calories 270 (Calories from Fat 110); Total Fat 12g (Saturated Fat 2.5g; Trans Fat 0g); Cholesterol 85mg; Sodium 760mg; Total Carbohydrate 8g (Dietary Fiber 1g; Sugars 0g); Protein 33g
% Daily Value: Vitamin A 0%; Vitamin C 0%; Calcium 2%; Iron 10%
Exchanges: ½ Starch, 4½ Very Lean Meat, 1½ Fat
Carbohydrate Choices: ½

KITCHEN TIPS

❂ If you are keeping an eye on salt intake, opt for low-sodium chicken broth, add ½ teaspoon garlic powder (or to taste) and leave out the salt.

Chicken Milano

Prep Time: 25 min Start to Finish: 25 min

Salad

1 cup tightly packed arugula leaves

$1/2$ cup diced tomatoes

2 tablespoons diced red onion

Dressing

1 tablespoon olive or vegetable oil

2 teaspoons red wine vinegar

$1/8$ teaspoon salt

Chicken

2 tablespoons Gold Medal all-purpose flour

1 cup Progresso Italian-style panko bread crumbs

1 egg

4 boneless, skinless chicken breasts (about $1/4$ pounds)

2 tablespoons olive or vegetable oil

$1/4$ cup crumbled tomato-basil feta cheese (1 ounce)

1. In medium bowl, place salad ingredients. In small bowl, beat dressing ingredients with wire whisk. Pour over salad; toss to coat.

2. On separate plates, place flour and bread crumbs. In medium bowl, beat egg with fork. Coat both sides of chicken with flour. Dip chicken into beaten egg, then coat well with bread crumbs.

3. In 12-inch nonstick skillet, heat 2 tablespoons oil over medium heat. Add chicken; cook 8 to 10 minutes, turning once, until juice of chicken is clear when center of thickest part is cut (170°F) and coating is golden brown. Serve chicken topped with salad and sprinkled with cheese.

4 servings
1 Serving: Calories 440 (Calories from Fat 210); Total Fat 24g (Saturated Fat 4g; Trans Fat 0g); Cholesterol 145mg; Sodium 650mg; Total Carbohydrate 21g (Dietary Fiber 0g; Sugars 1g); Protein 36g
% Daily Value: Vitamin A 8%; Vitamin C 4%; Calcium 6%; Iron 10%
Exchanges: 1 Starch, $1/2$ Other Carbohydrate, $4^1/2$ Very Lean Meat, 4 Fat
Carbohydrate Choices: $1^1/2$

KITCHEN TIPS

⊕ Short on time? Use 2 tablespoons purchased red wine vinaigrette dressing instead of making your own.

⊕ If you don't care for feta cheese, use mozzarella cheese instead.

Quick

Sunny Mediterranean Chicken

Prep Time: 30 min Start to Finish: 30 min

Chicken

- 1 cup Fiber One cereal
- 6 boneless, skinless chicken breasts (about 1¾ pounds)
- ½ teaspoon salt
- ¼ teaspoon pepper
- ¼ cup fat-free (skim) milk
- 1 tablespoon chopped fresh parsley

Vegetables

- ¼ cup olive or canola oil
- 1 medium zucchini, sliced (2 cups)
- 1 small unpeeled eggplant, cubed (2 cups)
- 1 jar (7 or 7.25 ounces) roasted red bell peppers, drained, cut into ½-inch strips
- ½ large red onion, sliced, separated into rings
- 1 large clove garlic, finely chopped
- 3 tablespoons water
- 4 teaspoons lime juice

Couscous

- 1½ cups water
- ¼ cup salt
- 1 cup uncooked whole wheat couscous

Garnish

- 1 lime, cut into 6 wedges

1. Place cereal in resealable plastic food-storage bag, seal bag and crush with rolling pin or meat mallet. Sprinkle both sides of chicken with ½ teaspoon salt and the pepper. In shallow dish, place milk. In another shallow dish, place cereal and parsley; dip chicken in milk, then coat with cereal.

2. In 12-inch nonstick skillet, heat 2 tablespoons of the oil over medium heat. Cook chicken in oil 15 minutes, turning once, until juice of chicken is clear when thickest part is cut (170°F). Remove chicken from skillet; cover to keep warm.

3. In same skillet, heat remaining 2 tablespoons oil over medium heat. Cook zucchini, eggplant, roasted peppers, onion and garlic in oil 3 minutes, stirring occasionally. Stir in 3 tablespoons water and the lime juice; cook about 1 minute or until vegetables are crisp-tender.

4. Meanwhile, in 2-quart saucepan, heat 1½ cups water and ¼ teaspoon salt to boiling. Stir in couscous. Cover; remove from heat and let stand 5 minutes or until water is absorbed. Fluff couscous with fork.

5. On large serving platter, place couscous. Top with chicken and vegetables. Serve with lime wedges.

6 servings
1 Serving: Calories 430 (Calories from Fat 130); Total Fat 14g (Saturated Fat 2.5g; Trans Fat 0g); Cholesterol 80mg; Sodium 410mg; Total Carbohydrate 41g (Dietary Fiber 9g; Sugars 5g); Protein 35g
% Daily Value: Vitamin A 35%; Vitamin C 50%; Calcium 8%; Iron 2%
Exchanges: 2 Starch, 1½ Vegetableetable, 4 Very Lean Meat, 2 Fat
Carbohydrate Choices: 3

Quick & Low Fat

Southwestern Chicken Scallopini

Prep Time: 30 min Start to Finish: 30 min

4	boneless, skinless chicken breasts (about 1¼ pounds)
¼	cup Gold Medal all-purpose flour
1	teaspoon ground cumin
½	teaspoon salt
1½	teaspoons canola oil
½	cup chicken broth
¼	teaspoon red pepper sauce, if desired
2	tablespoons lime juice
2	tablespoons chopped fresh cilantro

1. Between pieces of plastic wrap or waxed paper, place chicken breast half with smooth side down; gently pound with flat side of meat mallet or rolling pin until about ¼ inch thick. Repeat with remaining chicken. Cut chicken into smaller pieces if desired.

2. In shallow dish, mix flour, cumin and salt. Coat chicken with flour mixture. Reserve 1 teaspoon flour mixture.

3. In 12-inch nonstick skillet, heat oil over medium heat. Add chicken; cook 3 to 5 minutes on each side or until golden brown and no longer pink in center. Remove chicken from skillet; cover to keep warm.

4. In small bowl, stir reserved 1 teaspoon flour mixture into broth. Gradually stir both mixture and red pepper sauce into skillet. Heat to boiling; stir in lime juice and cilantro. Serve sauce over chicken.

4 servings
1 Serving: Calories 250 (Calories from Fat 90); Total Fat 10g (Saturated Fat 1.5g; Trans Fat 0g); Cholesterol 85mg; Sodium 500mg; Total Carbohydrate 7g (Dietary Fiber 0g; Sugars 0g); Protein 33g
% Daily Value: Vitamin A 0%; Vitamin C 0%; Calcium 2%; Iron 10%
Exchanges: ½ Starch, 4½ Very Lean Meat, 1½ Fat
Carbohydrate Choices: ½

KITCHEN TIPS

❀ Serve with corn bread or corn muffins, steamed green beans or broccoli, and fresh fruit for a scrumptious dinner.
❀ Instead of chicken, use 1 pound pork tenderloin. Cut into 4 pieces and flatten as directed for the chicken.

Italian Chicken Fingers

Prep Time: 40 min   Start to Finish: 40 min

- 1 package (14 ounces) uncooked chicken breast tenders (not breaded)
- 1 egg, beaten
- 1¼ cups Original Bisquick mix
- 1 teaspoon Italian seasoning
- 3 tablespoons butter or margarine, melted
- 1 cup tomato sauce, heated

1. Heat oven to 450°F. Spray 15 × 10 × 1-inch pan with cooking spray. In medium bowl, toss chicken and egg.

2. In resealable plastic food-storage bag, place Bisquick mix and Italian seasoning; seal bag and shake to mix. Add chicken; seal bag and shake to coat chicken with Bisquick mixture. Place chicken in single layer in pan. Drizzle with butter.

3. Bake 14 to 16 minutes, turning chicken after 6 minutes, until chicken is brown and crisp on the outside and no longer pink in center. Serve with warm tomato sauce for dipping.

4 servings
1 Serving: Calories 354 (Calories from Fat 143); Total Fat 16g (Saturated Fat 8g; Trans Fat 0g); Cholesterol 120mg; Sodium 913mg; Total Carbohydrate 27g (Dietary Fiber 2g; Sugars 3g); Protein 28g
% Daily Value: Vitamin A 10%; Vitamin C 8%; Calcium 8%; Iron 15%
Exchanges: 2 Fat, 1½ Starch, 1 Vegetable, 2 Meat
Carbohydrate Choices: 2

KITCHEN TIPS

⊕ Continue the finger shape theme by serving with carrot and celery sticks and French fries.

⊕ Use boneless, skinless turkey breast or tenderloin instead of chicken for a different kind of finger food.

Low Fat
Chicken with Oregano-Peach Sauce

Prep Time: 15 min   Start to Finish: 35 min

- ½ cup peach preserves
- ¼ cup raspberry vinegar
- 2 tablespoons chopped fresh oregano leaves
- 4 boneless, skinless chicken breasts (1¼ pounds)
- ½ teaspoon garlic-pepper blend
- ½ teaspoon seasoned salt

1. Heat gas or charcoal grill. In 1-quart saucepan, heat preserves and vinegar to boiling, stirring constantly, until melted. Spoon about ¼ cup mixture into small bowl or custard cup for brushing on chicken. Stir oregano into remaining mixture and reserve to serve with chicken.

2. Sprinkle chicken with garlic-pepper blend and seasoned salt.

3. Place chicken on grill over medium heat. Cover grill; cook 15 to 20 minutes, turning once and brushing with preserves mixture during last 10 minutes of cook time, until juice of chicken is clear when center of thickest pieces are cut (170°F). Discard any remaining preserves mixture brushed on chicken. Serve chicken with reserved preserves mixture with oregano.

4 servings
1 Serving: Calories 280 (Calories from Fat 40); Total Fat 4.5g (Saturated Fat 1.5g; Trans Fat 0g); Cholesterol 85mg; Sodium 260mg; Total Carbohydrate 28g (Dietary Fiber 0g; Sugars 20g); Protein 31g
% Daily Value: Vitamin A 0%; Vitamin C 4%; Calcium 4%; Iron 8%
Exchanges: 2 Other Carbohydrate, 4 Very Lean Meat, ½ Fat
Carbohydrate Choices: 2

KITCHEN TIPS

⊕ When buying fresh oregano, look for bright-green bunches with no sign of wilting or yellowing. Store it in the refrigerator in a plastic food-storage bag up to three days.

⊕ This elegant chicken dish makes an easy special-occasion meal when served with cooked orzo and grilled fresh asparagus. For dessert, spoon sherbet into dessert dishes and top with fresh blueberries.

Chicken with Oregano-Peach Sauce

Italian Chicken Fingers

Grilled Taco-Barbecue Chicken

Prep Time: 25 min Start to Finish: 25 min

- 2 tablespoons Old El Paso taco seasoning mix (from 1.25-ounce package)
- 1 teaspoon dried oregano leaves
- 4 boneless, skinless chicken breasts (about 1¼ pounds)
- 1 tablespoon olive or vegetable oil
- ¼ cup barbecue sauce
- 2 tablespoons chili sauce
- ½ teaspoon ground cumin

1. Heat gas or charcoal grill. In shallow bowl, combine taco seasoning mix and oregano. Brush chicken with oil; sprinkle with taco seasoning mixture.

2. Place chicken on grill. Cover grill; cook over medium heat 10 to 15 minutes or until juice of chicken is clear when center of thickest part is cut (170°F).

3. Meanwhile, in small microwavable bowl, mix barbecue sauce, chili sauce and cumin. Cover; microwave on High 30 to 60 seconds or until hot. Serve sauce with chicken.

Oven Directions: Heat oven to 375°F. Line shallow baking pan with aluminum foil or spray with cooking spray. Place coated chicken in pan. Bake 25 to 30 minutes or until juice of chicken is clear when center of thickest part is cut (170°F).

4 servings
1 Serving: Calories 240 (Calories from Fat 70); Total Fat 8g (Saturated Fat 2g; Trans Fat 0g); Cholesterol 85mg; Sodium 780mg; Total Carbohydrate 11g (Dietary Fiber 0g; Sugars 6g); Protein 31g
% Daily Value: Vitamin A 4%; Vitamin C 0%; Calcium 4%; Iron 10%
Exchanges: ½ Other Carbohydrate, 4½ Very Lean Meat, 1 Fat
Carbohydrate Choices: 1

KITCHEN TIPS

✹ Decrease the fat in this recipe by spraying the chicken breasts with olive oil-flavored cooking spray instead of brushing them with the 1 tablespoon olive oil.

✹ For zesty, make-your-own wrap sandwiches, slice the warm chicken into strips and serve with tortillas, shredded lettuce, sliced avocado and the sauce.

Easy Chicken and Garden Veggies

Prep Time: 35 min Start to Finish: 35 min

4 slices bacon, cut into ¹/₂-inch pieces

4 boneless, skinless chicken breasts (about 1¹/₄ pounds)

¹/₂ teaspoon garlic salt

¹/₄ teaspoon coarsely ground pepper

¹/₄ cup water

8 ounces fresh green beans, trimmed (leave whole)

1 medium yellow bell pepper, cut into ¹/₂-inch pieces

2 medium roma (plum) tomatoes, cut lengthwise in half, then sliced (about 1 cup)

¹/₂ cup balsamic vinaigrette dressing or Italian dressing

1. In 12-inch nonstick skillet, cook bacon over medium heat 3 to 4 minutes, stirring occasionally, until crisp.

2. Sprinkle both sides of chicken with garlic salt and pepper. Add chicken to bacon in skillet. Cook 3 to 5 minutes or until browned on both sides. Discard excess bacon drippings if necessary.

3. Add water and green beans to skillet. Cover and cook over medium-low heat 8 minutes. Stir in bell pepper. Cover and cook 3 to 5 minutes, turning and stirring vegetables occasionally, until juice of chicken is clear when center of thickest part is cut (170°F).

4. Stir in tomatoes and dressing. Cook uncovered about 2 minutes, stirring occasionally, until tomatoes are hot.

4 servings
1 Serving: Calories 370 (Calories from Fat 200); Total Fat 22g (Saturated Fat 4.5g; Trans Fat 0g); Cholesterol 95mg; Sodium 610mg; Total Carbohydrate 8g (Dietary Fiber 2g; Sugars 4g); Protein 35g
% Daily Value: Vitamin A 15%; Vitamin C 60%; Calcium 4%; Iron 10%
Exchanges: 1 Vegetableetable, 4¹/₂ Lean Meat, 2 Fat
Carbohydrate Choices: ¹/₂

KITCHEN TIPS

✿ Roma tomatoes are great for this dish because they will hold their shape when cooked and won't add a lot of extra liquid.

Chicken and Spinach-Stuffed Shells

Prep Time: 30 min Start to Finish: 1 hr 10 min

18 large pasta shells (from 16-ounce package)

1 container (15 ounces) whole-milk ricotta cheese

1 egg, slightly beaten

1/4 cup grated Parmesan cheese

2 cups frozen cut leaf spinach, thawed and squeezed to drain

1 cup chopped deli rotisserie chicken (from 2- to 2 1/2- pound chicken)

1 jar (26 ounces) tomato sauce

2 cups shredded Italian cheese blend (8 ounces)

1. Heat oven to 350°F. Cook and drain pasta as directed on package. Rinse with cool water; drain.

2. Meanwhile, in medium bowl, mix ricotta cheese, egg, Parmesan cheese, spinach and chicken.

3. Spread 1 cup of the tomato sauce in bottom of 13 × 9-inch (3-quart) glass baking dish. Spoon about 2 tablespoons ricotta mixture into each pasta shell. Arrange shells, filled sides up, on sauce in baking dish. Spoon remaining sauce over stuffed shells.

4. Cover dish with aluminum foil; bake 30 minutes. Sprinkle with Italian cheese blend. Bake uncovered 5 to 10 minutes longer or until cheese is melted.

6 servings (3 shells each)
1 Serving: Calories 656 (Calories from Fat 211); Total Fat 23g (Saturated Fat 14g; Trans Fat 0g); Cholesterol 120mg; Sodium 852mg; Total Carbohydrate 74g (Dietary Fiber 4g; Sugars 8g); Protein 33g
% Daily Value: Vitamin A 160%; Vitamin C 15%; Calcium 35%; Iron 25%
Exchanges: 2 Fat, 3 1/2 Meat, 1 Other Carbohydrate, 4 Starch, 1/2 Vegetable
Carbohydrate Choices: 6

KITCHEN TIPS

❂ Thaw the spinach overnight in the refrigerator or microwave about 2 minutes or just until thawed.
❂ Make this dish the night before. Cover and refrigerate until ready to bake. Add 5 to 10 minutes to the first bake time before topping with cheese.

Quick

Chicken Linguine Alfredo

Prep Time: 30 min Start to Finish: 30 min

8 ounces uncooked linguine
2 teaspoons butter or margarine
2 tablespoons finely chopped shallot
1 clove garlic, finely chopped
1 pint (2 cups) fat-free half-and-half
3 tablespoons Gold Medal all-purpose flour
1/2 cup reduced-fat sour cream
1/4 cup shredded fresh Parmesan cheese
1/2 teaspoon salt
1/8 teaspoon white pepper
1 1/4 pounds chicken breast strips for stir-fry
1 jar (7 ounces) roasted red bell peppers, drained, thinly sliced
1/3 cup shredded fresh Parmesan cheese
2 tablespoons chopped fresh parsley

1. In 4-quart Dutch oven, cook linguine as directed on package. Drain; rinse with hot water. Return to Dutch oven to keep warm.

2. Meanwhile, in 2-quart saucepan, melt butter over medium heat. Add shallot and garlic; cook and stir 1 minute. In medium bowl, beat half-and-half and flour with wire whisk; add to saucepan. Heat to boiling, stirring frequently. Beat in sour cream with wire whisk. Reduce heat to low; cook 1 to 2 minutes or until heated. Remove from heat; stir in 1/4 cup cheese, the salt and pepper.

3. Heat 12-inch nonstick skillet over medium-high heat. Add chicken; cook about 5 minutes, stirring frequently, until no longer pink in center.

4. Add chicken, bell peppers and sauce to linguine; stir to mix. Cook over low heat until hot. Garnish each serving with cheese and parsley.

6 servings
1 Serving: Calories 430 (Calories from Fat 110); Total Fat 12g (Saturated Fat 6g; Trans Fat 0g); Cholesterol 80mg; Sodium 710mg; Total Carbohydrate 47g (Dietary Fiber 2g; Sugars 8g); Protein 34g
% Daily Value: Vitamin A 40%; Vitamin C 45%; Calcium 25%; Iron 15%
Exchanges: 2 1/2 Starch, 1/2 Other Carbohydrate, 3 1/2 Lean Meat
Carbohydrate Choices: 3

KITCHEN TIPS

⚙ Instead of slicing the peppers with a knife, you can also cut them into slices with kitchen scissors.

Low Fat

Grilled Chicken Citrus Teriyaki

Prep Time: 25 min Start to Finish: 55 min

¼ cup teriyaki baste and glaze
(from 12-ounce bottle)

¼ cup frozen (thawed) orange juice
concentrate

2 teaspoons grated orange peel

½ pound uncooked chicken breast tenders
(not breaded)

1 cup snap pea pods

1 cup sliced fresh mushrooms (3 ounces)

1 medium zucchini, cut into ½-inch slices
(2 cups)

½ medium red bell pepper, cut into 1-inch
pieces (¾ cup)

1. In small bowl, mix teriyaki glaze, orange juice concentrate and orange peel. Reserve 2 tablespoons
mixture. Add chicken to remaining mixture; toss to
coat. Cover and refrigerate 30 minutes.

2. Meanwhile, heat gas or charcoal grill. Place grill
basket (grill "wok") on grill over medium heat.
Remove chicken from marinade; discard marinade.
Place chicken in grill basket. Cover grill; cook 6 to 8
minutes, shaking grill basket or stirring chicken occasionally, until chicken is brown.

3. Add remaining ingredients to grill basket. Cover grill;
cook 6 to 8 minutes, shaking basket or stirring occasionally, until vegetables are crisp-tender and
chicken is no longer pink in center. Add 2 tablespoons reserved marinade; stir to coat vegetables
and chicken. Cover grill; cook 2 to 3 minutes or
until hot.

2 servings
1 Serving: Calories 270 (Calories from Fat 10); Total Fat 1g (Saturated
Fat 0g; Trans Fat 0g); Cholesterol 50mg; Sodium 960mg; Total
Carbohydrate 34g (Dietary Fiber 3g; Sugars 28g); Protein 29g
% Daily Value: Vitamin A 35%; Vitamin C 110%; Calcium 8%; Iron 15%
Exchanges: 1½ Other Carbohydrate, 2 Vegetableetable, 3½ Very
Lean Meat
Carbohydrate Choices: 2

KITCHEN TIPS

✲ For a different citrus flavor, try using grated lime or lemon
peel instead of orange.

✲ Complete your meal by serving the mixture over hot
cooked rice.

Quick & Low-Fat

Sesame Chicken

Prep Time: 20 min Start to Finish: 20 min

1¼ cups water

⅛ teaspoon salt

1 cup uncooked instant brown rice

⅔ cup water

3 tablespoons reduced-sodium soy sauce

2 teaspoons lemon juice

1 tablespoon cornstarch

1 teaspoon toasted sesame oil

2 teaspoons canola or olive oil

1 package (14 ounces) uncooked chicken breast tenders (not breaded), pieces cut in half

1 bag (1 pound) frozen bell pepper and onion stir-fry, thawed, drained

1 tablespoon sesame seed

1. In 2-quart saucepan, heat 1¼ cups water and the salt to boiling over high heat. Stir in rice. Reduce heat to low. Cover; simmer about 10 minutes or until water is absorbed. Fluff with fork.

2. Meanwhile, in small bowl, stir ⅔ cup water, the soy sauce, lemon juice, cornstarch and sesame oil; set aside.

3. Heat nonstick wok or 12-inch skillet over medium-high heat. Add canola oil; rotate wok to coat side. Add chicken; stir-fry 2 to 3 minutes. Add stir-fry vegetables; stir-fry 3 to 5 minutes or until chicken is no longer pink in center and vegetables are crisp-tender.

4. Stir soy sauce mixture into chicken mixture; heat to boiling. Cook and stir until sauce is thickened. Sprinkle with sesame seed. Serve with rice.

4 servings
1 Serving: Calories 280 (Calories from Fat 50); Total Fat 5g (Saturated Fat 0g; Trans Fat 0g); Cholesterol 45mg; Sodium 600mg; Total Carbohydrate 34g (Dietary Fiber 2g; Sugars 5g); Protein 25g
% Daily Value: Vitamin A 2%; Vitamin C 30%; Calcium 2%; Iron 4%
Exchanges: 2 Starch, 1 Vegetableetable, 2½ Very Lean Meat, ½ Fat
Carbohydrate Choices: 2

KITCHEN TIPS

❂ Alter the flavor of this dish by using pork loin pieces instead of chicken.

Chicken Cacciatore

Prep Time: 15 min Start to Finish: 8 hr 25 min

2½ pounds boneless, skinless chicken thighs (about 12)

1 jar (4.5 ounces) Green Giant sliced mushrooms

2 cans (6 ounces each) Italian-style tomato paste

1 can (14 ounces) chicken broth

½ cup white wine, if desired

1½ teaspoons dried basil leaves

½ teaspoon salt

1 dried bay leaf

12 ounces uncooked linguine

¼ teaspoon dried thyme leaves

1 tablespoon cornstarch

Shredded Parmesan cheese, if desired

1. Spray 3- to 4-quart slow cooker with cooking spray. Place chicken in cooker. Add mushrooms, tomato paste, broth, wine, basil, salt and bay leaf; gently stir to mix.

2. Cover; cook on Low heat setting 8 to 10 hours.

3. About 15 minutes before serving, cook and drain linguine as directed on package. Remove chicken from slow cooker; cover to keep warm. Stir thyme into sauce in cooker. Increase heat setting to High. In small bowl, mix ¼ cup sauce from cooker and the cornstarch until smooth; stir into remaining sauce in cooker.

4. Cover; cook 10 minutes longer, stirring frequently. Remove bay leaf before serving. Serve chicken and sauce over linguine. Sprinkle with cheese.

6 servings
1 Serving: Calories 540 (Calories from Fat 120); Total Fat 13g (Saturated Fat 4g; Trans Fat 0g); Cholesterol 85mg; Sodium 1310mg; Total Carbohydrate 63g (Dietary Fiber 6g; Sugars 8g); Protein 42g
% Daily Value: Vitamin A 20%; Vitamin C 10%; Calcium 8%; Iron 35%
Exchanges: 3 Starch, 1 Other Carbohydrate, 4½ Lean Meat
Carbohydrate Choices: 4

KITCHEN TIPS

❂ Serve with sesame breadsticks and a simple salad of mixed greens drizzled with olive oil and balsamic vinegar.

❂ One 26-ounce jar of tomato sauce can be substituted for the tomato paste, chicken broth and white wine.

Chicken Cacciatore

Low Fat

Chicken in Red Wine

Prep Time: 20 min Start to Finish: 8 hr 50 min

   6   slices bacon
   8   boneless, skinless chicken thighs
       (about 1½ pounds)
   1   bag (16 ounces) ready-to-eat
       baby-cut carrots
   8   ounces tiny pearl onions
   1   teaspoon salt
 ¼   teaspoon pepper
   1   teaspoon dried thyme leaves
   2   cloves garlic, finely chopped
   2   dried bay leaves
 1¼   cups dry red wine or nonalcoholic red wine
 ¾   cup chicken broth
   1   pound fresh small whole mushrooms
   2   tablespoons Gold Medal all-purpose flour
   2   tablespoons cold water
 ¼   cup chopped fresh parsley

1. Line microwavable plate with microwavable paper towel. Add bacon; cover with paper towel. Microwave on high 3 to 5 minutes or until crisp. Crumble bacon.

2. Spray 5- to 6-quart slow cooker with cooking spray. Place chicken in cooker. Add carrots, onions, bacon, salt, pepper, thyme, garlic, bay leaves, wine and broth.

3. Cover; cook on Low heat setting 8 to 10 hours.

4. Skim any fat from surface of chicken mixture. Stir in mushrooms. In small bowl, mix flour and water; stir into chicken mixture. Stir in 2 tablespoons parsley.

5. Increase heat setting to High. Cover; cook about 30 minutes longer or until mixture is thickened. Remove bay leaves before serving. Sprinkle with remaining chopped parsley.

8 servings
1 Serving: Calories 230 (Calories from Fat 90); Total Fat 10g (Saturated Fat 3g; Trans Fat 0g); Cholesterol 60mg; Sodium 620mg; Total Carbohydrate 12g (Dietary Fiber 3g; Sugars 5g); Protein 23g
% Daily Value: Vitamin A 190%; Vitamin C 6%; Calcium 6%; Iron 15%
Exchanges: ½ Other Carbohydrate, 1 Vegetableetable, 3 Lean Meat
Carbohydrate Choices: 1

KITCHEN TIPS

❂ This robust chicken dish, known as Coq au Vin in France, gets it wonderful flavor and rich color from the red wine and bacon. It is usually prepared with bone-in chicken pieces, but we found that boneless chicken thighs work best in the slow cooker. The chicken becomes very tender and will fall apart into pieces for easier serving.

❂ If you prefer not to use red wine, you still can make a delicious chicken dish your family will love. Just increase the chicken broth to 2 cups and leave out the wine.

Quick

Slow Cooker Creamy Herbed Chicken Stew

Prep Time: 30 min Start to Finish: 7 hr 40 min

4 cups ready-to-eat baby-cut carrots

4 medium Yukon gold potatoes,
cut into 1½-inch pieces

1 large onion, chopped (1 cup)

2 medium stalks celery, sliced (1 cup)

1 teaspoon dried thyme leaves

½ teaspoon salt

½ teaspoon pepper

2 pound boneless, skinless chicken thighs

3 cups chicken broth

2 cups fresh snap pea pods

1 cup whipping cream

½ cup Gold Medal all-purpose flour

1 teaspoon dried thyme leaves

1. In 5- to 6-quart slow cooker, place carrots, potatoes, onion and celery. Sprinkle with 1 teaspoon thyme, the salt and pepper. Top with chicken. Pour in broth.

2. Cover; cook on Low heat setting 7 to 8 hours, adding pea pods for last 5 to 10 minutes of cooking.

3. Remove chicken and vegetables from cooker to serving bowl, using slotted spoon; cover to keep warm. Increase heat setting to High. In small bowl, combine whipping cream, flour and 1 teaspoon thyme; stir into liquid in cooker. Cover; cook about 10 minutes or until thickened. Pour sauce over chicken and vegetables.

10 servings
1 Serving: Calories 319 (Calories from Fat 115); Total Fat 13g (Saturated Fat 6g; Trans Fat 0g); Cholesterol 108mg; Sodium 546mg; Total Carbohydrate 27g (Dietary Fiber 3g; Sugars 5g); Protein 23g
% Daily Value: Vitamin A 140%; Vitamin C 35%; Calcium 6%; Iron 15%
Exchanges: 2 Fat, 1 Starch, 2 Vegetable, 2½ Meat
Carbohydrate Choices: 2

KITCHEN TIPS

✿ Chicken thighs are great for slow cooking because they stay moist and juicy, unlike chicken breasts, which can become dry and tough during the long cooking process.

✿ Instead of the baby-cut carrots, cut regular carrots into 2-inch lengths.

Betty Crocker
IN SEASON

Entertaining with Ease

Is there a party on your calendar?

Whether you're hosting a casual get-together with friends or a festive gathering with family, your slow cooker can lend a very helpful hand. It's a time-saving, low-tech appliance that's ideal for fix-and-forget cooking.

Use your slow cooker to cook part of the menu ahead, so you'll have plenty of time to prepare for your guests. Here are some tips for putting your "party helper" to work.

PARTY POINTERS

▶ Let your slow cooker work its magic while you prepare other dishes, arrange plates, napkins and silverware or do last-minute cleaning or decorating.

▶ When serving sandwiches, place the basket of buns or bread within easy reach of the slow cooker.

▶ Using more than one slow cooker? Avoid cord confusion by grouping your slow cookers together near an outlet.

▶ If you need to keep foods, such as a dip, warm during the party, transfer the hot food to your slow cooker and set on low heat.

FOOD SAFETY

Slow cooking is a safe cooking method, but it's also a good idea to follow these guidelines to make sure food stays safe.

Do's

▶ Refrigerate perishable ingredients that you've prepared ahead (such as meat and vegetables) in separate containers to avoid cross-contamination.

▶ Defrost meat or poultry before adding it to the slow cooker.

▶ Heat or microwave leftovers until thoroughly heated before placing in a preheated slow cooker to keep hot.

▶ Refrigerate leftovers in covered shallow containers within two hours after cooking is complete.

Don'ts

▶ Never put raw ground meat in your slow cooker. It must be cooked first.

▶ Don't slow cook whole chickens or meat loaf because they'd cook too slowly and remain in the harmful bacteria zone too long.

▶ Don't fully or partially cook meat and then refrigerate it before adding it to the slow cooker.

▶ Don't use your slow cooker to reheat leftovers straight from the fridge.

Traveling Tips

▶ Keep the lid in place by stretching rubber bands around the slow cooker handles and across the lid.

▶ Wrap the slow cooker in a towel or in newspaper to insulate it, then place it in a box to keep it steady. Or if you transport your slow cooker often, consider purchasing an insulated slow cooker tote.

▶ Once you arrive at your party, plug in the slow cooker and set on low. Serve food within two hours of toting it.

▶ Carry along an extension cord just in case there are no nearby outlets.

Dress It Up

Boost the color of slow cooker side dishes and appetizers with simple finishing touches such as chopped fresh parsley, basil or other herbs, bell pepper, green onion, zucchini or carrot.

Chopped green onions complement Spicy Chicken Nachos (page 60), while chopped fresh cilantro looks pretty on White Bean-Chicken Chili (page 183).

Serve sandwiches on hearty whole-grain buns, onion buns or on crusty rolls (Easy French Dip Sandwiches, page 114).

Arrange pineapple slices around a tray of Hawaiian Pork Ribs (page 199).

Spoon a dollop of sour cream, guacamole or salsa on chilies and soups. Or sprinkle with broken colored tortilla chips, corn chips, seasoned croutons or nuts.

Quick

Chicken Alfredo Stew

Prep Time: 10 min Start to Finish: 6 hr 10 min

- 1 jar (16 ounces) Alfredo pasta sauce
- ¾ cup water
- ½ teaspoon dried basil leaves
- ½ teaspoon salt
- 4 cups refrigerated cooked diced potatoes with onions (from 20-ounce bag)
- 1¼ pounds boneless, skinless chicken thighs, cut into 1-inch-wide strips
- 1 bag (1 pound) Green Giant frozen mixed vegetables

1. In small bowl, mix pasta sauce, water, basil and salt.

2. Spray 3- to 4-quart slow cooker with cooking spray. In cooker, layer half each of the potatoes, chicken strips, frozen vegetables and pasta sauce. Repeat layers, ending with pasta sauce.

3. Cover; cook on Low heat setting 6 to 8 hours.

6 servings
1 Serving: Calories 530 (Calories from Fat 280); Total Fat 31g (Saturated Fat 17g; Trans Fat 1g); Cholesterol 135mg; Sodium 730mg; Total Carbohydrate 33g (Dietary Fiber 5g; Sugars 3g); Protein 30g
% Daily Value: Vitamin A 80%; Vitamin C 8%; Calcium 20%; Iron 15%
Exchanges: 2 Starch, 1 Vegetableetable, 3 Very Lean Meat, 5½ Fat
Carbohydrate Choices: 2

KITCHEN TIPS

✿ Unbreaded chicken breast tenders can be used instead of the cut-up chicken thighs.
✿ If you like garlic, try using garlic-flavored Alfredo pasta sauce.

Quick & Low Fat

French Peasant Chicken Stew

Prep Time: 10 min Start to Finish: 35 min

- 2 cups ready-to-eat baby-cut carrots
- 1 cup sliced fresh mushrooms (about 3 ounces)
- 4 small red potatoes, cut into quarters
- 1 jar (12 ounces) chicken gravy
- 1 can (14.5 ounces) reduced-sodium chicken broth
- 1 teaspoon dried thyme leaves
- ½ cup Green Giant LeSueur® frozen baby sweet peas
- 1 deli rotisserie chicken (2- to 2½-pound), cut into serving pieces

1. In 4-quart saucepan, mix all ingredients except peas and chicken.

2. Heat to boiling over medium-high heat. Reduce heat to medium-low. Cover; simmer about 20 minutes or until vegetables are tender.

3. Stir in peas and chicken. Cover; simmer about 5 minutes or until peas are tender.

6 servings (1⅓ cups each)
1 Serving: Calories 276 (Calories from Fat 70); Total Fat 7.7g (Saturated Fat 2.2g; Trans Fat 0g); Cholesterol 88mg; Sodium 752mg; Total Carbohydrate 23g (Dietary Fiber 3g; Sugars 5g); Protein 29g
% Daily Value: Vitamin A 110%; Vitamin C 20%; Calcium 2%; Iron 4%
Exchanges: ½ Fat, 1 Starch, 1 Vegetable, 4 Meat
Carbohydrate Choices: 1½

KITCHEN TIPS

✿ Add 2 tablespoons white wine for a quick coq au vin.

French Peasant Chicken Stew

Chicken Alfredo Stew

Mexican Chicken Chili

White Bean Chicken Chili

Quick & Low-Fat
White Bean-Chicken Chili

Prep Time: 20 min Start to Finish: 20 min

- 2 tablespoons butter or margarine
- 1 large onion, coarsely chopped (1 cup)
- 2 cloves garlic, finely chopped
- 3 cups cubed deli rotisserie chicken (from 2- to 2$\frac{1}{2}$-pound chicken)
- $\frac{1}{2}$ teaspoon ground cumin
- 2 cans (14.5 ounces each) diced tomatoes with green chilies, undrained
- 1 can (15 to 16 ounces) great northern beans, drained, rinsed

  Sour cream, if desired

  Chopped fresh cilantro, if desired

1. In 4$\frac{1}{2}$- to 5-quart Dutch oven, melt butter over medium-high heat. Cook onion and garlic in butter, stirring occasionally, until onion is tender.

2. Stir in remaining ingredients except sour cream and cilantro. Heat to boiling; reduce heat to low. Simmer uncovered 2 to 3 minutes, stirring occasionally, until hot.

3. Top each serving with sour cream; sprinkle with cilantro.

6 servings
1 Serving: Calories 210 (Calories from Fat 56); Total Fat 6g (Saturated Fat 3g; Trans Fat 0g); Cholesterol 62mg; Sodium 817mg; Total Carbohydrate 17g (Dietary Fiber 4g; Sugars 0g); Protein 24g
% Daily Value: Vitamin A 15%; Vitamin C 30%; Calcium 40%; Iron 8%
Exchanges: 1 Fat, $\frac{1}{2}$ Starch, 2 Vegetable, 2$\frac{1}{2}$ Meat
Carbohydrate Choices: 1

KITCHEN TIPS

✿ Serve this chili with tortilla chips for a little crunch.
✿ A can of navy beans would be just as delicious as the great northern beans.

Quick
Mexican Chicken Chili

Prep Time: 10 min Start to Finish: 7 hr 10 min

- 1$\frac{3}{4}$ pounds boneless, skinless chicken thighs
- 1 medium onion, chopped ($\frac{1}{2}$ cup)
- 2 medium stalks celery, sliced ($\frac{3}{4}$ cup)
- 2 cans (14.5 ounces each) stewed tomatoes with garlic and onion, undrained
- 2 cans (15 ounces each) Progresso pinto beans, undrained
- 1 can (10 ounces) Old El Paso enchilada sauce
- 2 teaspoons chili powder
- 1 teaspoon ground cumin
- 1 cup scoop-shaped corn chips, if desired
- $\frac{1}{3}$ cup sour cream
- 2 tablespoons chopped fresh cilantro, if desired

1. Spray 4- to 5-quart slow cooker with cooking spray. In cooker, mix all ingredients except corn chips, sour cream and cilantro.

2. Cover; cook on Low heat setting 7 to 8 hours.

3. Stir mixture to break up chicken. Top each serving with corn chips, sour cream and cilantro.

6 servings (1$\frac{2}{3}$ cups each)
1 Serving: Calories 410 (Calories from Fat 100); Total Fat 11g (Saturated Fat 4g; Trans Fat 0g); Cholesterol 60mg; Sodium 860mg; Total Carbohydrate 47g (Dietary Fiber 13g; Sugars 10g); Protein 31g
% Daily Value: Vitamin A 15%; Vitamin C 10%; Calcium 15%; Iron 30%
Exchanges: 2 Starch, 1 Other Carbohydrate, 3$\frac{1}{2}$ Lean Meat
Carbohydrate Choices: 3

KITCHEN TIPS

✿ In place of the stewed tomatoes with garlic and onion, use regular stewed tomatoes and add a teaspoon of finely chopped garlic.

Nacho Chicken Casserole

Prep Time: 15 min Start to Finish: 1 hr 25 min

2 cups diced cooked chicken

$\frac{1}{2}$ cup uncooked instant rice

1 can (14.5 ounces) diced tomatoes, drained

1 can ($10\frac{3}{4}$ ounces) condensed reduced-fat reduced-sodium cream of chicken soup

1 can (11 ounces) Green Giant whole kernel corn with red and green peppers, undrained

1 teaspoon Old El Paso taco seasoning mix (from 1.25-ounce package)

$1\frac{1}{4}$ cups shredded reduced-fat Cheddar cheese (5 ounces)

1 cup tortilla chips

1. Heat oven to 350°F. Spray 2-quart casserole with cooking spray. In casserole, stir chicken, rice, tomatoes, soup, corn, taco seasoning mix and 1 cup of the cheese until well mixed.

2. Cover and bake about 1 hour or until rice is tender and mixture is heated through. Top with tortilla chips; sprinkle with remaining $\frac{1}{4}$ cup cheese. Bake about 10 minutes longer or until filling is bubbly and cheese is melted.

5 servings
1 Serving: Calories 330 (Calories from Fat 80); Total Fat 9g (Saturated Fat 3g; Trans Fat 0g); Cholesterol 55mg; Sodium 950mg; Total Carbohydrate 34g (Dietary Fiber 2g; Sugars 6g); Protein 28g
% Daily Value: Vitamin A 4%; Vitamin C 8%; Calcium 25%; Iron 15%
Exchanges: 2 Starch, 3 Lean Meat
Carbohydrate Choices: 2

Spinach and Turkey Enchiladas

Prep Time: 25 min Start to Finish: 1 hr 10 min

- 1 pound lean ground turkey
- 1 medium onion, chopped (½ cup)
- 1 box (9 ounces) Green Giant frozen spinach
- 1 can (4.5 ounces) Old El Paso chopped green chilies, undrained
- ½ teaspoon ground cumin
- ½ teaspoon garlic-pepper blend
- ½ cup fat-free sour cream
- 1 cup shredded reduced-fat Colby-Monterey Jack cheese blend (4 ounces)
- 1 can (10 ounces) Old El Paso enchilada sauce
- 1 package (11.5 ounces) Old El Paso flour tortillas (8 tortillas)
- ½ cup Old El Paso Thick n' Chunky salsa

1. Heat oven to 350°F. Spray 13 × 9-inch (3-quart) glass baking dish with cooking spray. In 12-inch nonstick skillet, cook turkey and onion over medium-high heat 5 to 7 minutes, stirring occasionally, until turkey is no longer pink.

2. Stir in spinach; cook, stirring frequently, until thawed. Stir in green chilies, cumin, garlic-pepper blend, sour cream and ½ cup of the cheese.

3. Spread about 1 teaspoon enchilada sauce on each tortilla. Top each with about ½ cup turkey mixture. Roll up tortillas; place seam side down in baking dish. In small bowl, mix remaining enchilada sauce and the salsa; spoon over enchiladas. Sprinkle with remaining ½ cup cheese.

4. Spray sheet of aluminum foil with cooking spray; cover baking dish with foil, sprayed side down. Bake 40 to 45 minutes or until thoroughly heated.

8 enchiladas
1 Enchilada: Calories 300 (Calories from Fat 100); Total Fat 11g (Saturated Fat 3.5g; Trans Fat 1g); Cholesterol 45mg; Sodium 910mg; Total Carbohydrate 31g (Dietary Fiber 1g; Sugars 3g); Protein 21g
% Daily Value: Vitamin A 80%; Vitamin C 4%; Calcium 25%; Iron 15%
Exchanges: 2 Starch, 2 Medium-Fat Meat
Carbohydrate Choices: 2

Tomato-Basil Turkey Casserole

Prep Time: 25 min Start to Finish: 1 hr 15 min

- 2 cups uncooked gemelli pasta (8 ounces)
- 2 cups diced cooked turkey
- 1 jar (26 ounces) tomato sauce (any hearty or thick variety)
- 1 medium zucchini, cut in half lengthwise, then cut into slices (1½ cups)
- 1 can (2¼ ounces) sliced ripe olives, drained
- 1 teaspoon dried basil leaves
- ¼ cup shredded fresh Parmesan cheese

1. Heat oven to 375°F. Spray 2-quart casserole with cooking spray. Cook and drain pasta as directed on package.

2. In casserole, mix pasta and remaining ingredients except cheese.

3. Cover; bake 30 minutes. Sprinkle with cheese. Bake uncovered 15 to 20 minutes longer or until bubbly and thoroughly heated.

6 servings
1 Serving: Calories 390 (Calories from Fat 110); Total Fat 12g (Saturated Fat 3g; Trans Fat 0g); Cholesterol 70mg; Sodium 960mg; Total Carbohydrate 49g (Dietary Fiber 3g; Sugars 13g); Protein 21g
% Daily Value: Vitamin A 15%; Vitamin C 15%; Calcium 10%; Iron 20%
Exchanges: 2 Starch, 1 Other Carbohydrate, 2 Lean Meat, 1 Fat
Carbohydrate Choices: 3

KITCHEN TIPS

✿ When shopping for zucchini, choose small zucchini, which tend to be younger, more tender and have thinner skins. The skin should be a vibrant color and free of blemishes.

✿ Gemelli is a pasta that looks like two strands of spaghetti twisted together. Rotini or penne pasta would work well in this recipe, too.

Turkey and Wild Rice Casserole

Prep Time: 25 min Start to Finish: 2 hr

2¹⁄₂	cups water
1	cup uncooked wild rice
4	cups cut-up cooked turkey
1	bag (1 pound) Green Giant frozen mixed vegetables, thawed
1¹⁄₂	cups uncooked instant brown rice
¹⁄₂	teaspoon salt
¹⁄₂	teaspoon dried thyme leaves
1	cup chicken broth, heated
3	containers (10 ounces each) refrigerated reduced-fat Alfredo pasta sauce
¹⁄₂	cup Progresso plain bread crumbs
¹⁄₄	cup finely chopped walnuts
3	tablespoons butter or margarine, melted

1. In 2-quart saucepan, heat water to rolling boil. Stir in wild rice; reduce heat. Cover; simmer 40 to 50 minutes or until rice is tender.

2. Heat oven to 350°F. Spray 3-quart casserole with cooking spray.

3. In large bowl, mix turkey, vegetables, cooked wild rice, uncooked brown rice, salt and thyme. Stir in heated broth and Alfredo sauce. Pour into casserole.

4. In small bowl, mix bread crumbs, walnuts and butter; sprinkle over turkey mixture.

5. Bake uncovered about 45 minutes or until hot.

8 servings
1 Serving: Calories 630 (Calories from Fat 220); Total Fat 25g (Saturated Fat 12g; Trans Fat 0.5g); Cholesterol 110mg; Sodium 920mg; Total Carbohydrate 65g (Dietary Fiber 8g; Sugars 7g); Protein 36g
% Daily Value: Vitamin A 60%; Vitamin C 0%; Calcium 25%; Iron 15%
Exchanges: 3 Starch, 1 Other Carbohydrate, 1 Vegetableleetable, 3¹⁄₂ Lean Meat, 2¹⁄₂ Fat
Carbohydrate Choices: 4

KITCHEN TIPS

✿ To heat the chicken broth, measure it into a 2-cup microwavable measuring cup and microwave on High 2 minutes 30 seconds to 3 minutes or until almost boiling.

✿ To save time, purchase cooked wild rice. It's available in 15-ounce cans and 10-ounce frozen packages; each contains 2 cups cooked rice.

Curried Turkey Stir-Fry

Prep Time: 30 min Start to Finish: 30 min

1¾ cups uncooked instant brown rice
2 teaspoons canola oil
1 pound turkey breast tenderloins, cut into 2 × 1-inch strips
1 medium red bell pepper, cut into thin strips
2 cups small broccoli florets
1¼ cups reduced-sodium chicken broth
4 teaspoons cornstarch
4 teaspoons curry powder
½ teaspoon ground ginger
¼ teaspoon salt

1. Cook rice as directed on package, omitting butter and salt.

2. Meanwhile, in 12-inch nonstick skillet, heat oil over medium-high heat. Add turkey; cook 5 to 8 minutes, stirring frequently, until browned. Stir in bell pepper and broccoli. Cook 2 minutes.

3. In small bowl, stir together remaining ingredients. Stir into turkey and vegetables. Heat to boiling; reduce heat. Cover and cook 2 to 3 minutes or until vegetables are crisp-tender and turkey is no longer pink in center. Serve over brown rice.

4 servings (1¼ cups stir-fry and ¾ cup rice each)
1 Serving: Calories 360 (Calories from Fat 45); Total Fat 5g (Saturated Fat 0.5g; Trans Fat 0g); Cholesterol 75mg; Sodium 400mg; Total Carbohydrate 46g (Dietary Fiber 4g; Sugars 2g); Protein 33g
% Daily Value: Vitamin A 25%; Vitamin C 80%; Calcium 6%; Iron 15%
Exchanges: 2½ Starch, 1 Vegetableeetable, 3 Very Lean Meat, ½ Fat
Carbohydrate Choices: 3

KITCHEN TIPS

✹ Because it's quick, instant rice is a great choice for busy cooks. When you have the time, make this stir-fry with regular brown rice. Brown rice cooks in 45 minutes and has a chewy, nutty texture. You can cook it ahead of time and refrigerate for up to three days or freeze for up to three months. Just heat and eat.

Pork and Beef Dishes

Rich and Delicious Suppers

Pork Chop Supper (page 193)

Sweet and Tangy Short Ribs (page 201)

Quick

Stir-Fried Pork with Mushrooms and Broccoli

Prep Time: 25 min   Start to Finish: 25 min

- 1½ cups uncooked instant brown rice
- 1 tablespoon cornstarch
- ¼ cup reduced-sodium teriyaki marinade
- ½ cup water
- ½ teaspoon ground ginger
- 3 teaspoons canola oil
- ¾ pound boneless pork loin, trimmed of fat, cut into 2-inch strips
- 2 cups fresh broccoli florets
- 1 small onion, cut into thin wedges
- 1 package (8 ounces) sliced fresh mushrooms (3 cups)
- 1 medium red, yellow or orange bell pepper, cut into 1-inch pieces
- 2 cloves garlic, finely chopped

1. Cook rice as directed on package, omitting butter and salt. Meanwhile, place cornstarch in small bowl or cup. Gradually stir in teriyaki marinade, water and ginger.

2. In 12-inch nonstick skillet or wok, heat 2 teaspoons of the oil over medium-high heat. Add pork; cook and stir 4 to 5 minutes or until no longer pink in center. Remove pork from skillet; keep warm.

3. Add remaining 1 teaspoon oil to skillet. Add broccoli, onion, mushrooms, bell pepper and garlic; cook and stir 4 to 5 minutes or until vegetables are crisp-tender.

4. Stir cornstarch mixture into broccoli mixture. Add pork; cook and stir until sauce is thickened. Serve over rice.

4 servings (1½ cups stir-fry and 1 cup rice each)
1 Serving: Calories 310 (Calories from Fat 100); Total Fat 11g (Saturated Fat 2.5g; Trans Fat 0g); Cholesterol 55mg; Sodium 380mg; Total Carbohydrate 30g (Dietary Fiber 3g; Sugars 7g); Protein 24g
% Daily Value: Vitamin A 25%; Vitamin C 80%; Calcium 4%; Iron 8%
Exchanges: 1 Starch, ½ Other Carbohydrate, 1½ Vegetableetable, 2½ Lean Meat, ½ Fat
Carbohydrate Choices: 2

Low Fat

Grilled Pork Tenderloin with Pineapple Salsa

Prep Time: 40 min Start to Finish: 40 min

Pork

2	teaspoons canola oil
2	pork tenderloins (³⁄₄ pound each)
1	teaspoon black pepper
¹⁄₄ to ¹⁄₂	teaspoon ground red pepper (cayenne)
¹⁄₂	teaspoon salt

Pineapple Salsa

1	can (8 ounces) pineapple tidbits, drained
4	medium green onions, sliced (¹⁄₄ cup)
¹⁄₄	cup chopped red bell pepper
2	tablespoons chopped fresh or 2 teaspoons dried mint leaves
¹⁄₂	teaspoon grated lime peel
2	teaspoons lime juice
¹⁄₄	teaspoon salt

1. Heat gas or charcoal grill. Rub 1 teaspoon oil onto each pork tenderloin; sprinkle with black and red pepper and ¹⁄₂ teaspoon salt.

2. Carefully brush grill rack with oil. Place pork on grill over medium heat. Cover grill; cook 20 to 30 minutes turning 3 times, until pork has slight blush of pink in center and meat thermometer inserted in center reads 160°F.

3. Meanwhile, in medium bowl, mix salsa ingredients. Cut pork into ¹⁄₂-inch slices. Serve with salsa.

Broil Directions: Set oven control to broil. Prepare pork as directed in step 1; place on rack in broiler pan. Broil with tops 4 to 5 inches from heat using times in recipe as a guide, turning 3 times, until pork has slight blush of pink in center and meat thermometer inserted in center reads 160°F. Continue as directed in step 3.

4 servings
1 Serving: Calories 270 (Calories from Fat 80); Total Fat 9g (Saturated Fat 2.5g; Trans Fat 0g); Cholesterol 110mg; Sodium 520mg; Total Carbohydrate 8g (Dietary Fiber 1g; Sugars 7g); Protein 39g
% Daily Value: Vitamin A 10%; Vitamin C 40%; Calcium 2%; Iron 15%
Exchanges: ¹⁄₂ Other Carbohydrate, 5¹⁄₂ Very Lean Meat, 1 Fat
Carbohydrate Choices: ¹⁄₂

Quick & Low-Fat
Pork and Sweet Potato Kabobs

Prep Time: 15 min Start to Finish: 15 min

1/3 cup orange marmalade

1 teaspoon finely chopped fresh rosemary leaves

1/4 teaspoon salt

1/2 pound dark-orange sweet potatoes, peeled, cut into 8 pieces

2 tablespoons water

1/2 pound pork tenderloin, cut into 1-inch pieces

1 small zucchini, cut into 8 slices

1. Heat gas or charcoal grill. In 1-quart saucepan, heat marmalade, rosemary and salt to boiling, stirring frequently. Remove from heat; set aside.

2. In 1-quart microwavable bowl, place sweet potato pieces and water. Cover loosely with microwavable paper towel. Microwave on High 2 to 3 minutes, stirring once, just until potatoes are tender. (Do not overcook.) Drain sweet potatoes; rinse with cold water.

3. On each of four 10- to 12-inch metal skewers, carefully thread pork, sweet potatoes and zucchini (with cut side facing out) alternately, leaving 1/4-inch space between each piece.

4. Place kabobs on grill over medium heat. Cover grill; cook 8 to 10 minutes, turning once and brushing with marmalade glaze during last 3 minutes, until pork is not pink in center.

2 servings (2 kabobs each)
1 Serving: Calories 370 (Calories from Fat 40); Total Fat 4.5g (Saturated Fat 1.5g; Trans Fat 0g); Cholesterol 70mg; Sodium 390mg; Total Carbohydrate 53g (Dietary Fiber 3g; Sugars 32g); Protein 28g
% Daily Value: Vitamin A 270%; Vitamin C 25%; Calcium 6%; Iron 15%
Exchanges: 1 1/2 Starch, 2 Other Carbohydrate, 3 Very Lean Meat, 1/2 Fat
Carbohydrate Choices: 3 1/2

KITCHEN TIPS

✿ For the best flavor, purchase dark-orange sweet potatoes, often called yams, at the grocery store.

Low Fat
Pork Chop Supper

Prep Time: 15 min Start to Finish: 6 hr 30 min

- 6 pork loin or rib chops, ½ inch thick
- 6 medium red potatoes (about 1½ pounds), cut into eighths
- 1 can (10¾ ounces) condensed cream of mushroom soup
- 1 jar (4.5 ounces) Green Giant sliced mushrooms, drained
- 2 tablespoons dry white wine or chicken broth
- ¼ teaspoon dried thyme leaves
- ½ teaspoon garlic powder
- ½ teaspoon Worcestershire sauce
- 3 tablespoons Gold Medal all-purpose flour
- 1 tablespoon diced pimientos (from 2-ounce jar)
- 2 cups Green Giant frozen sweet peas, rinsed, drained

1. Heat 12-inch nonstick skillet over medium-high heat. Cook pork chops in skillet 2 to 4 minutes, turning once, until brown.

2. Spray 4- to 5-quart slow cooker with cooking spray. Place potatoes in cooker. In medium bowl, mix soup, mushrooms, wine, thyme, garlic powder, Worcestershire sauce and flour. Spoon half of the soup mixture over potatoes. Place pork on potatoes; cover with remaining soup mixture.

3. Cover; cook on Low heat setting 6 to 7 hours.

4. Remove pork from cooker; keep warm. Stir pimientos and peas into cooker. Cover; cook on Low heat setting about 15 minutes longer or until peas are tender. Serve with pork.

6 servings
1 Serving: Calories 350 (Calories from Fat 100); Total Fat 11g (Saturated Fat 3.5g; Trans Fat 0g); Cholesterol 65mg; Sodium 510mg; Total Carbohydrate 34g (Dietary Fiber 5g; Sugars 4g); Protein 28g
% Daily Value: Vitamin A 20%; Vitamin C 15%; Calcium 6%; Iron 20%
Exchanges: 2 Starch, 1 Vegetableetable, 3 Lean Meat
Carbohydrate Choices: 2

KITCHEN TIPS

✿ Virtually any cream soup will work in this recipe. Try golden cream of mushroom, cream of chicken or cream of celery instead of the cream of mushroom.

✿ Apple juice also works as a substitute for the white wine.

Apple-Maple Brined Pork Tenderloin

Prep Time: 15 min Start to Finish: 8 hr 40 min

- 4 cups cold water
- 2 cups apple cider
- 1/2 cup maple-flavored or real maple syrup
- 1/4 cup salt
- 2 pork tenderloins (about 1 pound each)
- 1 tablespoon chopped fresh rosemary leaves
- 1/2 teaspoon coarsely ground pepper
- 1/2 teaspoon garlic powder

1. In large container or stockpot, stir water, cider, maple syrup and salt until salt is dissolved. Add pork to brine mixture. Cover and refrigerate at least 8 hours but no longer than 12 hours.

2. Heat gas or charcoal grill. Remove pork from brine mixture; rinse thoroughly under cool running water and pat dry. Discard brine. Sprinkle pork with rosemary, pepper and garlic powder.

3. Place pork on grill over medium heat. Cover grill; cook 20 to 25 minutes, turning occasionally, until pork has slight blush of pink in center and meat thermometer inserted in center reads 160°F.

6 servings
1 Serving: Calories 220 (Calories from Fat 50); Total Fat 6g (Saturated Fat 2g; Trans Fat 0g); Cholesterol 95mg; Sodium 470mg; Total Carbohydrate 8g (Dietary Fiber 0g; Sugars 5g); Protein 34g
% Daily Value: Vitamin A 0%; Vitamin C 0%; Calcium 0%; Iron 10%
Exchanges: 1/2 Other Carbohydrate, 4 1/2 Very Lean Meat, 1 Fat
Carbohydrate Choices: 1/2

KITCHEN TIPS

✷ Because you're using a brine solution to flavor and tenderize the pork, be sure to buy meat that hasn't been injected with a saline solution.

✷ Brining is an age-old process for preserving meats. Today, this simple method of soaking meat in a salt-water solution is used to make meat exceptionally moist, juicy and flavorful.

Southwestern Grilled Pork Chops with Peach Salsa

Prep Time: 25 min Start to Finish: 25 min

- 3 ripe medium peaches, peeled, chopped (about 1 1/2 cups)
- 1/4 cup finely chopped red bell pepper
- 2 tablespoons finely chopped red onion
- 1 tablespoon chopped fresh cilantro
- 2 teaspoons packed brown sugar
- 2 teaspoons fresh lime juice
- 1/4 teaspoon finely chopped serrano or jalapeño chili
- 1 tablespoon chili powder
- 4 bone-in pork loin chops, 1/2 inch thick (4 ounces each)

1. Heat gas or charcoal grill. In medium bowl, mix peaches, bell pepper, onion, cilantro, brown sugar, lime juice and chili; set aside.

2. Rub chili powder on both sides of each pork chop. Place pork on grill over medium heat. Cover grill; cook 6 to 9 minutes, turning once, until pork is no longer pink in center. Serve pork chops topped with salsa, or serve salsa on the side.

4 servings
1 Serving: Calories 180 (Calories from Fat 60); Total Fat 7g (Saturated Fat 2g; Trans Fat 0g); Cholesterol 50mg; Sodium 50mg; Total Carbohydrate 11g (Dietary Fiber 2g; Sugars 9g); Protein 19g
% Daily Value: Vitamin A 20%; Vitamin C 40%; Calcium 0%; Iron 6%
Exchanges: 1 Other Carbohydrate, 2 1/2 Lean Meat
Carbohydrate Choices: 1

KITCHEN TIPS

✷ Boneless pork chops can be used instead of bone-in chops.

✷ If ripe peaches are not available, you can substitute 1 1/2 cups chopped mango or pineapple.

Southwestern Grilled Pork Chops with Peach Salsa

Apple-Maple Brined Pork Tenderloin

Asian Pork Stew

Prep Time: 25 min Start to Finish: 7 hr 25 min

2 pounds boneless country-style pork ribs, cut into 2-inch pieces

3 medium carrots, cut into 1-inch slices

2 medium onions, cut into 1-inch wedges

1 package (8 ounces) fresh whole mushrooms, cut in half if large

1 can (8 ounces) whole water chestnuts, drained

1 can (8 ounces) bamboo shoots, drained

³/₄ cup hoisin sauce

¹/₃ cup reduced-sodium soy sauce

4 large cloves garlic, finely chopped

1 tablespoon finely chopped gingerroot

4 cups water

2 cups uncooked long-grain white rice

2 tablespoons cornstarch

3 tablespoons water

¹/₃ cup lightly packed coarsely chopped cilantro

1. Spray 5- to 6-quart slow cooker with cooking spray. In cooker, layer pork, carrots, onions, mushrooms, water chestnuts and bamboo shoots. In small bowl, stir together ¹/₂ cup of the hoisin sauce, the soy sauce, garlic and gingerroot; pour into slow cooker.

2. Cover; cook on Low heat setting 7 to 9 hours.

3. During last hour of cooking, in 3-quart saucepan, heat 4 cups water and the rice to boiling over high heat. Reduce heat to low. Cover; simmer 15 to 20 minutes or until rice is tender and water is absorbed.

4. Gently remove pork and vegetables with slotted spoon to large bowl; cover to keep warm. Skim any fat from liquid in cooker. Pour liquid in 1-quart saucepan. Stir remaining ¹/₄ cup hoisin sauce into liquid; heat to boiling. In small bowl, mix cornstarch and 3 tablespoons water; stir into liquid. Cook, stirring constantly, until thickened; pour over pork mixture and gently stir.

5. Sprinkle cilantro over stew. Serve over rice.

8 servings (1 cup stew and ³/₄ cup rice each)
1 Serving: Calories 510 (Calories from Fat 130); Total Fat 15g (Saturated Fat 5g; Trans Fat 0g); Cholesterol 70mg; Sodium 810mg; Total Carbohydrate 63g (Dietary Fiber 3g; Sugars 5g); Protein 30g
% Daily Value: Vitamin A 80%; Vitamin C 6%; Calcium 6%; Iron 20%
Exchanges: 3 Starch, 1 Other Carbohydrate, 1 Vegetableetable, 2¹/₂ Medium-Fat Meat
Carbohydrate Choices: 4

KITCHEN TIPS

✿ Keep cleanup to a minimum by using a heat-resistant slow cooker liner in your slow cooker.

✿ Hoisin sauce is often used in Chinese cuisine. The reddish brown sauce, flavored with soybeans, garlic, chilies and numerous spices, tastes spicy and sweet.

Ham with Tropical Fruit Sauce

Prep Time: 20 min Start to Finish: 6 hr 20 min

1 fully cooked smoked boneless ham
(4 ½ pounds)

¼ teaspoon pepper

1 jar (24 ounces) mango in extra-light syrup,
drained

1 jar (12 ounces) pineapple preserves

1 jalapeño chili, seeded and chopped

2 tablespoons white wine vinegar

¼ cup chopped fresh cilantro

1 can (20 ounces) sliced pineapple, drained,
each cut into 6 pieces

1. Spray inside of 4- to 5-quart slow cooker with
cooking spray. Place ham in slow cooker; sprinkle
with pepper. In blender, place mango, preserves, chili
and vinegar. Cover; blend on high speed 30 seconds;
pour over ham.

2. Cover; cook on Low heat setting 6 to 8 hours.

3. Remove ham from cooker; place on serving platter.
Sprinkle ham with 1 tablespoon of the cilantro. Stir
remaining 3 tablespoons cilantro and the pineapple
into sauce in cooker. Serve sauce with ham.

12 servings
1 Serving: Calories 393 (Calories from Fat 42); Total Fat 4.7g
(Saturated Fat 1.5g; Trans Fat 0g); Cholesterol 61mg; Sodium 1887mg;
Total Carbohydrate 32g (Dietary Fiber 1g; Sugars 22g); Protein 31g
% Daily Value: Vitamin A 2%; Vitamin C 25%; Calcium 0%; Iron 15%
Exchanges: 1 Fat, 1 Fruit, 1 Other Carbohydrate, 4 Meat
Carbohydrate Choices: 2

KITCHEN TIPS

✿ Out of cilantro? Chopped Italian parsley is a good
substitute.

✿ Put leftovers in a freezer container and freeze for up to 4
months. To thaw, place the container in the fridge for
about 8 hours or thaw in the microwave.

Grilled Slow-Cooker Ribs

Prep Time: 30 min Start to Finish: 8 hr 30 min

3½	pounds pork loin back ribs
2	cloves garlic, finely chopped
¼	cup packed brown sugar
1	teaspoon salt
½	teaspoon pepper
3	tablespoons liquid smoke
1	medium onion, sliced
½	cup cola carbonated beverage
1½	cups barbecue sauce

1. Spray inside of 4- to 5-quart slow cooker with cooking spray. Remove inner skin from ribs.

2. In small bowl, mix garlic, brown sugar, salt, pepper and liquid smoke. Rub mixture into ribs. Cut ribs into 4-inch pieces. Layer ribs and onion in slow cooker. Pour carbonated beverage over ribs.

3. Cover; cook on Low heat setting 8 to 9 hours.

4. Heat gas or charcoal grill. Remove ribs from slow cooker; drain and discard liquid. Place ribs on grill over medium heat; brush with barbecue sauce. Cover grill; cook 15 minutes.

6 servings
1 Serving: Calories 660 (Calories from Fat 350); Total Fat 39g (Saturated Fat 14g; Trans Fat 0g); Cholesterol 155mg; Sodium 1180mg; Total Carbohydrate 39g (Dietary Fiber 0g; Sugars 32g); Protein 38g
% Daily Value: Vitamin A 4%; Vitamin C 2%; Calcium 10%; Iron 20%
Exchanges: 2½ Other Carbohydrate, 5 High-Fat Meat
Carbohydrate Choices: 2½

KITCHEN TIPS

✿ Cola carbonated beverage adds a wonderful sweetness to the ribs, but you can use water instead of the cola.

✿ Serve the ribs with deli coleslaw, biscuits and glasses of iced tea.

Quick

Hawaiian Pork Ribs

Prep Time: 15 min Start to Finish: 6 hr 40 min

6 pounds pork loin back ribs
¾ cup ketchup
¾ cup pineapple preserves
½ cup teriyaki marinade and sauce
2 tablespoons packed brown sugar
2 cloves garlic, finely chopped
½ cup cornstarch
1 can (20 ounces) pineapple chunks in juice, drained, ⅓ cup juice reserved
1 bag (1 pound) frozen bell pepper and onion stir-fry

1. Spray 6-quart slow cooker with cooking spray. Cut ribs into 2- or 3-rib portions; place in cooker. In small bowl, mix ketchup, preserves, teriyaki marinade, brown sugar and garlic; pour over ribs.

2. Cover; cook on Low heat setting 6 to 7 hours.

3. Skim fat from liquid in cooker if necessary. Remove ribs from cooker; cover to keep warm or keep warm in 200°F oven. In small bowl, mix cornstarch and reserved ⅓ cup pineapple juice until smooth; stir into liquid in cooker. Increase heat setting to High. Cover; cook about 25 minutes or until thickened.

4. Meanwhile, in large microwavable bowl, mix pineapple chunks and stir-fry vegetables. Microwave uncovered on High 5 to 7 minutes or until thoroughly heated. Drain; stir vegetable mixture into sauce in cooker. Serve vegetable mixture over ribs.

10 servings
1 Serving: Calories 700 (Calories from Fat 360); Total Fat 40g (Saturated Fat 15g; Trans Fat 0g); Cholesterol 160mg; Sodium 820mg; Total Carbohydrate 44g (Dietary Fiber 1g; Sugars 30g); Protein 40g
% Daily Value: Vitamin A 6%; Vitamin C 20%; Calcium 8%; Iron 15%
Exchanges: 3 Other Carbohydrate, 5 High-Fat Meat
Carbohydrate Choices: 3

KITCHEN TIPS

✪ A clever trick for skimming fat from the cooked meat mixture is to place a slice of bread on top of the mixture for a few minutes to absorb the fat.

✪ To turn this main-dish recipe into a delicious riblet appetizer, ask the meat cutter at your supermarket to cut across the ribs horizontally.

Quick

Cola Barbecued Ribs

Prep Time: 10 min Start to Finish: 9 hr 10 min

3½ pounds pork spareribs or loin back ribs
¼ cup packed brown sugar
½ teaspoon hickory smoked salt
¼ teaspoon pepper
½ cup cola
1¼ cups barbecue sauce

1. Spray 4- to 5-quart slow cooker with cooking spray. Trim excess fat and remove membranes from ribs. In small bowl, mix brown sugar, hickory smoked salt and pepper; rub mixture into ribs. Cut ribs into 2- or 3-rib portions. Place ribs in cooker; pour cola around ribs.

2. Cover; cook on Low heat setting 8 to 9 hours.

3. Remove ribs from cooker; place in shallow baking pan. Drain liquid from cooker and discard. Brush both sides of ribs with barbecue sauce. Return ribs to cooker. Pour any remaining sauce over ribs.

4. Cover; cook on Low heat setting about 1 hour longer or until ribs are glazed and sauce is desired consistency. Cut into single-rib servings if desired.

4 servings
1 Serving: Calories 800 (Calories from Fat 420); Total Fat 47g (Saturated Fat 17g; Trans Fat 0g); Cholesterol 190mg; Sodium 1270mg; Total Carbohydrate 49g (Dietary Fiber 0g; Sugars 42g); Protein 46g
% Daily Value: Vitamin A 4%; Vitamin C 2%; Calcium 15%; Iron 25%
Exchanges: 3 Other Carbohydrate, 6 High-Fat Meat
Carbohydrate Choices: 3

KITCHEN TIPS

✿ For a comforting homemade dinner, serve with coleslaw and hot-from-the-oven corn bread. Don't forget to pass the butter to top off the corn bread!

✿ Hickory smoked salt adds a nice hint of barbecue flavor to these ribs. If you don't have smoky-flavored salt on hand, use ½ teaspoon garlic salt instead.

Sweet and Tangy Short Ribs

Prep Time: 35 min Start to Finish: 9 hr 35 min

Ribs

- 1 tablespoon vegetable oil
- 4 pounds beef short ribs
- 1 large sweet onion (such as Bermuda, Maui or Spanish), cut in half, halves sliced (about 3 1/2 cups)

Sauce

- 1 bottle (12 ounces) chili sauce
- 3/4 cup apricot preserves
- 2 tablespoons packed brown sugar
- 2 tablespoons cider vinegar
- 2 tablespoons Worcestershire sauce
- 2 teaspoons ground mustard
- 2 cloves garlic, finely chopped

1. In 12-inch nonstick skillet, heat oil over medium-high heat. Add ribs, in batches if necessary; cook 6 to 8 minutes, turning occasionally, until brown on all sides.

2. Spray 4- to 5-quart slow cooker with cooking spray. Place onion in cooker. Top with ribs. Cover; cook on Low heat setting 8 hours.

3. In 2-quart saucepan, cook sauce ingredients over low heat 15 to 20 minutes, stirring frequently, until sauce has thickened.

4. Drain excess liquid from cooker. Pour sauce over ribs. Increase heat setting to High. Cover; cook about 1 hour longer or until meat begins to separate from bones.

6 servings
1 Serving: Calories 470 (Calories from Fat 180); Total Fat 20g (Saturated Fat 7g; Trans Fat 1g); Cholesterol 90mg; Sodium 880mg; Total Carbohydrate 47g (Dietary Fiber 4g; Sugars 32g); Protein 24g
% Daily Value: Vitamin A 8%; Vitamin C 15%; Calcium 6%; Iron 15%
Exchanges: 3 Other Carbohydrate, 3 1/2 Medium-Fat Meat, 1/2 Fat
Carbohydrate Choices: 3

KITCHEN TIPS

✿ Make the sauce a day ahead. Store covered in the refrigerator and heat before adding to the ribs.

✿ These ribs are great with steamed broccoli and warm dinner rolls.

Easy Beef Short Rib Supper

Prep Time: 15 min Start to Finish: 8 hr 40 min

3 pounds beef short ribs, cut into rib sections

1/2 teaspoon seasoned salt

12 small whole red potatoes

1 1/2 cups ready-to-eat baby-cut carrots

1 can (10 3/4 ounces) condensed cream of celery soup

1/2 cup chili sauce

2 tablespoons Worcestershire sauce

1/2 teaspoon garlic-pepper blend

1 1/2 cups Green Giant frozen cut green beans, thawed

1. Spray 5- to 6-quart slow cooker and 12-inch skillet with cooking spray. Sprinkle ribs with seasoned salt. In skillet, cook ribs over medium-high heat 6 to 8 minutes, turning occasionally, until well browned.

2. Remove ribs from skillet with fork or tongs; place in cooker. Add potatoes and carrots to cooker. In small bowl, mix soup, chili sauce, Worcestershire sauce and garlic-pepper blend; pour over ribs and vegetables.

3. Cover; cook on Low heat setting 8 to 10 hours.

4. Skim fat from liquid in cooker if desired. Stir in green beans. Increase heat setting to High. Cover; cook 15 to 25 minutes longer or until beans are tender.

6 servings
1 Serving: Calories 530 (Calories from Fat 150); Total Fat 16g (Saturated Fat 6g; Trans Fat 0.5g); Cholesterol 70mg; Sodium 920mg; Total Carbohydrate 71g (Dietary Fiber 11g; Sugars 10g); Protein 24g
% Daily Value: Vitamin A 110%; Vitamin C 40%; Calcium 15%; Iron 40%
Exchanges: 3 Starch, 1 1/2 Other Carbohydrate, 1 Vegetableetable, 2 Lean Meat, 1 1/2 Fat
Carbohydrate Choices: 5

KITCHEN TIPS

⚙ Short ribs are trimmed from narrow beef rib and short plate sections. They're tasty but not tender, so slow cooking is great for tenderizing them.

⚙ Browning the short ribs before slow cooking gives the dish a rich, savory flavor and removes some of the fat.

Quick

Grilled Garlic Steak Salad

Prep Time: 25 min Start to Finish: 25 min

Dressing

- 1/4 cup olive or canola oil
- 2 tablespoons chopped fresh parsley
- 3 tablespoons red wine vinegar
- 1 tablespoon lemon juice
- 1 teaspoon chopped fresh or 1/2 teaspoon dried oregano leaves
- 1/2 teaspoon crushed red pepper flakes
- 2 cloves garlic, finely chopped

Salad

- 1 pound boneless beef sirloin steak, 1 to 1 1/2 inches thick
- 1 large bell pepper, cut into strips
- 1 cup sliced fresh mushrooms (3 ounces)
- 6 cups bite-size pieces salad greens

1. Heat gas or charcoal grill. In tightly covered container, shake dressing ingredients; set aside.

2. Place beef on grill over medium heat. Cover grill; cook 10 to 14 minutes, turning once, until desired doneness.

3. Meanwhile, in medium bowl, toss bell pepper and mushrooms with 2 tablespoons of the dressing. Place vegetables in grill basket (grill "wok"). Place basket on grill. Cover grill; cook vegetables 5 minutes, shaking grill basket or stirring vegetables occasionally, until bell pepper is crisp-tender.

4. Season beef to taste with salt and pepper; cut into 1/4-inch slices. In large bowl, toss beef and 1/4 cup of the dressing. Add salad greens and vegetables. Drizzle with remaining dressing; toss.

Broil Directions: Make dressing as directed. Set oven setting to broil. Place beef on rack in broiler pan. Broil with top 4 to 6 inches from heat 6 minutes. Meanwhile, in medium bowl, toss bell pepper and mushrooms with 2 teaspoons of the dressing. Turn beef over; add vegetables. Broil 5 minutes longer or until beef is desired doneness and bell pepper is crisp-tender. Continue as directed in step 4.

4 servings
1 Serving: Calories 200 (Calories from Fat 110); Total Fat 12g (Saturated Fat 2g; Trans Fat 0g); Cholesterol 45mg; Sodium 40mg; Total Carbohydrate 5g (Dietary Fiber 2g; Sugars 2g); Protein 19g
% Daily Value: Vitamin A 80%; Vitamin C 110%; Calcium 4%; Iron 15%
Exchanges: 1 Vegetableetable, 2 1/2 Lean Meat, 1 Fat
Carbohydrate Choices: 1/2

Latin-Style Flank Steak with Spicy Parsley Pesto

Prep Time: 20 min Start to Finish: 20 min

1 beef flank steak (1 pound)

¼ teaspoon pepper

¼ teaspoon salt

½ cup chopped fresh Italian (flat-leaf) or curly leaf parsley

2 teaspoons red wine vinegar

5 or 6 drops red pepper sauce

⅛ teaspoon ground cumin

1. Place oven rack in second position from the top. Set oven control to broil.

2. On rack in broiler pan, place beef. Sprinkle with pepper and half of the salt. Broil with top 4 to 6 inches from heat 10 to 12 minutes, turning once, until desired doneness.

3. In small bowl, mix parsley, vinegar, pepper sauce, cumin and remaining half of the salt.

4. Cut beef across grain into thin strips. Serve beef with parsley pesto.

4 servings
1 Serving: Calories 180 (Calories from Fat 70); Total Fat 8g (Saturated Fat 3g; Trans Fat 0g); Cholesterol 50mg; Sodium 190mg; Total Carbohydrate 0g (Dietary Fiber 0g; Sugars 0g); Protein 26g
% Daily Value: Vitamin A 15%; Vitamin C 8%; Calcium 0%; Iron 15%
Exchanges: 3½ Lean Meat
Carbohydrate Choices: 0

KITCHEN TIPS

✿ For easy cleanup, line the broiler pan with aluminum foil.
✿ Herb-Roasted Root Vegetables, page 233, are a good accompaniment to the steak, or choose your favorite vegetable.

Low Fat

Grilled Italian Steak and Vegetables

Prep Time: 25 min Start to Finish: 40 min

½ cup fat-free balsamic vinaigrette dressing
¼ cup chopped fresh basil leaves
1½ teaspoons peppered seasoned salt
2 beef boneless New York strip steaks, about 1 inch thick (8 to 10 ounces each)
1 pound asparagus spears, cut into 2-inch pieces
1 medium red onion, cut into thin wedges
1 yellow bell pepper, cut into 8 pieces

1. In large bowl, mix 2 tablespoons of the dressing, 2 tablespoons of the basil and ¾ teaspoon of the peppered seasoned salt; set aside for vegetables. In shallow glass or plastic dish or resealable plastic food-storage bag, mix remaining dressing, basil and peppered seasoned salt; add beef. Cover dish or seal bag; refrigerate 15 minutes to marinate.

2. Heat gas or charcoal grill. Add asparagus, onion and bell pepper to reserved dressing mixture; toss to coat. Place in disposable 8-inch square foil pan or grill basket (grill "wok"). Reserve dressing in bowl.

3. Remove beef from marinade; reserve marinade. Place pan of vegetables on grill. Cover grill; cook 5 minutes. Add beef to grill next to pan. Cover grill; cook beef and vegetables 10 to 12 minutes, turning beef once and stirring vegetables occasionally, until beef is desired doneness and vegetables are tender. Brush beef with reserved marinade during last 5 minutes of cooking.

4. Add vegetables to bowl with reserved dressing; toss to coat. Cut beef into thin slices. Discard any remaining marinade. Serve vegetables with beef. Drizzle with additional dressing if desired.

To Broil: Place pan of vegetables on rack in broiler pan; broil with top 4 to 6 inches from heat 5 minutes. Add beef to rack. Broil beef and vegetables 10 to 12 minutes, turning beef once and stirring vegetables occasionally, until beef is desired doneness and vegetables are tender. Brush beef with reserved marinade during last 5 minutes of cooking.

4 servings
1 Serving: Calories 240 (Calories from Fat 45); Total Fat 5g (Saturated Fat 2g; Trans Fat 0g); Cholesterol 90mg; Sodium 890mg; Total Carbohydrate 10g (Dietary Fiber 2g; Sugars 6g); Protein 38g
% Daily Value: Vitamin A 15%; Vitamin C 50%; Calcium 40%; Iron 25%
Exchanges: ½ Other Carbohydrate, 1 Vegetableetable, 5 Very Lean Meat
Carbohydrate Choices: ½

Szechuan Beef and Bean Sprouts

Strip Steaks with Chipotle-Peach Glaze

Strip Steaks with Chipotle-Peach Glaze

Prep Time: 15 min Start to Finish: 35 min

- ½ cup peach preserves
- ¼ cup lime juice
- 1 chipotle chili in adobo sauce (from 7-ounce can), seeded and chopped
- 1 teaspoon adobo sauce (from can of chilies)
- 2 tablespoons chopped fresh cilantro
- 8 beef boneless strip steaks, 1 inch thick (about 3 pounds)
- 1 teaspoon garlic-pepper blend
- ½ teaspoon ground cumin
- ½ teaspoon salt
- 4 peaches, cut in half and pitted, if desired
  Cilantro sprigs, if desired

1. Heat gas or charcoal grill.

2. In 1-quart saucepan, heat preserves, lime juice, chili and adobo sauce over low heat, stirring occasionally, until preserves are melted. Stir in chopped cilantro; set aside. Sprinkle each beef steak with garlic-pepper blend, cumin and salt.

3. Place beef on grill over medium heat. Cover grill; cook 15 to 18 minutes for medium doneness, turning once or twice and brushing top of beef with preserves mixture during last 2 minutes of cooking. Add peach halves to grill for last 2 to 3 minutes of cooking just until heated.

4. Heat any remaining preserves mixture to boiling; boil and stir 1 minute. Serve with beef and peaches. Garnish with cilantro sprigs.

8 servings
1 Serving: Calories 280 (Calories from Fat 50); Total Fat 6g (Saturated Fat 2g; Trans Fat 0g); Cholesterol 105mg; Sodium 230mg; Total Carbohydrate 15g (Dietary Fiber 0g; Sugars 10g); Protein 41g
% Daily Value: Vitamin A 0%; Vitamin C 4%; Calcium 0%; Iron 25%
Exchanges: 1 Other Carbohydrate, 6 Very Lean Meat
Carbohydrate Choices: 1

Low-Fat
Szechuan Beef and Bean Sprouts

Prep Time: 25 min Start to Finish: 35 min

- 1 pound boneless beef eye of round steak, trimmed of fat
- ¼ cup reduced-sodium chicken broth
- 1 tablespoon reduced-sodium soy sauce
- 1 tablespoon Szechuan sauce
- ⅛ teaspoon crushed red pepper flakes
- 4 roma (plum) tomatoes, cut into 8 pieces
- 2 cups fresh bean sprouts (4 ounces)
- 1 tablespoon chopped fresh cilantro

1. Cut beef with grain into 2-inch strips; cut strips across grain into ⅛-inch slices. (Beef is easier to cut if partially frozen, 30 to 60 minutes.) In medium bowl, stir together broth, soy sauce, Szechuan sauce and pepper flakes. Stir in beef. Let stand 10 minutes.

2. Drain beef; reserve marinade. Heat 12-inch nonstick skillet over medium-high heat. Add half of the beef to skillet; stir-fry 2 to 3 minutes or until brown. Remove beef from skillet. Repeat with remaining beef. Return all beef to skillet.

3. Add reserved marinade, the tomatoes and bean sprouts to beef in skillet; stir-fry about 1 minute or until vegetables are warm. Sprinkle with cilantro.

4 servings (1¼ cups each)
1 Serving: Calories 200 (Calories from Fat 50); Total Fat 6g (Saturated Fat 1.5g; Trans Fat 0g); Cholesterol 65mg; Sodium 340mg; Total Carbohydrate 6g (Dietary Fiber 1g; Sugars 3g); Protein 30g
% Daily Value: Vitamin A 10%; Vitamin C 10%; Calcium 2%; Iron 20%
Exchanges: 1 Vegetableeetable, 4 Very Lean Meat, 1 Fat
Carbohydrate Choices: ½

KITCHEN TIPS

✿ For the leanest cuts of meat, look for the words "round" or "loin" in the name—think eye of round, top round, sirloin or tenderloin.

✿ This dish is high in iron, an important mineral that transports oxygen to all the body's cells. Iron is more easily absorbed when eaten with a food high in vitamin C, like roma tomatoes.

Beef Fajitas

Prep Time: 20 min Start to Finish: 40 min

1 pound boneless beef sirloin steak, cut into thin strips

1 medium green bell pepper, cut into $\frac{1}{2}$-inch strips

1 medium red bell pepper, cut into $\frac{1}{2}$-inch strips

1 medium yellow bell pepper, cut into $\frac{1}{2}$-inch strips

1 medium onion, thinly sliced

1 package (1.25 ounces) fajita seasoning mix

$\frac{1}{3}$ cup water

8 Old El Paso flour tortillas for soft tacos & fajitas (from 10.5-ounce package)

$\frac{3}{4}$ cup Old El Paso Thick n' Chunky salsa, if desired

$\frac{3}{4}$ cup sour cream, if desired

1. Heat gas or charcoal grill. Cut 4 (20 × 18-inch) sheets of heavy-duty aluminum foil. In large bowl, mix beef, bell peppers, onion, seasoning mix and water.

2. Place $\frac{1}{4}$ of beef mixture on center of each foil sheet. Bring up 2 sides of foil over beef mixture so edges meet. Seal edges, making tight $\frac{1}{2}$-inch fold; fold again, allowing space for heat circulation and expansion. Fold other sides to seal.

3. Place packets on grill over low heat. Cover grill; cook 13 to 18 minutes, rotating packets $\frac{1}{2}$ turn after about 6 minutes, until beef is cooked to desired doneness and peppers are tender.

4. To serve, cut large X across top of each packet; carefully fold back to allow steam to escape. Serve beef mixture with tortillas, salsa and sour cream.

4 servings
1 Serving: Calories 460 (Calories from Fat 110); Total Fat 12g (Saturated Fat 3.5g; Trans Fat 2g); Cholesterol 65mg; Sodium 1270mg; Total Carbohydrate 55g (Dietary Fiber 2g; Sugars 5g); Protein 33g
% Daily Value: Vitamin A 25%; Vitamin C 110%; Calcium 15%; Iron 25%
Exchanges: 3 Starch, 1$\frac{1}{2}$ Vegetableetable, 3 Lean Meat
Carbohydrate Choices: 3$\frac{1}{2}$

KITCHEN TIPS

❂ To warm tortillas, wrap them in foil and place on the grill for 5 to 8 minutes.

❂ The fajita mixture can be mixed ahead of time and stored in the refrigerator.

Italian Beef and Ravioli Stew

Prep Time: 30 min Start to Finish: 1 hr 40 min

1 tablespoon olive or vegetable oil

1 medium onion, coarsely chopped (1/2 cup)

2 teaspoons finely chopped garlic

2 teaspoons chopped fresh rosemary leaves

1 medium yellow or green bell pepper, cut into 2-inch strips

2 pounds boneless beef chuck, trimmed of fat and cut into 1-inch pieces

2 cans (14.5 ounces each) diced tomatoes with balsamic vinegar, basil and olive oil, undrained

1/2 cup red wine or beef broth

1 1/2 cups Green Giant frozen cut green beans

1 package (9 ounces) refrigerated cheese-filled ravioli

1. In 4 1/2- to 5-quart Dutch oven, heat oil over medium-high heat. Cook onion, garlic, rosemary and bell pepper in oil 4 to 5 minutes, stirring frequently, until onion is softened. Stir in beef. Cook 6 to 8 minutes, stirring occasionally, until beef is lightly browned.

2. Stir in tomatoes and wine. Heat to boiling; reduce heat to medium-low. Cover; cook 45 to 50 minutes, stirring occasionally, until beef is tender.

3. Stir in frozen green beans and ravioli. Increase heat to medium-high. Cook 8 to 10 minutes, stirring occasionally, until ravioli are tender.

6 servings (1 1/3 cups each)
1 Serving: Calories 395 (Calories from Fat 100); Total Fat 11g (Saturated Fat 4g; Trans Fat 0g); Cholesterol 88mg; Sodium 539mg; Total Carbohydrate 17g (Dietary Fiber 3g; Sugars 7g); Protein 37g
% Daily Value: Vitamin A 15%; Vitamin C 90%; Calcium 8%; Iron 25%
Exchanges: 1/2 Fat, 1/2 Starch, 2 Vegetable, 5 Meat
Carbohydrate Choices: 1

KITCHEN TIPS

- It's hard to beat the flavor of rosemary in this stew, but if you like basil, go ahead and use chopped fresh basil instead.
- Warm Italian peasant bread and herb butter is a delicious combination with this one-dish stew. End the meal on a light note with vanilla frozen yogurt, cappuccino and chocolate-dipped biscotti.
- Top this robust stew with shaved curls of Parmesan cheese and a sprinkling of chopped fresh rosemary leaves.

Chili Mole

Prep Time: 15 min Start to Finish: 4 hr 15 min

1 pound lean (at least 80%) ground beef

1 medium onion, chopped (½ cup)

1 package (1.25 ounces) Tex-Mex chili seasoning mix

1 can (28 ounces) Progresso diced tomatoes, undrained

1 can (28 ounces) Progresso crushed tomatoes, undrained

1 can (15 ounces) spicy chili beans, undrained

1 ounce unsweetened baking chocolate, coarsely chopped

1. Spray 4- to 5-quart slow cooker with cooking spray. In 10-inch skillet, cook beef and onion over medium heat 8 to 10 minutes, stirring occasionally, until beef is thoroughly cooked; drain.

2. In cooker, mix beef mixture and remaining ingredients.

3. Cover; cook on Low heat setting 4 to 6 hours. Stir well before serving.

6 servings (1½ cups each)
1 Serving: Calories 310 (Calories from Fat 110); Total Fat 12g (Saturated Fat 5g; Trans Fat 0.5g); Cholesterol 45mg; Sodium 1100mg; Total Carbohydrate 29g (Dietary Fiber 8g; Sugars 10g); Protein 20g
% Daily Value: Vitamin A 15%; Vitamin C 20%; Calcium 10%; Iron 140%
Exchanges: 1½ Starch, 1 Vegetableetable, 2 Medium-Fat Meat
Carbohydrate Choices: 2

KITCHEN TIPS

✺ Mole (MOH-lay) refers to a Mexican sauce which is characterized by the addition of chocolate.

✺ Serve with wedges of warm corn bread and slices of Cheddar cheese.

Beef and Kasha Mexicana

Prep Time: 10 min Start to Finish: 25 min

1 pound extra-lean (at least 90%) ground beef

1 small onion, chopped ($^{1}/_{2}$ cup)

1 cup uncooked kasha (roasted buckwheat groats)

1 can (14.5 ounces) diced tomatoes, undrained

1 can (4.5 ounces) Old El Paso chopped green chilies, undrained

1 package (1.25 ounces) Old El Paso 40% less sodium taco seasoning mix

2 cups Green Giant Niblets frozen whole kernel corn (from 1-pound bag), thawed

$1^{1}/_{2}$ cups water

1 cup shredded reduced-fat Cheddar cheese (4 ounces)

2 tablespoons chopped fresh cilantro, if desired

2 tablespoons sliced ripe olives, if desired

1. In 12-inch skillet, cook beef and onion over medium-high heat 5 to 7 minutes, stirring occasionally, until beef is thoroughly cooked; drain. Stir in kasha until kernels are moistened by beef mixture.

2. Stir in tomatoes, chilies, taco seasoning mix, corn and water. Heat to boiling. Cover; reduce heat to low. Simmer 5 to 7 minutes, stirring occasionally, until kasha is tender.

3. Sprinkle cheese over kasha mixture. Cover; cook 2 to 3 minutes or until cheese is melted. Sprinkle with cilantro and olives.

6 servings ($1^{1}/_{3}$ cups each)
1 Serving: Calories 300 (Calories from Fat 80); Total Fat 8g (Saturated Fat 3.5g; Trans Fat 0g); Cholesterol 50mg; Sodium 720mg; Total Carbohydrate 33g (Dietary Fiber 4g; Sugars 5g); Protein 23g
% Daily Value: Vitamin A 6%; Vitamin C 15%; Calcium 20%; Iron 20%
Exchanges: $1^{1}/_{2}$ Starch, $^{1}/_{2}$ Other Carbohydrate, $2^{1}/_{2}$ Lean Meat
Carbohydrate Choices: 2

KITCHEN TIPS

✹ This mixture also tastes great as a filling for tortillas.

✹ Kasha, also known as buckwheat groats, is native to Russia and is one of the oldest and most traditional foods. It has a hearty flavor that works well with ginger. Its small size makes it ideal in main dishes because it cooks quickly.

Quick & Low Fat
Meatballs with Roasted Red Pepper Sauce

Prep Time: 15 min Start to Finish: 6 hr 15 min

1½ pounds frozen meatballs (from two 1-pound bags), thawed

1 jar (7.25 ounces) roasted red bell peppers, drained

¼ cup grated Parmesan cheese

¼ cup Italian dressing

1 jar (26 ounces) marinara sauce

16 small sandwich buns, if desired

1. Spray 3- to 4-quart slow cooker with cooking spray. Place meatballs in cooker.

2. In blender, cover and blend bell peppers until smooth. Add cheese and Italian dressing; cover and blend until mixed. Add marinara sauce; pulse until just blended. Pour sauce over meatballs.

3. Cover; cook on Low heat setting 6 to 7 hours.

4. Stir before serving. Meatballs can be kept warm on Low heat setting up to 2 hours; stir occasionally. Use appetizer picks to serve meatballs or, for mini sandwiches, serve meatballs on buns.

16 servings
1 Serving (3 meatballs): Calories 170 (Calories from Fat 80); Total Fat 9g (Saturated Fat 3g; Trans Fat 0g); Cholesterol 45mg; Sodium 530mg; Total Carbohydrate 14g (Dietary Fiber 1g; Sugars 6g); Protein 10g
% Daily Value: Vitamin A 20%; Vitamin C 20%; Calcium 6%; Iron 8%
Exchanges: ½ Starch, ½ Other Carbohydrate, 1 High-Fat Meat
Carbohydrate Choices: 1

KITCHEN TIPS

✺ Sprinkle freshly grated Parmesan cheese and chopped red or green bell pepper over the meatballs just before serving.

✺ Small sandwich buns are sometimes called dollar buns.

Spicy Parmesan Meatballs with Angel Hair Pasta

Prep Time: 50 min Start to Finish: 50 min

¾ cup Fiber One cereal

1 pound extra-lean (at least 90%) ground beef

¼ cup shredded Parmesan cheese (1 ounce)

¾ teaspoon Italian seasoning

¼ teaspoon garlic powder

1 can (8 ounces) tomato sauce

1 can (14.5 ounces) diced tomatoes with green pepper and onion, undrained

⅛ teaspoon ground red pepper (cayenne)

6 ounces uncooked whole wheat capellini (angel hair) pasta

Additional shredded Parmesan cheese, if desired

1 to 2 tablespoons chopped fresh parsley, if desired

1. Place cereal in resealable plastic food-storage bag; seal bag and finely crush with rolling pin or meat mallet.

2. In large bowl, mix cereal, beef, ¼ cup cheese, the Italian seasoning, garlic powder and ¼ cup of the tomato sauce until well blended. Shape into 16 (1½-inch) meatballs.

3. Spray 12-inch skillet with cooking spray. Cook meatballs in skillet over medium heat 8 to 10 minutes, turning occasionally, until browned. Drain if necessary. Add remaining tomato sauce, the tomatoes and red pepper to skillet; turn meatballs to coat.

4. Cover; cook over medium-low heat 15 to 20 minutes, stirring sauce and turning meatballs occasionally, until meatballs are thoroughly cooked and no longer pink in center.

5. Meanwhile, cook and drain pasta as directed on package. Serve meatballs over pasta. Top each serving with additional Parmesan cheese and parsley.

4 servings
1 Serving: Calories 460 (Calories from Fat 110); Total Fat 12g (Saturated Fat 5g; Trans Fat 0.5g); Cholesterol 75mg; Sodium 950mg; Total Carbohydrate 54g (Dietary Fiber 10g; Sugars 9g); Protein 33g
% Daily Value: Vitamin A 10%; Vitamin C 10%; Calcium 20%; Iron 40%
Exchanges: 2½ Starch, 1 Other Carbohydrate, 3½ Lean Meat
Carbohydrate Choices: 3½

Meatball Lasagna

Prep Time: 25 min Start to Finish: 9 hr 40 min

- 1 jar (26 ounces) tomato sauce (any variety)
- 1 can (14.5 ounces) diced tomatoes with Italian herbs, undrained
- 1 box (12 ounces) frozen cooked Italian-style meatballs (12 meatballs), thawed, each cut in half
- 1½ cups frozen bell pepper and onion stir-fry (from 1-pound bag), thawed, drained
- 1 container (15 ounces) ricotta cheese
- 1 egg, beaten
- 2 tablespoons chopped fresh basil leaves
- 8 uncooked lasagna noodles
- 3 cups shredded mozzarella cheese (12 ounces)
- ¼ cup shredded Parmesan cheese (1 ounce)

1. Spray 13 × 9-inch (3-quart) glass baking dish with cooking spray. In large bowl, mix pasta sauce and tomatoes. Reserve ½ cup tomato mixture. Stir meatballs and stir-fry vegetables into remaining tomato mixture.

2. In medium bowl, mix ricotta cheese, egg and basil.

3. Spoon and spread reserved ½ cup tomato mixture in bottom of baking dish. Top with 4 noodles. Top with about half of the ricotta mixture and half of the meatball mixture. Layer with remaining 4 noodles, remaining ricotta mixture, 1 cup mozzarella cheese and remaining meatball mixture. Sprinkle with remaining 2 cups mozzarella cheese and the Parmesan cheese. Spray sheet of aluminum foil with cooking spray; cover baking dish with foil. Refrigerate 8 hours or overnight.

4. Heat oven to 350°F. Bake covered lasagna 45 minutes. Uncover; bake 15 to 20 minutes longer or until bubbly, edges are golden brown and cheese is melted. Let stand 10 minutes before cutting.

8 servings
1 Serving: Calories 436 (Calories from Fat 194); Total Fat 22g (Saturated Fat 12g; Trans Fat 0g); Cholesterol 139mg; Sodium 844mg; Total Carbohydrate 32g (Dietary Fiber 1g; Sugars 9g); Protein 31g
% Daily Value: Vitamin A 30%; Vitamin C 20%; Calcium 40%; Iron 10%
Exchanges: 1½ Fat, 3 Meat, ½ Other Carbohydrate, ½ Starch, 1 Vegetable
Carbohydrate Choices: 2

KITCHEN TIPS

- Thaw the meatballs in the refrigerator overnight, or thaw in the microwave following the directions on the box.
- If desired, you can bake the lasagna right after preparing it.

On the
Side

Savory Side Dishes

Herb-Roasted Root Vegetables (page 233)

Broccoli, Pepper and Bacon Toss (page 223)

Grilled Cashew-Asparagus Packet

Prep Time: 20 min Start to Finish: 20 min

1 pound fresh asparagus spears
2 tablespoons butter or margarine
1/2 teaspoon salt
1/2 teaspoon pepper
1/4 cup chopped cashews

1. Heat gas or charcoal grill. Cut 18 × 18-inch sheet of heavy-duty aluminum foil. Break off tough ends of asparagus as far down as stalks snap easily. Place asparagus on center of foil. Top with butter, salt and pepper.

2. Bring up 2 sides of foil over asparagus so edges meet. Seal edges, making tight 1/2-inch fold; fold again, allowing space for heat circulation and expansion. Fold other sides to seal.

3. Place packet on grill over low heat. Cover grill; cook 10 to 15 minutes, rotating packet 1/2 turn after 4 minutes, until asparagus is tender.

4. To serve, cut large X across top of packet; carefully fold back foil to allow steam to escape. Sprinkle with cashews.

4 servings
1 Serving: Calories 120 (Calories from Fat 90); Total Fat 10g (Saturated Fat 4.5g; Trans Fat 0g); Cholesterol 15mg; Sodium 340mg; Total Carbohydrate 5g (Dietary Fiber 1g; Sugars 1g); Protein 3g
% Daily Value: Vitamin A 15%; Vitamin C 4%; Calcium 0%; Iron 6%
Exchanges: 1 Vegetableetable, 2 Fat
Carbohydrate Choices: 1/2

KITCHEN TIPS

✿ If your asparagus stalks are thin, cook for shorter time.
✿ Pair this dish with Grilled Ginger Salmon Fillets on page 158.

Asparagus and Corn with Honey-Mustard Glaze

Prep Time: 10 min Start to Finish: 20 min

1 pound fresh asparagus spears
1 cup Green Giant frozen whole kernel corn
2 teaspoons Dijon mustard
2 teaspoons honey
$\frac{1}{4}$ teaspoon lemon-pepper seasoning

1. Snap off tough ends of asparagus; cut stalks into 1-inch pieces.

2. In 2-quart saucepan, heat $\frac{1}{2}$ cup water to boiling. Add asparagus and corn; reduce heat. Simmer uncovered 5 to 8 minutes or until asparagus is crisp-tender; drain.

3. In small bowl, mix mustard, honey and lemon-pepper seasoning. Stir into hot vegetables.

5 servings (1$\frac{1}{2}$ cups each)
1 Serving: Calories 50 (Calories from Fat 0); Total Fat 0g (Saturated Fat 0g; Trans Fat 0g); Cholesterol 0mg; Sodium 75mg; Total Carbohydrate 11g (Dietary Fiber 1g; Sugars 4g); Protein 2g
% Daily Value: Vitamin A 10%; Vitamin C 4%; Calcium 0%; Iron 4%
Exchanges: $\frac{1}{2}$ Other Carbohydrate, 1 Vegetableetable
Carbohydrate Choices: 1

KITCHEN TIPS

☸ Green beans, cut into 1-inch pieces, can be substituted for the asparagus.
☸ This colorful side goes well with grilled steaks or chicken and crusty rolls.

Balsamic Green Beans and Fennel

Green Beans with Glazed Shallots in Lemon-Dill Butter

Green Beans with Glazed Shallots in Lemon-Dill Butter

Prep Time: 15 min Start to Finish: 15 min

- 1 pound fresh green beans, trimmed
- 2 tablespoons butter
- 2 shallots, finely chopped
- 1/2 teaspoon sugar
- 1 teaspoon lemon juice
- 1 tablespoon chopped fresh dill weed
- 1/4 teaspoon salt

1. In 4-quart Dutch oven, heat 1 to 2 inches water to boiling. Add beans; boil uncovered 8 to 10 minutes or until crisp-tender. Drain; return to Dutch oven.

2. Meanwhile, in 10-inch skillet, melt butter over medium heat. Add shallots; cook 2 to 3 minutes, stirring occasionally, until crisp-tender. Stir in sugar. Cook 2 to 3 minutes longer, stirring occasionally, until shallots are glazed and brown. Stir in lemon juice, dill weed and salt.

3. Add shallot mixture to green beans; toss to coat.

6 servings
1 Serving: Calories 60 (Calories from Fat 35); Total Fat 4g (Saturated Fat 2.5g; Trans Fat 0g); Cholesterol 10mg; Sodium 130mg; Total Carbohydrate 5g (Dietary Fiber 2g; Sugars 2g); Protein 1g
% Daily Value: Vitamin A 10%; Vitamin C 10%; Calcium 2%; Iron 4%
Exchanges: 1 Vegetableetable, 1 Fat
Carbohydrate Choices: 1/2

KITCHEN TIPS

✿ Shallots look like mini onions and taste like a mild mix of garlic and onion. You can usually find them near the onions in the produce section of the supermarket.

✿ You can substitute 1/4 cup finely chopped onion for the shallots.

Balsamic Green Beans and Fennel

Prep Time: 20 min Start to Finish: 20 min

- 2 teaspoons olive or canola oil
- 1 medium bulb fennel, cut into thin wedges
- 1 small onion, cut into thin wedges
- 2 cups Green Giant Select® frozen whole green beans
- 1/4 cup water
- 2 teaspoons packed brown sugar
- 1/4 teaspoon salt
- 1/4 teaspoon freshly ground black pepper
- 1 tablespoon balsamic vinegar

1. In 12-inch nonstick skillet, heat oil over medium heat. Add fennel and onion; cook 7 to 8 minutes, stirring frequently, until fennel is light golden brown.

2. Add beans and water; heat to boiling. Stir; reduce heat to low. Cover; simmer 6 to 8 minutes or until beans are crisp-tender.

3. Stir in remaining ingredients; cook and stir 15 to 30 seconds longer or until vegetables are coated.

4 servings
1 Serving: Calories 80 (Calories from Fat 25); Total Fat 2.5g (Saturated Fat 0g; Trans Fat 0g); Cholesterol 0mg; Sodium 180mg; Total Carbohydrate 13g (Dietary Fiber 4g; Sugars 6g); Protein 2g
% Daily Value: Vitamin A 8%; Vitamin C 10%; Calcium 6%; Iron 6%
Exchanges: 1/2 Other Carbohydrate, 1 Vegetableetable, 1/2 Fat
Carbohydrate Choices: 1

KITCHEN TIPS

✿ Fennel is cultivated in the Mediterranean and in the United States. Both the bulb and the stems can be eaten raw or cooked. The flavor is a little bit like anise but is sweeter and more delicate. The feathery greenery can be used as a garnish or snipped like dill weed and used for a last-minute flavor enhancer.

Green Beans with Pickled Onions

Prep Time: 25 min Start to Finish: 25 min

- 3 cups fresh green beans, strings removed
- 1/4 cup cider vinegar
- 1 tablespoon sugar
- 1/4 teaspoon salt
- 1/8 teaspoon pepper
- 1/2 medium red onion, very thinly sliced
- 2 teaspoons olive or vegetable oil

1. In 2-quart saucepan, heat 1/2 cup water to boiling over high heat. Add green beans; cover and return to boiling. Reduce heat; simmer covered 10 to 12 minutes or until tender. Drain; cool in colander under cold running water.

2. Meanwhile, in shallow bowl, stir vinegar, sugar, salt and pepper until sugar is dissolved. Add onion; toss to coat. Let stand 10 minutes, tossing occasionally. Drain, reserving 1 tablespoon vinegar mixture.

3. In medium serving bowl, place beans; top with onion. Drizzle with reserved vinegar mixture and the oil; toss to coat.

4 servings
1 Serving: Calories 70 (Calories from Fat 20); Total Fat 2.5g (Saturated Fat 0g; Trans Fat 0g); Cholesterol 0mg; Sodium 150mg; Total Carbohydrate 11g (Dietary Fiber 3g; Sugars 6g); Protein 2g
% Daily Value: Vitamin A 10%; Vitamin C 15%; Calcium 4%; Iron 4%
Exchanges: 1/2 Other Carbohydrate, 1 Vegetableetable, 1/2 Fat
Carbohydrate Choices: 1

KITCHEN TIPS

✿ Quick-pickling the onion tames its heat and gives a beautiful pink color. The flavors go well with grilled salmon, lamb or pork chops.

✿ You can cook the beans up to two days ahead, but for the brightest color, don't toss with the dressing until just before serving.

Company Broccoli Three-Cheese Bake

Prep Time: 10 min Start to Finish: 1 hr

- 1 can (2.8 ounces) French-fried onions
- 2 bags (24 ounces each) Green Giant frozen broccoli & three cheese sauce
- 1 package (3 ounces) cream cheese, cut into cubes
- 1/4 cup chopped red bell pepper, if desired
- 1/2 teaspoon red pepper sauce

1. Heat oven to 350°F. Reserve 1 cup French-fried onions for topping.

2. In 5-quart Dutch oven, mix remaining onions, the broccoli, cream cheese, bell pepper and red pepper sauce. Cover; cook over medium-low heat about 20 minutes, stirring once halfway through cooking, until sauce chips are melted. Transfer to ungreased 2- to 3-quart casserole.

3. Bake uncovered 20 to 25 minutes or until vegetables are tender. Sprinkle reserved onions around outer edge of casserole; bake 5 minutes longer.

14 servings
1 Serving: Calories 110 (Calories from Fat 60); Total Fat 6g (Saturated Fat 2.5g; Trans Fat 1g); Cholesterol 10mg; Sodium 430mg; Total Carbohydrate 9g (Dietary Fiber 2g; Sugars 3g); Protein 3g
% Daily Value: Vitamin A 0%; Vitamin C 20%; Calcium 4%; Iron 2%
Exchanges: 1/2 Other Carbohydrate, 1 Vegetableetable, 1 Fat
Carbohydrate Choices: 1/2

KITCHEN TIPS

✿ To make ahead, prepare recipe through step 2, then cover and refrigerate up to 24 hours. Add 5 to 10 minutes to the bake time to heat thoroughly.

Company Broccoli Three-Cheese Bake

Green Beans with Pickled Onions

Broccoli, Pepper and Bacon Toss

The Ultimate Creamed Corn

Quick

The Ultimate Creamed Corn

Prep Time: 5 min Start to Finish: 2 hr 5 min

- 2 bags (1 pound each) Green Giant Niblets frozen whole kernel corn
- 4 packages (3 ounces each) cream cheese, cut into cubes
- 1 cup milk
- 1/2 cup butter or margarine, melted
- 2 teaspoons sugar
- 1 teaspoon salt
- 1/4 teaspoon pepper

1. Spread corn over bottom of 3- to 4-quart slow cooker. Top with cream cheese cubes. In small bowl, stir together remaining ingredients; pour over corn and cream cheese.

2. Cover; cook on High heat setting 2 to 3 hours.

3. Stir well before serving. Corn will hold on Low heat setting up to 2 hours; stir occasionally.

10 servings
1 Serving: Calories 300 (Calories from Fat 200); Total Fat 22g (Saturated Fat 14g; Trans Fat 1g); Cholesterol 65mg; Sodium 410mg; Total Carbohydrate 20g (Dietary Fiber 2g; Sugars 5g); Protein 6g
% Daily Value: Vitamin A 20%; Vitamin C 2%; Calcium 6%; Iron 4%
Exchanges: 1 Other Carbohydrate, 1 Vegetableetable, 1/2 High-Fat Meat,
3 1/2 Fat
Carbohydrate Choices: 1

KITCHEN TIPS

- ✿ Sprinkle thinly sliced green onions on top of the creamed corn just before serving to give the dish a dash of color.
- ✿ Reduced-fat cream cheese (Neufchâtel) can be used in place of the regular cream cheese.

Quick

Broccoli, Pepper and Bacon Toss

Prep Time: 15 min Start to Finish: 15 min

- 1 bag (14 ounces) Green Giant Select frozen broccoli florets
- 2 cups frozen bell pepper and onion stir-fry (from 1-pound bag)
- 1/2 cup raisins
- 2 tablespoons reduced-fat coleslaw dressing
- 2 tablespoons real bacon pieces (from 2.8-ounce package)

1. Cook broccoli and bell pepper and onion stir-fry separately in microwave as directed on bags. Drain well.

2. In large bowl, toss broccoli, bell pepper and onion stir-fry, raisins and coleslaw dressing. Sprinkle with bacon. Serve warm.

6 servings (1/2 cup each)
1 Serving: Calories 110 (Calories from Fat 20); Total Fat 2g (Saturated Fat 0g; Trans Fat 0g); Cholesterol 0mg; Sodium 65mg; Total Carbohydrate 19g (Dietary Fiber 3g; Sugars 11g); Protein 4g
% Daily Value: Vitamin A 15%; Vitamin C 35%; Calcium 4%; Iron 4%
Exchanges: 1 Starch, 1 Vegetableetable
Carbohydrate Choices: 1

Chive-and-Onion Creamed Corn

Prep Time: 20 min Start to Finish: 3 hr

4 slices bacon

4½ cups Green Giant Niblets frozen whole kernel corn (from two 1-pound bags), thawed

½ medium red bell pepper, chopped (½ cup)

½ cup milk

¼ cup butter or margarine, melted

1 teaspoon sugar

½ teaspoon salt

⅛ teaspoon pepper

1 container (8 ounces) reduced-fat chive-and-onion cream cheese

1. In 12-inch nonstick skillet, cook bacon over medium-high heat, turning occasionally, until crisp. Drain on paper towels. Crumble bacon.

2. Spray 3- to 4-quart slow cooker with cooking spray. In cooker, mix corn, bell pepper, milk, butter, sugar, salt, pepper and half of the bacon. Refrigerate remaining bacon.

3. Cover; cook on High heat setting 2 hours to 2 hours 30 minutes.

4. Stir in cream cheese. Cook on High heat setting 10 minutes longer. Stir well; sprinkle with remaining bacon. Corn can be kept warm on Low heat setting up to 1 hour.

8 servings (½ cup each)
1 Serving: Calories 220 (Calories from Fat 110); Total Fat 12g (Saturated Fat 7g; Trans Fat 0g); Cholesterol 35mg; Sodium 460mg; Total Carbohydrate 21g (Dietary Fiber 2g; Sugars 6g); Protein 6g
% Daily Value: Vitamin A 20%; Vitamin C 15%; Calcium 6%; Iron 2%
Exchanges: 1½ Starch, 2 Fat
Carbohydrate Choices: 1½

KITCHEN TIPS

❂ Sprinkle with chopped fresh chives for an added burst of color.

❂ Company coming? Serve this with baked ham.

Quick

Grilled Corn on the Cob with Herb Butter

Prep Time: 30 min Start to Finish: 30 min

1/4 cup butter or margarine

1/2 teaspoon garlic salt

2 tablespoons chopped fresh chives

6 ears fresh sweet corn, husks removed, cleaned

1/4 cup grated Parmesan cheese

1. Heat gas or charcoal grill. Cut 30 × 18-inch sheet of heavy-duty aluminum foil. In small microwavable bowl, place butter, garlic salt and chives. Microwave uncovered on High 15 to 20 seconds or until butter is melted.

2. Brush butter mixture over each ear of corn. Place corn on center of foil. Pour any remaining butter mixture over corn. Sprinkle with cheese.

3. Bring up 2 sides of foil over corn so edges meet. Seal edges, making tight 1/2-inch fold; fold again, allowing space for heat circulation and expansion. Fold other sides to seal.

4. Place packet on grill over low heat. Cover grill; cook 12 to 18 minutes, rotating packet 1/2 turn after every 6 minutes, until corn is tender.

5. To serve, cut large X across top of packet; carefully fold back foil to allow steam to escape.

6 servings
1 Serving: Calories 210 (Calories from Fat 90); Total Fat 10g (Saturated Fat 6g; Trans Fat 0g); Cholesterol 25mg; Sodium 220mg; Total Carbohydrate 25g (Dietary Fiber 4g; Sugars 3g); Protein 5g
% Daily Value: Vitamin A 10%; Vitamin C 6%; Calcium 6%; Iron 4%
Exchanges: 1 1/2 Starch, 2 Fat
Carbohydrate Choices: 1 1/2

KITCHEN TIPS

✿ Cooking an entrée and vegetable packets on the same grill? Move packets to the top rack, and add 5 minutes to the recipe cooking time.

✿ If you've run out of heavy-duty foil, layer two sheets of standard foil to make your packet.

Quick

Grilled Savory Cheese Potatoes

Prep Time: 30 min Start to Finish: 30 min

4   cups frozen potatoes O'Brien with onions and peppers (from 28-ounce bag)

½   cup ranch dressing

1   cup shredded Cheddar-American cheese blend (4 ounces)

2   tablespoons grated Parmesan cheese

5 servings
1 Serving: Calories 280 (Calories from Fat 180); Total Fat 20g (Saturated Fat 7g; Trans Fat 0g); Cholesterol 35mg; Sodium 390mg; Total Carbohydrate 17g (Dietary Fiber 1g; Sugars 2g); Protein 8g
% Daily Value: Vitamin A 4%; Vitamin C 4%; Calcium 15%; Iron 0%
Exchanges: 1 Starch, ½ High-Fat Meat, 3 Fat
Carbohydrate Choices: 1

KITCHEN TIPS

✪ Slide the foil pan from the grill to a cutting board or tray to easily transport it to the table.
✪ Try using any of the popular cheese blends available, such as Mexican or Italian, for this recipe.

1. Heat gas or charcoal grill. Spray 12 × 8-inch foil pan with cooking spray. Place potatoes in pan. Drizzle with dressing; mix gently. Sprinkle with shredded cheese blend. Cover pan with foil.

2. Place pan on grill over medium heat. Cover grill; cook 20 to 25 minutes, rotating pan ½ turn after 10 minutes, until potatoes are tender.

3. To serve, carefully remove foil. Sprinkle with Parmesan cheese.

Classic Mashed Potatoes

Prep Time: 30 min Start to Finish: 55 min

4 pounds russet or white potatoes
(10 to 12 medium), peeled, cut into pieces

²/₃ to 1 cup milk, warmed

½ cup butter or margarine, softened

1 teaspoon salt

¼ teaspoon pepper

1. In 4-quart saucepan, place potatoes and add enough water to cover. Heat to boiling. Reduce heat; cover and cook 20 to 25 minutes or until potatoes are tender. (Cooking time will vary depending on size of potato pieces and type of potato used.) Drain and return to saucepan.

2. Heat potatoes over low heat about 1 minute, shaking pan often to keep potatoes from sticking and burning, to dry potatoes (this will help make mashed potatoes fluffier).

3. Mash potatoes in pan with potato masher until no lumps remain. Add milk in small amounts, mashing after each addition. (Amount of milk needed to make potatoes smooth and fluffy depends on type of potatoes used.) Add butter, salt and pepper. Mash vigorously until potatoes are light and fluffy.

16 servings
1 Serving: Calories 150 (Calories from Fat 50); Total Fat 6g (Saturated Fat 4g; Trans Fat 0g); Cholesterol 15mg; Sodium 200mg; Total Carbohydrate 21g (Dietary Fiber 2g; Sugars 1g); Protein 2g
% Daily Value: Vitamin A 4%; Vitamin C 6%; Calcium 2%; Iron 0%
Exchanges: 1 Starch, ½ Other Carbohydrate, 1 Fat
Carbohydrate Choices: 1½

KITCHEN TIPS

❂ Softening the butter and warming the milk before adding to the potatoes will make the mashed potatoes smoother and keep them warm longer.

❂ We based the serving size of this recipe on ½ cup. Because someone at your table may want a larger serving, it's helpful to know this recipe makes 8 cups or 16 (½-cup) servings.

Betty Crocker
MAKES IT EASY

Mashed Potatoes

Mashed potatoes should be light and fluffy with little or no potato lumps. You want to avoid sticky or gummy potatoes.

Smashing Mashed Potato Tips

▶ Russet potatoes will make fluffier mashed potatoes.

▶ Yellow, white and red potatoes will need a little extra TLC to turn them into mashed because they can become gummy.

▶ Leaving the skin on adds flavor and nutrients. Simply scrub skins with a vegetable brush, clean cloth or sponge.

▶ Cut potatoes into pieces of the same size before cooking.

▶ Cut potatoes can be stored in cold water up to 2 hours before cooking to prevent darkening.

▶ Cook potatoes over medium heat. When potatoes are fork-tender, drain them right away. Return to the same pan, and cook over low heat about 1 minute to remove excess water and to dry the potatoes, shaking the pan frequently to keep the potatoes from burning.

▶ Be sure to heat the milk to prevent potatoes from becoming sticky.

▶ Beat potatoes only until light and fluffy. Overbeating will cause potatoes to become gummy. If you use an electric mixer, be especially careful not to overbeat.

For Classic Mashed Potatoes recipe, see page 227.

Quick

Country Ranch Smashed Potatoes

Prep Time: 15 min Start to Finish: 5 hr 15 min

3 pounds small red potatoes

⅓ cup water

1 cup sour cream-and-chive potato topper (from 12-ounce container)

2 tablespoons ranch dressing and seasoning mix (from 1-ounce package)

⅓ cup half-and-half

12 servings (½ cup each)
1 Serving: Calories 140 (Calories from Fat 40); Total Fat 4g (Saturated Fat 2.5g; Trans Fat 0g); Cholesterol 5mg; Sodium 280mg; Total Carbohydrate 23g (Dietary Fiber 2g; Sugars 3g); Protein 3g
% Daily Value: Vitamin A 4%; Vitamin C 10%; Calcium 8%; Iron 10%
Exchanges: 1 Starch, ½ Other Carbohydrate, ½ Fat
Carbohydrate Choices: 1½

KITCHEN TIPS

❂ For Cheesy Smashed Potatoes, fold in 1 cup shredded Cheddar cheese after stirring in the half-and-half.

❂ Serve with sliced ham and steamed whole green beans.

1. Spray 5- to 6-quart slow cooker with cooking spray. Cut potatoes into halves or quarters as needed to make similar-size pieces. Place potatoes in cooker. Add water; mix well to coat all pieces.

2. Cover; cook on Low heat setting 5 to 6 hours.

3. Gently mash potatoes with fork or potato masher. Stir in potato topper and dry dressing mix. Stir in half-and-half until potatoes are soft consistency. Potatoes can be kept warm on Low heat setting up to 1 hour; stir occasionally.

The Ultimate Slow Cooker Potatoes

Prep Time: 15 min Start to Finish: 1 hr 45 min

3 cups boiling water

1½ cups milk

½ cup butter or margarine, cut into pieces

½ cup sour cream

1 package (8 ounces) cream cheese, cut into cubes

1 teaspoon garlic salt

¼ teaspoon pepper

4 cups Betty Crocker Potato Buds® mashed potatoes (dry)

Gravy or chopped fresh parsley, if desired

Stove-Top Directions: In 4-quart Dutch oven, heat water, milk and butter to boiling. Stir in sour cream and cream cheese until blended. Remove from heat. Add garlic salt, pepper and mashed potatoes (dry); whip with fork just until moistened. If potatoes become too thick, stir in additional milk, a couple tablespoons at a time.

1. Spray 3- to 4-quart slow cooker with cooking spray. In cooker, mix boiling water, milk, butter, sour cream and cream cheese with wire whisk until blended. Add garlic salt, pepper and mashed potatoes (dry); mix just until blended.

2. Cover; cook on Low heat setting 1 hour 30 minutes, stirring once after 1 hour.

3. Before serving, stir potatoes. Serve immediately, or hold in slow cooker on Low heat setting up to 3 hours, stirring every 30 minutes. If potatoes become too thick, stir in additional milk, a couple table-spoons at a time. Serve with gravy or sprinkle with chopped parsley.

12 servings
1 Serving: Calories 250 (Calories from Fat 150); Total Fat 17g (Saturated Fat 11g; Trans Fat 0.5g); Cholesterol 50mg; Sodium 230mg; Total Carbohydrate 20g (Dietary Fiber 1g; Sugars 2g); Protein 5g
% Daily Value: Vitamin A 10%; Vitamin C 0%; Calcium 6%; Iron 4%
Exchanges: 1½ Starch, 3 Fat
Carbohydrate Choices: 1

KITCHEN TIPS

✿ Add your own personal touch to delicious potatoes. Sprinkle with chopped fresh chives, canned French-fried onions or freshly grated Parmesan cheese.

✿ Toting these potatoes to a gathering? Loop a large, sturdy rubber band from handle to handle across the slow cooker cover to keep it sealed during transit.

Quick

Yummy Fries

Prep Time: 10 min Start to Finish: 35 min

- 1 bag (22 ounces) frozen waffle potato fries
- ¼ cup chopped fresh parsley
- 1 teaspoon garlic powder
- ½ teaspoon seasoned salt
- ¼ teaspoon pepper
- 6 tablespoons ranch dressing

1. Heat oven to 450°F. Arrange fries in single layer on cookie sheet. Bake 17 to 23 minutes or until desired crispness.

2. Meanwhile, in medium bowl, mix remaining ingredients except ranch dressing. Add baked fries; toss to coat. Serve with dressing.

6 servings
1 Serving: Calories 270 (Calories from Fat 150); Total Fat 16g (Saturated Fat 3g; Trans Fat 2.5g); Cholesterol 0mg; Sodium 570mg; Total Carbohydrate 27g (Dietary Fiber 2g; Sugars 2g); Protein 3g **% Daily Value:** Vitamin A 4%; Vitamin C 4%; Calcium 0%; Iron 6% **Exchanges:** 1 Starch, 1 Other Carbohydrate, 3 Fat **Carbohydrate Choices:** 2

KITCHEN TIPS

✿ Seasoned salt is a mixture of salt and spices, such as paprika, garlic, turmeric and onion, that jazzes up foods with a couple of shakes.

Mashed Sweet Potatoes with Bacon

Prep Time: 25 min   Start to Finish: 1 hr 45 min

3   pounds dark-orange sweet potatoes
     (about 4 potatoes)
8   slices bacon
1   large onion, chopped ($^3/_4$ cup)
$^1/_4$ cup half-and-half, warmed
1   teaspoon chopped fresh thyme leaves
$^1/_2$ teaspoon salt
$^1/_4$ teaspoon pepper
     Fresh thyme sprigs, if desired

1. Heat oven to 350°F. Pierce sweet potatoes all over
   with fork; place on cookie sheet with sides. Bake
   about 1 hour 15 minutes or until tender when pierced
   with fork. Let stand 15 minutes or until cool enough
   to handle.

2. Meanwhile, in 10-inch skillet, cook bacon over
   medium-high heat 4 minutes, turning occasionally,
   until brown. Remove bacon from skillet; place on
   paper towels to drain. Reserve 1 tablespoon drippings in skillet; discard remaining drippings. Add
   onion to skillet; cook over medium heat 5 to 8 minutes, stirring occasionally, until softened.

3. Peel sweet potatoes; place in large bowl. Mash until
   no lumps remain. Add warm half-and-half, thyme,
   salt and pepper; mash until very smooth.

4. Add onion to sweet potatoes. Crumble bacon;
   reserve 2 tablespoons for garnish. Add remaining
   bacon to potatoes; stir until blended. Garnish with
   reserved bacon and thyme sprigs.

10 servings
1 Serving: Calories 130 (Calories from Fat 30); Total Fat 3.5g
(Saturated Fat 1.5g; Trans Fat 0g); Cholesterol 10mg; Sodium 300mg;
Total Carbohydrate 19g (Dietary Fiber 3g; Sugars 8g); Protein 4g
% Daily Value: Vitamin A 320%; Vitamin C 15%; Calcium 4%; Iron 4%
Exchanges: 1 Starch, $^1/_2$ Other Carbohydrate, $^1/_2$ Fat
Carbohydrate Choices: 1

KITCHEN TIPS

❁ Two varieties of sweet potatoes are commercially grown
  in the United States, one with light yellow skin and pale
  yellow flesh and a darker-skinned variety with dark orange
  flesh. The darker of the two is often confused with yams
  of Africa and Central and South America.

❁ Store sweet potatoes in a cool, dark, dry place to keep
  them fresh.

Herb-Roasted Root Vegetables

Prep Time: 15 min Start to Finish: 1 hr 10 min

2 medium turnips, peeled, cut into 1-inch pieces (3 cups)

2 medium parsnips, peeled, cut into 1/2-inch pieces (1 1/2 cups)

1 medium red onion, cut into 1-inch wedges (1 cup)

1 cup ready-to-eat baby-cut carrots
   Cooking spray

2 teaspoons Italian seasoning

1/2 teaspoon coarse salt

1. Heat oven to 425°F. Spray 15 × 10 × 1-inch pan with cooking spray. Arrange vegetables in single layer in pan. Spray with cooking spray (2 or 3 seconds). Sprinkle with Italian seasoning and salt.

2. Bake uncovered 45 to 55 minutes, stirring once, until vegetables are tender.

6 servings (1/2 cup each)
1 Serving: Calories 70 (Calories from Fat 5); Total Fat 0.5g (Saturated Fat 0g; Trans Fat 0g); Cholesterol 0mg; Sodium 260mg; Total Carbohydrate 14g (Dietary Fiber 4g; Sugars 7g); Protein 1g
% Daily Value: Vitamin A 70%; Vitamin C 20%; Calcium 4%; Iron 4%
Exchanges: 1/2 Starch, 1 Vegetableetable
Carbohydrate Choices: 1

KITCHEN TIPS

❂ Roasting brings out the natural sweetness of vegetables. As some of the moisture is evaporated in the high heat, the sugar is concentrated, so the vegetables taste sweeter.

❂ Roasting is a great, low-fat way to cook because no fat is added. Other low-fat ways to cook are: broiling, boiling, grilling, braising and simmering.

Zucchini with Edamame and Tomatoes

Prep Time: 10 min Start to Finish: 15 min

1 small zucchini, cut lengthwise into fourths, then cut crosswise into $\frac{1}{2}$-inch slices

1 cup refrigerated fully cooked ready-to-eat shelled edamame or frozen (thawed) shelled edamame

1 medium tomato, coarsely chopped ($\frac{1}{2}$ cup)

2 teaspoons chopped fresh basil leaves

$\frac{1}{4}$ teaspoon garlic salt

$\frac{1}{8}$ teaspoon pepper

1 tablespoon shredded Parmesan cheese

1. In 2-quart saucepan, heat $\frac{1}{4}$ cup water to boiling over medium heat. Add zucchini and edamame; simmer 3 to 5 minutes or until vegetables are crisp-tender. Drain well; return to saucepan.

2. Stir in remaining ingredients except cheese. Cook and stir about 1 minute or until heated.

3. Place zucchini mixture in serving dish. Sprinkle with cheese.

4 servings ($\frac{1}{2}$ cup each)
1 Serving: Calories 60 (Calories from Fat 20); Total Fat 2.5g (Saturated Fat 0.5g; Trans Fat 0g); Cholesterol 0mg; Sodium 95mg; Total Carbohydrate 5g (Dietary Fiber 2g; Sugars 2g); Protein 5g
% Daily Value: Vitamin A 6%; Vitamin C 10%; Calcium 6%; Iron 4%
Exchanges: 1 Vegetableetable, $\frac{1}{2}$ Very Lean Meat, $\frac{1}{2}$ Fat
Carbohydrate Choices: $\frac{1}{2}$

Lemon-Spinach Couscous

Prep Time: 15 min Start to Finish: 20 min

2 teaspoons olive oil

$\frac{1}{2}$ cup chopped red bell pepper

2 cloves garlic, finely chopped

$1\frac{1}{3}$ cups water

$\frac{1}{2}$ teaspoon salt

$\frac{1}{8}$ teaspoon pepper

1 cup uncooked whole wheat couscous

2 teaspoons finely grated lemon peel

2 cups firmly packed fresh baby spinach leaves (3 ounces)

Lemon wedges, if desired

1. In 2-quart saucepan, heat oil over medium heat. Add bell pepper and garlic; cook 3 to 4 minutes, stirring frequently, until tender.

2. Stir in water, salt and pepper. Heat to boiling. Remove from heat; stir in couscous and lemon peel. Layer spinach on top of couscous. Cover; let stand about 5 minutes or until liquid is absorbed. With fork, stir spinach into couscous until spinach is wilted, about 1 minute. Serve with lemon wedges.

6 servings ($\frac{2}{3}$ cup each)
1 Serving: Calories 140 (Calories from Fat 20); Total Fat 2g (Saturated Fat 0g; Trans Fat 0g); Cholesterol 0mg; Sodium 210mg; Total Carbohydrate 25g (Dietary Fiber 3g; Sugars 0g); Protein 4g
% Daily Value: Vitamin A 35%; Vitamin C 20%; Calcium 2%; Iron 8%
Exchanges: $1\frac{1}{2}$ Starch, $\frac{1}{2}$ Fat
Carbohydrate Choices: $1\frac{1}{2}$

Zucchini with Edamame and Tomatoes

Lemon-Spinach Couscous

Pecan-Topped Corn Bread with Honey Butter

Quick

Pecan-Topped Corn Bread with Honey Butter

Prep Time: 20 min Start to Finish: 1 hr 15 min

Corn Bread

  1 cup cornmeal

  1 cup Gold Medal all-purpose flour

  1/3 cup sugar

  1/4 cup butter or margarine, melted

  2 teaspoons baking powder

  1/4 teaspoon salt

  3 eggs

  1 can (14.75 ounces) Green Giant cream-style corn

  1/4 cup chopped pecans

Honey Butter

  1/2 cup butter, softened (do not use margarine)

  1/4 cup honey

    Dash salt

1. Heat oven to 375°F. Spray 8- or 9-inch round cake pan with baking spray with flour. In medium bowl, stir all corn bread ingredients except pecans until well blended. Pour into pan. Sprinkle pecans evenly over top.

2. Bake 35 to 45 minutes or until toothpick inserted in center comes out clean.

3. Meanwhile, in small bowl, beat 1/2 cup butter with spoon until creamy. Slowly beat in honey and salt until well blended.

4. Serve warm corn bread with honey butter.

12 servings
1 Serving: Calories 300 (Calories from Fat 140); Total Fat 15g (Saturated Fat 8g; Trans Fat 0g); Cholesterol 85mg; Sodium 320mg; Total Carbohydrate 35g (Dietary Fiber 1g; Sugars 13g); Protein 5g
% Daily Value: Vitamin A 10%; Vitamin C 2%; Calcium 6%; Iron 8%
Exchanges: 1 Starch, 1 1/2 Other Carbohydrate, 3 Fat
Carbohydrate Choices: 2

KITCHEN TIPS

✪ Keep your cornmeal fresh by storing it in the refrigerator or freezer.

✪ Don't like pecans? Feel free to leave them out.

Low Fat
Cranberry-Raspberry Sauce

Prep Time: 20 min Start to Finish: 1 hr

   3   cups fresh cranberries (12 ounces)

1½ cups packed brown sugar

 ¾ cup water

 ½ cup seedless raspberry jam

1. In 2-quart saucepan, mix cranberries, brown sugar and water. Heat to boiling over high heat. Reduce heat to medium-high. Cook 8 to 10 minutes, stirring frequently, until mixture is thick and all cranberries have popped. Cool slightly, about 10 minutes.

2. Strain cranberry mixture, pressing berries to extract juice; discard berry skins. Stir jam into warm juice. Cool 30 minutes.

12 servings
1 Serving: Calories 140 (Calories from Fat 0); Total Fat 0g (Saturated Fat 0g; Trans Fat 0g); Cholesterol 0mg; Sodium 15mg; Total Carbohydrate 35g (Dietary Fiber 1g; Sugars 31g); Protein 0g
% Daily Value: Vitamin A 0%; Vitamin C 4%; Calcium 2%; Iron 4%
Exchanges: 2½ Other Carbohydrate
Carbohydrate Choices: 2

KITCHEN TIPS

✿ If you like a chunky sauce, skip the straining step.
✿ Granulated sugar can be substituted for the brown sugar.

Quick

Cranberry-Pear Chutney

Prep Time: 45 min Start to Finish: 3 hr 15 min

1 pound fresh or frozen cranberries (4 cups)
2 small pears, peeled, chopped (about 1½ cups)
1 large onion, chopped (1 cup)
1 cup granulated sugar
½ cup packed brown sugar
½ cup golden raisins
1 cup water
2 teaspoons ground cinnamon
1½ teaspoons ground ginger
¼ teaspoon ground cloves
¼ teaspoon ground allspice

1. In 3-quart saucepan, mix all ingredients. Heat to boiling over high heat, stirring frequently.

2. Reduce heat to medium. Cook 25 to 30 minutes, stirring occasionally, until thickened.

3. Cool at room temperature 30 minutes, then refrigerate at least 2 hours. Chutney will thicken more as it cools. Store in refrigerator up to 2 weeks.

16 servings
1 Serving: Calories 120 (Calories from Fat 0); Total Fat 0g (Saturated Fat 0g; Trans Fat 0g); Cholesterol 0mg; Sodium 0mg; Total Carbohydrate 29g (Dietary Fiber 2g; Sugars 25g); Protein 0g
% Daily Value: Vitamin A 0%; Vitamin C 4%; Calcium 0%; Iron 2%
Exchanges: 2 Other Carbohydrate
Carbohydrate Choices: 2

KITCHEN TIPS

✿ This chutney is very tart and goes well with any cooked meat. If you prefer your chutney on the sweeter side, increase the sugar to 1½ cups.

✿ Golden raisins come from the same grape as regular raisins, but golden raisins are treated with sulfur dioxide to prevent darkening and then dried with artificial heat to give a plumper, moister raisin with a pale gold color.

Quick

Three-Seed Flatbread

Prep Time: 10 min Start to Finish: 1 hr 15 min

6 frozen unbaked large whole wheat rolls (from 48-ounce package)
2 teaspoons olive or canola oil
3 cloves garlic, finely chopped
1 teaspoon ground flaxseed or flaxseed meal
$\frac{1}{2}$ teaspoon black sesame seed or poppy seed
$\frac{1}{2}$ teaspoon white sesame seed
$\frac{1}{2}$ teaspoon salt
$\frac{1}{4}$ teaspoon dried basil leaves
2 tablespoons shredded Parmesan cheese

1. On microwavable plate, place frozen rolls. Cover with microwavable plastic wrap; microwave on High 25 seconds. Turn rolls over; rotate plate $\frac{1}{2}$ turn. Microwave on High 25 seconds longer to thaw.

2. Spray 13 × 9-inch pan with cooking spray. On lightly floured surface, knead roll dough together. Pat dough in bottom of pan; brush with oil. Sprinkle with remaining ingredients.

3. Cover; let rise in warm place about 40 minutes or until slightly puffy.

4. Heat oven to 350°F. Bake 20 to 22 minutes or until golden brown. Cut into 12 squares.

12 servings
1 Serving: Calories 70 (Calories from Fat 20); Total Fat 2g (Saturated Fat 0.5g; Trans Fat 0g); Cholesterol 0mg; Sodium 230mg; Total Carbohydrate 10g (Dietary Fiber 1g; Sugars 2g); Protein 3g
% Daily Value: Vitamin A 0%; Vitamin C 0%; Calcium 4%; Iron 4%
Exchanges: $\frac{1}{2}$ Starch, $\frac{1}{2}$ Fat
Carbohydrate Choices: $\frac{1}{2}$

KITCHEN TIPS

✪ Olive oil is a great choice for this three-seed bread. It contains monounsaturated fat and antioxidants. A simple change, like replacing butter with olive oil, can help lower cholesterol.

Cupcakes, Bars and Cookies

Delectable Bites

Snow-Capped Gingersnaps (page 268)

Lemon Burst Cupcakes (page 245)

Turkey Cupcakes

Prep Time: 30 min Start to Finish: 1 hr 30 min

1 box Betty Crocker SuperMoist® devil's food cake mix

Water, vegetable oil and eggs called for on cake mix box

2 containers (1 pound each) Betty Crocker Rich & Creamy milk chocolate frosting

1 tube (4.25 ounces) Betty Crocker white decorating icing

1 bag (11 ounces) candy corn (1$\frac{2}{3}$ cups)

$\frac{1}{2}$ cup Betty Crocker chocolate candy sprinkles

1. Heat oven to 350°F for shiny metal pans (or 325°F for dark or nonstick pans). Make and bake 24 cupcakes as directed on box, using water, oil and eggs. Cool in pan 10 minutes; remove from pan to cooling rack. Cool completely, about 30 minutes.

2. Frost cupcakes with frosting. Place remaining frosting in corner of resealable plastic freezer bag; seal bag. Cut small tip off one bottom corner of bag.

3. To decorate each cupcake, pipe 1-inch mound of frosting on one side of cupcake for head of turkey. Make eyes with white decorating icing. Using a toothpick, add a dot of chocolate frosting to each eye. Add candy corn for beak. To make feathers, pipe frosting on opposite side from "head" to hold candy corn; place candy corn upright on frosting to look like feathers. Sprinkle chocolate candy sprinkles near head and at base of feathers. If desired, add candy corn at base of cupcake for feet. Store loosely covered at room temperature.

24 cupcakes
1 Cupcake: Calories 290 (Calories from Fat 110); Total Fat 13g (Saturated Fat 3.5g; Trans Fat 2.5g); Cholesterol 25mg; Sodium 280mg; Total Carbohydrate 42g (Dietary Fiber 0g; Sugars 32g); Protein 2g
% Daily Value: Vitamin A 0%; Vitamin C 0%; Calcium 0%; Iron 10%
Exchanges: $\frac{1}{2}$ Starch, 2 Other Carbohydrate, 2$\frac{1}{2}$ Fat
Carbohydrate Choices: 3

KITCHEN TIPS

✿ If you don't need all 24 frosted and decorated cupcakes, freeze the remaining unfrosted ones for a later use. Frost and decorate when needed—frozen cupcakes are also easier to frost!

✿ Get a head start on these cupcakes by baking them in advance. Tightly cover the unfrosted cupcakes and freeze up to 2 months.

Teddy-at-the-Beach Cupcakes

Prep Time: 30 min Start to Finish: 1 hr 35 min

1 box Betty Crocker SuperMoist cake mix (any flavor)

Water, vegetable oil and eggs called for on cake mix box

2 drops blue food color

1 cup Betty Crocker Whipped vanilla frosting (from 12-ounce container)

1 roll (from 4.5-ounce box) Betty Crocker Fruit by the Foot® chewy fruit snack (any flavor)

½ cup teddy bear-shaped graham snacks, crushed, or brown sugar

1 tablespoon blue sugar or edible glitter, if desired

12 teddy bear-shaped graham snacks

12 paper drink umbrellas or small plastic umbrellas, if desired

12 ring-shaped gummy candies

12 multi-colored fish-shaped crackers

1. Heat oven to 350°F for shiny metal pans (or 325°F for dark or nonstick pans). Place paper baking cup in each of 24 regular-size muffin cups.

2. In large bowl, make cake mix as directed on box, using water, oil and eggs. Divide batter evenly among muffin cups.

3. Bake as directed on box or until toothpick inserted in center comes out clean. Cool 10 minutes; remove from pan to cooling rack. Cool completely, about 30 minutes. Tightly wrap 12 cupcakes; freeze for a later use.

4. Stir blue food color into frosting until blended. Frost cupcakes with frosting.

5. Cut 12 (1½-inch) pieces from fruit snack roll; peel off paper backing. Use fruit snack, crushed graham snacks, blue sugar, teddy bear-shaped snacks, umbrellas, gummy candies and fish-shaped crackers to decorate cupcakes as shown in photo or as desired.

12 cupcakes
1 Frosted Cupcake (Undecorated): Calories 190 (Calories from Fat 80); Total Fat 9g (Saturated Fat 2.5g; Trans Fat 1.5g); Cholesterol 25mg; Sodium 160mg; Total Carbohydrate 28g (Dietary Fiber 0g; Sugars 19g); Protein 1g
% Daily Value: Vitamin A 0%; Vitamin C 0%; Calcium 4%; Iron 2%
Exchanges: ½ Starch, 1½ Other Carbohydrate, 1½ Fat
Carbohydrate Choices: 2

KITCHEN TIPS

✿ If you have Betty Crocker decorating icing (in 4.25-ounce tubes), use the writing tip to pipe swimsuits on the bears.

✿ The small plastic umbrellas can be found at www.fancyflours.com.

Pirate's Hidden Treasure Cupcakes

Prep Time: 50 min Start to Finish: 1 hr 55 min

1 box Betty Crocker SuperMoist chocolate fudge cake mix

1 cup water

½ cup vegetable oil

3 eggs

24 miniature chocolate-covered peanut butter cup candies (from 12-ounce bag), unwrapped

1 container (1 pound) Betty Crocker Rich & Creamy vanilla frosting

2 rolls (from 4.5-ounce box) Betty Crocker Fruit by the Foot chewy fruit snack (any red color)

24 pieces Cheerios® cereal or small ring-shaped candies (about 4 teaspoons)

3 tablespoons miniature candy-coated semisweet chocolate baking bits

1 tablespoon semisweet chocolate chips

2 pieces black string licorice (each 34 inches long)

1. Heat oven to 350°F for shiny metal pans (or 325°F for dark or nonstick pans). Place paper baking cup in each of 24 regular-size muffin cups.

2. In large bowl, make cake mix as directed on box—except use 1 cup water, the oil and eggs. Divide batter evenly among muffin cups. Place 1 peanut butter cup candy in top of batter for each cupcake (candies will sink as cupcakes bake).

3. Bake 17 to 22 minutes or until toothpick inserted in cake comes out clean. Cool 10 minutes; remove from pan to cooling rack. Cool completely, about 30 minutes.

4. Frost cupcakes with frosting. Cut 12-inch piece from 1 fruit snack roll; set aside. From remaining fruit snack, cut 24 (2-inch) pieces; cut crescent-shaped piece from each. Peel off paper backing; add 1 piece to each cupcake for top of kerchief.

5. Cut reserved fruit snack into 12 (1-inch) pieces; peel off paper backing. Cut each piece in half lengthwise. Twist each piece in middle; add to 1 end of crescent-shaped fruit snack on each cupcake, forming tie of kerchief. Add 1 piece of cereal under each tie for earring. Use baking bit, chocolate chips and licorice to make facial features and eye patches.

24 cupcakes
1 Frosted Cupcake (Undecorated): Calories 250 (Calories from Fat 110); Total Fat 12g (Saturated Fat 3g; Trans Fat 1.5g); Cholesterol 25mg; Sodium 240mg; Total Carbohydrate 33g (Dietary Fiber 0g; Sugars 24g); Protein 2g
% Daily Value: Vitamin A 0%; Vitamin C 0%; Calcium 2%; Iron 4%
Exchanges: ½ Starch, 1½ Other Carbohydrate, 2½ Fat
Carbohydrate Choices: 2

KITCHEN TIPS

✺ These cupcakes are great to serve at a kid's birthday party. Complete the theme by having eye patches and red kerchiefs available for the kids to wear.

✺ You can skip the pirate theme and just keep things simple by topping the cupcakes with vanilla frosting.

Lemon Burst Cupcakes

Prep Time: 30 min Start to Finish: 1 hr 15 min

1   box Betty Crocker SuperMoist white cake mix

Water, vegetable oil and egg whites called for on cake mix box

1   jar (10 to 12 ounces) lemon curd

1   container (12 ounces) Betty Crocker Whipped fluffy white frosting

¼   cup Betty Crocker yellow candy sprinkles

¼   cup Betty Crocker white candy sprinkles

1. Heat oven to 350°F for shiny metal pans or (325°F for dark or nonstick pans). Place paper baking cup in each of 24 regular-size muffin cups.

2. In large bowl, make cake mix as directed on box, using water, oil and egg whites. Divide batter evenly among muffin cups.

3. Bake as directed on box or until toothpick inserted in center comes out clean. Cool 10 minutes; remove from pan to cooling rack. Cool completely, about 30 minutes.

4. Spoon lemon curd into corner of resealable heavy-duty plastic food-storage bag. Cut about ¼ inch off corner of bag. Gently push cut corner of bag into center of cupcake. Squeeze about 2 teaspoons lemon curd into center of each cupcake for filling, being careful not to split cupcake.

5. Frost cupcakes with frosting. To decorate, roll edge of each cupcake in candy sprinkles. Store loosely covered at room temperature.

24 cupcakes
1 Cupcake: Calories 240 (Calories from Fat 90); Total Fat 10g (Saturated Fat 3g; Trans Fat 1.5g); Cholesterol 10mg; Sodium 180mg; Total Carbohydrate 36g (Dietary Fiber 0g; Sugars 26g); Protein 1g
% Daily Value: Vitamin A 0%; Vitamin C 0%; Calcium 2%; Iron 2%
Exchanges: ½ Fruit, 2 Other Carbohydrate, 2 Fat
Carbohydrate Choices: 2½

KITCHEN TIPS

✪ Look for lemon curd near the jams and preserves or by the canned pie filling.

✪ Canned lemon pie filling can be substituted for the lemon curd.

Lemon-Blueberry Cupcakes

Prep Time: 25 min Start to Finish: 1 hr 55 min

Cupcakes

- 1 box Betty Crocker SuperMoist lemon cake mix
- $\frac{3}{4}$ cup water
- $\frac{1}{3}$ cup vegetable oil
- 1 tablespoon grated lemon peel
- 2 eggs
- 1 package (3 ounces) cream cheese, softened
- $1\frac{1}{2}$ cups fresh blueberries

Frosting and Garnish

- $2\frac{1}{2}$ cups powdered sugar
- $\frac{3}{4}$ cup unsalted butter, softened
- 1 teaspoon grated lemon peel
- $\frac{1}{2}$ teaspoon kosher (coarse) salt
- $1\frac{1}{4}$ teaspoons vanilla
- 1 tablespoon milk
- 1 cup fresh blueberries
  Lemon peel, if desired
  Fresh mint leaves, if desired

1. Heat oven to 375°F for shiny metal pans (or 350°F for dark or nonstick pans). Place paper baking cup in each of 24 regular-size muffin cups.

2. In large bowl, beat all cupcake ingredients except blueberries with electric mixer on low speed 30 seconds. Beat on medium speed 2 minutes, scraping bowl occasionally. Fold $1\frac{1}{2}$ cups blueberries into batter. Divide batter evenly among muffin cups.

3. Bake 18 to 22 minutes or until tops are light golden brown. Cool 5 minutes; remove from pan to cooling rack. Cool completely, about 1 hour.

4. In medium bowl, beat powdered sugar, butter, 1 teaspoon lemon peel, the salt, vanilla and 1 tablespoon milk on high speed about 4 minutes or until smooth and well blended, adding more milk by teaspoonfuls if needed. Frost cupcakes with frosting. Garnish with 1 cup blueberries, the lemon peel and mint leaves. Store in airtight container at room temperature.

24 cupcakes
1 Cupcake: Calories 250 (Calories from Fat 110); Total Fat 12g (Saturated Fat 6g; Trans Fat 1g); Cholesterol 35mg; Sodium 210mg; Total Carbohydrate 32g (Dietary Fiber 0g; Sugars 23g); Protein 2g
% Daily Value: Vitamin A 6%; Vitamin C 0%; Calcium 4%; Iron 2%
Exchanges: $\frac{1}{2}$ Starch, $1\frac{1}{2}$ Other Carbohydrate, $2\frac{1}{2}$ Fat
Carbohydrate Choices: 2

KITCHEN TIPS

✪ Unsalted butter tastes a little sweeter than the more common salted butter. We added the coarse salt for small bursts of saltiness to complement the sweetness of the other ingredients and to bring out the lemon flavor. If you don't have unsalted butter, use salted butter and omit the kosher salt.

✪ For decorative cupcake liners, surf to www.fancyflours.com.

Lemon-Blueberry Cupcakes

Hot Chocolate Cupcakes

Prep Time: 20 min Start to Finish: 1 hr 25 min

1¾ cups Betty Crocker SuperMoist devil's food cake mix (from 18.25-ounce box)

½ cup water

3 tablespoons vegetable oil

1 egg

1 cup Betty Crocker Whipped vanilla frosting (from 12-ounce container)

½ cup marshmallow creme

¼ teaspoon unsweetened baking cocoa

6 miniature pretzel twists, broken in half

1. Heat oven to 350°F for shiny metal pan (or 325°F for dark or nonstick pan). Place paper baking cup in each of 12 regular-size muffin cups.

2. In large bowl, beat cake mix, water, oil and egg with electric mixer on low speed 30 seconds. Beat on medium speed 2 minutes, scraping bowl occasionally. Divide batter evenly among muffin cups.

3. Bake 17 to 22 minutes or until toothpick inserted in center comes out clean. Cool in pan 10 minutes; remove from pan to cooling rack. Cool completely, about 30 minutes.

4. In small bowl, mix frosting and marshmallow creme. Spoon into small resealable plastic food-storage bag; seal bag. Cut ⅜-inch top off one corner of bag. (Or spoon mixture onto cupcakes instead of piping.)

5. Pipe 3 small dollops of frosting mixture on top of each cupcake to resemble melted marshmallows. Sprinkle with cocoa. Press pretzel half into side of each cupcake for cup handle.

12 cupcakes
1 Cupcake: Calories 240 (Calories from Fat 80); Total Fat 9g (Saturated Fat 2.5g; Trans Fat 1.5g); Cholesterol 20mg; Sodium 300mg; Total Carbohydrate 37g (Dietary Fiber 0g; Sugars 22g); Protein 2g
% Daily Value: Vitamin A 0%; Vitamin C 0%; Calcium 0%; Iron 6%
Exchanges: 2½ Other Carbohydrate, 2 Fat
Carbohydrate Choices: 2½

KITCHEN TIPS

❊ If you like peppermint, frost these fun cupcakes with the frosting mixture, and sprinkle the tops with crushed candy canes.

Espresso Cupcakes

Prep Time: 40 min Start to Finish: 1 hr 40 min

Cupcakes

- 1 box Betty Crocker SuperMoist chocolate fudge cake mix
- 1⅓ cups water
- ½ cup vegetable oil
- 3 eggs
- 1 tablespoon instant espresso coffee powder

Filling

- 1 container (8 ounces) mascarpone cheese
- 2 teaspoons milk
- 2 teaspoons instant espresso coffee powder
- 1 cup powdered sugar

Frosting and Garnish

- 4 ounces semisweet baking chocolate, finely chopped
- 6 tablespoons butter or margarine, softened
- 3 tablespoons milk
- 1 teaspoon instant espresso coffee powder
- ½ teaspoon vanilla
  Dash of salt
- 3 cups powdered sugar
  Chocolate-covered espresso beans, if desired

1. Heat oven to 350°F for shiny metal pans (or 325°F for dark or nonstick pans). Place paper baking cup in each of 24 regular-size muffin cups.

2. In large bowl, beat cake mix, water, oil and eggs with electric mixer on low speed 30 seconds. Beat on medium speed 2 minutes, scraping bowl occasionally. Gently stir in 1 tablespoon espresso powder just until blended. Divide batter evenly among muffin cups.

3. Bake 18 to 23 minutes or until toothpick inserted in center comes out clean. Cool 5 minutes; remove from pan to cooling rack. Cool completely, about 30 minutes.

4. In medium bowl, beat mascarpone cheese, 2 teaspoons milk, 2 teaspoons espresso powder and 1 cup powdered sugar on medium speed until smooth. Spoon mixture into decorating bag fitted with ¼-inch (#9) writing tip.

5. To fill each cupcake, insert tip of bag into center of cooled cupcake, gently squeeze bag until cupcake expands slightly but does not burst (each cupcake should be filled with about 1 tablespoon filling).

6. In small microwavable bowl, microwave chocolate uncovered on High 45 seconds, stir. Continue microwaving and stirring at 15-second intervals until melted. Cool slightly, about 5 minutes.

7. In another medium bowl, beat butter, 3 tablespoons milk, 1 teaspoon espresso powder, the vanilla and salt on low speed until well blended. Beat in 3 cups powdered sugar, 1 cup at a time, until smooth. Stir in melted chocolate until blended. Spoon mixture into decorating bag fitted with ¾-inch (#824) star tip. Pipe frosting over tops of cupcakes. Garnish with espresso beans. Store covered in refrigerator.

24 cupcakes
1 Cupcake: Calories 310 (Calories from Fat 130); Total Fat 14g (Saturated Fat 6g; Trans Fat 0g); Cholesterol 45mg; Sodium 210mg; Total Carbohydrate 42g (Dietary Fiber 0g; Sugars 32g); Protein 2g
% Daily Value: Vitamin A 4%; Vitamin C 0%; Calcium 4%; Iron 4%
Exchanges: ½ Starch, 2½ Other Carbohydrate, 2½ Fat
Carbohydrate Choices: 3

Chai Latte Cupcakes

Chai Latte Cupcakes

Prep Time: 25 min Start to Finish: 1 hr 50 min

Cake

- 1 box Betty Crocker SuperMoist French vanilla cake mix
- 1½ cups water
- ⅓ cup vegetable oil
- 3 eggs
- 1 package (1.1 ounces) instant chai tea latte mix (or 3 tablespoons from larger container)

Frosting and Garnish

- 4 ounces white chocolate baking bars (from 6-ounce package), chopped
- ⅓ cup butter or margarine, softened
- 4 cups powdered sugar
- ¼ cup milk
- ½ teaspoon vanilla
  Ground cinnamon, if desired

1. Heat oven to 350°F for shiny metal pans (or 325°F for dark or nonstick pans). Place paper baking cup in each of 24 regular-size muffin cups.

2. In large bowl, beat cake ingredients with electric mixer on low speed 30 seconds. Beat on medium speed 2 minutes, scraping bowl occasionally. Divide batter evenly among muffin cups.

3. Bake 18 to 23 minutes or until toothpick inserted in center comes out clean. Cool 10 minutes; remove from pan to cooling rack. Cool completely, about 1 hour.

4. In medium microwavable bowl, microwave baking bars on High 30 seconds; stir until melted. If necessary, microwave 15 seconds longer or until melted and smooth. Stir in butter until smooth. Add powdered sugar, milk and vanilla; stir until well blended.

5. Frost cupcakes with frosting. Sprinkle with cinnamon. Store loosely covered at room temperature.

24 cupcakes
1 Cupcake: Calories 260 (Calories from Fat 90); Total Fat 10g (Saturated Fat 3.5g; Trans Fat 0.5g); Cholesterol 35mg; Sodium 180mg; Total Carbohydrate 41g (Dietary Fiber 0g; Sugars 33g); Protein 2g
% Daily Value: Vitamin A 2%; Vitamin C 0%; Calcium 6%; Iron 2%
Exchanges: ½ Starch, 2 Other Carbohydrate, 2 Fat
Carbohydrate Choices: 3

KITCHEN TIPS

✹ Instant chai tea mix comes in a variety of flavors. Experiment to find your favorite.

Chocolate Cupcakes with Penuche Filling

Prep Time: 40 min Start to Finish: 2 hr 10 min

Cupcakes

- 1 box Betty Crocker SuperMoist chocolate fudge cake mix
- 1⅓ cups water
- ½ cup vegetable oil
- 3 eggs
- 1 teaspoon vanilla

Filling and Garnish

- 1 cup butter or margarine
- 2 cups packed brown sugar
- ½ cup milk
- 4 cups powdered sugar
- 1 ounce grated semisweet baking chocolate, if desired

1. Heat oven to 350°F for shiny metal pans (or 325°F for dark or nonstick pans). Spray bottoms only of 24 regular-size muffin cups with baking spray with flour.

2. In large bowl, beat cake mix, water, oil, eggs and vanilla with electric mixer on low speed 30 seconds. Beat on medium speed 2 minutes, scraping bowl occasionally. Divide batter evenly among muffin cups.

3. Bake 18 to 24 minutes or until toothpick inserted in center comes out clean. Cool 15 minutes; remove from pan to cooling rack. Cool completely, about 30 minutes.

4. Meanwhile, in 2-quart saucepan, melt butter over medium heat. Stir in brown sugar. Heat to boiling, stirring constantly; reduce heat to low. Boil and stir 2 minutes. Stir in milk. Heat to boiling; remove from heat. Pour mixture into medium bowl; refrigerate about 30 minutes or until lukewarm.

5. Beat powdered sugar into cooled brown sugar mixture on low speed until smooth. If frosting becomes too stiff, stir in additional milk, 1 teaspoon at a time.

6. Using serrated knife, cut each cupcake in half horizontally, being careful not to break either half. Place heaping 1 tablespoon filling on each cupcake base. Replace rounded cupcake tops. Pipe or spoon 1 rounded tablespoon frosting onto cupcake tops. Garnish with grated chocolate. Store in airtight container at room temperature.

24 cupcakes
1 Cupcake: Calories 360 (Calories from Fat 130); Total Fat 15g (Saturated Fat 6g; Trans Fat 0.5g); Cholesterol 45mg; Sodium 240mg; Total Carbohydrate 56g (Dietary Fiber 0g; Sugars 48g); Protein 2g
% Daily Value: Vitamin A 6%; Vitamin C 0%; Calcium 4%; Iron 6%
Exchanges: ½ Starch, 3 Other Carbohydrate, 3 Fat
Carbohydrate Choices: 4

KITCHEN TIPS

✿ The word penuche comes from a Mexican word meaning "raw sugar" or "brown sugar." It is used to describe a fudgelike candy made from brown sugar, butter, milk or cream and vanilla.

Adorable Applesauce Cupcakes

Prep Time: 30 min Start to Finish: 1 hr 25 min

Cupcakes

- 1 box Betty Crocker SuperMoist yellow cake mix
- ½ teaspoon ground cinnamon
- 1 cup apple juice
- ⅓ cup unsweetened applesauce
- 3 eggs

Frosting

- ½ teaspoon red paste food color
- 1 container (1 pound) Betty Crocker Rich & Creamy vanilla frosting

Decorations

- 12 large pretzel twists, broken into pieces
- 16 spearmint leaf gumdrops
- 12 gummy worm candies, cut in half, if desired

1. Heat oven to 350°F for shiny metal pans (or 325°F for dark or nonstick pans). Place paper baking cup in each of 24 regular-size muffin cups.

2. In large bowl, beat cupcake ingredients with electric mixer on low speed 30 seconds. Beat on medium speed 2 minutes, scraping bowl occasionally. Divide batter evenly among muffin cups.

3. Bake 18 to 22 minutes or until tops spring back when lightly touched. Cool 10 minutes; carefully remove from pan to cooling rack. Cool completely, about 30 minutes.

4. Stir paste food color into frosting in container. Spread frosting over cupcakes.

5. To decorate cupcakes, poke 1 pretzel piece into each cupcake for stem. Cut each gumdrop leaf into 3 slices. Poke 2 gumdrop leaves into top of each cupcake on either side of pretzel stem. Poke half of gummy worm into each cupcake.

24 cupcakes
1 Cupcake: Calories 200 (Calories from Fat 60); Total Fat 6g (Saturated Fat 2g; Trans Fat 2g); Cholesterol 25mg; Sodium 200mg; Total Carbohydrate 34g (Dietary Fiber 0g; Sugars 24g); Protein 1g
% Daily Value: Vitamin A 0%; Vitamin C 0%; Calcium 4%; Iron 2%
Exchanges: ½ Starch, 2 Other Carbohydrate, 1 Fat
Carbohydrate Choices: 2

KITCHEN TIPS

✿ If you don't have unsweetened applesauce on hand, the regular kind will taste great in these cupcakes, too.

Baklava Bars

Prep Time: 25 min Start to Finish: 2 hr 50 min

Cookie Base

- 1 pouch (1 pound 1.5 ounces) Betty Crocker sugar cookie mix
- $\frac{1}{2}$ cup butter or margarine, softened
- $\frac{1}{2}$ teaspoon grated lemon peel
- 1 egg

Filling

- $1\frac{1}{2}$ cups chopped walnuts
- $\frac{1}{3}$ cup granulated sugar
- $\frac{1}{4}$ cup butter or margarine, softened
- 1 teaspoon ground cinnamon
- $\frac{1}{8}$ teaspoon salt
- 8 frozen mini fillo shells (from 2.1-ounce package)

Glaze

- $\frac{1}{3}$ cup honey
- 2 tablespoons butter or margarine, softened
- 1 tablespoon packed brown sugar
- $\frac{1}{2}$ teaspoon lemon juice
- $\frac{1}{4}$ teaspoon ground cinnamon
- 1 teaspoon vanilla

Garnish

- 5 tablespoons honey

1. Heat oven to 350°F. Spray bottom only of 13 × 9-inch pan with cooking spray.

2. In large bowl, stir cookie base ingredients until soft dough forms. Press dough in bottom of pan. Bake 15 minutes.

3. Meanwhile, in medium bowl, stir walnuts, granulated sugar, $\frac{1}{4}$ cup butter, 1 teaspoon cinnamon and the salt with fork until mixture is well mixed and crumbly.

4. Sprinkle nut mixture evenly over partially baked base. With hands, crumble frozen fillo shells evenly over nut mixture. Bake 18 to 20 minutes longer or until golden brown.

5. Meanwhile, in small microwavable bowl, microwave $\frac{1}{3}$ cup honey, 2 tablespoons butter, the brown sugar, lemon juice and $\frac{1}{4}$ teaspoon cinnamon uncovered on High 1 minute or until bubbly. Stir in vanilla.

6. Drizzle glaze evenly over fillo. Cool completely, about 2 hours.

7. For bars, cut into 6 rows by 4 rows. Before serving, drizzle about $\frac{1}{2}$ teaspoon honey over each bar. Store covered at room temperature.

24 bars
1 Bar: Calories 250 (Calories from Fat 130); Total Fat 14g (Saturated Fat 5g; Trans Fat 1g); Cholesterol 25mg; Sodium 115mg; Total Carbohydrate 29g (Dietary Fiber 0g; Sugars 21g); Protein 2g
% Daily Value: Vitamin A 4%; Vitamin C 0%; Calcium 0%; Iron 4%
Exchanges: $\frac{1}{2}$ Starch, $1\frac{1}{2}$ Other Carbohydrate, $2\frac{1}{2}$ Fat
Carbohydrate Choices: 2

KITCHEN TIPS

✿ This was a prize-winning recipe in the 2007 Betty Crocker Cookie Contest.
✿ You can find mini fillo shells in the freezer section of your supermarket.

Double-Chocolate Rocky Road Cookie Bars

Prep Time: 30 min Start to Finish: 3 hr 30 min

Cookie Base
- 1 pouch (1 pound 1.5 ounces) Betty Crocker double chocolate chunk cookie mix
- ¼ cup vegetable oil
- 2 tablespoons water
- 1 egg

Filling
- 1 package (8 ounces) cream cheese, softened
- ½ cup granulated sugar
- ¼ cup butter or margarine, softened
- 2 tablespoons Gold Medal all-purpose flour
- 1 teaspoon vanilla
- 1 egg
- ¼ cup chopped pecans
- 1 cup semisweet chocolate chips (6 ounces)
- 1½ cups miniature marshmallows

Frosting
- ½ cup butter or margarine
- ¼ cup unsweetened baking cocoa
- ⅓ cup milk
- 3 cups powdered sugar
- 1 teaspoon vanilla
- 1 cup chopped pecans

1. Heat oven to 350°F. Spray bottom and sides of 13 × 9-inch pan with cooking spray.

2. In large bowl, stir cookie base ingredients until soft dough forms. Press dough in bottom of pan. Set aside.

3. In large bowl, beat cream cheese, granulated sugar, ¼ cup butter, the flour, 1 teaspoon vanilla and the egg with electric mixer on medium speed until smooth. Stir in ¼ cup pecans. Spread over cookie base. Sprinkle with chocolate chips.

4. Bake 26 to 28 minutes or until filling is set. Sprinkle evenly with marshmallows. Bake 2 minutes longer.

5. In 2-quart saucepan, melt ½ cup butter over medium heat. Stir in cocoa and milk. Heat to boiling, stirring constantly. Remove from heat. With wire whisk, gradually stir in powdered sugar until well blended. Stir in 1 teaspoon vanilla and 1 cup pecans. Immediately pour over marshmallows, spreading gently to cover. Cool 30 minutes.

6. Refrigerate about 2 hours or until chilled. For bars, cut into 6 rows by 4 rows. Store covered in refrigerator.

24 bars
1 Bar: Calories 370 (Calories from Fat 180); Total Fat 20g (Saturated Fat 8g; Trans Fat 1g); Cholesterol 45mg; Sodium 130mg; Total Carbohydrate 45g (Dietary Fiber 1g; Sugars 34g); Protein 3g
% Daily Value: Vitamin A 6%; Vitamin C 0%; Calcium 2%; Iron 6%
Exchanges: 1 Starch, 2 Other Carbohydrate, 4 Fat
Carbohydrate Choices: 3

KITCHEN TIPS

- Line the baking pan with aluminum foil so the bars can be removed easily and cleanup will be a snap.
- This was a prize-winning recipe in the 2007 Betty Crocker Cookie Contest.

Betty Crocker
MAKES IT EASY

Bake & Send with Love

Want to make your college son or daughter the most popular one in the dorm? For all you seasoned bakers, food gifts are a wonderful way to send your love to those who are miles away but near in your heart.

Brown Paper Packages Tied Up with . . .

▶ Wrap cookies in pairs, back to back. Brownies and bars will remain fresher if left uncut; just wrap the whole rectangle or square in plastic wrap or aluminum foil. (Include a plastic knife, especially for the college student.)

▶ Rigid plastic containers, firm-sided cardboard boxes or sturdy metal cans are great for shipping. Before adding treats, line them with plastic wrap or foil.

▶ Fill each container until almost full, allowing space at the top to cushion with crumpled waxed paper, paper towels or packing peanuts to prevent food from breaking or crumbling; seal container with lid or top.

▶ Pack filled containers in a firm cardboard box. Cushion with bubble wrap, crumpled paper, shredded paper or packing peanuts.

Toffee-Pecan Bars

Prep Time: 30 min Start to Finish: 2 hr

Crust

- ¾ cup butter or margarine, softened
- ⅓ cup packed brown sugar
- 1 egg
- 2 cups Gold Medal all-purpose flour

Filling

- 1 cup butter or margarine
- ¾ cup packed brown sugar
- ¼ cup light corn syrup
- 2 cups coarsely chopped pecans
- 1 cup swirled milk chocolate and caramel chips (from 10-ounce bag)

1. Heat oven to 375°F. Grease bottom and sides of 15 × 10 × 1-inch pan with shortening or cooking spray (do not use dark pan).

2. In large bowl, beat ¾ cup butter and ⅓ cup brown sugar with electric mixer on medium speed until light and fluffy. Add egg; beat until well blended. On low speed, beat in flour until dough begins to form. Press dough in pan.

3. Bake 12 to 17 minutes or until edges are light golden brown. Meanwhile, in 2-quart saucepan, heat 1 cup butter, ¾ cup brown sugar and the corn syrup to boiling over medium heat, stirring frequently. Boil 2 minutes without stirring.

4. Quickly stir pecans into corn syrup mixture; spread over partially baked crust. Bake 20 to 23 minutes or until filling is golden brown and bubbly.

5. Immediately sprinkle chocolate chips evenly over hot bars. Let stand 5 minutes to soften. With rubber spatula, gently swirl melted chips over bars. Cool completely, about 1 hour. For bars, cut into 24 squares (6 rows by 4 rows), then cut each square in half to make triangles. Store covered in refrigerator.

48 bars
1 Bar: Calories 150 (Calories from Fat 100); Total Fat 11g (Saturated Fat 5g; Trans Fat 0g); Cholesterol 20mg; Sodium 50mg; Total Carbohydrate 12g (Dietary Fiber 0g; Sugars 7g); Protein 1g
% Daily Value: Vitamin A 4%; Vitamin C 0%; Calcium 0%; Iron 2%
Exchanges: 1 Other Carbohydrate, 2 Fat
Carbohydrate Choices: 1

KITCHEN TIPS

- Try using raspberry-flavored chocolate chips instead of the swirled chips.
- Coarsely chopped walnuts can be used instead of the pecans.

Chocolate Chip-Cherry Bars

Prep Time: 20 min Start to Finish: 1 hr 45 min

Bars

- 1 jar (10 ounces) maraschino cherries
- 1 cup powdered sugar
- 1 cup butter or margarine, softened
- 1 teaspoon vanilla
- 2 eggs
- 2 cups Gold Medal all-purpose flour
- 1 teaspoon baking soda
- $\frac{1}{2}$ teaspoon salt
- 1 cup semisweet chocolate chips (6 ounces)

Topping

- 1 cup semisweet chocolate chips (6 ounces)

Drizzle

- 1 cup powdered sugar
- 2 tablespoons butter or margarine, softened
  Reserved cherry juice

1. Heat oven to 325°F. Grease bottom and sides of 13 × 9-inch pan with shortening or cooking spray. Drain maraschino cherries, reserving juice for drizzle; set juice aside. Finely chop cherries; pat dry with paper towel.

2. In large bowl, beat 1 cup powdered sugar and 1 cup butter with electric mixer on medium speed until well mixed. Beat in vanilla and eggs. On low speed, beat in flour, baking soda and salt. Stir in 1 cup chocolate chips and the cherries. Spread in pan.

3. Bake 30 to 35 minutes or until top is golden brown. Immediately sprinkle with 1 cup chocolate chips. Let stand 5 minutes or until chocolate is softened. Spread chocolate evenly over crust.

4. In small bowl, mix 1 cup powdered sugar, 2 tablespoons butter and 2 to 3 tablespoons reserved cherry juice until smooth and thin enough to drizzle. Drizzle over chocolate. Cool completely, about 45 minutes. For bars, cut into 8 rows by 4 rows.

32 bars
1 Bar: Calories 190 (Calories from Fat 90); Total Fat 10g (Saturated Fat 6g; Trans Fat 0g); Cholesterol 30mg; Sodium 130mg; Total Carbohydrate 24g (Dietary Fiber 1g; Sugars 16g); Protein 2g
% Daily Value: Vitamin A 4%; Vitamin C 0%; Calcium 0%; Iron 4%
Exchanges: $\frac{1}{2}$ Starch, 1 Other Carbohydrate, 2 Fat
Carbohydrate Choices: $1\frac{1}{2}$

KITCHEN TIPS

- Fill a resealable plastic food-storage bag with the cherry drizzle, and cut off a tiny bottom corner of the bag to easily drizzle over the chocolate.
- Make sure you dry the cherries with a paper towel to eliminate excess moisture.

Brownie Goody Bars

Prep Time: 15 min Start to Finish: 2 hr 55 min

1 box (1 pound, 3.8 ounces) Betty Crocker fudge brownie mix

Water, vegetable oil and eggs called for on brownie mix box

1 container (1 pound) Betty Crocker Rich & Creamy or Whipped vanilla frosting

¾ cup salted peanuts, coarsely chopped

3 cups crisp rice cereal

1 cup creamy peanut butter

1 bag (12 ounces) semisweet chocolate chips (2 cups)

1. Heat oven to 350°F. Grease bottom only of 13 × 9-inch pan with shortening or cooking spray. Make and bake brownie mix as directed on box for 13 × 9-inch pan. Cool completely, about 1 hour.

2. Frost brownies with frosting. Sprinkle with peanuts; refrigerate while making cereal mixture.

3. Measure cereal into large bowl; set aside. In 1-quart saucepan, melt peanut butter and chocolate chips over low heat, stirring constantly. Pour over cereal in bowl, stirring until evenly coated. Spread over frosted brownies. Cool completely before cutting, about 1 hour. For bars, cut into 5 rows by 4 rows. Store tightly covered at room temperature.

20 bars
1 Bar: Calories 490 (Calories from Fat 240); Total Fat 27g (Saturated Fat 8g; Trans Fat 2g); Cholesterol 20mg; Sodium 240mg; Total Carbohydrate 55g (Dietary Fiber 2g; Sugars 41g); Protein 7g
% Daily Value: Vitamin A 0%; Vitamin C 0%; Calcium 4%; Iron 15%
Exchanges: 2 Starch, 1½ Other Carbohydrate, 5 Fat
Carbohydrate Choices: 3½

KITCHEN TIPS

✪ Drizzle caramel topping over the top of these bars for an even sweeter treat.

✪ Instead of peanuts, try using chopped walnuts or pecans.

Cranberry-Apricot Bars

Prep Time: 20 Min Start to Finish: 1 hr 40 min

Crust
1¼ cups Gold Medal all-purpose flour
½ cup butter or margarine, softened
¼ cup sugar

Filling
½ cup chopped dried apricots
½ cup sweetened dried cranberries
¼ cup sugar
1 tablespoon cornstarch
¼ cup honey
3 tablespoons orange juice

1. Heat oven to 350°F. Line 8-inch square pan with aluminum foil; spray foil with cooking spray. In large bowl, beat crust ingredients with electric mixer on low speed until mixture looks like coarse crumbs. Press in pan.

2. Bake 28 to 30 minutes or until light golden brown. Meanwhile, in medium bowl, mix filling ingredients.

3. Remove partially baked crust from oven. Reduce oven temperature to 325°F. Spread filling evenly over crust.

4. Bake 9 to 12 minutes longer or until mixture is set and appears glossy. Cool completely, about 45 minutes. For bars, cut into 4 rows by 4 rows.

16 bars
1 Bar: Calories 160 (Calories from Fat 50); Total Fat 6g (Saturated Fat 3.5g; Trans Fat 0g); Cholesterol 15mg; Sodium 40mg; Total Carbohydrate 24g (Dietary Fiber 0g; Sugars 16g); Protein 1g
% Daily Value: Vitamin A 6%; Vitamin C 0%; Calcium 0%; Iron 4%
Exchanges: ½ Starch, 1 Other Carbohydrate, 1 Fat
Carbohydrate Choices: 1½

KITCHEN TIPS

✪ To soften butter, let it stand at room temperature 30 to 45 minutes.

✪ You can use sweetened dried cherries instead of the cranberries.

Cranberry-Apricot Bars

Brownie Goody Bars

Best Chocolate Chip Cookies

Cookie Dough Brownies

Cookie Dough Brownies

Prep Time: 15 min Start to Finish: 1 hr 50 min

- 1 box (1 pound 4.75 ounce) Betty Crocker Supreme turtle brownie mix
- 2 tablespoons water
- 1/2 cup vegetable oil
- 2 eggs
- 1 roll (16.5 ounce) Pillsbury refrigerated chocolate chip cookies
- 1 container (1 pound) Betty Crocker Rich & Creamy chocolate frosting

1. Heat oven to 350°F. Grease bottom and sides of 13 × 9-inch pan with shortening or cooking spray. See Kitchen Tip regarding disposable foil pan. Set caramel pouch from brownie mix aside. In large bowl, stir brownie mix, water, oil, and eggs with spoon until well blended. Spread half of batter in pan.

2. Break cookie dough into small pieces. Sprinkle pieces evenly over brownie batter in pan; lightly press into batter. Open pouch of caramel from brownie mix; squeeze caramel between pieces of cookie dough, using entire pouch. Spoon remaining brownie batter over caramel and cookie dough.

3. Bake 28 to 35 minutes or until toothpick inserted in center comes out clean. Cool completely, about 1 hour.

4. Frost with chocolate frosting. For brownies, cut into 8 rows by 6 rows.

48 brownies
1 Brownie: Calories 150 (Calories from Fat 60); Total Fat 7g (Saturated Fat 1.5g; Trans Fat 1g); Cholesterol 10mg; Sodium 100mg; Total Carbohydrate 22g (Dietary Fiber 0g; Sugars 15g); Protein 1g
% Daily Value: Vitamin A 0%; Vitamin C 0%; Calcium 0%; Iron 4%
Exchanges: 1 1/2 Other Carbohydrate, 1 1/2 Fat
Carbohydrate Choices: 1 1/2

KITCHEN TIPS

✿ Bake this in a disposable foil pan to send in a care package. Send a plastic knife and the can of frosting so the bars can be frosted and cut once they are received.

✿ Brownies can be frozen up to 6 months; just wrap tightly and label.

Best Chocolate Chip Cookies

Prep Time: 1 hr 25 min Start to Finish: 1 hr 40 min

- 1 1/2 cups butter or margarine, softened
- 1 1/4 cups granulated sugar
- 1 1/4 cups packed brown sugar
- 1 tablespoon vanilla
- 2 eggs
- 4 cups Gold Medal all-purpose flour
- 2 teaspoons baking soda
- 1/2 teaspoon salt
- 1 bag (24 ounces) semisweet chocolate chips (4 cups)

1. Heat oven to 375°F. In large bowl, mix butter, sugars, vanilla and eggs with electric mixer on medium speed, or mix with spoon, until light and fluffy. Stir in flour, baking soda and salt (dough will be stiff). Stir in chocolate chips.

2. On ungreased cookie sheets, drop dough by level 1/4 cupfuls about 2 inches apart. Flatten slightly with fork.

3. Bake 12 to 15 minutes or until light brown (centers will be soft). Cool slightly; remove from cookie sheets to cooling rack.

3 1/2 dozen
1 Cookie: Calories 240 (Calories from Fat 110); Total Fat 12g (Saturated Fat 7g; Trans Fat 0g); Cholesterol 30mg; Sodium 140mg; Total Carbohydrate 32g (Dietary Fiber 1g; Sugars 21g); Protein 2g
% Daily Value: Vitamin A 3%; Vitamin C 0%; Calcium 0%; Iron 6%
Exchanges: 1/2 Starch, 1 1/2 Other Carbohydrate, 2 1/2 Fat
Carbohydrate Choices: 4

KITCHEN TIPS

✿ Making these cookies will go a lot faster if you use a cookie/ice-cream scoop. Level off the cookie dough in the scoop on the edge of the bowl.

✿ Sir in 2 cups coarsely chopped nuts with the chocolate chips.

Monster-Style Cookies

Prep Time: 45 min Start to Finish: 45 min

3/4 cup creamy peanut butter

1/2 cup butter or margarine, softened

3/4 cup packed brown sugar

1/2 cup granulated sugar

1 teaspoon vanilla

2 eggs

1 1/4 cups Gold Medal all-purpose flour

1 teaspoon baking soda

2 1/2 cups quick-cooking or old-fashioned oats

1/2 cup white vanilla baking chips

1/2 cup sweetened dried cranberries

1. Heat oven to 375°F. In large bowl, beat peanut butter and butter with electric mixer on medium speed until creamy. Add brown and granulated sugars; beat until fluffy. Beat in vanilla and eggs until well mixed. On low speed, beat in flour and baking soda. Stir in oats, baking chips and cranberries.

2. On ungreased cookie sheets, drop dough by 1/4 cupfuls 3 inches apart.

3. Bake 11 to 15 minutes or until edges are golden brown. Cool 1 minute; remove from cookie sheets to cooling rack.

1 1/2 dozen
1 Cookie: Calories 300 (Calories from Fat 120); Total Fat 14g (Saturated Fat 6g; Trans Fat 0g); Cholesterol 35mg; Sodium 180mg; Total Carbohydrate 38g (Dietary Fiber 2g; Sugars 22g); Protein 7g
% Daily Value: Vitamin A 4%; Vitamin C 0%; Calcium 4%; Iron 8%
Exchanges: 1/2 Starch, 2 Other Carbohydrate, 1/2 High-Fat Meat
Carbohydrate Choices: 2 1/2

KITCHEN TIPS

✪ To make 3 1/2 dozen smaller cookies, drop dough by tablespoonfuls instead of 1/4 cupfuls. Bake 8 to 10 minutes.

✪ Have semisweet chocolate chips on hand? Go ahead and use them instead of the vanilla chips.

Low Fat
Apple-Date Swirl Cookies
Prep Time: 1 hr 10 min Start to Finish: 3 hr 20 min

Filling

1	cup chopped dates
³⁄₄	cup finely chopped peeled apple
¹⁄₄	cup granulated sugar
1	teaspoon grated orange peel
¹⁄₄	cup orange juice

Cookies

¹⁄₂	cup granulated sugar
¹⁄₂	cup packed brown sugar
¹⁄₂	cup butter or margarine, softened
¹⁄₂	teaspoon vanilla
1	egg
1²⁄₃	cups Gold Medal all-purpose flour
¹⁄₂	teaspoon baking soda
¹⁄₄	teaspoon salt
¹⁄₄	teaspoon ground cinnamon

1. In 1-quart saucepan, mix filling ingredients. Cook over medium-high heat, stirring constantly, until mixture boils and thickens. Boil and stir 5 minutes. Cool.

2. In large bowl, beat ¹⁄₂ cup granulated sugar, the brown sugar, butter, vanilla and egg with electric mixer on medium speed, or mix with spoon, until well blended. Stir in flour, baking soda, salt and cinnamon.

3. Between sheets of waxed paper or plastic wrap, roll or pat dough into 16 × 8-inch rectangle. Remove top paper. Spread cooled filling over dough. Roll up dough with filling inside, starting with 16-inch side and using waxed paper to lift and roll. Wrap tightly. Refrigerate 2 to 3 hours or until firm.

4. Heat oven to 375°F. Cut roll with sharp knife into ¹⁄₄-inch slices, occasionally cleaning off knife. On ungreased cookie sheets, place slices about 1 inch apart. Bake 8 to 11 minutes or until lightly browned. Remove from cookie sheets to cooling rack.

5 dozen
1 Cookie: Calories 60 (Calories from Fat 15); Total Fat 1.5g (Saturated Fat 1g; Trans Fat 0g); Cholesterol 10mg; Sodium 35mg; Total Carbohydrate 10g (Dietary Fiber 0g; Sugars 6g); Protein 0g
% Daily Value: Vitamin A 0%; Vitamin C 0%; Calcium 0%; Iron 0%
Exchanges: ¹⁄₂ Other Carbohydrate, ¹⁄₂ Fat
Carbohydrate Choices: ¹⁄₂

KITCHEN TIPS

❂ Shape up your cookies! Rotate the roll slightly with each cut so the roll stays rounded.

❂ Use a kitchen scissors to make quick work of chopping the dates.

Pumpkin Cookies with Browned Butter Frosting

Prep Time: 1 hr 10 min Start to Finish: 1 hr 55 min

Cookies

2/3	cup granulated sugar
2/3	cup packed brown sugar
3/4	cup butter or margarine, softened
1	teaspoon vanilla
1/2	cup (from 15-ounce can) pumpkin (not pumpkin pie mix)
2	eggs
2 1/4	cups Gold Medal all-purpose flour
1	teaspoon baking soda
1	teaspoon ground cinnamon
1/2	teaspoon salt

Browned Butter Frosting

3	cups powdered sugar
1	teaspoon vanilla
3 to 4	tablespoons milk
1/3	cup butter (do not use margarine or spread; it will burn)

1. Heat oven to 375°F. In large bowl, beat granulated sugar, brown sugar, 3/4 cup butter and 1 teaspoon vanilla with electric mixer on medium speed, scraping bowl occasionally, until well blended. Beat in pumpkin and eggs until well mixed. On low speed, beat in flour, baking soda, cinnamon and salt.

2. On ungreased cookie sheets, drop dough by heaping tablespoonfuls.

3. Bake 10 to 12 minutes or until almost no indentation remains when touched in center. Immediately remove from cookie sheets to cooling rack. Cool completely, about 45 minutes.

4. In medium bowl, place powdered sugar, 1 teaspoon vanilla and 3 tablespoons milk. In 1-quart saucepan, heat 1/3 cup butter over medium heat, stirring constantly, just until light brown.

5. Pour browned butter over powdered sugar mixture. Beat on low speed about 1 minute or until smooth. Gradually add just enough of the remaining 1 tablespoon milk to make frosting creamy and spreadable. Generously frost cooled cookies.

2 1/2 dozen
1 Cookie: Calories 190 (Calories from Fat 60); Total Fat 7g (Saturated Fat 4.5g; Trans Fat 0g); Cholesterol 30mg; Sodium 135mg; Total Carbohydrate 29g (Dietary Fiber 0g; Sugars 21g); Protein 2g
% Daily Value: Vitamin A 15%; Vitamin C 0%; Calcium 0%; Iron 4%
Exchanges: 1/2 Starch, 1 1/2 Other Carbohydrate, 1 1/2 Fat
Carbohydrate Choices: 2

KITCHEN TIPS

✿ Instead of making Browned Butter Frosting, use a 1-pound container of Betty Crocker Rich & Creamy dulce de leche (caramel) frosting.

✿ Spice up these cookies by adding 1/8 teaspoon each ground cloves and ground ginger with the flour.

Pumpkin Cookies with Browned Butter Frosting

Snow-Capped Gingersnaps

Prep Time: 1 hr 20 min Start to Finish: 2 hr 30 min

1 cup packed brown sugar
¾ cup shortening
¼ cup molasses
1 egg
2¼ cups Gold Medal all-purpose flour
2 teaspoons baking soda
1 teaspoon ground ginger
1 teaspoon ground cinnamon
½ teaspoon ground cloves
¼ teaspoon salt
    Granulated sugar
1 cup white vanilla baking chips (6 ounces)
1 tablespoon shortening
    Chopped crystallized ginger, if desired

1. In large bowl, mix brown sugar, ¾ cup shortening, the molasses and egg. Stir in flour, baking soda, ground ginger, cinnamon, cloves and salt. Cover; refrigerate at least 1 hour.

2. Heat oven to 375°F. Lightly grease cookie sheets with shortening or cooking spray. Shape dough by rounded teaspoonfuls into balls; dip tops into granulated sugar. Place balls, sugared sides up, about 3 inches apart on cookie sheets.

3. Bake 9 to 12 minutes or just until set. Remove from cookie sheets to cooling rack. Cool completely, about 30 minutes.

4. Cover cookie sheet with waxed paper. In small microwavable bowl, microwave baking chips and 1 tablespoon shortening uncovered on Medium-High (70%) 1 minute 30 seconds to 2 minutes, stirring every 15 seconds, until smooth. Dip half of each cookie into melted mixture; sprinkle with crystallized ginger. Place on waxed paper; let stand until coating is firm.

4 dozen
1 Cookie: Calories 100 (Calories from Fat 40); Total Fat 4.5g (Saturated Fat 1.5g; Trans Fat 0.5g); Cholesterol 0mg; Sodium 75mg; Total Carbohydrate 13g (Dietary Fiber 0g; Sugars 8g); Protein 1g
% Daily Value: Vitamin A 0%; Vitamin C 0%; Calcium 0%; Iron 2%
Exchanges: 1 Other Carbohydrate, 1 Fat
Carbohydrate Choices: 1

KITCHEN TIPS

⚙ Before measuring molasses, spray the measuring cup with cooking spray; the molasses will come out of the cup much easier.

⚙ After baking, these spicy cookies have a crackly top. They are very nice served with ice cream, fresh fruit, sorbet or coffee.

Pecan Crisps

Prep Time: 1 hr 15 min Start to Finish: 1 hr 30 min

2 cups packed brown sugar
1 cup butter or margarine, softened
1 teaspoon vanilla
2 eggs
3 cups Gold Medal all-purpose flour
$\frac{1}{2}$ teaspoon baking soda
1 cup chopped pecans, toasted

5 dozen
1 Cookie: Calories 90 (Calories from Fat 40); Total Fat 4.5g (Saturated Fat 2g; Trans Fat 0g); Cholesterol 15mg; Sodium 35mg; Total Carbohydrate 12g (Dietary Fiber 0g; Sugars 7g); Protein 1g
% Daily Value: Vitamin A 2%; Vitamin C 0%; Calcium 0%; Iron 2%
Exchanges: $\frac{1}{2}$ Starch, 1 Fat
Carbohydrate Choices: 1

1. Heat oven to 350°F. In large bowl, beat brown sugar, butter, vanilla and eggs with electric mixer on medium speed, or mix with spoon, until well blended. Stir in flour, baking soda and pecans.

2. Shape dough into 1¼-inch balls. On ungreased cookie sheets, place balls 2 inches apart.

3. Bake 10 to 14 minutes or until edges are light golden brown. Remove from cookie sheets to cooling rack.

KITCHEN TIPS

❂ To toast nuts, bake in shallow pan at 350°F for 6 to 10 minutes, stirring occasionally, until light brown.
❂ Crisp and delicate, these cookies beg for a cup of steaming tea or warm apple cider.

PB&J Sandwich Cookies

Prep Time: 45 min Start to Finish: 1 hr 10 min

1 pouch (1 pound 1.5 ounces) Betty Crocker peanut butter cookie mix

Vegetable oil and egg called for on cookie mix pouch

$^1\!/_3$ cup Betty Crocker Rich & Creamy vanilla frosting (from 1-pound container)

2 tablespoons peanut butter

$^1\!/_3$ cup jam or preserves

1. Heat oven to 375°F. Make cookies as directed on pouch, using oil and egg. Cool completely, about 30 minutes.

2. In small bowl, stir frosting and peanut butter until smooth.

3. For each sandwich cookie, spread generous teaspoon frosting mixture on bottom of 1 cookie; spread scant teaspoon jelly over peanut butter mixture. Top with another cookie, bottom side down.

18 cookies
1 Sandwich Cookie: Calories 200 (Calories from Fat 80); Total Fat 9g (Saturated Fat 2g; Trans Fat 0g); Cholesterol 10mg; Sodium 170mg; Total Carbohydrate 28g (Dietary Fiber 0g; Sugars 18g); Protein 3g
% Daily Value: Vitamin A 0%; Vitamin C 0%; Calcium 0%; Iron 2%
Exchanges: 1 Starch, 1 Other Carbohydrate, 1$^1\!/_2$ Fat
Carbohydrate Choices: 2

KITCHEN TIPS

❀ You can make sandwich cookies with Betty Crocker oatmeal, chocolate chip or sugar cookie mixes, too.

❀ Keep a stash of baked cookies in the freezer, ready to be filled and served.

Cakes

Cakes

From Simple to Sublime

Lemon Pound Cake (page 279)

Spice Cake with Raspberry Filling and Cream Cheese Frosting
(page 300)

Roller Coaster Cake

Prep Time: 40 min Start to Finish: 2 hr 10 min

Cake

- 1 box Betty Crocker SuperMoist butter recipe yellow cake mix
- 1¼ cups water
- ½ cup butter, softened
- 3 eggs

Frosting and Decorations

- 1 container (12 ounces) Betty Crocker Whipped vanilla frosting
- Blue food color
- 1 roll Betty Crocker Fruit by the Foot chewy fruit snack (from 4.5-ounces box)
- 21 thin pretzel sticks
- 3 fruit slice candies (flat)
- 6 miniature brown candy-coated semisweet chocolate baking bits
- 1 tablespoon Betty Crocker Rich & Creamy chocolate frosting (from 1-pound container)
- 3 thin candy wafers (1-inch diameter)
- ½ teaspoon Betty Crocker candy sprinkles
- 3 miniature red candy-coated semisweet chocolate baking bits
- 6 oblong (1 inch) candy-coated licorice pieces

1. Heat oven to 350°F for shiny metal pan (or 325°F for dark or nonstick pan). Spray bottom only of 15 × 10 × 1-inch pan with baking spray with flour.

2. In large bowl, make cake mix as directed on box, using water, butter and eggs. Pour into pan. Bake 23 to 28 minutes or until toothpick inserted in center comes out clean. Cool completely, about 1 hour.

3. Frost cake with vanilla frosting. With toothpick, lightly draw shape of roller coaster on cake (see photo). Squeeze drops of food color in several places on frosting above roller coaster outline; use knife to swirl into frosting for sky.

4. Tear or cut fruit snack in half lengthwise; place strips on cake to make track of roller coaster. Add pretzels for supports. Add fruit slice candies just above track for cars; place 2 brown baking bits under each car for wheels.

5. In small microwavable bowl, microwave chocolate frosting uncovered on Medium (50%) 15 seconds; stir. Dip top third of each candy wafer into melted frosting; top with sprinkles for hair. Place 1 wafer "face" on top of each car.

6. Place remaining melted frosting in small resealable plastic food-storage bag; seal bag. Cut small hole in bottom corner of bag. Add dot of frosting to each red baking bit; add to wafers for mouths. Add licorice candies on both sides of each wafer candy for arms.

24 servings
1 Serving (Cake and Frosting): Calories 190 (Calories from Fat 80); Total Fat 9g (Saturated Fat 4g; Trans Fat 1.5g); Cholesterol 35mg; Sodium 190mg; Total Carbohydrate 26g (Dietary Fiber 0g; Sugars 18g); Protein 1g
% Daily Value: Vitamin A 4%; Vitamin C 0%; Calcium 4%; Iron 2%
Exchanges: 1½ Other Carbohydrate, 2 Fat
Carbohydrate Choices: 2

Sports Party Cake

Prep Time: 35 min Start to Finish: 3 hr 25 min

1 box Betty Crocker SuperMoist cake mix (any flavor)

Water, vegetable oil and eggs called for on cake mix box

Tray or cardboard (15 × 12 inch), covered

2 cups Betty Crocker Whipped fluffy white frosting (from two 12-ounce containers)

Food colors

1. Heat oven to 350°F for shiny metal or glass pan (or 325°F for dark or nonstick pan). Spray bottom only of 13 × 9-inch pan with baking spray with flour.

2. Make and bake cake as directed on box for 13 × 9-inch pan, using water, oil and eggs. Cool 10 minutes; remove from pan to cooling rack. Cool completely, about 1 hour.

3. Use toothpicks to mark sections of cake to be cut. Cut cake into sections with serrated knife. Cut neck hole from top of cake.

4. On tray, place largest piece of cake. Using frosting, attach 2 small rectangular pieces on each side of top of cake to form sleeves. Position sleeves in place. Cover; freeze cake 1 hour or until firm.

5. Tint 1½ cups of the frosting with food color as desired for your favorite team's jersey color. Remove cake from freezer; frost sides and top of cake with jersey frosting. Tint remaining ½ cup frosting as desired; pipe onto cake to create numbers, name and trim. Store loosely covered at room temperature.

15 servings
1 Serving: Calories 310 (Calories from Fat 130); Total Fat 14g (Saturated Fat 4g; Trans Fat 2.5g); Cholesterol 40mg; Sodium 260mg; Total Carbohydrate 44g (Dietary Fiber 0g; Sugars 30g); Protein 2g
% Daily Value: Vitamin A 0%; Vitamin C 0%; Calcium 6%; Iron 4%
Exchanges: 3 Other Carbohydrate, 3 Fat
Carbohydrate Choices: 3

Sparkling Fourth of July Cake

Prep Time: 40 min Start to Finish: 2 hr 20 min

1 box Betty Crocker SuperMoist white cake mix

1¼ cups water

⅓ cup vegetable oil

3 egg whites

½ teaspoon red food color

½ teaspoon blue food color

1 container (12 ounces) Betty Crocker Whipped fluffy white or whipped cream frosting

1 tablespoon Betty Crocker blue sugar

2 tablespoons Betty Crocker red sugar

White star candies, if desired

Fourth of July candles

1. Heat oven to 350°F for metal or glass pan (or 325°F for dark or nonstick pan). Spray bottom only of 13 × 9-inch pan with baking spray with flour. Place paper baking cup in 1 regular-size muffin cup.

2. Make cake mix as directed on box, using water, oil and egg whites. In small bowl, place ½ cup batter; stir in red food color. In another small bowl, place ½ cup batter; stir in blue food color.

3. Fill muffin cup with ¼ cup white batter; set aside. Pour remaining white batter into 13 × 9-inch pan. Randomly drop generous teaspoonfuls of red and blue batters over white batter in pan. For swirled design, cut through batters with knife in S-shaped curves in one continuous motion; turn pan ¼ turn and repeat.

4. Place muffin pan and cake pan in oven. Bake muffin cup 12 to 13 minutes or until toothpick inserted in center comes out clean; place pan on cooling rack. Continue baking 13 × 9-inch cake 14 to 18 minutes longer or until toothpick inserted in center comes out clean. Cool cake in pan 10 minutes. Remove cake and cupcake from pans to cooling rack. Cool completely, about 1 hour.

5. Reserve 2 tablespoons frosting. Frost cake with remaining frosting. In upper left-hand corner of cake, lightly score 5 × 3½-inch rectangle in frosting for blue area of flag; sprinkle with blue sugar. Cut 2 strips of clean white paper, 13 inches long and 1½ inches wide. Cut a third strip, 8 inches long and 1½ inches wide. Place strips lightly on cake to cover area for white stripes. Sprinkle red sugar on cake for red stripes. Remove paper strips. Top blue sugar with candy stars.

6. Frost cupcake with reserved frosting; place in center of cake. Arrange candles in cupcake.

15 servings
1 Serving: Calories 300 (Calories from Fat 110); Total Fat 13g (Saturated Fat 3g; Trans Fat 2g); Cholesterol 0mg; Sodium 270mg; Total Carbohydrate 43g (Dietary Fiber 0g; Sugars 29g); Protein 2g
% Daily Value: Vitamin A 0%; Vitamin C 0%; Calcium 4%; Iron 4%
Exchanges: ½ Starch, 2½ Other Carbohydrate, 2½ Fat
Carbohydrate Choices: 3

KITCHEN TIPS

✿ The star candies are available on www.shopbakersnook.com.

Peanut Butter Tandy Cake

Prep Time: 20 min Start to Finish: 1 hr 25 min

1 box Betty Crocker SuperMoist yellow cake mix

1¼ cups water

⅓ cup vegetable oil

3 eggs

1½ cups creamy peanut butter

½ cup semisweet chocolate chips

2 tablespoons butter or margarine

1 container (1 pound) Betty Crocker Rich & Creamy chocolate frosting

1. Heat oven to 350°F for shiny metal pan (or 325°F for dark or nonstick pan). Spray bottom and sides of 15 × 10 × 1-inch pan with baking spray with flour.

2. In large bowl, beat cake mix, water, oil and eggs with electric mixer on low speed 30 seconds. Beat on medium speed 2 minutes, scraping bowl occasionally. Pour batter into pan.

3. Bake 22 to 28 minutes or until toothpick inserted in center comes out clean. Cool in pan on cooling rack 30 minutes.

4. In small microwavable bowl, microwave peanut butter uncovered on High 20 seconds or until softened and spreadable. Drop by teaspoonfuls onto surface of warm cake; spread carefully to cover top. Freeze cake to harden the peanut butter, about 15 minutes.

5. Meanwhile, in medium microwavable bowl, microwave chocolate chips and butter uncovered on High 30 seconds. Stir; continue to microwave on High 10 to 20 seconds longer, stirring after 10 seconds until chips are melted. Stir in frosting.

6. Spread frosting over peanut butter layer on cake.

24 servings
1 Serving: Calories 330 (Calories from Fat 170); Total Fat 18g (Saturated 5g; Trans 1.5g); Cholesterol 30mg; Sodium 280mg; Total Carbohydrate 35g (Dietary Fiber 1g; Sugars 23g); Protein 5g
% Daily Value: Vitamin A 0%; Vitamin C 0%; Calcium 4%; Iron 6%
Exchanges: ½ Starch, 2 Other Carbohydrate, ½ High-Fat Meat, 2½ Fat
Carbohydrate Choices: 2

KITCHEN TIPS

✿ This is our version of a "Tandy Kake," a white cake made with peanut butter and chocolate that was popular in the 1930s.

✿ For flavor reminiscent of a popular candy bar, substitute milk chocolate chips for the semisweet.

Yule Log

Prep Time: 35 min Start to Finish: 2 hr 5 min

Cake

- 3 eggs
- 1¾ cups Betty Crocker SuperMoist devil's food cake mix (from 18.25-ounce box)
- ⅓ cup water
- 2 tablespoons vegetable oil
- 1 tablespoon powdered sugar

Rich Chocolate Frosting

- ½ cup whipping cream
- 1 cup semisweet chocolate chips (6 ounces)
- 1 tablespoon corn syrup
- ¼ teaspoon vanilla

Filling

- 1 container (12 ounces) Betty Crocker Whipped vanilla frosting

1. Heat oven to 375°F for shiny metal pan (or 350°F for dark or nonstick pan). Line bottom only of 15 × 10 × 1-inch pan with aluminum foil or waxed paper; spray with baking spray with flour.

2. In large bowl, beat eggs with electric mixer on high speed about 5 minutes or until thick and lemon colored. Add cake mix, water and oil; beat on low speed 30 seconds, then on medium speed 1 minute, scraping bowl occasionally. Pour into pan.

3. Bake 11 to 14 minutes or until cake springs back when lightly touched in center. If necessary, run knife around edges of pan to loosen cake. Turn cake upside down onto clean kitchen towel sprinkled generously with powdered sugar; carefully remove foil. While hot, carefully roll up cake and towel from narrow end. Cool completely on cooling rack, about 1 hour.

4. Meanwhile, in medium microwavable bowl, microwave whipping cream uncovered on High 1 minute to 1 minute 30 seconds or until it just starts to boil. Stir in chocolate chips and corn syrup; let stand 3 minutes. Beat gently with wire whisk until smooth. Beat in vanilla. Refrigerate about 1 hour, stirring every 15 minutes, until spreading consistency.

5. Unroll cake carefully and remove towel. Spread filling evenly over cake; roll up cake. Place cooling rack on sheet of waxed paper. Place cake roll on cooling rack; frost cake. Using fork, drag tines through frosting to resemble log. Let stand 15 minutes. Transfer cake to serving platter. Store loosely covered in refrigerator. Let stand at room temperature 30 minutes before serving.

12 servings
1 Serving: Calories 360 (Calories from Fat 160); Total Fat 18g (Saturated Fat 8g; Trans Fat 2g); Cholesterol 65mg; Sodium 220mg; Total Carbohydrate 46g (Dietary Fiber 1g; Sugars 35g); Protein 3g
% Daily Value: Vitamin A 4%; Vitamin C 0%; Calcium 4%; Iron 8%
Exchanges: 1 Starch, 2 Other Carbohydrate, 3½ Fat
Carbohydrate Choices: 3

KITCHEN TIPS

✿ For a garnish, brush cranberries with water and roll in coarse white or gold sugar. Add fresh mint leaves.

Yule Log

Key Lime Pie Poke Cake

Prep Time: 20 min Start to Finish: 1 hr 55 min

Cake

1	box Betty Crocker SuperMoist white cake mix
1¼	cups water
1	tablespoon vegetable oil
4	eggs

Key Lime Filling

1	can (14 ounces) sweetened condensed milk (not evaporated)
¾	cup whipping cream
½	cup Key lime juice or regular lime juice
1	teaspoon grated lime peel
4	drops yellow food color
1	drop green food color

Frosting

1	container (12 ounces) Betty Crocker Whipped vanilla frosting
2	teaspoons grated lime peel
	Garnish, if desired
	Fresh strawberries
	Key lime slices
	Lemon leaves

1. Heat oven to 350°F for shiny metal or glass pan (or 325°F for dark or nonstick pan). Spray bottom only of 13 × 9-inch pan with baking spray with flour.

2. In large bowl, beat cake ingredients with electric mixer on low speed 30 seconds. Beat on medium speed 2 minutes, scraping bowl occasionally. Pour into pan.

3. Bake 26 to 30 minutes or until toothpick inserted in center comes out clean. Cool 5 minutes. With handle of wooden spoon (¼ to ½ inch in diameter), poke holes almost to bottom of cake every ½ inch, wiping spoon handle occasionally to reduce sticking.

4. In medium bowl, stir together filling ingredients (mixture will thicken). Pour over cake; spread evenly over surface, working back and forth to fill holes. (Some filling should remain on top of cake.) Refrigerate 1 hour.

5. Spread frosting over cake; sprinkle with lime peel. Garnish with strawberries, lime slices and lemon leaves. Store loosely covered in refrigerator.

15 servings
1 Serving: Calories 390 (Calories from Fat 150); Total Fat 16g (Saturated Fat 7g; Trans Fat 2.5g); Cholesterol 80mg; Sodium 310mg; Total Carbohydrate 56g (Dietary Fiber 0g; Sugars 41g); Protein 6g
% Daily Value: Vitamin A 6%; Vitamin C 2%; Calcium 10%; Iron 4%
Exchanges: ½ Starch, 3 Other Carbohydrate, ½ High-Fat Meat, 2½ Fat
Carbohydrate Choices: 4

KITCHEN TIPS

❀ Key lime pie is not green in color unless food color is added. If you'd prefer a greener filling in this cake, add a couple drops of green food color to the filling before pouring it over the cake.

❀ If Key limes aren't available in your grocery store, look for bottled Key lime juice near the other bottled lime juices.

Lemon Pound Cake

Prep Time: 15 min Start to Finish: 2 hr 25 min

1 box Betty Crocker SuperMoist yellow cake mix
1 package (3 ounces) cream cheese, softened
¾ cup water
1 tablespoon grated lemon peel
3 eggs
¼ cup Betty Crocker Rich & Creamy lemon frosting (from 1-pound container)

1. Heat oven to 325°F for shiny metal or glass pan (or 300°F for dark or nonstick pan). Generously spray bottom only of 9 × 5-inch loaf pan with baking spray with flour.

2. In medium bowl, beat cake mix, cream cheese, water, grated lemon peel and eggs with electric mixer on low speed 1 minute, scraping bowl frequently. Beat on medium speed 2 minutes, scraping bowl occasionally. Pour into pan.

3. Bake 55 to 60 minutes or until toothpick inserted in center comes out clean. Cool in pan 10 minutes.

Remove from pan to cooling rack or heatproof serving plate. Cool completely, about 1 hour.

4. In small microwavable bowl, microwave frosting uncovered on High 10 to 15 seconds or until frosting is thin enough to drizzle; stir. Spoon frosting evenly over cake, allowing frosting to drip down sides.

1 loaf cake (12 slices)
1 Slice: Calories 240 (Calories from Fat 70); Total Fat 8g (Saturated Fat 3g; Trans Fat 1.5g); Cholesterol 60mg; Sodium 330mg; Total Carbohydrate 38g (Dietary Fiber 0g; Sugars 22g); Protein 4g
% Daily Value: Vitamin A 4%; Vitamin C 0%; Calcium 8%; Iron 6%
Exchanges: 1 Starch, 1½ Other Carbohydrate, 1½ Fat
Carbohydrate Choices: 2½

KITCHEN TIPS

✿ If you have leftover cake, cut it into slices and place individually in sandwich-size food-storage plastic bags. Seal bags and freeze. You'll have a quick treat when you need it!

Creamy Orange Cake

Prep Time: 25 min Start to Finish: 2 hr

1 cup boiling water

1 box (4-serving size) orange-flavored gelatin

1 box Betty Crocker SuperMoist white cake mix

¾ cup frozen (thawed) orange juice concentrate

⅓ cup vegetable oil

¼ cup water

4 egg whites

1 container (12 ounces) Betty Crocker Whipped vanilla frosting

1 container (8 ounces) frozen whipped topping, thawed

1. Heat oven to 350°F for shiny metal or glass pan (or 325°F for dark or nonstick pan). Spray bottom only of 13 × 9-inch pan with baking spray with flour. In small bowl, mix boiling water and gelatin until gelatin is completely dissolved. Cool slightly, about 5 minutes.

2. In large bowl, beat cake mix, ¼ cup of the gelatin mixture, ¼ cup of the orange juice concentrate, the oil, water and egg whites with electric mixture on low speed 30 seconds. Beat on medium speed 2 minutes, scraping bowl occasionally. Pour into pan. Reserve remaining gelatin mixture and orange juice concentrate.

3. Bake 30 to 35 minutes or until toothpick inserted in center comes out clean. Poke warm cake every inch with fork. Place 1 tablespoon of the reserved gelatin mixture in microwavable custard cup or small bowl; set aside. Into remaining gelatin mixture, stir remaining ½ cup orange juice concentrate; pour slowly over cake. Cool cake completely, about 1 hour.

4. In medium bowl, gently stir together frosting and whipped topping; frost cake. Microwave 1 tablespoon gelatin mixture uncovered on High 10 seconds to liquefy. Using ¼ teaspoon measuring spoon, place small drops of gelatin mixture over frosting. With spoon or toothpick, swirl gelatin into frosting. Store covered in refrigerator.

12 servings
1 Serving: Calories 470 (Calories from Fat 180); Total Fat 20g (Saturated Fat 7g; Trans Fat 3g); Cholesterol 0mg; Sodium 370mg; Total Carbohydrate 69g (Dietary Fiber 0g; Sugars 49g); Protein 5g
% Daily Value: Vitamin A 0%; Vitamin C 20%; Calcium 6%; Iron 4%
Exchanges: 1½ Starch, 3 Other Carbohydrate, 4 Fat
Carbohydrate Choices: 4½

KITCHEN TIPS

✿ Pour the leftover thawed frozen orange juice concentrate over a cup of fresh fruit for a quick snack.

Coconut Cake with White Chocolate Frosting

Prep Time: 25 min Start to Finish: 2 hr

1 can (14 ounces) coconut milk (not cream of coconut)
1 box Betty Crocker SuperMoist white cake mix
¼ cup water
3 egg whites
¾ cup large flaked coconut
1 cup white vanilla baking chips (6 ounces)
1¾ cups powdered sugar
⅓ cup butter or margarine, softened
½ teaspoon vanilla

1. Heat oven to 350°F for shiny metal or glass pan (or 325°F for dark or nonstick pan). Spray bottom only of 13 × 9-inch pan with baking spray with flour. Reserve ⅓ cup coconut milk for frosting.

2. In large bowl, beat cake mix, remaining coconut milk (1⅓ cups), the water and egg whites with electric mixer on low speed 30 seconds. Beat on medium speed 2 minutes, scraping bowl occasionally. Stir in ½ cup of the coconut until well combined. Pour into pan.

3. Bake 28 to 33 minutes or until toothpick inserted in center comes out clean. Cool completely, about 1 hour.

4. Meanwhile, in 2-quart bowl, microwave vanilla baking chips uncovered on High 30 seconds or until melted. Stir; if chips are not completely melted, microwave 15 seconds longer, then stir until all chips are melted. Stir in powdered sugar, butter, reserved ⅓ cup coconut milk and the vanilla. Cover; refrigerate 30 to 60 minutes. (If frosting becomes too firm to spread, microwave uncovered on High 10 to 15 seconds to soften; stir until smooth.)

5. Spread frosting over cake. Immediately sprinkle top with ¼ cup coconut. Store loosely covered at room temperature.

15 servings
1 Serving: Calories 370 (Calories from Fat 150); Total Fat 16g (Saturated Fat 11g; Trans Fat 1g); Cholesterol 10mg; Sodium 320mg; Total Carbohydrate 51g (Dietary Fiber 0g; Sugars 37g); Protein 4g
% Daily Value: Vitamin A 2%; Vitamin C 0%; Calcium 4%; Iron 4%
Exchanges: 1 Starch, 2½ Other Carbohydrate, 3 Fat
Carbohydrate Choices: 3½

KITCHEN TIPS

✿ Don't waste those egg yolks! Place them in a small container, adding enough water to cover yolks completely (to prevent drying). Cover tightly and refrigerate up to 24 hours. Drain water before using. Add them to scrambled eggs.

✿ Regular flaked coconut can be used instead of the large flakes.

No-Cholesterol Carrot Cake

Prep Time: 30 min Start to Finish: 2 hr 40 min

1 box Betty Crocker SuperMoist yellow cake mix

2 teaspoons ground cinnamon

1 cup fat-free egg product

²⁄₃ cup applesauce

¹⁄₃ cup vegetable oil

3 cups freshly shredded carrots (4 to 5 large)

¹⁄₂ cup raisins

1 container (12 ounces) Betty Crocker Whipped cream cheese frosting (no cholesterol)

2 drops red food color

1 drop yellow food color

2 drops green food color

1. Heat oven to 350°F for shiny metal or glass pan (or 325°F for dark or nonstick pan). Spray bottom only of 13 × 9-inch pan with baking spray with flour.

2. In medium bowl, beat cake mix, cinnamon, egg product, applesauce and oil with electric mixer on low speed 30 seconds, scraping bowl frequently. Beat on medium speed 2 minutes, scraping bowl occasionally. Add carrots; beat about 1 minute or until well blended. Stir in raisins. Pour batter into pan; spread evenly.

3. Bake 33 to 38 minutes or until center of cake feels firm or toothpick inserted in center comes out clean. Cool cake in pan or cooling rack at least 1 hour.

4. Reserve ¹⁄₂ cup of the frosting. Spread remaining frosting over top of cake. Spoon ¹⁄₄ cup of the reserved frosting into small resealable plastic freezer bag; spoon remaining frosting into second bag. Add red and yellow food colors to one bag; add green food color to other bag. Seal bags; squeeze bags to tint frosting evenly.

5. Pull tip of knife through frosting on top of the cake to score 16 serving pieces (4 rows by 4 rows). Cut ¹⁄₈-inch tip off one bottom corner of bag with orange frosting. Diagonally on each scored cake piece, pipe a carrot by squeezing frosting in a thick line, letting up on pressure at end to draw to a point.

Cut off tiny corner of bag with green frosting. At top of each carrot, pipe loops of green frosting for carrot tops. Refrigerate until frosting is firm before serving, about 30 minutes. Store loosely covered in refrigerator.

16 servings
1 Serving: Calories 300 (Calories from Fat 110); Total Fat 12g (Saturated Fat 3g; Trans Fat 2g); Cholesterol 0mg; Sodium 290mg; Total Carbohydrate 47g (Dietary Fiber 1g; Sugars 31g); Protein 3g
% Daily Value: Vitamin A 70%; Vitamin C 0%; Calcium 6%; Iron 6%
Exchanges: 1 Starch, 2 Other Carbohydrate, 2¹⁄₂ Fat
Carbohydrate Choices: 3

KITCHEN TIPS

❋ There's no cholesterol in the cake or frosting—really!

❋ If you like to use decorating bags and tips, use a #4 writing tip to form the carrots and a #67 leaf tip to make the leaves.

Honey Bun Cake

Prep Time: 15 min Start to Finish: 2 hr 5 min

Cake

- 1 box Betty Crocker SuperMoist yellow cake mix
- 2/3 cup vegetable oil
- 4 eggs
- 1 container (8 ounces) sour cream (1 cup)
- 1 cup packed brown sugar
- 1/3 cup chopped pecans
- 2 teaspoons ground cinnamon

Icing

- 1 cup powdered sugar
- 1 tablespoon milk
- 1 teaspoon vanilla

1. Heat oven to 350°F for shiny metal or glass pan (or 325°F for dark or nonstick pan). Spray bottom only of 13 × 9-inch pan with baking spray with flour.

2. In large bowl, beat cake mix, oil, eggs and sour cream with electric mixer on low speed 30 seconds; beat on medium speed 2 minutes, scraping bowl occasionally. Spread half of the batter in pan.

3. In small bowl, stir together brown sugar, pecans and cinnamon; sprinkle over batter in pan. Carefully spread remaining batter evenly over pecan mixture.

4. Bake 44 to 48 minutes or until deep golden brown.

5. In small bowl, stir icing ingredients until thin enough to spread. Prick surface of warm cake several times with fork. Spread icing over cake. Cool completely, about 1 hour. Store covered at room temperature.

12 servings
1 Serving: Calories 480 (Calories from Fat 210); Total Fat 23g (Saturated Fat 6g; Trans Fat 1g); Cholesterol 85mg; Sodium 320mg; Total Carbohydrate 65g (Dietary Fiber 0g; Sugars 48g); Protein 4g
% Daily Value: Vitamin A 4%; Vitamin C 0%; Calcium 10%; Iron 8%
Exchanges: 1 Starch, 3½ Other Carbohydrate, 4 Fat
Carbohydrate Choices: 4

KITCHEN TIPS

✿ Spread the batter over the pecan mixture with ease! Simply drizzle the batter over the pecan mixture from one end of the pan to the other, then spread to fill in the uncovered spaces.

✿ In a pinch, chopped walnuts or almonds can be substituted for the pecans.

Quick

German Chocolate Picnic Cake

Prep Time: 15 min Start to Finish: 1 hr 25 min

1¾ cups Betty Crocker SuperMoist German chocolate cake mix (from 18.25-ounce box)

½ cup water

2 tablespoons vegetable oil

1 egg

½ cup packed brown sugar

⅓ cup Gold Medal all-purpose flour

⅓ cup quick-cooking or old-fashioned oats

3 tablespoons butter or margarine, softened

¾ teaspoon ground cinnamon

¼ teaspoon ground nutmeg

1. Heat oven to 350°F for shiny metal or glass pan (or 325°F for dark or nonstick pan). Spray bottom only of 8- to 9-inch square pan with baking spray with flour.

2. In large bowl, beat cake mix, water, oil and egg with electric mixer on low speed 30 seconds. Beat on medium speed 2 minutes, scraping bowl occasionally. Pour batter into pan.

3. In medium bowl, stir remaining ingredients until well mixed; sprinkle evenly over batter in pan.

4. Bake 32 to 36 minutes or until toothpick inserted in center of cake comes out clean. Cool at least 30 minutes before serving. Serve warm or cool.

9 servings
1 Serving: Calories 260 (Calories from Fat 90); Total Fat 10g (Saturated Fat 4g; Trans Fat 0g); Cholesterol 35mg; Sodium 260mg; Total Carbohydrate 41g (Dietary Fiber 1g; Sugars 26g); Protein 3g
% Daily Value: Vitamin A 4%; Vitamin C 0%; Calcium 4%; Iron 6%
Exchanges: 1 Starch, 1½ Other Carbohydrate, 2 Fat
Carbohydrate Choices: 3

KITCHEN TIPS

❂ If you plan to tote this cake to a picnic, bake it in a disposable foil pan. Then you don't have to carry the dirty pan home.

❂ Use the other half of the cake mix to make Chocolate Zucchini Snack Cake, opposite page.

Quick

Chocolate Zucchini Snack Cake

Prep Time: 15 min Start to Finish: 1 hr 50 min

1¾ cups Betty Crocker SuperMoist German chocolate cake mix (from 18.25-ounce box)

1 cup shredded unpeeled zucchini (about 1 medium)

½ teaspoon ground cinnamon

⅛ teaspoon ground cloves

¼ cup buttermilk

2 tablespoons vegetable oil

1 egg

¼ cup chopped nuts

¼ cup miniature semisweet chocolate chips

1. Heat oven to 350°F for shiny metal or glass pan (or 325°F for dark or nonstick pan). Spray bottom and side of 8- to 9-inch round cake pan with baking spray with flour.

2. In large bowl, beat cake mix, zucchini, cinnamon, cloves, buttermilk, oil and egg with electric mixer on low speed until moistened. Beat on medium speed 2 minutes, scraping bowl occasionally. Pour into pan. Sprinkle evenly with nuts and chocolate chips.

3. Bake 30 to 35 minutes or until toothpick inserted in center comes out clean. Cool completely, about 1 hour.

6 servings
1 Serving: Calories 310 (Calories from Fat 120); Total Fat 14g (Saturated Fat 3.5g; Trans Fat 0.5g); Cholesterol 35mg; Sodium 350mg; Total Carbohydrate 42g (Dietary Fiber 2g; Sugars 26g); Protein 5g
% Daily Value: Vitamin A 0%; Vitamin C 4%; Calcium 6%; Iron 8%
Exchanges: 1 Starch, 2 Other Carbohydrate, 2½ Fat
Carbohydrate Choices: 3

KITCHEN TIPS

✪ Out of buttermilk? Use ¾ teaspoon lemon juice or vinegar plus milk to make ¼ cup. Let stand for about 5 minutes before using.

✪ Use the other half of the cake mix to make German Chocolate Picnic Cake, opposite page.

✪ Bake and serve the cake in a pretty, oven-safe ceramic pan.

Ginger-Carrot Cake

Prep Time: 25 min Start to Finish: 2 hr

Cake

1	tablespoon Gold Medal all-purpose flour
¼	cup finely chopped crystallized ginger
1¼	cups Gold Medal all-purpose flour
¾	cup granulated sugar
1	teaspoon baking soda
2	teaspoons ground cinnamon
½	teaspoon salt
¼	teaspoon ground nutmeg
¾	cup vegetable oil
2	teaspoons vanilla
2	eggs
1½	cups grated or finely shredded carrots (about 3 medium)

Cream Cheese Frosting

1	package (3 ounces) cream cheese, softened
¼	cup butter or margarine, softened
2	cups powdered sugar
1	teaspoon vanilla
	Finely chopped crystallized ginger, if desired

1. Heat oven to 350°F. Grease bottom and sides of 8- or 9-inch square pan with shortening or cooking spray.

2. In small bowl, toss 1 tablespoon flour and the ginger to coat. In large bowl, beat remaining cake ingredients except carrots with electric mixer on low speed 30 seconds. Beat on medium speed 3 minutes. Stir in carrots and ginger-flour mixture. Pour into pan.

3. Bake 30 to 35 minutes or until toothpick inserted in center comes out clean. Cool completely on cooling rack, about 1 hour.

4. In medium bowl, beat cream cheese and butter on medium speed until smooth. Gradually stir in powdered sugar and vanilla until smooth and spreadable. Frost cake. Sprinkle with finely chopped crystallized ginger. Store covered in refrigerator.

9 servings
1 Serving: Calories 530 (Calories from Fat 250); Total Fat 28g (Saturated Fat 8g; Trans Fat 0g); Cholesterol 70mg; Sodium 360mg; Total Carbohydrate 65g (Dietary Fiber 1g; Sugars 44g); Protein 4g
% Daily Value: Vitamin A 70%; Vitamin C 0%; Calcium 4%; Iron 8%
Exchanges: 1 Starch, 3½ Other Carbohydrate, 5½ Fat
Carbohydrate Choices: 4

KITCHEN TIPS

✪ Crystallized ginger gives the unique flavor to this traditional carrot cake recipe.
✪ Look for packages of shredded carrots in the produce section of your grocery store.

Carrot-Mandarin Orange Cake

Prep Time: 35 min Start to Finish: 2 hr 50 min

Cake

- 1 box Betty Crocker SuperMoist yellow or golden vanilla cake mix
- 1 cup vegetable oil
- 2 teaspoons ground cinnamon
- 1 teaspoon ground allspice
- 3 eggs
- 1 can (11 ounces) mandarin orange segments, undrained
- 1 cup finely shredded carrots (2 large)
- 1 cup flaked coconut

Topping

- 1 package (8 ounces) cream cheese, softened
- 1 container (1 pound) Betty Crocker Rich & Creamy vanilla frosting
- ½ cup finely chopped pecans, if desired

1. Heat oven to 350°F (or 325°F for dark or nonstick pan). Spray bottom only of 13 × 9-inch pan with baking spray with flour.

2. In large bowl, beat all cake ingredients except carrots and coconut with electric mixer on low speed 30 seconds. Beat on medium speed 2 minutes. Stir in carrots and coconut. Pour into pan.

3. Bake 40 to 45 minutes or until toothpick inserted in center comes out clean. Cool completely, about 1 hour.

4. In large bowl, beat cream cheese on medium speed until smooth and creamy. Stir in frosting until well mixed. Spread frosting over cake. Sprinkle with pecans (or top with additional mandarin orange segments just before serving). Refrigerate 30 minutes before serving. Store covered in refrigerator.

15 servings
1 Serving: Calories 510 (Calories from Fat 290); Total Fat 32g (Saturated Fat 10g; Trans Fat 3.5g); Cholesterol 60mg; Sodium 370mg; Total Carbohydrate 53g (Dietary Fiber 0g; Sugars 38g); Protein 4g
% Daily Value: Vitamin A 35%; Vitamin C 6%; Calcium 8%; Iron 6%
Exchanges: 1 Starch, 2½ Other Carbohydrate, 6 Fat
Carbohydrate Choices: 3½

KITCHEN TIPS

 Buy an extra can of mandarin orange segments for the garnish.

Italian Orange Cake

Prep Time: 20 min Start to Finish: 2 hr 10 min

1 box Betty Crocker SuperMoist white cake mix

1¼ cups water

⅓ cup light olive oil

¼ cup sweet Marsala, Muscat or sherry dessert wine, or orange juice

1 tablespoon grated orange peel

3 eggs

1 container (12 ounces) Betty Crocker Whipped whipped cream or vanilla frosting

1½ teaspoons grated orange peel

1 tablespoon sweet Marsala, Muscat or sherry dessert wine, or orange juice

1 tablespoon grated orange peel

1. Heat oven to 325°F for shiny metal pan (or 300°F for dark or nonstick pan). Generously spray bottom only of 10- or 12-inch springform pan with baking spray with flour.

2. In large bowl, beat cake mix, water, olive oil, ¼ cup wine, 1 tablespoon orange peel and the eggs with electric mixer on low speed 30 seconds. Beat on medium speed 2 minutes, scraping bowl occasionally. Pour batter into pan.

3. Bake 10-inch pan 45 to 50 minutes, 12-inch pan 35 to 40 minutes, or until toothpick inserted near center comes out clean. (Top of cake may appear very dark brown and rippled with a crack in center of cake.) Cool completely, about 1 hour.

4. Carefully run knife around side of pan to loosen; remove side of pan. Transfer cake to serving plate. In medium bowl, stir frosting, 1½ teaspoons orange peel and 1 tablespoon wine until well blended. Frost top and side of cake. Garnish with 1 tablespoon orange peel. Store loosely covered in refrigerator.

12 servings
1 Serving: Calories 380 (Calories from Fat 150); Total Fat 17g (Saturated Fat 4g; Trans Fat 3g); Cholesterol 55mg; Sodium 340mg; Total Carbohydrate 51g (Dietary Fiber 0g; Sugars 34g); Protein 4g
% Daily Value: Vitamin A 0%; Vitamin C 0%; Calcium 4%; Iron 6%
Exchanges: 1 Starch, 2½ Other Carbohydrate, 3½ Fat
Carbohydrate Choices: 3½

KITCHEN TIPS

✿ If a springform pan is unavailable, bake the cake in a 13 × 9-inch pan for 30 to 35 minutes.

Lemon-Ginger Bundt Cake

Prep Time: 25 min Start to Finish: 2 hr 20 min

Cake

- 1 box Betty Crocker SuperMoist lemon cake mix
- ¾ cup water
- ½ cup vegetable oil
- ½ cup sour cream
- 1 teaspoon ground ginger
- 3 eggs
- ½ cup finely chopped crystallized ginger (about 2½ ounces)

Frosting

- 1 cup powdered sugar
- ½ teaspoon grated fresh lemon peel
- 4 teaspoons fresh lemon juice

1. Heat oven to 350°F for shiny metal pan (or 325°F for dark or nonstick pan). Generously spray 12-cup fluted tube cake pan with baking spray with flour.

2. In medium bowl, beat cake mix, water, oil, sour cream, ground ginger and eggs with electric mixer on low speed 30 seconds. Beat on medium speed 2 minutes, scraping bowl occasionally. Stir in crystallized ginger. Pour batter into pan.

3. Bake 40 to 45 minutes or until toothpick inserted in center comes out clean. Cool 10 minutes. Place cooling rack or heatproof serving plate upside down on pan; turn rack and pan over. Remove pan. Cool completely, about 1 hour.

4. In small bowl, stir frosting ingredients until well blended. Spoon over cake. Store loosely covered at room temperature.

16 servings
1 Serving: Calories 270 (Calories from Fat 110); Total Fat 12g (Saturated Fat 3g; Trans Fat 1g); Cholesterol 45mg; Sodium 230mg; Total Carbohydrate 38g (Dietary Fiber 0g; Sugars 23g); Protein 2g
% Daily Value: Vitamin A 2%; Vitamin C 0%; Calcium 6%; Iron 4%
Exchanges: ½ Starch, 2 Other Carbohydrate, 2½ Fat
Carbohydrate Choices: 2½

KITCHEN TIPS

- Check your produce department for clear plastic bags of crystallized ginger. Buying ginger this way costs much less than buying it in a jar from the spice section.
- Garnish with additional crystallized ginger. (If you purchase a 3-ounce package, there will be 2 tablespoons left over for this.)

Caramel Latte Cake

Prep Time: 30 min Start to Finish: 3 hr 15 min

Cake

- 1 box Betty Crocker SuperMoist yellow cake mix
- 1¼ cups warm water
- 1 tablespoon instant espresso coffee granules
- ⅓ cup butter or margarine, melted
- 3 eggs

Filling

- 1 can (13.4 ounces) dulce de leche (caramelized sweetened condensed milk)
- ½ cup hot water
- 3 tablespoons instant espresso coffee granules
- 1 tablespoon dark rum or 1 teaspoon rum extract plus 2 teaspoons water

Frosting and Garnish

- 1 cup whipping cream
- ¼ cup powdered sugar
- 2 ounces semisweet baking chocolate, chopped, or 1 teaspoon cocoa

1. Heat oven to 350°F for shiny metal or glass pan (or 325°F for dark or nonstick pan). Spray bottom only of 13 × 9-inch pan with baking spray with flour.

2. In large bowl, place cake mix. In 2-cup glass measuring cup, stir 1¼ cups warm water and 1 tablespoon espresso granules until granules are dissolved. Add espresso mixture, butter and eggs to cake mix. Beat with electric mixer on low speed 30 seconds; scrape bowl. Beat on medium speed 2 minutes longer. Pour batter into pan.

3. Bake 30 to 35 minutes or until toothpick inserted in center comes out clean. Cool cake in pan on cooling rack 15 minutes.

4. Meanwhile, pour dulce de leche into medium microwavable bowl. In small bowl, mix ½ cup hot water, 3 tablespoons espresso granules and the rum; stir into dulce de leche until smooth. Microwave uncovered on High 2 to 3 minutes, stirring after about 1 minute with wire whisk, until pourable. Set aside while cake cools.

5. Poke cooled cake every ½ inch with handle end of wooden spoon. Pour dulce de leche mixture evenly over cake; spread mixture over top of cake with metal spatula to fill holes. Run knife around sides of pan to loosen cake. Cover; refrigerate 2 hours.

6. In medium bowl, beat whipping cream and powdered sugar on high speed until stiff. Spread whipped cream evenly over chilled cake. Sprinkle with chopped chocolate or cocoa. Store covered in refrigerator.

16 servings
1 Serving: Calories 330 (Calories from Fat 130); Total Fat 14g (Saturated Fat 8g; Trans Fat 1g); Cholesterol 65mg; Sodium 280mg; Total Carbohydrate 45g (Dietary Fiber 0g; Sugars 30g); Protein 4g
% Daily Value: Vitamin A 8%; Vitamin C 0%; Calcium 15%; Iron 4%
Exchanges: 1 Starch, 2 Other Carbohydrate, 3 Fat
Carbohydrate Choices: 3

Mojito Cake

Prep Time: 30 min Start to Finish: 2 hr 20 min

Cake

- 1 box Betty Crocker SuperMoist white cake mix
- 1 cup unflavored carbonated water
- 1/3 cup vegetable oil
- 1/4 cup rum or 1 teaspoon rum extract plus 1/4 cup water
- 3 tablespoons chopped fresh mint leaves
- 2 teaspoons grated lime peel
- 3 egg whites

Glaze

- 1/2 cup butter or margarine
- 1/4 cup water
- 1 cup granulated sugar
- 1/2 cup rum or 2 teaspoons rum extract plus 1/2 cup water

Garnish

- 1 cup whipping cream
- 2 tablespoons powdered sugar
- 15 fresh mint leaves, if desired
- Shredded lime peel, if desired

1. Heat oven to 350°F for shiny metal or glass pan (or 325°F for dark or nonstick pan). Spray bottom only of 13 × 9-inch pan with baking spray with flour.

2. In large bowl, beat cake ingredients with electric mixer on low speed 30 seconds. Beat on medium speed 2 minutes, scraping bowl occasionally. Pour batter into pan.

3. Bake 28 to 33 minutes or until toothpick inserted in center comes out clean. Cool 15 minutes.

4. Meanwhile, in 2-quart saucepan, mix glaze ingredients. Heat to boiling over high heat, stirring frequently. Reduce heat to medium; continue to boil 3 minutes, stirring frequently, until glaze has thickened slightly.

5. Poke warm cake every inch with fork tines. Pour glaze slowly over cake. Cool completely, about 1 hour.

6. In small bowl, beat whipping cream and powdered sugar on high speed until soft peaks form. Garnish each serving with whipped cream, mint leaf, and shredded lime peel. Store loosely covered at room temperature.

15 servings
1 Serving: Calories 350 (Calories from Fat 170); Total Fat 19g (Saturated Fat 8g; Trans Fat 1g); Cholesterol 35mg; Sodium 290mg; Total Carbohydrate 41g (Dietary Fiber 0g; Sugars 29g); Protein 3g
% Daily Value: Vitamin A 8%; Vitamin C 0%; Calcium 4%; Iron 4%
Exchanges: 1 Starch, 1 1/2 Other Carbohydrate, 4 Fat
Carbohydrate Choices: 3

KITCHEN TIPS

- A mojito typically refers to a cocktail made with lime juice, sugar, mint leaves and rum. We've taken those same flavors and turned them into a tasty cake.
- In a pinch, use purchased frozen whipped topping, thawed, instead of making your own whipped cream.

Chunky Apple Cake with Browned Butter Frosting

Prep Time: 25 min Start to Finish: 3 hr

Cake

1	cup butter or margarine, softened
2	cups granulated sugar
3	eggs
½	teaspoon vanilla
2½	cups Gold Medal all-purpose flour
2	teaspoons baking soda
½	teaspoon salt
2	teaspoons ground cinnamon
3	cups coarsely chopped peeled baking apples (3 medium)
1	cup chopped walnuts

Frosting

½	cup butter (do not use margarine)
3¼	cups powdered sugar
1	teaspoon vanilla
1 to 3	tablespoons milk

1. Heat oven to 350°F. Spray 12-cup fluted tube cake pan with baking spray with flour.

2. In large bowl, beat 1 cup butter and the granulated sugar with electric mixer on medium speed until light and fluffy. Beat in eggs, one at a time, until blended. Stir in ½ teaspoon vanilla. Stir in flour, baking soda, salt and cinnamon. Stir in apples and walnuts. Spoon into pan.

3. Bake 55 to 65 minutes or until toothpick inserted in center of cake comes out clean. Cool 10 minutes. Remove from pan to cooling rack. Cool completely, about 1 hour 30 minutes.

4. In 2-quart saucepan, heat ½ cup butter over medium heat, stirring constantly, until golden brown. Gradually beat in powdered sugar with spoon. Stir in 1 teaspoon vanilla and enough milk until frosting is smooth and desired spreading consistency. Generously spread frosting over top and partially down side of cake. To serve, cut cake with serrated knife.

16 servings
1 Serving: Calories 670 (Calories from Fat 280); Total Fat 31g (Saturated Fat 16g; Trans Fat 1g); Cholesterol 115mg; Sodium 490mg; Total Carbohydrate 91g (Dietary Fiber 2g; Sugars 68g); Protein 6g
% Daily Value: Vitamin A 15%; Vitamin C 0%; Calcium 4%; Iron 10%
Exchanges: 2 Starch, 4 Other Carbohydrate, 6 Fat
Carbohydrate Choices: 6

KITCHEN TIPS

- The best baking apples are slightly tart. Top choices are Granny Smith, Braeburn, Cortland, Northern Spy and Rome Beauty.
- Browned butter frosting has a sweet, nutty flavor that pairs well with this apple cake.

Banana-Ginger-Macadamia Cake

Prep Time: 25 min Start to Finish: 2 hr

Cake
- 2 cups Gold Medal all-purpose flour
- 1½ teaspoons baking powder
- 1 teaspoon baking soda
- 2 teaspoons ground ginger
- 1 teaspoon ground nutmeg
- ¼ teaspoon salt
- 1½ cups granulated sugar
- ½ cup butter or margarine, softened
- 2 eggs
- 1¼ cups mashed ripe bananas (2 to 3 medium)
- ¾ cup buttermilk
- ½ cup finely chopped macadamia nuts (not toasted)

Frosting
- 4 ounces (half 8-ounce package) cream cheese, softened
- ½ cup butter, softened (do not use margarine)
- 4 cups powdered sugar
- 1 teaspoon vanilla

Garnish
- ¼ cup coarsely chopped toasted macadamia nuts

1. Heat oven to 350°F. Grease bottom only of 2 (9-inch) round cake pans with shortening or cooking spray. Line bottom with cooking parchment paper; grease and flour paper and sides of pans. In medium bowl, stir together flour, baking powder, baking soda, ginger, nutmeg and salt.

2. In large bowl, beat granulated sugar and ½ cup butter with electric mixer on medium speed 3 to 4 minutes or until fluffy. On low speed, beat in eggs, one at a time, beating well after each addition. Beat in bananas. (Mixture will look curdled.) Alternately beat in flour mixture and buttermilk, beginning and ending with flour mixture. Stir in ½ cup nuts. Spread batter evenly in pans.

3. Bake 30 to 35 minutes or until dark golden brown and cakes begin to pull away from sides of pans. Cool 5 minutes; remove from pans to cooling racks. Cool completely, about 1 hour.

4. In large bowl, beat frosting ingredients with electric mixer on medium speed until smooth.

5. On serving plate, place 1 cake layer, rounded side down. Spread with half of frosting. Place remaining cake layer, rounded side up, on frosting, pressing gently to secure (frosting should show around edge). Spread frosting on top of cake, leaving side unfrosted. Sprinkle ¼ cup nuts around top edge of cake.

12 servings
1 Serving: Calories 600 (Calories from Fat 230); Total Fat 25g (Saturated Fat 13g; Trans Fat 0.5g); Cholesterol 85mg; Sodium 380mg; Total Carbohydrate 89g (Dietary Fiber 2g; Sugars 68g); Protein 5g
% Daily Value: Vitamin A 15%; Vitamin C 0%; Calcium 8%; Iron 10%
Exchanges: 1 Starch, 5 Other Carbohydrate, 5 Fat
Carbohydrate Choices: 6

Quick

Triple-Ginger Pound Cake

Prep Time: 20 min Start to Finish: 3 hr 40 min

   3   cups Gold Medal all-purpose flour
   2   teaspoons ground ginger
   1   teaspoon baking powder
 ¼   teaspoon salt
 2½   cups sugar
 1¼   cups butter, softened (do not use margarine)
   1   tablespoon grated gingerroot
   1   teaspoon vanilla
   5   eggs
 ¾   cup milk
 ½   cup finely chopped crystallized ginger

1. Heat oven to 350°F. Spray 12-cup fluted tube cake pan or 10-inch angel food cake pan with baking spray with flour.

2. In medium bowl, mix flour, ground ginger, baking powder and salt; set aside. In large bowl, beat sugar, butter, gingerroot, vanilla and eggs with electric mixer on low speed 30 seconds, scraping bowl constantly. Beat on high speed 5 minutes, scraping bowl occasionally. On low speed, beat in flour mixture alternately with milk. Fold in crystallized ginger until evenly mixed. Spread in pan.

3. Bake 50 to 60 minutes or until toothpick inserted in center comes out clean. Cool 10 minutes. Remove cake from pan to cooling rack. Cool completely, about 2 hours.

24 servings
1 Serving: Calories 250 (Calories from Fat 100); Total Fat 11g (Saturated Fat 7g; Trans Fat 0g); Cholesterol 70mg; Sodium 130mg; Total Carbohydrate 35g (Dietary Fiber 0g; Sugars 21g); Protein 3g
% Daily Value: Vitamin A 8%; Vitamin C 0%; Calcium 4%; Iron 6%
Exchanges: 1 Starch, 1½ Other Carbohydrate, 2 Fat
Carbohydrate Choices: 2

KITCHEN TIPS

✿ Crystallized ginger is fresh gingerroot that has been cooked in a sugar syrup, then coated with sugar. It has that great ginger bite along with the sweet flavor.

✿ Pound cake freezes beautifully. Wrap the cooled cake in heavy-duty aluminum foil, then place it in a resealable plastic bag. Freeze up to one month.

✿ Serve the cake on a pedestal plate and garnish with fresh fruit.

Caramel-Apple Upside Down Cake

Prep Time: 25 min Start to Finish: 1 hr 45 min

Topping

- ¼ cup butter or margarine
- ⅔ cup packed brown sugar
- ½ teaspoon ground cinnamon
- 2 medium apples, peeled, cut into ½-inch wedges

Cake

- 1⅓ cups Gold Medal all-purpose flour
- 1 teaspoon baking powder
- ½ teaspoon ground cinnamon
- ¼ teaspoon salt
- 1 cup granulated sugar
- ½ cup butter or margarine, softened
- 2 eggs
- ½ teaspoon vanilla
- ¼ cup milk

Whipped Cream

- 1 cup whipping cream
- 2 tablespoons granulated sugar

1. Heat oven to 325°F. Spray bottom and sides of 8- or 9-inch square pan with cooking spray.

2. In 1-quart saucepan, melt ¼ cup butter over medium heat, stirring occasionally. Stir in brown sugar. Heat to boiling; remove from heat. Stir in ½ teaspoon cinnamon. Pour into pan; spread evenly. Arrange apple wedges over brown sugar mixture, overlapping tightly and making 2 layers if necessary.

3. In medium bowl, mix flour, baking powder, ½ teaspoon cinnamon and the salt; set aside. In large bowl, beat 1 cup granulated sugar and ½ cup butter with electric mixer on medium speed, scraping bowl occasionally, until fluffy. Beat in eggs, one at a time, until smooth. Add vanilla. Gradually beat in flour mixture alternately with milk, beating after each addition until smooth. Spread batter over apple wedges in brown sugar mixture.

4. Bake 55 to 65 minutes or until toothpick inserted in center comes out clean. Cool on cooling rack 15 minutes. Meanwhile, in medium bowl, beat whipping cream on high speed until it begins to thicken. Gradually add 2 tablespoons granulated sugar, beating until soft peaks form.

5. Run knife around sides of pan to loosen cake. Place heatproof serving plate upside down over pan; turn plate and pan over. Remove pan. Serve warm cake with whipped cream. Store cake loosely covered.

8 servings
1 Serving: Calories 550 (Calories from Fat 250); Total Fat 28g (Saturated Fat 17g; Trans Fat 1g); Cholesterol 135mg; Sodium 290mg; Total Carbohydrate 68g (Dietary Fiber 1g; Sugars 50g); Protein 5g
% Daily Value: Vitamin A 20%; Vitamin C 0%; Calcium 10%; Iron 10%
Exchanges: 1 Starch, 3½ Other Carbohydrate, 5½ Fat
Carbohydrate Choices: 4½

KITCHEN TIPS

✿ To serve leftover dessert warm, scoop servings into small microwavable bowls and microwave individual servings on High for 15 to 20 seconds.

Betty Crocker
IN SEASON

Baking with Confidence

Baking isn't rocket science, but it is a science. Not to worry—even if you dreaded the subject in school, these tips will help ensure your success in the kitchen.

Picking the Right Pans

There are many types of pans to choose from, including shiny aluminum, insulated, nonstick and dark surface pans.

Shiny smooth-surface or textured aluminum pans are recommended for baking. These pans reflect heat, letting foods bake evenly and brown properly. The recipes in this book were tested using shiny aluminum pans.

Insulated pans help prevent foods from turning too dark on the bottom or overbaking if the oven is too hot. Food baked in these pans may take longer to bake and may not brown properly.

Nonstick and dark surface pans may cause foods to overbrown or to be fully baked in the minimum or less than the minimum time. Overbaking can also cause dryness in baked goods.

Get the Scoop

To make drop cookies uniform in size and shape, use a spring-handled cookie scoop. Look for scoops at the grocery store or kitchen specialty shops. Select the size of the scoop based on how large or small you like your cookies.

Housewares Help

Is the beater from your mixer MIA? Having caffeine withdrawal because the coffee carafe broke? Culinary Parts Unlimited comes to the rescue. The company stocks thousands of factory original parts and accessories for more than forty well-known brands of kitchen appliances. Reach them at www.culinaryparts.com or 1-866-PART-HELP. All orders are shipped within 24 hours.

Grease Is the Word

The next time a recipe directs you to grease and flour a baking pan, try baking spray with flour, available in aerosol cans in the baking aisle of the supermarket. This one-step solution is easy and less messy than the alternative.

Butter Basics

Butter is a flavorful choice for baking. Sweet butter is available in both salted and unsalted choices. Our recipes were tested with salted butter. Stick margarine can be substituted for butter  with good results in most recipes. Whipped or low-fat butters, margarine or spreads often contain more air and sometimes water or oil, making them less successful when baking.

To soften butter: Let the butter soften at room temperature for 30 to 45 minutes. Perfectly softened butter should give gently to pressure but it shouldn't be soft in appearance (still holds its stick shape).

Apple Pickin'

Here are eight apple varieties, ranging from sweet to tart, that are good for baking.

▶ Cortland—slightly tart, slightly crisp

▶ Crispin/Matsu—sweet, crisp

▶ Granny Smith—tart, crisp

▶ Haralson—tart, crisp

▶ Honeycrisp—sweet, crisp

▶ Jonagold—sweet-tart, crisp

▶ Northern Spy—slightly tart, crisp

Black Forest Cake

Prep Time: 25 min Start to Finish: 2 hr 15 min

Cake

1	box Betty Crocker SuperMoist devil's food cake mix
	Water, vegetable oil and eggs called for on cake mix box

Filling and Topping

1	pint (2 cups) whipping cream
¹⁄₂	cup powdered sugar
2 to 3	tablespoons brandy, if desired
1	can (21 ounces) cherry pie filling
¹⁄₂	teaspoon almond extract
2	tablespoons sliced almonds

1. Heat oven to 350°F for shiny metal pans (or 325°F for dark or nonstick pans). Spray bottoms and sides of 2 (8- or 9-inch) round cake pans with baking spray with flour.

2. Make and bake cake as directed on box for 8- or 9-inch rounds, using water, oil and eggs. Cool 10 minutes; remove from pans to cooling rack. Cool completely, about 1 hour.

3. In medium bowl, beat whipping cream with electric mixer on high speed until slightly thickened. Gradually beat in powdered sugar until stiff peaks form. Fold in brandy. In another small bowl, mix pie filling and almond extract.

4. On serving plate, place 1 cake layer, rounded side down. Spread with half of whipped cream and 1 cup cherry mixture to within 1 inch of edge. Top with second cake layer, rounded side up. Frost top with remaining whipped cream. Spoon remaining cherry mixture over top. Sprinkle with sliced almonds. Store covered in refrigerator.

12 servings
1 Serving: Calories 390 (Calories from Fat 150); Total Fat 16g (Saturated Fat 4.5g; Trans Fat 0.5g); Cholesterol 60mg; Sodium 370mg; Total Carbohydrate 55g (Dietary Fiber 2g; Sugars 39g); Protein 5g
% Daily Value: Vitamin A 4%; Vitamin C 0%; Calcium 6%; Iron 10%
Exchanges: 1¹⁄₂ Starch, 2 Other Carbohydrate, 3 Fat
Carbohydrate Choices: 3¹⁄₂

KITCHEN TIPS

✿ "Black Forest" usually describes desserts made with chocolate, cherries and whipping cream.

✿ If you start with a chilled bowl, the whipping cream will whip up much faster.

Chocolate-Orange Cake

Prep Time: 25 min Start to Finish: 2 hr 15 min

Cake

1	box Betty Crocker SuperMoist devil's food cake mix
2	tablespoons freshly grated orange peel
1⅓	cups orange juice
½	cup vegetable oil
3	eggs

Frosting

1½	containers (12 ounces each) Betty Crocker Whipped vanilla frosting
2	tablespoons freshly grated orange peel
½	teaspoon orange extract
⅓	cup orange marmalade

Garnishes, If Desired

Orange peel strips

Corn syrup

Sugar

1. Heat oven to 350°F for shiny metal pans (or 325°F for dark or nonstick pans). Spray bottoms and sides of 2 (8- or 9-inch) round cake pans with baking spray with flour.

2. In large bowl, beat cake mix, 2 tablespoons orange peel, the orange juice, oil and eggs with electric mixer on low speed 30 seconds, scraping bowl occasionally, until light and fluffy. Divide batter between pans.

3. Bake 8-inch pans 32 to 36 minutes, 9-inch pans 30 to 35 minutes, or until toothpick inserted in center comes out clean. Cool 10 minutes on cooling rack. Remove from pans to cooling rack. Cool completely, about 1 hour.

4. In medium bowl, stir frosting, 2 tablespoons orange peel and the orange extract until blended. On serving plate, place 1 cake layer, rounded side down. Spread ½ cup frosting over cake layer; spread marmalade over frosting. Add other cake layer, rounded side up. Frost side and top of cake with remaining frosting. For garnish, cut strips of orange peel. Brush strips with corn syrup and sprinkle with sugar. Top cake with sugared orange peel. Store loosely covered at room temperature.

16 servings
1 Serving: Calories 370 (Calories from Fat 150); Total Fat 17g (Saturated Fat 4.5g; Trans Fat 2.5g); Cholesterol 40mg; Sodium 300mg; Total Carbohydrate 53g (Dietary Fiber 1g; Sugars 39g); Protein 3g
% Daily Value: Vitamin A 0%; Vitamin C 8%; Calcium 4%; Iron 8%
Exchanges: 1 Starch, 2½ Other Carbohydrate, 3 Fat
Carbohydrate Choices: 3½

KITCHEN TIPS

✿ A pedestal plate makes any cake look extra-special.

Spice Cake with Raspberry Filling and Cream Cheese Frosting

Prep Time: 35 min Start to Finish: 2 hr 20 min

1 box Betty Crocker SuperMoist spice cake mix

Water, vegetable oil and eggs called for on cake mix box

1 package (8 ounces) cream cheese, softened

½ cup butter or margarine, softened

3½ cups powdered sugar

1 teaspoon vanilla

2 cups fresh raspberries

¼ cup red currant jelly, if desired

Fresh mint leaves if desired

1. Heat oven to 350°F for shiny metal pans (or 325°F for dark or nonstick pans). Spray bottoms and sides of 2 (8- or 9-inch) round cake pans with baking spray with flour.

2. Make and bake cake mix as directed on box for 8- or 9-inch rounds, using water, oil and eggs. Cool 10 minutes. Run knife around side of pans to loosen cakes; remove from pans to cooling rack. Cool completely, about 1 hour.

3. In medium bowl, beat cream cheese and butter with electric mixer on medium speed until fluffy. Beat in powdered sugar and vanilla.

4. On serving plate, place 1 cake, rounded side down. Spread with 1 cup frosting. Sprinkle 1 cup of the raspberries over frosting. Top with second cake, rounded side up.

5. Frost side and top of cake with remaining frosting. Arrange remaining 1 cup raspberries on top of cake along edge.

6. In 1-quart saucepan, heat jelly over medium heat, stirring constantly, until melted. Brush melted jelly over berries. Garnish with mint leaves. Store covered in refrigerator.

16 servings
1 Serving: Calories 410 (Calories from Fat 170); Total Fat 19g (Saturated Fat 8g; Trans Fat 1g); Cholesterol 70mg; Sodium 310mg; Total Carbohydrate 57g (Dietary Fiber 1g; Sugars 44g); Protein 3g
% Daily Value: Vitamin A 8%; Vitamin C 4%; Calcium 8%; Iron 6%
Exchanges: 1 Starch, 3 Other Carbohydrate, 3½ Fat
Carbohydrate Choices: 4

KITCHEN TIPS

✿ Save time by using Betty Crocker Rich & Creamy cream cheese frosting instead of making the frosting from scratch.

✿ To soften cream cheese, simply let it come to room temperature, about 30 minutes.

Strawberry-Lime Layer Cake

Prep Time: 1 hr Start to Finish: 2 hr 30 min

Cake

- 1 box Betty Crocker SuperMoist white cake mix

  Water, vegetable oil and egg whites called for on cake mix box

- 2 tablespoons grated fresh lime peel

Filling and Frosting

- 1 quart (4 cups) fresh strawberries
- 1/2 cup butter or margarine, softened
- 4 cups powdered sugar
- 1 1/3 cups whipping cream

1. Heat oven to 350°F for shiny metal pans (or 325°F for dark or nonstick pans). Generously spray bottoms and sides of 2 (8- or 9-inch) round cake pans with baking spray with flour.

2. Make cake mix as directed on box, using water, oil and egg whites; stir lime peel into batter. Divide batter between pans.

3. Bake as directed on box for 8- or 9-inch rounds. Cool in pans 10 minutes. Remove from pans to cooling rack. Cool completely, around 1 hour.

4. Reserve 3 whole strawberries for garnish. Cut remaining strawberries into thin slices. Finely chop enough of the sliced strawberries to equal 1/2 cup.

5. In medium bowl, beat butter with electric mixer on low speed about 30 seconds to soften, then beat on high speed until fluffy. Add chopped strawberries and powdered sugar; beat on low speed until sugar has been incorporated. Increase speed to medium; beat until frosting is fluffy. Divide frosting into fourths.

6. With long, sharp knife, split each cooled cake layer horizontally in half. Place 1 layer, cut side up, on serving plate. Spread with 1/4 of the frosting; top with half of the sliced strawberries. Add second layer, cut side down. Spread with 1/4 of the frosting. Add third layer, cut side up. Spread with 1/4 of the frosting; top with remaining sliced strawberries. Add remaining cake layer, cut side down. Frost top of cake with remaining frosting.

7. In medium bowl, beat whipping cream with electric mixer on high speed until stiff peaks form. Frost side of cake with whipped cream. Refrigerate at least 1 hour before serving. Garnish top of cake with whole strawberries just before serving. Store covered in refrigerator.

12 servings
1 Serving: Calories 560 (Calories from Fat 240); Total Fat 26g (Saturated Fat 12g; Trans Fat 1.5g); Cholesterol 50mg; Sodium 370mg; Total Carbohydrate 78g (Dietary Fiber 1g; Sugars 60g); Protein 4g
% Daily Value: Vitamin A 10%; Vitamin C 60%; Calcium 8%; Iron 6%
Exchanges: 1 Starch, 4 Other Carbohydrate, 5 Fat
Carbohydrate Choices: 5

KITCHEN TIPS

✪ This cake can be cut most easily after being chilled.
✪ To cut fresh strawberries into even slices, use an egg slicer.

Decadent Chocolate Torte

Prep Time: 40 min Start to Finish: 5 hr 40 min

Cake

- 6 eggs
- 1 box Betty Crocker SuperMoist devil's food cake mix
- $2/3$ cup water
- $1/4$ cup vegetable oil
- 2 tablespoons powdered sugar

Filling

- 1 cup plus 2 tablespoons whipping cream
- 2 packages (3 ounces each) cream cheese, softened
- $1/4$ cup powdered sugar
- 1 cup white vanilla baking chips
- 4 bars (1.4 ounces each) chocolate-covered English toffee candy, coarsely chopped

Glaze

- $3/4$ cup butter, softened (do not use margarine)
- 4 envelopes (1 ounce each) premelted unsweetened baking chocolate
- $1\frac{1}{2}$ cups powdered sugar

1. Heat oven to 375°F for shiny metal pans (or 350°F for dark or nonstick pans). Line bottoms only of 2 (15 × 10 × 1-inch) pans with aluminum foil or waxed paper; spray with baking spray with flour.

2. In large bowl, beat eggs with electric mixer on high speed about 5 minutes or until thick and lemon colored. Add cake mix, water and oil; beat on low speed 30 seconds, then on medium speed 1 minute, scraping bowl occasionally. Spread half the batter (about $2\frac{1}{4}$ cups) in each pan.

3. Bake 10 to 15 minutes or until cake springs back when lightly touched in center. Run knife around edges of pans to loosen cakes if necessary. Turn each cake upside down onto clean kitchen towel each sprinkled with 1 tablespoon powdered sugar; carefully remove foil. Cool completely, about 45 minutes.

4. In medium bowl, beat 1 cup of the whipping cream on high speed until stiff peaks form; set aside. In another medium bowl, beat cream cheese and $1/4$ cup powdered sugar on medium speed until smooth; set aside.

5. In small microwavable bowl, microwave baking chips and 2 tablespoons whipping cream on High 30 seconds; stir. Microwave 15 to 30 seconds longer; stir until chips are melted. Stir melted chips into cream cheese mixture. Add whipped cream and toffee candy to mixture; stir until well blended. Cover; refrigerate at least 1 hour.

6. Trim edges of cakes to make even. Cut each cake in half lengthwise. Place 1 cake piece on serving platter; spread one-third of the filling (about 1 cup). Repeat layers twice. Top with remaining cake piece. Gently press in sides to neaten; if necessary, trim sides until even. Cover; refrigerate 30 minutes.

7. In medium microwavable bowl, beat butter on medium speed until smooth. On low speed, beat in remaining glaze ingredients until well blended. Reserve 1 cup of the glaze for garnish; cover and let stand at room temperature about 30 minutes or until thick enough to pipe. Meanwhile, microwave remaining glaze on High about 10 seconds or until slightly warm and spreading consistency. Spread over top of torte, letting some drip down sides. Refrigerate torte about 30 minutes or until glaze is set.

8. Spoon reserved 1 cup glaze into decorating bag fitted with small star tip. Pipe decorative border around edges of torte. Refrigerate at least 2 hours. (Torte can be made 2 days ahead; wrap sides tightly with plastic wrap and refrigerate.) Let cake stand at room temperature 20 minutes before serving. Store covered in refrigerator.

16 servings
1 Serving: Calories 560 (Calories from Fat 310); Total Fat 35g (Saturated Fat 20g; Trans Fat 1g); Cholesterol 140mg; Sodium 430mg; Total Carbohydrate 56g (Dietary Fiber 2g; Sugars 42g); Protein 7g
% Daily Value: Vitamin A 15%; Vitamin C 0%; Calcium 8%; Iron 15%
Exchanges: 1 Starch, $2\frac{1}{2}$ Other Carbohydrate, $1/2$ High-Fat Meat, 6 Fat
Carbohydrate Choices: 4

Decadent Chocolate Torte

Brownie Ice Cream Cake

Prep Time: 25 min Start to Finish: 3 hr 55 min

1 box (1 pound 6.5 ounces) Betty Crocker Original Supreme brownie mix (with chocolate syrup pouch)

Water, vegetable oil and eggs called for on brownie mix box

1/2 gallon (8 cups) vanilla ice cream, slightly softened

1 cup hot fudge topping, warmed if desired

2 tablespoons candy sprinkles

16 red maraschino cherries with stems, drained

1. Heat oven to 350°F. Line 2 (9-inch) round cake pans with aluminum foil; grease bottoms only with shortening or cooking spray.

2. Make brownie mix as directed on box—except divide batter evenly between pans. Bake 22 to 26 minutes or until toothpick inserted 2 inches from side of pan comes out almost clean. Cool completely in pans, about 1 hour. Do not remove from pans.

3. Spread slightly softened ice cream evenly on brownies in pans. Freeze at least 2 hours or until ice cream is firm.

4. Remove desserts from pans; remove foil. Place on serving plates. Cut each dessert into 8 wedges. Drizzle each wedge with hot fudge topping. Decorate with candy sprinkles and cherries. Store covered in freezer.

16 servings
1 Serving: Calories 370 (Calories from Fat 140); Total Fat 15g (Saturated Fat 6g; Trans Fat 1g); Cholesterol 60mg; Sodium 200mg; Total Carbohydrate 54g (Dietary Fiber 2g; Sugars 39g); Protein 5g
% Daily Value: Vitamin A 6%; Vitamin C 0%; Calcium 10%; Iron 8%
Exchanges: 1 Starch, 2 1/2 Other Carbohydrate, 3 Fat
Carbohydrate Choices: 3 1/2

KITCHEN TIPS

✪ Set up a dessert bar with ice cream toppings and syrups and extras such as fresh strawberries, sliced bananas, chopped nuts and candies. Let guests create their own desserts.

✪ Use your favorite flavor of ice cream or a combination of ice creams to make this frozen dessert.

Black Forest Brownie Dessert

Prep Time: 20 min Start to Finish: 1 hr 20 min

1 pouch (10.25 ounces) Betty Crocker fudge brownie mix

1/3 cup vegetable oil

2 tablespoons water

1 egg

1 can (21 ounces) cherry pie filling

2 tablespoons almond-flavored liqueur, if desired

1 cup whipping cream

1 tablespoon powdered sugar

1/4 teaspoon cocoa, if desired

1. Heat oven to 350°F. Spray 9-inch glass pie plate with baking spray with flour. Make brownie mix as directed on pouch, using oil, water and egg. Pour batter into pie plate.

2. Bake 24 to 26 minutes or until toothpick inserted in center comes out almost clean. Cool 30 minutes.

3. In small bowl, stir together pie filling and liqueur. Cut brownie into 6 wedges. Place each wedge on individual serving plate. Spoon about 1/3 cup cherry mixture over each wedge.

4. In medium bowl, beat whipping cream and powdered sugar with electric mixer on high speed until stiff peaks form. Add dollop of whipped cream to each serving. Sprinkle with cocoa.

6 servings
1 Serving: Calories 540 (Calories from Fat 250); Total Fat 28g (Saturated Fat 10g; Trans Fat 1g); Cholesterol 80mg; Sodium 190mg; Total Carbohydrate 70g (Dietary Fiber 3g; Sugars 53g); Protein 4g
% Daily Value: Vitamin A 10%; Vitamin C 4%; Calcium 8%; Iron 10%
Exchanges: 1 Starch, 3 1/2 Other Carbohydrate, 5 1/2 Fat
Carbohydrate Choices: 4 1/2

KITCHEN TIPS

✪ The name of these brownies stems from the same flavors found in an exquisite chocolate-cherry torte, which was embellished with cherry liqueur (Kirsch) and whipped cream that originated in Germany's Black Forest region.

Brownie Ice Cream Cake

Black Forest Brownie Dessert

Apricot Petits Fours

Prep Time: 1 hr 20 min Start to Finish: 4 hr 20 min

Cake

- 1 box Betty Crocker SuperMoist yellow cake mix
- 1 cup apricot nectar or juice
- 1/3 cup vegetable oil
- 1 teaspoon grated orange peel
- 2 eggs
- 2 tablespoons orange-flavored liqueur or apricot nectar

Icing

- 9 cups powdered sugar
- 3/4 cup apricot nectar or water
- 1/2 cup light corn syrup
- 1/3 cup butter or margarine, melted
- 2 teaspoons almond extract

Decorations, If Desired

- Sliced almonds
- Orange peel

1. Heat oven to 350°F for shiny metal pan (or 325°F for dark or nonstick pan). Spray bottom and sides of 15 × 10 × 1-inch pan with baking spray with flour.

2. In large bowl, beat all cake ingredients except liqueur with electric mixer on low speed 30 seconds. Beat on medium speed 2 minutes, scraping bowl occasionally. Pour batter into pan.

3. Bake 22 to 28 minutes or until cake springs back when touched lightly in center. Brush liqueur over top of cake. Cool completely, about 20 minutes. To avoid cake crumbs when adding icing, freeze cake 1 hour before cutting.

4. In large bowl, beat icing ingredients on low speed until powdered sugar is moistened. Beat on high speed until smooth. If necessary, add 2 to 3 teaspoons more apricot nectar until icing is pourable.

5. Place cooling rack on cookie sheet or waxed paper to catch icing drips. Cut cake into 9 rows by 6 rows. Working with 6 pieces at a time, remove cake pieces from pan and place on cooling rack. Spoon icing evenly over top and sides of cake pieces, letting icing coat sides. (Icing that drips off can be reused.) Let stand until icing is set, about 2 hours.

6. Decorate with almonds and orange peel as desired. Store in single layer in airtight plastic container at room temperature.

54 petits fours
1 Petit Four: Calories 160 (Calories from Fat 30); Total Fat 3.5g (Saturated Fat 1.5g; Trans Fat 0g); Cholesterol 10mg; Sodium 75mg; Total Carbohydrate 31g (Dietary Fiber 0g; Sugars 26g); Protein 0g
% Daily Value: Vitamin A 4%; Vitamin C 0%; Calcium 0%; Iron 0%
Exchanges: 2 Other Carbohydrate, 1 Fat
Carbohydrate Choices: 2

KITCHEN TIPS

✿ You can make the cakes up to 2 weeks earlier and freeze, but wait to add the icing until shortly before you serve them.

✿ Apricot nectar sounds like an exotic ingredient, but you can find it in the juice aisle of the supermarket.

Cranberry Mousse Torte

Prep Time: 35 min Start to Finish: 6 hr 40 min

Brownie Base

- 1 box (1 pound 2.3 ounces) Betty Crocker fudge brownie mix
- $\frac{1}{4}$ cup water
- $\frac{2}{3}$ cup vegetable oil
- 2 eggs
- $\frac{1}{2}$ cup miniature semisweet chocolate chips

Filling

- 2 tablespoons water
- 1 envelope ($2\frac{1}{2}$ teaspoons) unflavored gelatin
- 1 can (16 ounces) jellied cranberry sauce
- $\frac{1}{2}$ cup sugar
- 1 teaspoon grated orange peel
- $1\frac{1}{2}$ cups whipping cream
- 3 drops red food color, if desired

Cranberry Sauce

- $\frac{1}{2}$ cup sugar
- 4 teaspoons cornstarch
- 1 can (11.5 ounces) frozen cranberry juice cocktail concentrate, thawed

1. Heat oven to 350°F. Wrap aluminum foil around outside of bottom and side of 10-inch springform pan to catch drips. Spray bottom only of pan with cooking spray. In large bowl, beat all base ingredients except chocolate chips with spoon 50 strokes; fold in chocolate chips. Spread in pan. Bake 35 to 40 minutes or until base pulls away from side of pan; do not overbake. Cool completely, about 1 hour 30 minutes.

2. Meanwhile, place 2 tablespoons water in 2-quart saucepan; sprinkle gelatin over water. Let stand 1 minute to soften. Spoon cranberry sauce and $\frac{1}{2}$ cup sugar over gelatin. Heat to rolling boil over medium-high heat. Cook over medium-high heat, stirring frequently, until gelatin is completely dissolved. Stir in orange peel. Cool at room temperature 20 minutes. Cover; refrigerate 1 hour 30 minutes to 2 hours, stirring every 30 minutes, until mixture is slightly thickened.

3. In medium bowl, beat whipping cream with electric mixer on high speed until stiff peaks form. Fold into cranberry mixture. Fold in food color. Spoon mixture over cooled brownie base. Cover; refrigerate about 2 hours or until set.

4. Meanwhile, in $1\frac{1}{2}$-quart saucepan, mix $\frac{1}{2}$ cup sugar and the cornstarch. Stir in cranberry juice concentrate. Heat to boiling over high heat, stirring constantly. Boil 4 to 5 minutes, stirring constantly, until slightly thickened. Cool 20 minutes at room temperature. Pour sauce into small resealable container. Refrigerate about 1 hour 30 minutes or until chilled.

5. To serve, spoon sauce over each serving of torte.

16 servings
1 Serving: Calories 460 (Calories from Fat 180); Total Fat 20g (Saturated Fat 7g; Trans Fat 0g); Cholesterol 50mg; Sodium 140mg; Total Carbohydrate 69g (Dietary Fiber 2g; Sugars 57g); Protein 3g
% Daily Value: Vitamin A 6%; Vitamin C 10%; Calcium 2%; Iron 8%
Exchanges: $\frac{1}{2}$ Starch, 4 Other Carbohydrate, 4 Fat
Carbohydrate Choices: $4\frac{1}{2}$

Peach Melba Shortcakes

Peach Melba Shortcakes

Prep Time: 25 min Start to Finish: 1 hr 10 min

Fruit

- 3 peaches, peeled and sliced into thin wedges, or 1 bag (1 pound) frozen sliced peaches, thawed
- 1 container (6 ounces) fresh raspberries (1$\frac{1}{2}$ cups)
- $\frac{3}{4}$ cup granulated sugar

Shortcakes

- 2$\frac{1}{2}$ cups Gold Medal all-purpose flour
- $\frac{1}{2}$ cup granulated sugar
- 2 teaspoons baking powder
- $\frac{1}{2}$ teaspoon salt
- $\frac{1}{2}$ cup firm butter or margarine
- $\frac{2}{3}$ cup milk
- $\frac{1}{2}$ teaspoon almond extract
- 1 egg, slightly beaten
- 1 tablespoon milk
- $\frac{1}{4}$ cup sliced almonds
- 3 tablespoons coarse sugar

Ice Cream

- 1 pint (2 cups) vanilla ice cream

1. In medium bowl, mix peaches, raspberries and $\frac{3}{4}$ cup sugar. Let stand 1 hour so fruit will become juicy.

2. Meanwhile, heat oven to 400°F. In medium bowl, mix flour, $\frac{1}{2}$ cup sugar, baking powder and salt. Cut in butter, using pastry blender (or pulling 2 table knives through ingredients in opposite directions), until mixture looks like coarse crumbs. Using wooden spoon, stir in $\frac{2}{3}$ cup milk, almond extract and egg just until blended. (Dough will be stiff.)

3. On ungreased cookie sheet, drop dough by 8 spoonfuls about 2 inches apart. Brush with 1 tablespoon milk; sprinkle almonds over tops of each. Sprinkle with coarse sugar.

4. Bake 14 to 16 minutes or until light golden brown. Remove from cookie sheet; cool 10 minutes.

5. Cut shortcakes in half. Spoon about $\frac{1}{4}$ cup ice cream onto bottom of each shortcake. Top each with $\frac{1}{2}$ cup of the peach mixture; add tops of shortcakes.

8 servings
1 Serving: Calories 520 (Calories from Fat 170); Total Fat 19g (Saturated Fat 10g; Trans Fat 0.5g); Cholesterol 75mg; Sodium 400mg; Total Carbohydrate 79g (Dietary Fiber 4g; Sugars 45g); Protein 8g
% Daily Value: Vitamin A 15%; Vitamin C 15%; Calcium 15%; Iron 15%
Exchanges: 2$\frac{1}{2}$ Starch, $\frac{1}{2}$ Fruit, 2 Other Carbohydrate, 3$\frac{1}{2}$ Fat
Carbohydrate Choices: 5

KITCHEN TIPS

✿ For light golden brown shortcakes, make sure you use a shiny cookie sheet and bake the shortcakes on the center oven rack.

✿ Top each shortcake with a dollop of whipped cream, if desired.

Molten Butterscotch Cakes

Impossible Easy Cheesecake

Molten Butterscotch Cakes

Prep Time: 15 min Start to Finish: 35 min

- 6 teaspoons graham cracker crumbs
- 1 cup butterscotch chips (6 ounces)
- $^2/_3$ cup butter or margarine
- 3 whole eggs
- 3 egg yolks
- $^3/_4$ cup packed brown sugar
- $^1/_2$ cup Gold Medal all-purpose flour

1. Heat oven to 450°F. Spray bottoms and sides of 6 (6-ounce) custard cups with baking spray with flour. Sprinkle 1 teaspoon cracker crumbs onto bottom and around side of each cup.

2. In 1-quart saucepan, melt butterscotch chips and butter over medium heat, stirring constantly. Remove from heat; cool slightly, about 5 minutes.

3. Meanwhile, in large bowl, beat whole eggs and egg yolks with wire whisk or egg beater until well blended. Beat in brown sugar. Beat in melted butterscotch mixture and flour until well blended. Divide batter evenly among custard cups. Place cups on cookie sheet with sides.

4. Bake 12 to 14 minutes or until sides are set and centers are still soft (tops will be puffed and cracked). Let stand 3 minutes. Run small knife or metal spatula along sides of cakes to loosen. Immediately place individual dessert plate upside down over top of each cup; turn plate and cup over. Remove cup. Serve warm.

6 servings
1 Serving: Calories 550 (Calories from Fat 300); Total Fat 34g (Saturated Fat 21g; Trans Fat 1g); Cholesterol 265mg; Sodium 230mg; Total Carbohydrate 56g (Dietary Fiber 0g; Sugars 47g); Protein 6g
% Daily Value: Vitamin A 20%; Vitamin C 0%; Calcium 6%; Iron 8%
Exchanges: $^1/_2$ Starch, 3 Other Carbohydrate, $^1/_2$ High-Fat Meat, 6 Fat
Carbohydrate Choices: 4

KITCHEN TIPS

✿ This luscious dessert tastes even better when served with a big scoop of praline pecan ice cream.
✿ Look for boxes of graham cracker crumbs in the baking aisle of your supermarket.

Impossible Easy Cheesecake

Prep Time: 15 min Start to Finish: 4 hr

Cheesecake
- $^3/_4$ cup milk
- 2 teaspoons vanilla
- 2 eggs
- 1 cup sugar
- $^1/_2$ cup Original Bisquick mix
- 2 packages (8 ounces each) cream cheese, cut into about $^1/_2$-inch cubes, softened

Topping, If Desired
- 1 cup sour cream
- 2 tablespoons sugar
- 2 teaspoons vanilla
- Fresh fruit, if desired

1. Heat oven to 350°F. Grease 9-inch glass pie plate with shortening or cooking spray. In blender, place all cheesecake ingredients except cream cheese. Cover; blend on high speed 15 seconds. Add cream cheese. Cover; blend 2 minutes longer or until smooth. Pour into pie plate.

2. Bake 40 to 45 minutes or until knife inserted in center comes out clean. Cool at room temperature 1 hour. Refrigerate at least 2 hours until chilled.

3. In small bowl, stir sour cream, 2 tablespoons sugar and vanilla until blended. Spread on top of completely cooled cheesecake. Serve with fruit. Store covered in refrigerator.

8 servings
1 Serving: Calories 360 (Calories from Fat 200); Total Fat 22g (Saturated Fat 13g; Trans Fat 1g); Cholesterol 115mg; Sodium 280mg; Total Carbohydrate 33g (Dietary Fiber 0g; Sugars 28g); Protein 7g
% Daily Value: Vitamin A 20%; Vitamin C 0%; Calcium 8%; Iron 6%
Exchanges: $^1/_2$ Starch, $1^1/_2$ Other Carbohydrate, 1 High-Fat Meat, 3 Fat
Carbohydrate Choices: 2

KITCHEN TIPS

✿ For a deliciously decadent cheesecake, drizzle it with fudge and caramel toppings and sprinkle with chopped pecans.
✿ Garnish each slice of cheesecake with fresh fruit or edible flowers, such as pansies or nasturtiums.

Almond Cheesecake

Prep Time: 40 min Start to Finish: 7 hr 45 min

Crust

1 box Betty Crocker SuperMoist yellow cake mix

$^1\!/_2$ cup butter or margarine, softened

Filling

3 packages (8 ounces each) cream cheese, softened

$^3\!/_4$ cup sugar

1 cup whipping cream

1 teaspoon almond extract

3 eggs

Garnish

$^1\!/_4$ cup sliced almonds

4 teaspoons sugar

Fresh raspberries, if desired

1. Heat oven to 350°F for shiny metal pan (or 325°F for dark or nonstick pan). Spray bottom and side of 10-inch springform pan with baking spray with flour. Wrap outside of side and bottom of pan with aluminum foil.

2. Reserve $^1\!/_2$ cup of the cake mix; set aside. In large bowl, beat remaining cake mix and butter with electric mixer on low speed until crumbly. Press in bottom and $1^1\!/_2$ inches up side of pan. Bake 15 minutes or until edges are golden brown. Reduce oven temperature to 325°F for shiny metal pan (or 300°F for dark or nonstick pan).

3. In same large bowl, beat reserved $^1\!/_2$ cup cake mix and cream cheese on medium speed until well blended. Beat in $^3\!/_4$ cup sugar, the whipping cream and almond extract on medium speed until smooth and creamy. On low speed, beat in eggs, one at a time, until well blended. Pour batter over crust. Place springform pan in large roasting pan; place on oven rack. Pour enough boiling water into roasting pan to cover half of side of springform pan.

4. Bake 55 to 60 minutes or until edge is set but center jiggles slightly when moved. Cool in pan (in water bath) on cooling rack 20 minutes. Remove pan from water bath. Carefully run knife around side of pan to loosen, but do not remove side of pan. Cool 1 hour 30 minutes at room temperature.

5. Cover loosely; refrigerate at least 4 hours or overnight.

6. Meanwhile, in 1-quart saucepan, cook almonds and 4 teaspoons sugar over low heat about 10 minutes, stirring constantly, until sugar is melted and almonds are coated. Cool on waxed paper; break apart.

7. Remove side of pan before serving. Garnish cheesecake with sugared almonds and raspberries. Store covered in refrigerator.

16 servings
1 Serving: Calories 440 (Calories from Fat 270); Total Fat 30g (Saturated Fat 17g; Trans Fat 1.5g); Cholesterol 120mg; Sodium 390mg; Total Carbohydrate 39g (Dietary Fiber 0g; Sugars 27g); Protein 6g
% Daily Value: Vitamin A 20%; Vitamin C 0%; Calcium 10%; Iron 6%
Exchanges: 1 Starch, $1^1\!/_2$ Other Carbohydrate, $^1\!/_2$ High-Fat Meat, 5 Fat
Carbohydrate Choices: $2^1\!/_2$

Hot Buttered Rum Cheesecake
with Brown Sugar–Rum Sauce

Prep Time: 45 min Start to Finish: 15 hr 20 min

Crust

- 1¼ cups graham cracker crumbs
- ¼ cup butter or margarine, melted

Filling

- 5 packages (8 ounces each) cream cheese, softened
- 1¼ cups granulated sugar
- ⅓ cup whipping cream
- 2 tablespoons rum
- ¼ teaspoon ground cinnamon
- ⅛ teaspoon ground cloves
- ⅛ teaspoon ground nutmeg
- 3 eggs

Sauce

- ½ cup packed brown sugar
- ¼ cup butter or margarine
- ⅓ cup whipping cream
- ¼ cup rum
- ¼ cup golden raisins, if desired

1. Heat oven to 350°F. In small bowl, mix crust ingredients. Press firmly in bottom of ungreased 9-inch springform pan. Bake 10 minutes. Cool completely. Reduce oven temperature to 325°F.

2. While crust is cooling, in large bowl, beat all filling ingredients except eggs with electric mixer on medium speed about 1 minute or until smooth. On low speed, beat in eggs until well blended. Pour over crust; smooth top.

3. Bake 1 hour 15 minutes to 1 hour 25 minutes or until edge is set and center is still soft. Turn off oven; leave oven door open about 4 inches. Leave cheesecake in oven 30 minutes. Remove from oven; cool in pan on cooling rack away from drafts 30 minutes.

4. Without releasing or removing side of pan, run metal spatula carefully along side of cheesecake to loosen. Refrigerate uncovered about 3 hours or until chilled. Cover; continue refrigerating at least 9 hours but no longer than 48 hours.

5. In 1½-quart saucepan, mix sauce ingredients. Heat to boiling over medium heat, stirring constantly. Boil 3 to 4 minutes, stirring constantly, until slightly thickened.

6. To serve, run metal spatula along side of cheesecake to loosen again; remove side of pan. Serve with warm sauce. Store cheesecake and sauce covered in refrigerator.

16 servings
1 Serving: Calories 470 (Calories from Fat 320); Total Fat 35g (Saturated Fat 22g; Trans Fat 1.5g); Cholesterol 145mg; Sodium 300mg; Total Carbohydrate 30g (Dietary Fiber 0g; Sugars 27g); Protein 7g
% Daily Value: Vitamin A 25%; Vitamin C 0%; Calcium 8%; Iron 6%
Exchanges: 2 Other Carbohydrate, 1 High-Fat Meat, 5½ Fat
Carbohydrate Choices: 2

Chocolate Grasshopper Cheesecake

Prep Time: 30 min   Start to Finish: 7 hr 35 min

Crust

30	fudge mint cookies, crushed (about 1¾ cups)
2	tablespoons butter or margarine, melted

Filling

4	ounces semisweet baking chocolate
3	packages (8 ounces each) cream cheese, softened
1	cup sugar
4	eggs
⅓	cup green crème de menthe liqueur

Topping and Garnish, If Desired

Sweetened whipped cream

Crème de menthe thin rectangular candies for garnish, unwrapped, cut in half diagonally

1. Heat oven to 300°F. Wrap aluminum foil around bottom and side of ungreased 9-inch springform pan. In large bowl, mix crust ingredients with fork until crumbly. Press in bottom and 1 inch up side of pan. Bake 12 minutes. Cool 30 minutes.

2. In small microwavable bowl, microwave chocolate on High 45 to 60 seconds, stirring once halfway through microwaving, until melted. If necessary, continue to microwave on High in 15-second increments, stirring until smooth. Set aside.

3. In large bowl, beat cream cheese and sugar with electric mixer on medium speed, scraping bowl frequently, until smooth and creamy. Add eggs, one at a time, beating until smooth after each addition. Stir in liqueur. Pour filling evenly over crust.

4. Drop 8 to 10 teaspoonfuls melted chocolate randomly onto filling, allowing chocolate to sink into filling. With table knife or small spatula, cut through chocolate and filling to swirl for marbled design.

5. Bake 1 hour 10 minutes to 1 hour 20 minutes or until set 2 inches from edge of pan. Remove from oven; run knife around side of cheesecake to loosen. Return to oven; turn oven off and open door slightly. Cool cheesecake in oven 1 hour. Remove from oven to cooling rack; cool at room temperature 1 hour. Refrigerate 3 hours.

6. To serve, remove side of pan. Spoon whipped cream into decorating bag with large star tip; squeeze bag to pipe cream around top edge of cheesecake. Garnish with candies.

16 servings
1 Serving: Calories 340 (Calories from Fat 210); Total Fat 23g (Saturated Fat 15g; Trans Fat 0.5g); Cholesterol 105mg; Sodium 190mg; Total Carbohydrate 28g (Dietary Fiber 0g; Sugars 23g); Protein 6g
% Daily Value: Vitamin A 15%; Vitamin C 0%; Calcium 4%; Iron 6%
Exchanges: ½ Starch, 1½ Other Carbohydrate, ½ High-Fat Meat, 3½ Fat
Carbohydrate Choices: 2

KITCHEN TIPS

✿ One teaspoon peppermint extract and 4 to 6 drops green food color can be substituted for the crème de menthe liqueur.

✿ This decadent dessert is the perfect do-ahead because it needs to be chilled at least 3 hours before serving.

✿ For easy cutting, dip your knife into hot water.

Pies and
Other Desserts

Luscious Finales

Ginger-Almond Pears (page 340)

Fudgy Brownie Pie with Caramel Sauce (page 320)

Dutch Pear Pie

Prep Time: 20 min Start to Finish: 1 hr 40 min

Crust

1   Pillsbury refrigerated pie crust (from 15-ounce box), softened as directed on box

Filling

1   cup sour cream

$^{1}/_{2}$ cup granulated sugar

1   tablespoon Gold Medal all-purpose flour

1   teaspoon vanilla

1   egg, beaten

3   cups coarsely chopped fresh pears (2 to 3 medium pears)

Crumb Topping

1   cup Gold Medal all-purpose flour

$^{1}/_{2}$ cup packed brown sugar

$^{1}/_{2}$ cup butter or margarine

1. Heat oven to 425°F. Make pie crust as directed on box for One-Crust Baked Shell using 9-inch glass pie plate; do not prick crust. Carefully line pastry with a double thickness of aluminum foil, gently pressing foil to bottom and side of pastry. Let foil extend over edge to prevent excessive browning. Bake 10 minutes. Carefully remove foil; bake 2 to 4 minutes longer or until pastry just begins to brown and has become set. If crust bubbles, gently push bubbles down with back of spoon.

2. Meanwhile, in medium bowl, mix filling ingredients. Pour into warm baked pie shell.

3. In medium bowl, mix crumb topping ingredients with pastry blender or fork until mixture looks like fine crumbs; sprinkle topping evenly over filling.

4. Reduce oven temperature to 350°F. Bake 40 to 50 minutes or until top is light golden brown. After 30 minutes of baking, cover top of pie with foil to prevent excessive browning. Cool at least 30 minutes before serving. Store in refrigerator.

8 servings
1 Serving: Calories 490 (Calories from Fat 220); Total Fat 25g (Saturated Fat 13g; Trans Fat 0.5g); Cholesterol 80mg; Sodium 220mg; Total Carbohydrate 62g (Dietary Fiber 2g; Sugars 33g); Protein 4g
% Daily Value: Vitamin A 10%; Vitamin C 2%; Calcium 6%; Iron 6%
Exchanges: 1 Starch, 3 Other Carbohydrate, 5 Fat
Carbohydrate Choices: 4

KITCHEN TIPS

✿ Purchase pears ahead of time to ensure ripeness. To speed ripening, place pears in a paper or plastic bag at room temperature for several days. Pears are ready when they yield slightly when pressed.

✿ Serve each slice with a dollop of whipped cream or a scoop of vanilla ice cream.

Peach Crumble Pie

Prep Time: 35 min Start to Finish: 2 hr 30 min

Crust

- 1 cup Gold Medal all-purpose flour
- 1/2 teaspoon salt
- 1/3 cup plus 1 tablespoon shortening
- 2 to 3 tablespoons cold water

Filling

- 4 cups quartered peeled peaches (8 to 10 medium)
- 1/2 cup granulated sugar
- 1/2 teaspoon ground nutmeg
- 2 tablespoons whipping cream
- 1 egg

Topping

- 1/2 cup Gold Medal all-purpose flour
- 1/4 cup packed brown sugar
- 1/4 teaspoon ground cinnamon
- 1/4 teaspoon ground nutmeg
- 1/4 cup butter or margarine, softened

1. In medium bowl, mix 1 cup flour and the salt. Cut in shortening, using pastry blender (or pulling 2 table knives through ingredients in opposite directions), until particles are size of small peas. Sprinkle with cold water, 1 tablespoon at a time, tossing with fork until all flour is moistened and pastry almost cleans side of bowl (1 to 2 teaspoons more water can be added if necessary).

2. Gather pastry into a ball. On lightly floured surface, shape pastry into flattened disk. Wrap in plastic wrap; refrigerate about 45 minutes or until dough is firm and cold, yet pliable. (If refrigerated longer, let dough soften slightly before rolling.)

3. Heat oven to 425°F. On lightly floured surface, roll pastry with floured rolling pin into round 2 inches larger than upside-down 9-inch glass pie plate. Fold pastry into quarters; place in pie plate. Unfold and ease into plate, pressing firmly against bottom and side. Trim overhanging edge of pastry 1 inch from rim of plate. Fold and roll pastry under, even with plate; press edge with tines of fork or flute if desired.

4. Place peaches in pastry-lined plate. Mix granulated sugar and 1/2 teaspoon nutmeg; sprinkle over peaches. In small bowl, beat whipping cream and egg with fork or wire whisk until blended; pour over peaches. In another small bowl, mix topping ingredients with fork until crumbly; sprinkle over peaches.

5. Cover edge of pastry with 2- to 3-inch-wide strip of aluminum foil to prevent excessive browning; remove foil for last 15 minutes of baking. Bake 35 to 40 minutes or until top is golden brown. Cool 30 minutes. Serve warm.

8 servings
1 Serving: Calories 360 (Calories from Fat 160); Total Fat 18g (Saturated Fat 7g; Trans Fat 2g); Cholesterol 45mg; Sodium 200mg; Total Carbohydrate 46g (Dietary Fiber 2g; Sugars 27g); Protein 4g
% Daily Value: Vitamin A 10%; Vitamin C 4%; Calcium 2%; Iron 8%
Exchanges: 1 Starch, 1/2 Fruit, 1 1/2 Other Carbohydrate, 3 1/2 Fat
Carbohydrate Choices: 3

Dulce de Leche-Banana Pie

Dulce de Leche-Banana Pie

Prep Time: 20 min Start to Finish: 1 hr 5 min

Crust

1	cup Gold Medal all-purpose flour
½	teaspoon salt
⅓	cup plus 1 tablespoon shortening
2 to 3	tablespoons cold water

Filling

1	can (13.4 ounces) dulce de leche
3	ripe medium bananas
1	cup whipping cream
¼	cup powdered sugar
½	cup semisweet chocolate chips
1	teaspoon vegetable oil

1. Heat oven to 450°F. In medium bowl, mix flour and salt. Cut in shortening, using pastry blender (or pulling 2 table knives through ingredients in opposite directions), until particles are size of small peas. Sprinkle with water, 1 tablespoon at a time, tossing with fork until all flour is moistened and dough almost leaves sides of bowl (1 to 2 teaspoons more water can be added if necessary).

2. On lightly floured surface, shape dough into a ball. Flatten ball to ½-inch thickness, rounding and smoothing edges. With floured rolling pin, roll dough into 11-inch round, rolling from center to edge. Fold dough in half; place in 9-inch glass pie plate. Unfold; gently press in bottom and up side of plate, being careful not to stretch dough.

3. Fold and roll edge of dough under, even with plate; flute edge. Prick bottom and side of dough generously with fork. Bake 9 to 12 minutes or until light golden brown. Cool completely, about 30 minutes.

4. Spoon contents of can of dulce de leche into center of cooled crust; gently spread to edge. Thinly slice bananas; arrange over dulce de leche.

5. In medium bowl, beat whipping cream and powdered sugar with electric mixer on high speed until stiff peaks form. Spread over bananas.

6. In small resealable plastic freezer bag, place chocolate chips and oil; seal bag. Microwave on High 30 seconds; knead bag to mix melted chips and unmelted chips. Microwave 15 to 30 seconds longer or until all chips are melted and smooth. Snip off tiny corner of bag. Pipe melted chocolate mixture over whipped cream. Store pie in refrigerator.

8 servings
1 Serving: Calories 500 (Calories from Fat 230); Total Fat 26g (Saturated Fat 12g; Trans Fat 2g); Cholesterol 35mg; Sodium 210mg; Total Carbohydrate 60g (Dietary Fiber 2g; Sugars 38g); Protein 7g
% Daily Value: Vitamin A 10%; Vitamin C 4%; Calcium 15%; Iron 6%
Exchanges: 1 Starch, 3 Other Carbohydrate, ½ High-Fat Meat, 4 Fat
Carbohydrate Choices: 4

KITCHEN TIPS

❀ Dulce de leche is a traditional Spanish confection made from milk. It's a popular culinary reference to rich caramel flavors. Look for canned dulce de leche in the Hispanic section of the supermarket.

Fudgy Brownie Pie with Caramel Sauce

Prep Time: 15 min Start to Finish: 2 hr 5 min

Crust

1 Pillsbury refrigerated pie crust (from 15-ounce box), softened as directed on box

Filling

1 cup butter or margarine

2 cups sugar

2 teaspoons vanilla

4 eggs, slightly beaten

1½ cups Gold Medal all-purpose flour

¾ cup unsweetened baking cocoa

¼ teaspoon salt

1 cup semisweet chocolate chunks (from 11.5- or 12-ounce bag)

1 cup chopped pecans

Sauce

1 bag (14 ounce) caramels, unwrapped

⅔ cup half-and-half

1. Heat oven to 350°F. Place pie crust in 9-inch glass pie plate as directed on box for One-Crust Filled Pie.

2. In 2-quart saucepan, melt butter over low heat; remove from heat. Stir in sugar, vanilla and eggs until well blended. Stir in flour, cocoa and salt until smooth. Stir in chocolate chunks and pecans. Spread evenly in pie crust.

3. Bake 45 to 60 minutes or until set. Cool 1 hour.

4. Meanwhile, in 2-quart saucepan, heat caramels and half-and-half over low heat, stirring constantly, until caramels are melted and mixture is smooth. Serve hot caramel sauce over each serving.

16 servings
1 Serving: Calories 560 (Calories from Fat 250); Total Fat 28g (Saturated Fat 13g; Trans Fat 0.5g); Cholesterol 90mg; Sodium 260mg; Total Carbohydrate 70g (Dietary Fiber 3g; Sugars 43g); Protein 6g
% Daily Value: Vitamin A 10%; Vitamin C 0%; Calcium 6%; Iron 10%
Exchanges: 1 Starch, 3½ Other Carbohydrate, ½ Medium-Fat Meat, 5 Fat
Carbohydrate Choices: 4½

KITCHEN TIPS

✿ Short on time? Use caramel topping instead of making the sauce from scratch.
✿ If you don't like pecans, feel free to leave them out.

Bourbon Pecan Pie with Pecan Crust

Prep Time: 30 min Start to Finish: 4 hr

Crust

- ⅓ cup finely chopped pecans
- 2 tablespoons Gold Medal all-purpose flour
- 1 Pillsbury refrigerated pie crust (from 15-ounce box), softened as directed on box

Filling

- 3 eggs
- ¾ cup packed brown sugar
- 3 tablespoons Gold Medal all-purpose flour
- 1 cup dark corn syrup
- 2 tablespoons butter or margarine, melted
- 2 tablespoons bourbon
- 1½ cups pecan halves

Topping

- ¾ cup whipping cream
- 2 tablespoons packed brown sugar
- 1 teaspoon vanilla

1. Heat oven to 325°F. In bottom of ungreased 9-inch glass pie plate, mix ⅓ cup chopped pecans and 2 tablespoons flour. Place pie crust over pecan mixture in pie plate as directed on box for One-Crust Filled Pie.

2. In large bowl, beat eggs slightly with hand beater or wire whisk. Beat in ¾ cup brown sugar, 3 tablespoons flour, the corn syrup, butter and bourbon until smooth. Stir in pecan halves. Pour into crust-lined pie plate.

3. Bake 15 minutes. Cover top of crust with aluminum foil to prevent excessive browning; bake 40 to 45 minutes longer or until filling is set and center of pie is puffed and golden brown. Cool completely on cooling rack, about 2 hours 30 minutes.

4. In chilled medium bowl, beat topping ingredients with electric mixer on high speed until soft peaks form. Serve pie topped with whipped cream.

8 servings
1 Serving: Calories 650 (Calories from Fat 320); Total Fat 36g (Saturated Fat 11g; Trans Fat 1g); Cholesterol 115mg; Sodium 200mg; Total Carbohydrate 77g (Dietary Fiber 2g; Sugars 41g); Protein 6g
% Daily Value: Vitamin A 8%; Vitamin C 0%; Calcium 6%; Iron 8%
Exchanges: 2 Starch, 3 Other Carbohydrate, 7 Fat
Carbohydrate Choices: 5

KITCHEN TIPS

- If you purchase pecan pieces for the crust, you will need to chop them a bit smaller. You can do this with a sharp knife, or use a small food processor or nut chopper.
- Dark corn syrup has caramel flavor and color added, which give it a darker color and stronger flavor.

Classic Pumpkin Pie

Prep Time: 25 min Start to Finish: 6 hr 45 min

Pie Crust

1	cup Gold Medal all-purpose flour
1/2	teaspoon salt
1/3	cup plus 1 tablespoon shortening
2 to 3	tablespoons cold water

Filling

2	eggs
1/2	cup sugar
1	teaspoon ground cinnamon
1/2	teaspoon salt
1/2	teaspoon ground ginger
1/8	teaspoon ground cloves
1	can (15 ounces) pumpkin (not pumpkin pie mix)
1	can (12 ounces) evaporated milk

Topping

1/2	cup whipping cream
1	tablespoon sugar
1/4	teaspoon pumpkin pie spice or ground cinnamon

1. In medium bowl, mix flour and 1/2 teaspoon salt. Cut in shortening, using pastry blender (or pulling 2 table knives through ingredients in opposite directions), until particles are size of small peas. Sprinkle with cold water, 1 tablespoon at a time, tossing with fork until all flour is moistened and pastry almost leaves side of bowl (1 to 2 teaspoons more water can be added if necessary).

2. Gather pastry into a ball. On lightly floured surface, shape dough into flattened round. Wrap pastry in plastic wrap; refrigerate about 45 minutes or until dough is firm and cold, yet pliable.

3. Heat oven to 425°F. On lightly floured surface, roll pastry with floured rolling pin into round 2 inches larger than upside-down 9-inch glass pie plate. Fold pastry into fourths; place in pie plate. Unfold and ease into plate, pressing firmly against bottom and side. Trim overhanging edge of pastry 1 inch from rim of pie plate. Fold and roll pastry under, even with plate; flute as desired.

4. In medium bowl, beat eggs slightly with wire whisk. Beat in remaining filling ingredients. Place pastry-lined pie plate on oven rack to prevent spilling the filling. Pour filling into pie plate. Cover edge of crust with 2- to 3-inch strip of aluminum foil to prevent excessive browning.

5. Bake 15 minutes. Reduce oven temperature to 350°F. Bake about 45 minutes longer, removing foil during last 15 minutes of baking, until knife inserted in center comes out clean. Cool 30 minutes. Refrigerate about 4 hours or until chilled.

6. In chilled small bowl, beat topping ingredients with electric mixer on high speed until soft peaks form. Serve pie topped with whipped cream.

8 servings
1 Serving: Calories 350 (Calories from Fat 180); Total Fat 20g (Saturated Fat 8g; Trans Fat 2g); Cholesterol 85mg; Sodium 370mg; Total Carbohydrate 36g (Dietary Fiber 2g; Sugars 21g); Protein 7g
% Daily Value: Vitamin A 170%; Vitamin C 2%; Calcium 15%; Iron 10%
Exchanges: 1 Starch, 1 1/2 Other Carbohydrate, 1/2 High-Fat Meat, 3 Fat
Carbohydrate Choices: 2 1/2

Sweet Potato Pie with Cornmeal Pastry

Prep Time: 30 min Start to Finish: 4 hr 15 min

Pastry

$2/3$	cup Gold Medal all-purpose flour
$1/3$	cup cornmeal
$1/4$	teaspoon salt
$1/3$	cup plus 1 tablespoon shortening
2 to 3	tablespoons cold water

Filling and Topping

2	eggs
2	cups mashed cooked sweet potatoes
$3/4$	cup granulated sugar
$1 2/3$	cups evaporated milk (from two 12-ounce cans)
1	teaspoon ground cinnamon
$1/2$	teaspoon salt
$1/2$	teaspoon ground ginger
$1/4$	teaspoon ground cloves
	Sweetened whipped cream, if desired

Cinnamon-Pecan Streusel

$1/3$	cup packed brown sugar
$1/3$	cup chopped pecans
1	tablespoon butter or margarine, softened
$1/2$	teaspoon ground cinnamon

1. In medium bowl, mix flour, cornmeal and $1/4$ teaspoon salt. Cut in shortening, using pastry blender (or pulling 2 table knives through ingredients in opposite directions), until particles are size of small peas. Sprinkle with cold water, 1 tablespoon at a time, tossing with fork until all flour is moistened and pastry almost leaves side of bowl (1 to 2 teaspoons more water can be added if necessary).

2. Gather pastry into a ball. On lightly floured surface, shape dough into flattened round. Wrap pastry in plastic wrap; refrigerate about 45 minutes or until dough is firm and cold, yet pliable.

3. Heat oven to 425°F. On lightly floured surface, roll pastry with floured rolling pin into round 2 inches larger than upside-down 9-inch deep-dish glass pie plate. Fold pastry into fourths; place in pie plate.

Unfold and ease into plate, pressing firmly against bottom and side. Trim overhanging edge of pastry $1/2$ inch from rim of plate. Fold and roll pastry under, even with plate; flute as directed.

4. In medium bowl, beat eggs slightly with wire whisk. Stir in remaining filling ingredients except whipped cream. Pour into pastry-lined pie plate. Cover edge of crust with 2- to 3-inch strip of aluminum foil to prevent excessive browning.

5. Bake 15 minutes. Reduce oven temperature to 350°F. Bake 35 minutes longer.

6. Meanwhile, in small bowl, mix streusel ingredients until crumbly. Sprinkle streusel over pie. Remove foil from crust. Bake about 10 minutes longer or until knife inserted in center comes out clean. Place pie on cooling rack. Cool completely, about 2 hours. Serve with whipped cream.

8 servings
1 Serving: Calories 450 (Calories from Fat 180); Total Fat 20g (Saturated Fat 7g; Trans Fat 2g); Cholesterol 70mg; Sodium 320mg; Total Carbohydrate 58g (Dietary Fiber 3g; Sugars 37g); Protein 8g
% Daily Value: Vitamin A 210%; Vitamin C 8%; Calcium 20%; Iron 10%
Exchanges: 1 Starch, 3 Other Carbohydrate, $1/2$ High-Fat Meat, 3 Fat
Carbohydrate Choices: 4

Nectarine-Plum Crostata

Quick

Nectarine-Plum Crostata

Prep Time: 20 min Start to Finish: 2 hr 30 min

Crust

1½	cups Gold Medal all-purpose flour
1	teaspoon sugar
¼	teaspoon salt
½	cup firm butter or margarine, cut into pieces
1	egg yolk
4 to 5	tablespoons cold water

Filling

½	cup sugar
3	tablespoons Gold Medal all-purpose flour
¼	teaspoon ground cinnamon
3	cups sliced nectarines (about 3 medium)
2	cups sliced plums (about 2 medium)
1	tablespoon lemon juice
2	tablespoons butter or margarine, softened
1	tablespoon sugar, if desired

1. Heat oven to 425°F. In medium bowl, mix 1½ cups flour, 1 teaspoon sugar and the salt. Cut in ½ cup butter, using pastry blender (or pulling 2 table knives through ingredients in opposite directions), until mixture is crumbly. Stir in egg yolk with fork. Sprinkle with water, 1 tablespoon at a time, tossing with fork until ball of pastry forms. Gather pastry into a ball; flatten to ½-inch thickness. Wrap in plastic wrap; refrigerate 30 minutes.

2. On lightly floured surface, roll pastry into 13-inch round, about ⅛ inch thick. Place on ungreased large cookie sheet.

3. In large bowl, mix ½ cup sugar, 3 tablespoons flour and the cinnamon. Stir in nectarines and plums until coated. Sprinkle with lemon juice; mix. Spoon fruit mixture onto center of pastry, spreading to within 3 inches of edge. Dot with 2 tablespoons butter. Fold edge of pastry up over fruit mixture, making pleats. Brush edge of pastry with small amount of water; sprinkle with 1 tablespoon sugar.

4. Bake 30 to 40 minutes or until crust is golden brown and fruit is tender. Cool completely, about 1 hour.

8 servings
1 Serving: Calories 330 (Calories from Fat 140); Total Fat 15g (Saturated Fat 9g; Trans Fat 0.5g); Cholesterol 65mg; Sodium 180mg; Total Carbohydrate 44g (Dietary Fiber 2g; Sugars 21g); Protein 4g
% Daily Value: Vitamin A 15%; Vitamin C 6%; Calcium 0%; Iron 8%
Exchanges: 1 Starch, 1 Fruit, 1 Other Carbohydrate, 3 Fat
Carbohydrate Choices: 3

KITCHEN TIPS

✿ You can keep a fruit crostata at room temperature for 2 days; after that, store it loosely covered in the fridge up to 2 days longer. In warm climates, always store fruit crostatas in the fridge.

✿ Serve the crostata with ice cream or whipped cream.

Strawberry-Cream Puff Kabobs

Prep Time: 15 min Start to Finish: 25 min

6 (10-inch) bamboo skewers
18 tiny frozen cream puffs (from 13.2-ounce box), thawed
12 fresh medium strawberries (about ²⁄₃ pound), stems removed if desired
2 tablespoons semisweet chocolate chips
1 tablespoon butter or margarine

1. Line cookie sheet with waxed paper. On each skewer, alternately thread 3 cream puffs and 2 strawberries.

2. In small resealable plastic freezer bag, place chocolate chips and butter. Seal bag. Microwave on High about 30 seconds or until melted. Squeeze bag to mix melted chips and butter.

3. Cut small tip from corner of bag. Drizzle chocolate mixture over kabobs. Place on cookie sheet. Refrigerate about 10 minutes or until set. Store in refrigerator.

6 kabobs
1 Kabob: Calories 150 (Calories from Fat 90); Total Fat 10g (Saturated Fat 6g; Trans Fat 0.5g); Cholesterol 25mg; Sodium 20mg; Total Carbohydrate 13g (Dietary Fiber 1g; Sugars 11g); Protein 2g
% Daily Value: Vitamin A 0%; Vitamin C 25%; Calcium 0%; Iron 0%
Exchanges: ¹⁄₂ Starch, ¹⁄₂ Other Carbohydrate, 2 Fat
Carbohydrate Choices: 1

KITCHEN TIPS

❁ Frozen cream puffs can be found in the frozen food department in large supermarkets and club stores.
❁ Kabobs can be covered with plastic wrap and refrigerated up to 24 hours before serving. Use white vanilla baking chips instead of the chocolate chips.

Strawberry-Cream Puff Kabobs

Tiramisu Tart

Prep Time: 35 min Start to Finish: 3 hr 5 min

Crust
1	cup Gold Medal all-purpose flour
1/2	cup cold butter or margarine, cut into 1/8-inch slices
1/4	cup powdered sugar

Chocolate Layer
1	bar (4 ounces) bittersweet baking chocolate, coarsely chopped
2	teaspoons vegetable oil

Filling
1/2	cup granulated sugar
2	tablespoons Gold Medal all-purpose flour
1	cup whipping cream
1	tablespoon instant espresso coffee granules
1	egg
1/2	teaspoon vanilla

Topping
1	package (8 ounces) cream cheese, softened
1/2	cup whipping cream
1/2	cup powdered sugar

1. Heat oven to 350°F. In food processor, place crust ingredients. Cover; process until soft dough forms. Spread dough evenly with fingers on bottom and up side of ungreased 9- or 10-inch tart pan. Bake 12 to 15 minutes or until edge begins to brown. Cool 5 minutes.

2. In small bowl, reserve 3 tablespoonfuls of the chopped chocolate. In 1-cup glass measuring cup, microwave remaining chocolate uncovered on High about 45 seconds; stir until chocolate is melted. Stir in oil. Spread mixture over baked crust. Place in freezer to cool chocolate.

3. Meanwhile, in medium bowl, mix granulated sugar and 2 tablespoons flour; set aside. In 2-cup liquid measuring cup, beat 1 cup whipping cream, the coffee granules, egg and vanilla with wire whisk until well blended. Beat cream mixture into sugar mixture until well blended. Pour over chocolate in pan.

4. Bake 35 to 40 minutes or until edge is golden brown and center is set. Cool completely in pan on cooling rack, about 1 hour 30 minutes.

5. In medium bowl, beat topping ingredients with electric mixer on medium speed about 2 minutes or until fluffy. Spread over top of cooled tart in pan. Sprinkle with reserved chopped chocolate. Remove side of pan before serving. Store covered in refrigerator.

12 servings
1 Serving: Calories 410 (Calories from Fat 270); Total Fat 30g (Saturated Fat 18g; Trans Fat 1g); Cholesterol 90mg; Sodium 130mg; Total Carbohydrate 29g (Dietary Fiber 2g; Sugars 17g); Protein 5g
% Daily Value: Vitamin A 15%; Vitamin C 0%; Calcium 6%; Iron 15%
Exchanges: 1/2 Starch, 1 1/2 Other Carbohydrate, 1/2 High-Fat Meat, 5 Fat
Carbohydrate Choices: 2

KITCHEN TIPS

✿ Tiramisu means "carry me up" in Italian, and refers to the dessert's ethereal texture. This recipe transforms traditional tiramisu flavors into an elegant tart.

Fabulous Three-Berry Tart

Prep Time: 30 min Start to Finish: 2 hr 30 min

Crust

- 1 bag (8 ounces) animal crackers
- 1/3 cup butter or margarine, melted
- 1 teaspoon ground cinnamon
- 2 tablespoons sugar

Filling

- 1 package (8 ounces) cream cheese, softened
- 1/2 cup sugar
- 2 tablespoons lemon juice
- 1 cup whipping cream
- 1/2 pint (1 cup) fresh blackberries
- 1/2 pint (1 cup) fresh blueberries
- 1/2 pint (1 cup) fresh raspberries
- 1/4 cup strawberry jam
- 1 tablespoon orange juice

1. Heat oven to 350°F. Place animal crackers in food processor; cover and process about 1 minute or until crumbs are finely ground. In medium bowl, mix cracker crumbs, butter, cinnamon and 2 tablespoons sugar. Press mixture in bottom and up side of un-greased 9-inch tart pan with removable bottom. Bake 8 to 12 minutes or until golden brown. Cool completely, about 20 minutes.

2. In large bowl, beat cream cheese, 1/2 cup sugar and the lemon juice with electric mixer on low speed until blended. Add whipping cream; beat on high speed 3 to 5 minutes or until light and fluffy. Spread mixture in tart shell. Refrigerate at least 2 hours.

3. Arrange berries on chilled filling. In small microwavable bowl, microwave jam uncovered on High about 20 seconds or until warm. Stir in orange juice; mix well with fork. Brush strawberry glaze over berries.

10 servings
1 Serving: Calories 380 (Calories from Fat 235); Total Fat 26g (Saturated Fat 15g; Trans Fat 0g); Cholesterol 74mg; Sodium 209mg; Total Carbohydrate 33g (Dietary Fiber 2g; Sugars 16g); Protein 4g
% Daily Value: Vitamin A 0%; Vitamin C 15%; Calcium 6%; Iron 6%
Exchanges: 4 1/2 Fat, 1/2 Fruit, 1/2 Other Carbohydrate, 1 Starch
Carbohydrate Choices: 2

KITCHEN TIPS

✿ Make the crust and filling a day ahead and refrigerate it. Add the fresh berries just before serving time.

✿ To quickly soften cream cheese, use your microwave. Remove foil wrapper and place cream cheese in a microwavable bowl. Microwave uncovered on Medium (50%) 1 minute to 1 minute 30 seconds.

Pear Tartlets

Prep Time: 10 min Start to Finish: 40 min

- 1 sheet frozen puff pastry (from 17.3-ounce package), thawed as directed on package
- 1 ripe pear
- ¼ cup peach preserves

1. Heat oven to 400°F. Cut pastry into 4 squares. Place pastry squares on ungreased cookie sheet.

2. Peel pear and cut into quarters; remove seeds. Slice each pear quarter into very thin slices. Arrange pear slices over pastry squares, leaving ½-inch border.

3. Bake about 20 minutes or until pastry is puffed and browned. Spread 1 tablespoon preserves over top of each warm tartlet to cover pears. Cool on cookie sheet 10 minutes before serving.

4 tartlets
1 Tartlet: Calories 420 (Calories from Fat 210); Total Fat 24g (Saturated Fat 8g; Trans Fat 2.5g); Cholesterol 75mg; Sodium 160mg; Total Carbohydrate 48g (Dietary Fiber 2g; Sugars 14g); Protein 5g
% Daily Value: Vitamin A 0%; Vitamin C 2%; Calcium 2%; Iron 15%
Exchanges: 1½ Starch, 1½ Other Carbohydrate, 4½ Fat
Carbohydrate Choices: 3

KITCHEN TIPS

✿ Thaw the frozen puff pastry on the counter about 15 minutes. The pastry should be chilled but still pliable when you're ready to work with it. If the pastry gets too warm, the butter layers will flatten and the pastry won't puff as high when it bakes.

✿ This is the perfect dessert to make when you're short on time. Keep puff pastry in the freezer for those occasions when you need a quick dessert.

Brownie Pops

Prep Time: 30 min Start to Finish: 2 hr 30 min

- 1 box (1 pound 6.5 ounces) Betty Crocker Original Supreme brownie mix (with chocolate syrup pouch)
  Water, vegetable oil and eggs called for on brownie mix box
- 24 craft sticks (flat wooden sticks with round ends)
- 1 cup semisweet chocolate chips (6 ounces)
- 2 teaspoons shortening
  Assorted Betty Crocker Decor Selects decors or sprinkles

1. Heat oven to 350°F. Line 13 × 9-inch pan with aluminum foil so foil extends about 2 inches over sides of pan. Spray foil with cooking spray. Make brownie mix as directed on box for 13 × 9-inch pan. Cool completely, about 1 hour.

2. Place brownies in freezer for 30 minutes. Remove brownies from pan by lifting foil; peel foil from sides of brownies. Cut brownies into 24 rectangular bars, 6 strips lengthwise and 4 rows across, each about 1½ by 3¼ inches. Gently insert stick into end of each bar, peeling foil from bars. Place on baking sheet; freeze 30 minutes.

3. In microwavable bowl, microwave chocolate chips and shortening uncovered on High about 1 minute; stir until smooth. If necessary, microwave additional 5 seconds at a time. Dip top one-third to one-half of each brownie into chocolate; sprinkle with decors. Lay flat on waxed paper or foil to dry.

24 pops
1 Pop: Calories 180 (Calories from Fat 70); Total Fat 7g (Saturated Fat 2.5g; Trans Fat 0g); Cholesterol 20mg; Sodium 95mg; Total Carbohydrate 28g (Dietary Fiber 1g; Sugars 20g); Protein 2g
% Daily Value: Vitamin A 0%; Vitamin C 0%; Calcium 0%; Iron 6%
Exchanges: 2 Other Carbohydrate, 1½ Fat
Carbohydrate Choices: 2

KITCHEN TIPS

✿ Visit a cake-decorating supply store or catalog to find an array of candy sprinkles.

✿ For more contrast, use white vanilla baking chips instead of the chocolate chips. Or, melt dark and white chocolate for variety.

Brownie Pops

Pear Tartlets

Brownie 'n Berries Dessert Pizza

Prep Time: 20 min Start to Finish: 2 hr 50 min

- 1 box (1 pound 6.5 ounces) Betty Crocker Original Supreme brownie mix
- Water, vegetable oil and eggs called for on brownie mix box
- 1 package (8 ounces) cream cheese, softened
- 1/3 cup sugar
- 1/2 teaspoon vanilla
- 2 cups sliced fresh strawberries
- 1 cup fresh blueberries
- 1 cup fresh raspberries
- 1/2 cup apple jelly

1. Heat oven to 350°F (or 325°F for dark or nonstick pan). Grease bottom only of 12-inch pizza pan with cooking spray or shortening.

2. In medium bowl, stir brownie mix, pouch of chocolate syrup, water, oil and eggs until well blended. Spread in pan.

3. Bake 28 to 30 minutes or until toothpick inserted 2 inches from side of pan comes out clean or almost clean. Cool completely, about 1 hour.

4. In small bowl, beat cream cheese, sugar and vanilla with electric mixer on medium speed until smooth. Spread mixture evenly over brownie base. Arrange berries over cream cheese mixture. Stir jelly until smooth; brush over berries. Refrigerate about 1 hour or until chilled. Cut into wedges. Store covered in refrigerator.

16 servings
1 Serving: Calories 310 (Calories from Fat 110); Total Fat 12g (Saturated Fat 4.5g; Trans Fat 0g); Cholesterol 40mg; Sodium 180mg; Total Carbohydrate 47g (Dietary Fiber 2g; Sugars 34g); Protein 3g
% Daily Value: Vitamin A 4%; Vitamin C 25%; Calcium 2%; Iron 10%
Exchanges: 1 Starch, 2 Other Carbohydrate, 2 1/2 Fat
Carbohydrate Choices: 3

KITCHEN TIPS

✪ For easy cleanup, bake the brownie in a 12-inch disposable foil pizza pan. Slide the pan onto a cookie sheet when you remove the brownie from the oven. Place the brownie dessert on a tray when you take it to the table.

✪ Any cut-up fresh fruit can be used for this dessert. Substitute 4 cups cut-up fresh fruit for the berries.

Turtle Tart

Prep Time: 25 min Start to Finish: 3 hr 15 min

Cookie Base

- 1   pouch Betty Crocker oatmeal cookie mix
- $^1/_2$ cup butter or margarine, softened
- 1   tablespoon water
- 1   egg
- 1   cup chopped pecans

Filling

- 40   caramels, unwrapped
- $^1/_3$ cup whipping cream
- $^3/_4$ cup chopped pecans

Topping

- 1   bag (11.5 ounces) milk chocolate chips (2 cups)
- $^1/_3$ cup whipping cream
- $^1/_4$ cup chopped pecans

1. Heat oven to 350°F. In large bowl, stir cookie mix, butter, water and egg until soft dough forms. Stir in 1 cup pecans. Press dough in bottom and up side of ungreased 9-inch tart pan with removable bottom.

2. Bake 19 to 21 minutes or until light golden brown. Cool 10 minutes.

3. Meanwhile, in medium microwavable bowl, microwave caramels and $^1/_3$ cup whipping cream on High 2 to 4 minutes, stirring twice, until caramels are melted. Stir in $^3/_4$ cup pecans. Spread over cooled crust. Refrigerate 15 minutes.

4. In another medium microwavable bowl, microwave chocolate chips and $^1/_3$ cup whipping cream on High 1 to 2 minutes, stirring every 30 seconds, until chocolate is smooth. Pour over filling. Sprinkle with $^1/_4$ cup pecans. Refrigerate 2 hours or until set. To serve, let stand at room temperature 10 minutes before cutting. Store covered in refrigerator.

16 servings
1 Serving: Calories 520 (Calories from Fat 260); Total Fat 29g (Saturated Fat 10g; Trans Fat 0g); Cholesterol 45mg; Sodium 240mg; Total Carbohydrate 59g (Dietary Fiber 3g; Sugars 37g); Protein 7g
% Daily Value: Vitamin A 8%; Vitamin C 0%; Calcium 10%; Iron 8%
Exchanges: $^1/_2$ Starch, $3^1/_2$ Other Carbohydrate, $^1/_2$ High-Fat Meat, 5 Fat
Carbohydrate Choices: 4

KITCHEN TIPS

- This recipe was one of 15 winners in the 2007 Mix It Up with Betty! Cookie Mix Recipe Contest.
- No tart pan? Use a 13 × 9-inch pan, and cut into squares instead of wedges.
- If you loosen the crust from the pan before adding the filling, the tart will be easier to remove from the pan.

Cool and Creamy Lime Dessert

Prep Time: 10 min   Start to Finish: 2 hr 55 min

Crust

  1   cup Gold Medal all-purpose flour
 1/2 cup firm butter or margarine
 1/2 cup finely chopped walnuts or pecans
  1   teaspoon grated lime peel

Filling

  1   can (14 ounces) sweetened condensed milk
      (not evaporated)
 1/2 cup Key lime juice or regular lime juice
  2   teaspoons grated lime peel, if desired
  2   cups whipping cream
      Few drops green food color, if desired

1. Heat oven to 350°F. Place flour in medium bowl. Cut in butter, using pastry blender (or pulling 2 table knives through flour in opposite directions), until evenly mixed. Stir in walnuts and 1 teaspoon lime peel. Press evenly in bottom of ungreased 9-inch square pan.

2. Bake about 15 minutes or until light brown. Cool completely, about 30 minutes.

3. In medium bowl, mix condensed milk, lime juice and 2 teaspoons lime peel; set aside. In chilled large bowl, beat whipping cream and food color with electric mixer on high speed until stiff.

4. Fold lime mixture into whipped cream just until blended. Pour over crust. Cover; refrigerate at least 2 hours until chilled but no longer than 48 hours. Store covered in refrigerator.

9 servings
1 Serving: Calories 490 (Calories from Fat 310); Total Fat 35g (Saturated Fat 20g; Trans Fat 1g); Cholesterol 100mg; Sodium 150mg; Total Carbohydrate 38g (Dietary Fiber 0g; Sugars 25g); Protein 7g
% Daily Value: Vitamin A 20%; Vitamin C 4%; Calcium 20%; Iron 6%
Exchanges: 1 1/2 Starch, 1 Other Carbohydrate, 7 Fat
Carbohydrate Choices: 2 1/2

KITCHEN TIPS

❂ This is an easy-to-prepare version of Key Lime Pie because the crust is pressed into the pan instead of fluted.
❂ Garnish each serving with a dollop of whipped cream sprinkled with chopped walnuts.

Low Fat

Summer Fruit-Topped Sorbet Sundae

Prep Time: 10 min Start to Finish: 40 min

1 nectarine, chopped (1 cup)
¾ cup fresh raspberries
¾ cup fresh blueberries
2 tablespoons sugar
2 teaspoons orange-flavored liqueur or orange juice
1 pint (2 cups) lemon sorbet
4 thin ginger cookies

4 servings
1 Serving: Calories 250 (Calories from Fat 10); Total Fat 1g (Saturated Fat 0g; Trans Fat 0g); Cholesterol 0mg; Sodium 50mg; Total Carbohydrate 57g (Dietary Fiber 3g; Sugars 44g); Protein 1g
% Daily Value: Vitamin A 2%; Vitamin C 20%; Calcium 0%; Iron 4%
Exchanges: ½ Fruit, 3 Other Carbohydrate, 1 Fat
Carbohydrate Choices: 4

KITCHEN TIPS

1. In small bowl, mix nectarine, raspberries, blueberries, sugar and liqueur. Refrigerate at least 30 minutes but no longer than 4 hours.

2. Into each of 4 serving dishes, scoop ½ cup sorbet. Stir fruit mixture; spoon over sorbet. Garnish each serving with 1 cookie.

✿ When purchasing nectarines, look for smooth, unblemished skins. A good nectarine will be firm but not rock hard. For optimum eating, ripen them at room temperature for two or three days until they are slightly soft along the seam.

✿ Use any combination of fresh summer fruit, such as chopped strawberries and peaches, in this delightful sundae topping.

Quick

Red, White and Blueberry Sundaes

Prep Time: 10 min Start to Finish: 10 min

1/3 cup seedless strawberry jam

2 tablespoons light corn syrup

2 teaspoons balsamic vinegar, if desired

1 cup fresh blueberries

1 cup quartered small to medium fresh strawberries

1 quart (4 cups) vanilla ice cream

White chocolate curls, if desired

8 servings
1 Serving: Calories 220 (Calories from Fat 70); Total Fat 8g (Saturated Fat 5g; Trans Fat 0g); Cholesterol 30mg; Sodium 65mg; Total Carbohydrate 35g (Dietary Fiber 1g; Sugars 24g); Protein 3g
% Daily Value: Vitamin A 6%; Vitamin C 15%; Calcium 10%; Iron 0%
Exchanges: 2 Other Carbohydrate, 1/2 Low-Fat Milk, 1 Fat
Carbohydrate Choices: 2

KITCHEN TIPS

1. In medium bowl, beat jam, corn syrup and vinegar with wire whisk until smooth. Fold in blueberries and strawberries until coated.

2. Scoop ice cream into 8 dessert bowls. Top with berry mixture. Garnish with white chocolate.

✿ Blueberries pack a huge nutritional punch. One cup of fresh blueberries gives you 3.5 grams of fiber and is an excellent source of vitamin C.

✿ Strawberry ice cream is also delicious with the fresh berries and white chocolate.

✿ To make the chocolate curls, melt 1/2 cup chips with 1 teaspoon oil in microwave or over low heat. Pour into a small bowl lined with aluminum foil. Refrigerate 20 minutes or until set. Peel off foil. Use vegetable peeler to make curls.

Quick

Caramel-Orange Ice Cream Sundaes

Prep Time: 15 min Start to Finish: 15 min

3 tablespoons butter or margarine

½ cup packed dark brown sugar

2 tablespoons light or dark corn syrup

½ cup whipping cream

2 tablespoons orange juice

¼ teaspoon grated orange peel

2 pints (4 cups) vanilla ice cream

½ cup coarsely chopped toasted macadamia nuts

1. In 2-quart saucepan, melt butter over medium heat. Add brown sugar and corn syrup; cook 2 to 3 minutes, stirring constantly, until sugar is dissolved. Stir in whipping cream and orange juice; cook 3 minutes, stirring constantly, until well blended. Stir in orange peel. (Sauce can be served immediately or cooled to room temperature, about 30 minutes, before refrigerating. If sauce has been refrigerated, stir well before serving.)

2. Serve sauce over scoops of ice cream. Garnish sundaes with nuts. Store sauce covered in refrigerator.

8 servings
1 Serving: Calories 360 (Calories from Fat 200); Total Fat 22g (Saturated Fat 11g; Trans Fat 0.5g); Cholesterol 60mg; Sodium 100mg; Total Carbohydrate 36g (Dietary Fiber 1g; Sugars 29g); Protein 3g
% Daily Value: Vitamin A 10%; Vitamin C 0%; Calcium 10%; Iron 4%
Exchanges: 1 Starch, 1½ Other Carbohydrate, 4 Fat
Carbohydrate Choices: 2½

KITCHEN TIPS

❀ To toast nuts, sprinkle nuts in ungreased heavy skillet. Cook over medium heat 5 to 7 minutes, stirring frequently until nuts begin to brown, then stirring constantly until nuts are light brown.

❀ Garnish each sundae with an orange twist.

❀ Scoop ice cream early in the day. Place scoops on a plastic-wrapped tray and freeze. Pop the scoops into dishes for easy serving.

Orange Marmalade Crème Brûlée

Prep Time: 20 min Start to Finish: 7 hr

¼ cup orange marmalade

6 egg yolks

2 cups whipping cream

⅓ cup sugar

1 teaspoon vanilla

  Boiling water

8 teaspoons sugar

1. Heat oven to 350°F. Spoon 1 tablespoon marmalade into bottom of each of 4 (6-ounce) ceramic ramekins.*

2. In small bowl, slightly beat egg yolks with wire whisk. In large bowl, stir whipping cream, ⅓ cup sugar and the vanilla until well mixed. Add egg yolks to cream mixture; beat with wire whisk until evenly colored and well blended.

2. In 13 × 9-inch pan, place ramekins. Pour cream mixture evenly into ramekins. Carefully place pan with ramekins in oven. Pour enough boiling water into pan, being careful not to splash water into ramekins, until water covers two-thirds of the height of the ramekins.

4. Bake 30 to 40 minutes or until tops are light golden brown and sides are set (centers will be jiggly).

5. Carefully transfer ramekins to cooling rack, using tongs or grasping tops of ramekins with pot holder. Cool 2 hours or until room temperature. Cover tightly with plastic wrap; refrigerate until chilled, at least 4 hours but no longer than 2 days.

6. Uncover ramekins; gently blot any condensation on custards with paper towel. Sprinkle 2 teaspoons sugar over each custard. Holding kitchen torch 3 to 4 inches from custard, caramelize sugar on each custard by heating with torch about 2 minutes, moving flame continuously over sugar in circular motion, until sugar is melted and light golden brown. Serve immediately, or refrigerate up to 8 hours before serving.

Note *Do not use glass custard cups or glass pie plates; they cannot withstand the heat from the kitchen torch and may break.*

4 servings
1 Serving: Calories 590 (Calories from Fat 390); Total Fat 44g (Saturated Fat 25g; Trans Fat 1.5g); Cholesterol 440mg; Sodium 60mg; Total Carbohydrate 43g (Dietary Fiber 0g; Sugars 38g); Protein 7g
% Daily Value: Vitamin A 30%; Vitamin C 2%; Calcium 10%; Iron 4%
Exchanges: 3 Other Carbohydrate, 1 High-Fat Meat, 7 Fat
Carbohydrate Choices: 3

KITCHEN TIPS

❀ Make this spectacular dessert a day ahead. Prepare through step 5; refrigerate up to 24 hours. All you'll need to do at the last minute is caramelize the sugar.

❀ Pair this mouthwatering dessert with purchased pirouette cookies.

Orange Marmalade Crème Brûlée

Low Fat
Ginger-Almond Pears
Prep Time: 50 min Start to Finish: 3 hr 25 min

$1\frac{1}{2}$ cups sugar

$1\frac{1}{2}$ cups water

$\frac{1}{3}$ cup chopped crystallized ginger

2 tablespoons lemon juice

$\frac{1}{8}$ teaspoon almond extract

4 Anjou pears, peeled, cut in half lengthwise and cored

$\frac{1}{4}$ cup sliced almonds

4 teaspoons sugar

1 cup vanilla frozen yogurt

1. In 4-quart Dutch oven, mix $1\frac{1}{2}$ cups sugar, the water, ginger and lemon juice. Heat to boiling over medium-high heat. Boil 2 minutes, stirring occasionally, until sugar is melted. Stir in almond extract. Add pear halves; cover and return to boiling. Reduce heat; simmer covered 8 to 10 minutes or until pears are tender when pierced with tip of knife. Remove pears from liquid, using slotted spoon, to bowl; cover and refrigerate until serving.

2. Boil remaining pear liquid over high heat 8 to 10 minutes, stirring occasionally, until slightly thickened and syrupy. Cool 30 to 40 minutes or until warm. Refrigerate 2 hours or until serving.

3. Meanwhile, in 10-inch nonstick skillet, cook almonds over medium heat 4 to 6 minutes, stirring constantly, until just beginning to brown. Sprinkle 4 teaspoons sugar over almonds. Continue cooking and stirring 2 to 3 minutes longer or until sugar is melted and almonds are coated. Spread almond mixture on sheet of aluminum foil sprayed with cooking spray. Cool 2 to 3 minutes; break apart.

4. Place pear halves, cut sides up, in individual dessert bowls. (If desired, cut thin slice from rounded side of each pear half so that it won't roll around in bowl.)

5. Place small scoop (about 2 tablespoons) frozen yogurt in center of each pear half. Spoon syrup over top. Sprinkle with almonds.

8 servings
1 Serving: Calories 280 (Calories from Fat 20); Total Fat 2g (Saturated Fat 0g; Trans Fat 0g); Cholesterol 0mg; Sodium 20mg; Total Carbohydrate 62g (Dietary Fiber 3g; Sugars 53g); Protein 2g **% Daily Value:** Vitamin A 0%; Vitamin C 4%; Calcium 6%; Iron 0% **Exchanges:** $\frac{1}{2}$ Starch, $\frac{1}{2}$ Fruit, 3 Other Carbohydrate, $\frac{1}{2}$ Fat **Carbohydrate Choices:** 4

KITCHEN TIPS

✺ A small (#50) ice cream scoop works great for scooping ice cream onto pears.

Blueberry-Peach Cobbler with Walnut Biscuits

Prep Time: 30 min Start to Finish: 1 hr 40 min

Fruit Mixture

- 8 medium fresh peaches (about 2 pounds), peeled, each cut into 6 wedges
- 1 cup fresh blueberries
- 1 tablespoon cornstarch
- 1/2 cup granulated sugar
- 1 tablespoon lemon juice
- 1/4 teaspoon ground cinnamon
- Dash of salt

Biscuit Topping

- 1 cup Original Bisquick mix
- 1/4 teaspoon ground nutmeg
- 2 tablespoons milk
- 2 tablespoons butter or margarine, softened
- 2 tablespoons granulated sugar
- 2/3 cup chopped walnuts
- 2 teaspoons milk, if desired
- 1 tablespoon coarse sugar

6 servings
1 Serving: Calories 380 (Calories from Fat 140); Total Fat 15g (Saturated Fat 4g; Trans Fat 1g); Cholesterol 10mg; Sodium 300mg; Total Carbohydrate 55g (Dietary Fiber 4g; Sugars 37g); Protein 5g
% Daily Value: Vitamin A 10%; Vitamin C 10%; Calcium 6%; Iron 8%
Exchanges: 1½ Starch, 1 Fruit, 1 Other Carbohydrate, 3 Fat
Carbohydrate Choices: 3½

KITCHEN TIPS

- Two bags (16 ounces each) frozen sliced peaches, thawed, can be used in place of the fresh peaches if you like.
- Serve with dulce de leche or cinnamon ice cream.

1. Heat oven to 400°F. In medium bowl, stir together fruit mixture ingredients; let stand 10 minutes to allow sugar to pull juices from peaches. Transfer to ungreased 8-inch square (2-quart) glass baking dish. Bake uncovered about 10 minutes or until fruit is bubbling. Remove from oven; stir. Bake 10 to 12 minutes longer or until bubbly around edges (fruit must be hot in middle so biscuit topping bakes completely).

2. Meanwhile, in medium bowl, stir all biscuit topping ingredients except 2 teaspoons milk and coarse sugar until firm dough forms.

3. Drop dough by 6 spoonfuls onto warm fruit mixture. Brush dough with 2 teaspoons milk. Sprinkle with coarse sugar.

4. Bake 25 to 30 minutes or until biscuits are deep golden brown and center biscuit is no longer doughy on bottom. Cool 10 minutes on cooling rack. Serve warm.

Apple Bread Pudding with Warm Butter Sauce

Apple Bread Pudding with Warm Butter Sauce

Prep Time: 25 min Start to Finish: 2 hr 20 min

Bread Pudding

- 4 whole eggs
- 1 egg yolk
- ³⁄₄ cup granulated sugar
- 2¹⁄₂ cups milk
- 2¹⁄₂ cups whipping cream
- 1 tablespoon vanilla
- 1 teaspoon ground cinnamon
- 3 medium apples, peeled, cubed (2 cups)
- 12 ounces French or other firm bread, cut into ¹⁄₂-inch slices, then cut into 1¹⁄₂-inch pieces (10 cups)
- 2 tablespoons butter or margarine, melted
- 2 tablespoons granulated sugar
- ¹⁄₂ teaspoon ground cinnamon

Sauce

- ¹⁄₂ cup butter or margarine
- ¹⁄₂ cup granulated sugar
- ¹⁄₂ cup packed brown sugar
- ¹⁄₂ cup half-and-half

1. Heat oven to 325°F. Spray bottom and sides of 13 × 9-inch (3-quart) glass baking dish with cooking spray.

2. In large bowl, beat 4 whole eggs, 1 egg yolk and ³⁄₄ cup granulated sugar with wire whisk until well blended. Beat in milk, whipping cream, vanilla and 1 teaspoon cinnamon until well blended. Stir in apples and 7 cups of the bread pieces. Let stand 20 minutes.

3. Pour apple mixture into baking dish. Lightly press remaining 3 cups bread pieces on top of mixture in baking dish. Brush top of bread with melted butter. In small bowl, mix 2 tablespoons granulated sugar and ¹⁄₂ teaspoon cinnamon; sprinkle over top.

4. Bake 55 to 65 minutes or until top is puffed and light golden brown (center will jiggle slightly). Cool 30 minutes.

5. In 1-quart saucepan, heat sauce ingredients to boiling over high heat, stirring constantly, just until butter is melted and sauce is hot. Serve warm bread pudding with sauce.

12 servings
1 Serving: Calories 520 (Calories from Fat 270); Total Fat 30g (Saturated Fat 18g; Trans Fat 1g); Cholesterol 175mg; Sodium 300mg; Total Carbohydrate 54g (Dietary Fiber 1g; Sugars 39g); Protein 8g
% Daily Value: Vitamin A 20%; Vitamin C 0%; Calcium 15%; Iron 8%
Exchanges: 1 Starch, 2¹⁄₂ Other Carbohydrate, ¹⁄₂ High-Fat Meat, 5 Fat
Carbohydrate Choices: 3¹⁄₂

KITCHEN TIPS

- Using bread that is a day or two old is best; it will be firmer and drier than fresh bread. Bread that is too fresh and soft will give you a bread pudding that is too moist and soggy.
- If you like, skip making the sauce and top with caramel topping instead.

Quick

Apple Crisp

Prep Time: 20 min Start to Finish: 1 hr

6 medium tart cooking apples (Greening, Rome, Granny Smith), sliced (about 6 cups)

¾ cup packed brown sugar

½ cup Gold Medal all-purpose flour

½ cup quick-cooking or old-fashioned oats

1 teaspoon ground cinnamon

½ teaspoon ground nutmeg

⅓ cup butter or margarine

Cream or ice cream, if desired

1. Heat oven to 375°F. Spread apples in ungreased 8-inch square pan.

2. In medium bowl, mix brown sugar, flour, oats, cinnamon and nutmeg. Cut in butter, using pastry blender (or pulling 2 table knives through ingredients in opposite directions), until mixture is crumbly. Sprinkle evenly over apples.

3. Bake 35 to 40 minutes or until topping is golden brown and apples are tender when pierced with fork. Serve warm with cream or ice cream.

Blueberry Crisp: Substitute 6 cups fresh or frozen (thawed and drained) blueberries for the apples.

Rhubarb Crisp: Substitute 6 cups cut-up fresh rhubarb for the apples. Sprinkle ½ cup granulated sugar over rhubarb; stir to combine. Continue as directed in step 2. If rhubarb is frozen, thaw and drain.

6 servings
1 Serving: Calories 330 (Calories from Fat 100); Total Fat 11g (Saturated Fat 7g; Trans Fat 0g); Cholesterol 25mg; Sodium 85mg; Total Carbohydrate 55g (Dietary Fiber 4g; Sugars 38g); Protein 3g
% Daily Value: Vitamin A 8%; Vitamin C 4%; Calcium 4%; Iron 8%
Exchanges: 1 Starch, 1 Fruit, 1½ Other Carbohydrate, 2 Fat
Carbohydrate Choices: 3½

KITCHEN TIPS

❂ Other baking apple varieties that work well are Cortland, Haralson and Honey Crisp.

❂ Leftover apple crisp makes a tasty breakfast treat. Serve it with a dollop of plain yogurt.

Helpful Nutritional and Cooking Information

Nutrition Guidelines

We provide nutrition information for each recipe, which includes calories, fat, cholesterol, sodium, carbohydrate, fiber and protein. Individual food choices can be based on this information.

Recommended intake for a daily diet of 2,000 calories as set by the Food and Drug Administration

Total Fat	Less than 65g
Saturated Fat	Less than 20g
Cholesterol	Less than 300mg
Sodium	Less than 2,400mg
Total Carbohydrate	300g
Dietary Fiber	25g

criteria used for calculating nutrition information

- The first ingredient was used wherever a choice is given (such as $1/3$ cup sour cream or plain yogurt).
- The first ingredient amount was used wherever a range is given (such as 3- to $3^1/_2$-pound cut-up broiler-fryer chicken).
- The first serving number was used wherever a range is given (such as 4 to 6 servings).
- "If desired" ingredients and recipe variations were not included (such as, sprinkle with brown sugar, if desired).
- Only the amount of a marinade or frying oil that is estimated to be absorbed by the food during preparation or cooking was calculated.

ingredients used in recipe testing and nutrition calculations

- Ingredients used for testing represent those that the majority of consumers use in their homes: large eggs, 2% milk, 80% lean ground beef, canned ready-to-use chicken broth and vegetable oil spread containing not less than 65 percent fat.
- Fat-free, low-fat or low-sodium products were not used, unless otherwise indicated.
- Solid vegetable shortening (not butter, margarine, nonstick cooking sprays or vegetable oil spread because they can cause sticking problems) was used to grease pans, unless otherwise indicated.

equipment used in recipe testing

We use equipment for testing that the majority of consumers use in their homes. If a specific piece of equipment (such as a wire whisk) is necessary for recipe success, it is listed in the recipe.

- Cookware and bakeware without nonstick coatings were used, unless otherwise indicated.

- No dark-colored, black or insulated bakeware was used.

- When a pan is specified in a recipe, a metal pan was used; a baking dish or pie plate means ovenproof glass was used.

- An electric hand mixer was used for mixing only when mixer speeds are specified in the recipe directions. When a mixer speed is not given, a spoon or fork was used.

cooking terms glossary

Beat: Mix ingredients vigorously with spoon, fork, wire whisk, hand beater or electric mixer until smooth and uniform.

Boil: Heat liquid until bubbles rise continuously and break on the surface and steam is given off. For a rolling boil, the bubbles form rapidly.

Chop: Cut into coarse or fine irregular pieces with a knife, food chopper, blender or food processor.

Cube: Cut into squares $1/2$ inch or larger.

Dice: Cut into squares smaller than $1/2$ inch.

Grate: Cut into tiny particles using small rough holes of grater (citrus peel or chocolate).

Grease: Rub the inside surface of a pan with shortening, using pastry brush, piece of waxed paper or paper towel, to prevent food from sticking during baking (as for some casseroles).

Julienne: Cut into thin, matchlike strips, using knife or food processor (vegetables, fruits, meats).

Mix: Combine ingredients in any way that distributes them evenly.

Sauté: Cook foods in hot oil or margarine over medium-high heat with frequent tossing and turning motion.

Shred: Cut into long, thin pieces by rubbing food across the holes of a shredder, as for cheese, or by using a knife to slice very thinly, as for cabbage.

Simmer: Cook in liquid just below the boiling point on top of the stove, usually after reducing heat from a boil. Bubbles will rise slowly and break just below the surface.

Stir: Mix ingredients until consistency is uniform. Stir once in a while for stirring occasionally, often for stirring frequently and continuously for stirring constantly.

Toss: Tumble ingredients (such as green salad) lightly with a lifting motion, usually to coat evenly or mix with another food.

metric conversion chart

Volume

U.S. Units	Canadian Metric	Australian Metric
¼ teaspoon	1 mL	1 ml
½ teaspoon	2 mL	2 ml
1 teaspoon	5 mL	5 ml
1 tablespoon	15 mL	20 ml
¼ cup	50 mL	60 ml
⅓ cup	75 mL	80 ml
½ cup	125 mL	125 ml
⅔ cup	150 mL	170 ml
¾ cup	175 mL	190 ml
1 cup	250 mL	250 ml
1 quart	1 liter	1 liter
1½ quarts	1.5 liters	1.5 liters
2 quarts	2 liters	2 liters
2½ quarts	2.5 liters	2.5 liters
3 quarts	3 liters	3 liters
4 quarts	4 liters	4 liters

Weight

U.S. Units	Canadian Metric	Australian Metric
1 ounce	30 grams	30 grams
2 ounces	55 grams	60 grams
3 ounces	85 grams	90 grams
4 ounces (¼ pound)	115 grams	125 grams
8 ounces (½ pound)	225 grams	225 grams
16 ounces (1 pound)	455 grams	500 grams
1 pound	455 grams	½ kilogram

Measurements

Inches	Centimeters
1	2.5
2	5.0
3	7.5
4	10.0
5	12.5
6	15.0
7	17.5
8	20.5
9	23.0
10	25.5
11	28.0
12	30.5
13	33.0

Temperatures

Fahrenheit	Celsius
32°	0°
212°	100°
250°	120°
275°	140°
300°	150°
325°	160°
350°	180°
375°	190°
400°	200°
425°	220°
450°	230°
475°	240°
500°	260°

Note: The recipes in this cookbook have not been developed or tested using metric measures. When converting recipes to metric, some variations in quality may be noted.

Index

Underscored page references indicate boxed text or tips. **Boldfaced** page references indicate photographs.

P

Pancakes
  Corn Bread Pancakes with Butter-Pecan Syrup, 18, **18**
  Peach Melba Pancakes, **16**, 17
Pasta and noodles. *See also* Couscous
  Asian Beef and Noodle Soup, 98, **98**
  Chicken and Spinach–Stuffed Shells, 170, **170**
  Chicken Cacciatore, 174, **175**
  Chicken-Gorgonzola Pasta Salad, 82, **82**
  Chicken Linguine Alfredo, 171, **171**
  Hearty Soybean and Cheddar Pasta Salad, 126, **126**
  Italian Beef and Ravioli Stew, 209, **209**
  Marinara Sauce with Spaghetti, 136, **137**
  Meatball Lasagna, 214, **214**
  Noodle and Chicken Bowl, 85, **85**
  Noodles and Peanut Sauce Salad Bowl, 127, **127**
  Primavera Pasta Salad, **76**, 77
  Salmon-Pasta Toss, 160, **160**
  Shrimp Summer Rolls with Dipping Sauce, 146, **146**
  Slow Cooker Steak and Pasta Soup, 94, **95**
  Spicy Parmesan Meatballs with Angel Hair Pasta,
    213, **213**
  Spinach Pasta Salad, 78, **78**
  Tomato-Basil Turkey Casserole, 186, **186**
Peaches
  Blueberry-Peach Cobbler with Walnut Biscuits, 341, **341**
  Chicken with Oregano-Peach Sauce, 166, **167**
  Creamy Peach Smoothie, 36, **36**
  Peach Crumble Pie, 317, **317**
  Peach Melba Pancakes, **16**, 17
  Peach Melba Shortcakes, **308**, 309
  Southwestern Grilled Pork Chops with Peach Salsa,
    194, **195**
  Strip Steaks with Chipotle-Peach Glaze, **206**, 207
Peanut butter
  Brownie Goody Bars, 260, **261**
  Green Beans with Peanut-Ginger Dip, 38, **38**
  Monster-Style Cookies, 264, **264**
  Noodles and Peanut Sauce Salad Bowl, 127, **127**
  Peanut Butter Tandy Cake, 275, **275**
  Tempeh Stir-Fry with Yogurt-Peanut Sauce, 135, **135**
  Whole Wheat Waffles with Honey–Peanut Butter Syrup,
    20, **20**
Peanuts
  Brownie Goody Bars, 260, **261**
  Chicken-Filled Lettuce Wraps, 37, **37**
Pears
  buying and ripening, 316
  Cranberry-Pear Chutney, 239, **239**
  Dutch Pear Pie, 316, **316**
  Ginger-Almond Pears, 340, **340**
  Pear Tartlets, 330, **331**
  Spanish Fruit and Cheese Stacks, 44, **44**

Peas
  Asian Tossed Salad, 73, **73**
  Chicken-Filled Lettuce Wraps, 37, **37**
  Grilled Chicken Citrus Teriyaki, 172, **172**
  Pork Chop Supper, 193, **193**
  Primavera Pasta Salad, **76**, 77
  Sesame Shrimp Stir-Fry, **148**, 149
Pecans
  Bourbon Pecan Pie with Pecan Crust, 321, **321**
  Cool and Creamy Lime Dessert, 334, **334**
  Corn Bread Pancakes with Butter-Pecan Syrup, 18, **18**
  Double-Chocolate Rocky Road Cookie Bars, 255, **255**
  Fudgy Brownie Pie with Caramel Sauce, 320, **320**
  Honey Bun Cake, 283, **283**
  Mixed-Berry Butter Crunch Parfaits, 30, **30**
  Pecan Crisps, 269, **269**
  Pecan-Topped Corn Bread with Honey Butter, **236**, 237
  Summer Layered Chicken Salad, 81, **81**
  Toffee-Pecan Bars, 258, **258**
  Turtle Tart, 333, **333**
Peppers. *See* Bell peppers; Chile peppers
Phyllo pastry
  Baklava Bars, 254, **254**
  Cashew-Chicken Firecrackers, 49, **49**
  Curried Chicken Salad Cups, 42, **43**
Pies
  Bourbon Pecan Pie with Pecan Crust, 321, **321**
  Classic Pumpkin Pie, 322, **322**
  Dulce de Leche–Banana Pie, **318**, 319
  Dutch Pear Pie, 316, **316**
  Fudgy Brownie Pie with Caramel Sauce, 320, **320**
  Nectarine-Plum Crostata, **324**, 325
  Peach Crumble Pie, 317, **317**
  Sweet Potato Pie with Cornmeal Pastry, 323, **323**
Pillsbury® cookie dough
  Cookie Dough Brownies, **262**, 263
Pineapple
  choosing, tip for, 70
  Coconut, Pineapple and Macadamia Scones, 12, **13**
  Fall Fruit Medley, 65, **65**
  Grilled Pork Tenderloin with Pineapple Salsa, 191, **191**
  Ham with Tropical Fruit Sauce, 197, **197**
  Hawaiian Pork Ribs, 199, **199**
  Pineapple and Carrot Surprise Muffins, 9, **9**
  Pineapple-Berry Salad with Honey-Mint Dressing, 70, **71**
Pistachios
  Mascarpone and Pistachio Toasts, 102, **103**
Pizza
  Barbecue Pizza Wedges, 101, **101**
  Brownie 'n Berries Dessert Pizza, 332, **332**
  Canadian Bacon Brunch Pizza with Cheddar-Dijon Sauce,
    1, 27
  Grilled Bacon and Tomato Pizza Wedges, 102, **103**
  Turkey Taco Pizza, 100, **100**